The Social Life of Gender

Dedicated to Saba Mahmood, whose brilliant scholarship has challenged and inspired our thinking about the meaning and goals of feminism.

The Social Life of Gender

Raka Ray
University of California, Berkeley

Jennifer Carlson
The University of Arizona

Abigail Andrews
University of California, San Diego

SAGE

Los Angeles | London | New Delhi
Singapore | Washington DC | Melbourne

SAGE

FOR INFORMATION:

SAGE Publications, Inc.
2455 Teller Road
Thousand Oaks, California 91320
E-mail: order@sagepub.com

SAGE Publications Ltd.
1 Oliver's Yard
55 City Road
London, EC1Y 1SP
United Kingdom

SAGE Publications India Pvt. Ltd.
B 1/I 1 Mohan Cooperative Industrial Area
Mathura Road, New Delhi 110 044
India

SAGE Publications Asia-Pacific Pte. Ltd.
3 Church Street
#10-04 Samsung Hub
Singapore 049483

Printed in the United States of America.

Library of Congress Cataloging-in-Publication Data

Names: Ray, Raka, author. | Carlson, Jennifer, author. | Andrews, Abigail, author.

Title: The social life of gender / Raka Ray, University of California, Berkeley, Jennifer D. Carlson, The University of Arizona, Abigail Andrews, University of California, San Diego.

Description: Thousand Oaks, California : SAGE, 2018. | Includes bibliographical references.

Identifiers: LCCN 2017037893 | ISBN 9781452286976 (pbk. : alk. paper)

Subjects: LCSH: Sex role. | Sexism. | Sex differences. | Women—Social conditions.

Classification: LCC HQ1075 .R38 2018 | DDC 305.3—dc23 LC record available at https://lccn.loc.gov/2017037893

This book is printed on acid-free paper.

MIX
Paper from responsible sources
FSC® C012947
FSC www.fsc.org

Acquisitions Editor: Joshua Perigo
Editorial Assistant: Alexandra Randall
Production Editor: Laureen Gleason
Copy Editor: Erin Livingston
Typesetter: Hurix Digital
Proofreader: Caryne Brown
Cover Designer: Scott Van Atta
Marketing Manager: Kara Kindstrom

17 18 19 20 21 10 9 8 7 6 5 4 3 2 1

Contents

Acknowledgments **xi**

Author Biographies **xiii**

Introduction: Conceptualizing Gender **xv**

The Missing Feminist Revolution in Sociology xvi

Conceptualizing Gender: A Category and a Lens xvii

Breeders and Criminals: Gendering U.S. Immigration Control xviii

Providers and Protectors: Gendering U.S. Gun Culture xix

Banning Burqas and Burkinis: Gendering Foreign Policy and National Identity xx

Beginning Our Gendered Analysis xxi

Power xxii

Position xxii

Representation xxii

Practice xxii

Note xxiv

Chapter 1 Power **1**

Abigail Andrews

Introduction 1

The Gender Orders of Institutions 4

How Institutions Reinforce Inequalities 5

Gender Hegemonies 7

Masculine and Feminine as Signifiers of Power 7

A History of Gender Hegemonies 9

Feudalism and Dependency 9

Industrialization and the Independent Male Worker-Citizen 10

Colonialism and the Family of Man 11

The Welfare State: From Private to Public Patriarchy 13

Neoliberal Globalization and the Responsible Woman Worker 13

The Ambiguities of "Progress" 15

Keywords 16

Questions 16

Associated Readings 17

Chapter 2 Position **19**

Abigail Andrews

Introduction 19

Thinking through Difference: Beyond Universality and Objectivity 21

Standpoint Theory: A Sociology for Women 24
From Thinking Gender to Thinking Difference 26
Beyond Binary Thinking 29
An Epistemology of Difference 30
Keywords 31
Questions 31
Associated Readings 32

Chapter 3 Representation 33
Jennifer Carlson
Introduction 33
Emphasized Femininity 35
The Power of Images 36
Imperial Advertising and Commodity Fetishism 38
Gendered Advertising and the Growth of Industrial Capitalism in the U.S. 40
Norms of Neoliberalism 42
How Images Harm 45
Representing Hegemonic Masculinity 47
Marginalized Masculinities 50
Conclusion: Shifting Gendered Norms 53
Keywords 54
Questions 54
Associated Readings 55
Note 55

Chapter 4 Practice 57
Jennifer Carlson
Introduction 57
From Gender Identities to Gender Practices 59
Gender Accountability 61
Interrogating the Science of Sexual Difference 64
Embodiment: Bodies as the Effect of Gender 67
Doing/Undoing Gender and Sex 71
Keywords 72

Questions 72

Associated Readings 73

Chapter 5 Gendering Sexuality **75**

Oluwakemi M. Balogun and Kimberly Kay Hoang

Introduction 75

The Development of Human Sexuality as a Field of Inquiry 77

Early Feminist Interventions: Force versus Consent 78

Contemporary Debates around Sex Trafficking 81

The Politics of Sexual Rights: LGBTQ Rights Movement 82

From Sexuality to Sexualities: Power and Play 84

Doing Gender, Doing Sexuality 86

Sexualized Intersections: Sexuality, Race, Class, and Nation 88

Globalizing Sexualities 90

Conclusion 92

Keywords 92

Questions 93

Associated Readings 93

Chapter 6 Gendering Crime and Justice **95**

Jennifer Carlson

Introduction 95

From Violence against Women to Sexual Violence and Intimate Partner Violence 96

Rape Myths 99

The Social Construction of Victims and Criminals 102

The Paradox of Women's Violence: Blurring Victimhood and Criminality 104

The Gender Gap in Violence: Men and Masculinity 106

Gendering Justice 108

The Police 109

The Courts 111

The Prison 113

Undoing Violence, Recognizing Gender 116

Keywords 118

Questions 118

Associated Readings 119

Chapter 7 Gendering Social Reproduction **121**

Dawn Dow and Katherine Mason

Introduction 121

The Social Organization of Biological Reproduction: Historical and Global Perspectives 122

Adoption and Fosterage: Decoupling Biological Reproduction from Child-Rearing 123

Outsourcing Reproduction and Reproducing Inequality 124

Who Is Responsible for Social Reproduction? Historical and Global Perspectives 126

What Does Reproductive Labor Entail? 132

Debating Reproductive Labor 136

The Stalled Revolution: Persisting Gender Differences in Reproductive Labor 137

The Mommy Wars and the "Opt-Out Revolution" 138

New Family Forms, New Forms of Social Reproduction? Legal and Technological Innovations 140

Conclusion 143

Keywords 144

Questions 144

Associated Readings 144

Notes 145

Chapter 8 Gendering Exploitation **147**

Abigail Andrews and Raka Ray

Introduction 147

Gender Norms and Inequities in Today's Workplace 149

Occupational Segregation by Sex 151

The Glass Ceiling and the Glass Escalator 152

Explaining Sex Segregation at Work 153

The Gender Wage Gap 154

Other Forms of Discrimination 156

Barriers to Union Organizing 157

Gendering Neoliberal Globalization 158

Gendered Migration and the Global Care Chain 159
The Global Factory and the New Feminine Worker 160
Microfinance, the "Responsible Woman," and the Triple Burden of Public Service 161
Gender Transformations in the Informal Economy 163
Reconstructing Masculinities on the Margins 165
The End of Men? Or More Glass Ceiling? 166
Beyond the Gendered Economy 168
Keywords 169
Questions 169
Associated Readings 170
Notes 170

Chapter 9 Politicizing Gender 171
Gowri Vijayakumar and Katherine Maich

Introduction 171
Rethinking the History of Feminism: Waves and Currents 172
Nineteenth- and Early 20th-Century Gender Activism in the United States 174
Feminisms in the United States during the 1960s and 1970s 176
Black Women's Organizing: "A Woman's Place Is in the Struggle" 178
Speaking, Singing, and Performing Gender: Creatively Challenging the "Relations of Ruling" 180
The 1980s and 1990s: Critiques of White Feminism, Queer Politics, and Transnational Solidarities 181
The Politics of Sexuality in the 1980s and 1990s 183
The Sounds of Feminist Politics in the 1980s and 1990s: Women as Cultural Producers 184
Thinking Globally: Transnational Feminisms and North–South Alliances 185
The 2000s and Beyond: Institutionalization, Backlash, and New Directions 186
The F Word: The Feminist Backlash 186
Bridging Locations, Interests, and Movements 187
New Struggles over Sexuality around the World 189
Conclusion 191
Keywords 191
Questions 191

Associated Readings 192

Note 192

Chapter 10 Decolonizing Gender **193**

Raka Ray

Introduction 193

Constructing the Global World Order 194

How Colonialism Reconstituted Gender Hegemonies 195

Breaking the Power of Indigenous Women: Colonialism in North America 198

The Effects of Struggles around Decolonization 199

Colonial Positions and the Politics of Knowledge 201

The Geopolitical Construction of Gender 203

Contextualizing Our Concepts: Ideas Mediated by Culture 206

Freedom 207

Agency 209

The Problem of Female Genital Surgeries 210

Conclusion 212

Keywords 213

Questions 213

Associated Readings 214

References **215**

Acknowledgments

From Raka Ray: As a new young assistant professor at Berkeley in 1993, I stepped into what seemed a paradise of feminist sociology led by Nancy Chodorow, Arlie Hochschild, Kristin Luker, and Barrie Thorne. For a few important years, we were also joined by the brilliant Dawne Moon. In a field in which social inequality was largely studied through social stratification, these sociologists created an intellectual world that brought psychology, emotion, and narrative to the sociology of gender through deep and incisive ethnographic work. They interrogated religion and sexuality, motherhood, the division of labor in families and at work, the creation of gender identity in schools, and social movements. At the same time, Michael Burawoy's attention to labor, and his nurturing of gender scholars, produced sociologists who wrote singularly important work on gendered labor market processes. Together, these scholars produced scores of students who created a Berkeley tradition in the sociology of gender. With my arrival, the scope of the work extended to a consideration of the effects of global forces on gender. Today, the University of California, Berkeley sociology department has developed a particular perspective on the study of gender that takes seriously individual life stories, cultural location, and global political economy. In writing this book, we hope to introduce American undergraduates to a fundamentally new way of thinking about gender, based both on our research and our collective teaching practice. In doing so, we acknowledge with gratitude our colleagues and teachers who have written with us, mentored us, and worked side by side with us, as well as those we have taught. I thank my former students, stellar scholars all, who have come together to write this book. There are no words to thank, in particular, Jennifer Carlson and Abigail Andrews, for the idea of the book, for its planning and execution, for their brilliant writing, and for the privilege of being able to transition so easily from their teacher to their colleague.

From Jennifer Carlson and Abigail Andrews: In the last decade, Raka Ray has become the pillar of the University of California, Berkeley department of sociology's contributions to the sociology of gender. In addition to her own pathbreaking scholarship, she is the supervisor of some of the most innovative, and oftentimes award-winning, new feminist studies in the field, many of which are discussed in this book. In the mid-2000s, many of her future advisees came to Berkeley as graduate students, inspired by its tradition of feminist sociology. When we arrived, Dawne Moon, Raka, and Barrie Thorne inspired us by teaching our first classes in gender and feminist theory. Whether in office hours or during seminars, Barrie insisted that we push disciplinary bounds, fight the so-called male mafia, and never let anyone dismiss our work by saying it was not "real" sociology. Meanwhile, Dawne compelled us to think within but also beyond the disciplinary boundaries of sociology and taught us how to read Judith Butler and Michel Foucault.

Sadly, due to a confluence of factors, many of Berkeley's luminaries in the sociology of gender—Nancy Chodorow, Arlie Hochschild, Dawne Moon, and Barrie Thorne—left Berkeley shortly before or after our arrival.

Raka ended up chairing more than ten dissertations at once. She adapted as a true feminist, bringing us students together to mentor each other. For several years, we regularly convened as a group to eat, drink, and discuss the work of one another. We jokingly referred to this group as *Team Raka*. Its impact on our intellectual development cannot be overstated. Raka taught us to open up our minds, intellectually and to one another. With her guidance, we became more than the sum of our parts. We pushed each other to ask bigger questions and to see connections in the complex, gendered politics occurring around the world, from Michigan to Mexico, India to Nigeria, and beyond. Not least, Raka taught us how to hang our hearts in the balance. Giving us roots and wings, Raka and the ties among us have carried us through personal trials, inspired us to question our certainties about feminist theories and politics, and compelled us to think globally.

This book emerges out of that intellectual space, which alongside Raka Ray (coeditor and author) included Abigail Andrews (coeditor and author), Oluwakemi Balogun (author), Jennifer Carlson (coeditor and author), Dawn Dow (author), Katie Hasson, Kimberly Hoang (author), Katherine Maich (author), Kate Mason (author), Jordanna Matlon, Sarah Anne Minkin, Nazanin Shahrokni, and Gowri Vijayakumar (author). As coeditors, Jennifer and Abigail are especially grateful for the labor of love from all members of this group, which has made possible this collective text.

Finally, the editors would like to acknowledge Jeff Lasser and the excellent editorial team at SAGE for providing thoughtful guidance and encouragement throughout the development of this book. We are especially grateful to Jessica Cobb, who immeasurably improved the quality of the manuscript with her acute sociological eye and attentive editorial acumen. Last but not least, we are thankful to our friends and families who, through their love and labor, supported us throughout the book writing process.

Author Biographies

Abigail Andrews is an assistant professor of sociology and urban studies at the University of California–San Diego. She received a PhD in sociology from the University of California, Berkeley in 2014. Her research focuses on gender, political sociology, globalization, and migration between Mexico and the United States. Her work on undocumented migrant communities and transnational politics appears in *Gender & Society, World Development,* and the *Journal of Contemporary Ethnography.*

Oluwakemi M. Balogun is an assistant professor in the departments of women's gender and sexuality studies and sociology at the University of Oregon. She received a PhD in sociology from the University of California, Berkeley in 2012. Her research and teaching interests focus on gender, globalization, nationalism, race/ethnicity, migration, and Africana Studies. Her scholarship appears in *Gender & Society* and *Ethnicities.*

Jennifer Carlson is an assistant professor in sociology and government and public policy at the University of Arizona. She received a PhD in sociology from the University of California, Berkeley in 2013. Her work examines the gendered dynamics of American gun culture, policing and public law enforcement, and conservative politics. She is the author of *Citizen-Protectors: The Everyday Politics of Guns in an Age of Decline*. In addition to writing for popular audiences in venues such as the *Los Angeles Times* and the *Washington Post*, her work also appears in *Gender & Society, Social Problems,* and other scholarly outlets.

Dawn M. Dow is an assistant professor of sociology at the University of Maryland, College Park. She received a PhD in sociology from the University of California, Berkeley in 2012 and also earned a JD from Columbia University, School of Law. Dow's research examines intersections of race, class, and gender within the context of the family, the workplace, educational settings, the law, and political mobilization. Her work has been published in journals including *Gender & Society*, *Journal of Marriage and Family,* and *Sociology of Race & Ethnicity*.

Kimberly Kay Hoang is an assistant professor of sociology and the College at the University of Chicago. She received her PhD in sociology in 2011 from the University of California, Berkeley. Her research interests center on sociology of gender, globalization, economic sociology, and qualitative methods. A central focus of her work is to understand the gendered dynamics of deal brokering in Southeast Asia's emerging markets. She is the author of the award-winning *Dealing in Desire: Asian Ascendancy, Western Decline and the Hidden Currencies of Global Sex Work*, and her work also appears in *Social Problems, Gender & Society*, *Journal of Contemporary Ethnography,* and other venues.

Katherine Maich is a postdoctoral scholar at the Center for Global Workers' Rights at the Pennsylvania State University. She received her PhD in sociology from the University of California, Berkeley in 2017, where she was also a Berkeley Empirical Legal Studies Fellow. Her research uses ethnographic methods to explore labor informality and the reproduction of gender and racial inequality. Her work has been published in *Social Development Issues*, *The Sociology of Work*, and *Doméstica: Housemaids*.

Katherine Mason is an assistant professor of sociology and women's and gender studies at Wheaton College in Norton, Massachusetts. She received her PhD in sociology from the University of California, Berkeley in 2012. Her work on bodies, gender, and the reproduction of social inequality has been published in journals including *Social Problems, Social Politics,* and *Sexuality Research and Social Policy*.

Raka Ray is professor of sociology, South and Southeast Asia studies, and geography at the University of California, Berkeley. Her areas of specialization are gender and feminist theory, inequality, emerging middle classes, cultures of servitude, social movements, and postcolonial sociology. Her publications include *Fields of Protest: Women's Movements in India*, *Social Movements in India: Poverty, Power, and Politics* (coedited with Mary Katzenstein), *Cultures of Servitude: Modernity, Domesticity and Class in India* (with Seemin Qayum), *Both Elite and Everyman: The Cultural Politics of the Indian Middle Classes* (coedited with Amita Baviskar), *The Handbook of Gender,* and many articles.

Gowri Vijayakumar is an assistant professor of sociology and South Asian studies at Brandeis University. She received her PhD in sociology from the University of California, Berkeley in 2016. Her research and teaching focus on the sociology of gender, sexuality, social movements, and development in transnational perspective. Her scholarship has been published in *Gender & Society* and *Global Labor Journal*.

Introduction: Conceptualizing Gender

Gender refers to the concepts societies create about differences between men and women. Though gender categories are sometimes rooted in beliefs about biological characteristics, gender is not innate. Instead, gendered ideas organize power and resources unequally based on the assumption that there are two mutually exclusive categories of men and women.

Around the world, social systems of gender place women at a disadvantage. In the United States, for example, women earn only 80 cents for every dollar men earn,[1] and married women with children spend almost three times as much time on housework as married men with children (28 hours vs. 10 hours per week; Lachance-Grzela and Bouchard 2010).

These disadvantages are justified by ideas about how men and women behave. People in many contemporary societies stereotype women as emotional or as caretakers. Whether consciously or not, people often expect women to find joy in assisting others, rather than treating them as workers, thinkers, or doers in their own right. By contrast, these societies often stereotype men as breadwinners and protectors who think objectively, even in the face of danger. While men are not expected to find the same joy as women in caring relationships, they are often seen as natural leaders.

Though these stereotypes may appear commonsense, a comparison across time and place reveals very different configurations of gendered expectations. For example, in the United States today, people often see secretarial and clerical work as female occupations, while in the earlier part of the 20th century, many considered these occupations "naturally" male. Meanwhile, in indigenous Zapotec villages in rural Mexico, farmers consider planting and plowing to be masculine activities and weeding and harvesting to be feminine. Even though stereotypes and expectations differ across societies, most gendered systems share a common feature: the belief that men and women are different and that these differences complement each other. The institution of heterosexual marriage, which is at the nucleus of gender relations in many societies, maintains this idea of gender complementarity. Heterosexual marriage also provides a concrete system for organizing household economies. In turn, other institutions such as families, schools, and workplaces rely on the organization of the household, reinforcing the dominant framework of gender relations.

This book examines such inequalities and the ideas that support them. The authors look at realms often associated with gender, such as care work, family, and love. In doing so, we understand gender as a category that organizes social relationships. But we also see gender as a mode of critical analysis—a lens through which we understand the social world. Therefore, we also look at areas that appear to have little to do with gender, such as the economy and politics. To set this approach in context, we begin by discussing how sociology, as a discipline, has incorporated gender analysis.

The Missing Feminist Revolution in Sociology

Like popular cultures, academic disciplines reflect and reproduce dominant frameworks of gender in a given society. In sociology, many classical canonical thinkers saw gender as foundational to social difference. But like the broader public, they assumed that these distinctions were natural, and they failed to comprehend how gender was socially constructed.

Take Émile Durkheim, for example. Durkheim argued that differences between people (especially the social division of labor) helped build interdependence and "organic solidarity," which he believed was the key feature of a healthy modern society. In his sociological classic, *The Division of Labor in Society* ([1893] 1997), Durkheim wrote,

> It is because men and women differ from one another that they seek out one another with such passion . . . in fact, men and women in isolation from each other are only different parts of the same concrete whole, which they reconstitute by uniting with each other . . . in other words, it is the sexual division of labor which is the source of conjugal solidarity. . . . Nowadays, among civilized peoples the woman leads an existence entirely different from the man's. It might be said that the two great functions of psychological life had become as if dissociated from each other, one sex having taken over the affective, the other the intellectual function.

Here, Durkheim used what he presumed were fundamental differences between men and women as a conceptual device to introduce his central argument. Organic solidarity, he suggested, had its roots in gender difference: As individual men and women joined in marriage, they constituted their own small society characterized by interdependence. Though Durkheim understood that gender differences can be socially created, his argument was premised on the assumption that heterosexual unions are based on natural contrasts between men and women and that the heterosexual union is at the heart of modern society.

Karl Marx—the founder of critical sociology—also saw the division of labor between women and men as a fundamental expression of social difference. Unlike Durkheim's harmonious view of male–female differences, Marx saw these differences as the first example of economic oppression and class antagonism. Before capitalism, he argued, men benefited from women's labor within families, creating "the latent slavery in the family." This exploitation intensified under capitalism, he suggested: "The bourgeois [or capitalist] sees in his wife a mere instrument of production" (Marx and Engels 2002: 27). By highlighting the unfairness of this arrangement, Marx provided a set of important tools for a sociology of gender.

Yet Marx—and many Marxist scholars—failed to see how gender was a distinct form of inequality from class. Instead, they assumed that the problem of gender was subsumed by class. They argued that capitalism would level the differences between men and women, turning both into members of the working class. Communism, they hoped, would then do away with *all* forms of oppression—both class and gender. Thus, Marx suggested, "The bourgeois family will vanish as a matter of course . . . with the vanishing of capital" (Marx and Engels 2002: 100). However, a worldwide communist revolution never happened. Far from undermining gender difference, capitalism has created profitable industries of cosmetics, dieting, plastic surgery, and fashion and treated women and men as different sorts of workers who are paid unequal wages.

By using distinctions between men and women to illustrate their theories of modern society, both Durkheim and Marx underscored the importance of gender as foundational to social difference. Nevertheless, neither provided a clear understanding of the relationship between masculinity and femininity as social categories or explained why these categories were socially significant. As a result, they gave little insight into how gender organized social life.

Assumptions about gender persist among many researchers in sociology today. First, similar to Durkheim and Marx, scholars often treat gender as if it refers to already-existing categories of *men* and *women*. Second, they subsume gender differences under other social inequalities, such as class, failing to understand gender in its own right. Third, they assume that the way they look at the world is objective, without marking their analyses as coming from a particular, gendered point of view. Finally, they neglect the ways gender shapes institutional arrangements and relations of power.

Feminist sociologists Judith Stacey and Barrie Thorne critiqued these assumptions in their 1985 essay, "The Missing Feminist Revolution in Sociology." They argued that, instead, gender should form the basis of a *critical sociology*. This means treating gender not only as a variable but also as an analytical perspective. As historian Joan Scott notes, gender is more than a category that describes men and women. Rather, gender is a device—a lens, if you will—that men and women use to interpret and imagine social reality. The social world is saturated with gender meaning, in reference to everything from cars (Mazda Miatas versus Hummers) to occupations (administrative assistants versus chief executive officers [CEOs]) and even to concepts (peace versus war). Scott argues that people use gender as a basic device to recognize and reinforce power and subordination. For instance, politicians often use gendered imagery to disparage opponents and their ideas as well as to legitimate those in power. Such an approach exposes how even social phenomena that are seemingly unrelated to gender are informed by and reproduce the distinction between masculinity and femininity.

Conceptualizing Gender: A Category and a Lens

In this book, we use the term *gender* in two ways.

First, gender refers to *categories*, particularly the stereotypes and norms that everyday people use to make sense of and participate in social life. These ideas about gender are rooted in the supposed opposition between two categories: masculinity and femininity. The social organization of this binary relationship shapes who does what and who gets what, often in unequal ways. It also influences behavior and beliefs, such as which bathroom people enter, which occupations and careers they pursue, and how they present themselves and relate to one another. In turn, these categories intertwine with and reinforce unequal relations of race, class, sexuality, colonial domination, and other lines of difference.

Second, gender is a *lens* through which people interpret the world and imagine society. This lens shapes how people make sense of moral values such as authority, independence, humility, and power and how they view institutions such as the military, the economy, the criminal justice system, and domestic and international politics.

To illustrate the distinction between gender as a category and gender as a lens for understanding the world, consider the following three examples.

Breeders and Criminals: Gendering U.S. Immigration Control

At first glance, immigration enforcement appears to have little to do with gender. Popular accounts suggest that the United States government creates and enforces immigration laws to protect national security and the U.S. economy. These laws mark migrants who cross the border without authorization as "illegal." To enforce such policies, the U.S. patrols the border and deports unauthorized immigrants. However, such laws employ gendered *lenses* both to determine who should be deported and to legitimize policing these groups. Immigration enforcement also has unequal implications across gendered *categories,* that is, for immigrant men and women. Finally, the gendered lenses and categories used in immigration control change over time.

In their 2013 article, "Latino Immigrant Men and the Deportation Crisis: A Gendered, Racial Removal Program," Tanya Golash-Boza and Pierrette Hondagneu-Sotelo flesh out some of this logic. They point out that during the 1990s, U.S. political campaigns framed immigrants as dangerous due to their potential to reproduce. Politicians targeted immigrant women in particular as "breeders" who might come to the United States to bear children who would eventually help them earn citizenship. Using this logic, federal and state lawmakers shrank the safety net for immigrant women, including access to welfare and government support.

After September 11, 2001, however, the dominant tropes in immigration policy shifted. As the United States waged a "War on Terror," the media and policymakers began to frame Mexican and Central American immigrants—particularly men—as potential criminals and terrorists. This masculine version of gendered threat helped reframe immigration enforcement as a matter of national security, an idea that may seem like common sense today. In turn, the U.S. began to promote mass deportation in order to "protect" the U.S. from threats of crime and terror by racialized immigrant men. Of the roughly 400,000 people deported each year, more than 90% were men, most of them Latinos. While women immigrants were deported less frequently, men's deportation left women to cope with *de facto* single motherhood, the loss of male income, and personal trauma.

Viewing gender as a category highlights the different impacts immigration enforcement has on immigrant men and women. Viewing gender as a lens, meanwhile, reveals how even state policies that appear to be gender neutral, such as border patrol and deportation, use gendered terms for legitimacy. In particular, framing immigrants as *breeders* or *criminals* helps position the state, immigration agents, and police as good, masculine protectors of U.S. citizens while justifying the expulsion and withdrawal of benefits from migrant groups.

As chapters in *The Social Life of Gender* will show, these gendered imaginaries intersect with and reinforce racial inequities between whites and Latino migrants as well as global inequalities between the United States and countries in Latin America.

Providers and Protectors: Gendering U.S. Gun Culture

In contrast to immigration politics, the gendering of American gun culture seems straightforward: The vast majority of gun owners and gun carriers are men, and guns are often seen as masculine-marked objects. But a closer look at why men understand guns as objects of safety and security suggests a more complicated story.

The United States is a gun-rich country, and it is becoming more so. According to recent estimates, the U.S. now has more guns than people. The frequency of Federal Bureau of Investigation (FBI) background checks—a way to measure the scope of gun sales in the absence of more direct measures—suggests that Americans bought guns in record numbers after President Obama's election in 2008. Americans are not only owning guns; they are also carrying them. More than 13 million Americans are licensed to carry guns in public.

Only recently have men turned to guns primarily for personal protection rather than for hunting. In *Citizen-Protectors: The Everyday Politics of Guns in an Age of Decline*, Jennifer Carlson (2015) traces this shift in motivation to changes in men's roles in the economy. During the 20th century, men's social identities revolved around their obligations as providers. In the latter half of the 20th century, however, deindustrialization eroded men's access to stable, well-paying jobs, especially in manufacturing. In places such as Michigan, men could no longer rely on providing income to demonstrate that they were good fathers, good husbands, and good men. Instead, men found alternative ways to fulfill the demands of masculinity. Today, many men embrace guns as tools of family protection. By carrying guns, they assert themselves as dutiful, useful, and even authoritative within their households. This gendered experience of social insecurity helps explain the overwhelming representation of men among gun owners and gun carriers.

Nevertheless, a meaningful, if small, minority of gun carriers are women. In contrast to men in Carlson's study, who emphasized insecurity, women gun carriers tended to see guns as objects of individual empowerment. Women gun carriers had different reasons from men because they started from a different place: exclusion from gun culture rather than marginalization in the labor market.

Viewing gender as a category allows us to appreciate the gender disparity in gun ownership and gun carrying, but it cannot tell us how guns matter to their owners. Viewing gender as a lens provides a deeper understanding of the social meaning of guns. This gendered lens helps link macro-level dynamics such as deindustrialization to micro-level practices such as the choice to carry a firearm. *The Social Life of Gender* follows several such linkages between macro and micro levels. It suggests that connecting social phenomena as seemingly distinct as the economy, violence, and the family enriches sociological insights into varying arenas, both within the U.S. and beyond.

Banning Burqas and Burkinis: Gendering Foreign Policy and National Identity

Finally, gender relations can play out in more complex ways, as illustrated by the controversies around Muslim women's apparel around the world. "Burkinis," for instance, are bathing suits that cover women's heads, arms, and legs, and many Muslim women wear them to swim in more modest clothing. In July 2016, several towns in France banned the wearing of burkinis on public beaches. The mayor of the city of Cannes went so far as to call the burkini "the uniform of extremist Islamism," framing it as a symbol of "backward" gender practices. These bans on burkinis follow an earlier ban throughout France on burqas, which are coverings that start at the head and cover the entire body. In the name of secular and liberal values, France declared these items of clothing oppressive to women. Through its decision to ban the burqa and the burkini, France presented itself to the world as a liberator of women.

To many people in the West, the practice of veiling represents a constraint on women's self-expression. In the U.S., as in France, political leaders and journalists often frame veiling as a patriarchal practice. Others suggest that U.S. development efforts and even military interventions will help liberate women from such forms of control. Ironically, in terms that recall the U.S. feminist movements of the 1970s, these leaders assume that women around the world are seeking freedom and choice. But many Muslim women emphasize that they *want* to be veiled and that they see the veil not as a form of submission to patriarchy but as a way of being pious.

Viewing gender as a category often reveals striking gender differences in social expectations about what men and women wear. But it does not explain why people in France care so much about burkinis, while saying little, say, about bikinis. Viewing gender as a lens makes sense of this difference by attending to how gender animates global geopolitical orders and justifies power relations across religion, ethnicity, and beyond. In Muslim communities from the Middle East to South Asia to immigrant enclaves in the U.S. and France, veiling is intertwined with a more complicated set of power relations. For one, policies such as the burkini ban use gender to express French anxiety about militant Islam and immigration from Muslim countries. They also legitimate Western intervention in the Middle East and state control over Muslim immigrants in the West. *The Social Life of Gender* highlights that gendered inequalities not only involve differences between women and men but are also implicated in varying relationships of power within and across different societies.

***

These three examples begin to illustrate what is gained if gender is taken seriously as a social category and as a lens of analysis. Attention to gender as a category helps us notice patterns and ask sociological questions, such as *Why are men migrants now deported more often than women? Why do men disproportionately own guns?* and *why do burkinis animate more heated debates than bikinis?* Using gender as a lens of analysis helps answer such questions in a nuanced way, which goes beyond obvious gendered arenas such as the family or clothing. For instance, immigration control is legitimated by gender ideologies that mark migrants as a masculine, criminal threat; many men turn to guns to navigate changes in their socioeconomic possibilities; and women's bodies are sometimes used to justify foreign policies or a nation's place in the world.

The sociology of gender provides much more than an additional set of binary variables to describe social reality. Gender is not only about the differences or inequalities between people called *women* and *men*. Rather, the sociology of gender provides critical tools of analysis that can be applied far beyond the analysis of women versus men. This is what Stacey and Thorne (1985) mean when they suggest that analyzing gender "leads feminists to rethink the basic conceptual and theoretical frameworks of their respective fields" (302).

In this book, you will grapple with inequalities between men and women and arguments for more equity, but you will also learn to see gender beyond men and women. You will examine how ideas about masculinity and femininity legitimize relations of power, race, and wealth. You will look at how gender offers a reference point for who "should" be dominant and who "should" be submissive and consider how these ideas are dynamic, historically constructed, and contested. You will look at gender in the United States and from varied global perspectives. This gender analysis may even lead you to question some widely held markers of gender equity as biased toward certain perspectives and particular groups. In the end, you will learn to treat gender as a set of structuring principles and ideologies that work in and through institutions, states, and families to legitimate broader relationships of power.

Beginning Our Gendered Analysis

The Social Life of Gender breaks the gendered lens into four distinct analytical arenas, each of which inspires a particular kind of critical inquiry. First, an analysis of *power* allows us to think historically about masculinity and femininity and to ask how gender ideologies shape, and are shaped by, power relations. Second, an analysis of *position* alerts us to how the world is differently understood from different points of view. Third, an analysis of *representation* allows us to see how gendered norms constrain how we see ourselves and others. Fourth, an analysis of *practice* allows us to think about how, through our daily practices, we recreate or challenge gender. The first portion of this book takes you through these four key theoretical components of gender, teaching you to raise questions about power, position, representation, and practice. These approaches then give you a foundation to explore other theoretical concepts, shape your research methods, and think critically about practices of feminism, enabling you to better grasp the complex ways in which the world is gendered.

Power

"Chapter 1: Power" explores how people use ideas about masculinity and femininity to explain or justify relations of inequality. It examines the gendered dynamics of power in different historical moments as people respond to changing configurations of capitalism, colonialism, and the state. This chapter shows how gendered ideologies reinforce and naturalize power relations and practices. It also highlights how relations of power can make gender norms appear natural, such as the idea that care work is feminine and wage labor is masculine. But power is not unchanging. As social processes around the family, the state, the economy, and other institutions change and people fight over power, gender ideologies also change.

Position

"Chapter 2: Position" moves from thinking about power broadly to thinking about gendered power dynamics within research. In particular, it walks through the ways gender inquiry is grounded in social difference. Knowledge is always produced from a particular social location, the chapter shows. By virtue of people's varying gender, racial, and class identities—to name a few—they have different perspectives on the world and different ways of knowing. After all, there is no such thing as *woman*; rather, there are white, middle-class, able-bodied, straight American women; there are straight, upper-class women of color from the Global South; there are working-class, African American lesbian women; there are women who identify sometimes as men; and there are those who reject the identity of *woman* and embrace *trans*, *queer*, *womyn*, *zhe*, or *man*. The chapter begins by discussing early feminist standpoint theorists who highlighted the importance of position in shaping what we know and how we know it. It then calls attention to diversity between, across, and among women and men as well as to the shortcomings of gender binaries. Thus, it uses position to build a sociology of knowledge.

Representation

While gender is a standpoint from which we understand the world, it is also a constraining force. Gender organizes expectations—or norms—for how people should look and behave and what they should desire. "Chapter 3: Representation" analyzes these norms and their circulation, particularly as they perpetuate understandings about "ideal" men and "ideal" women who implicitly embody other lines of social privilege. Tying gendered representation to class and race, this chapter shows that the impacts of gender norms go far beyond narrowing the range of possible gender expression. Dominant social standards of masculinity and femininity also impose psychic, social, economic, and physical losses (and, at times, rewards).

Practice

"Chapter 4: Practice" examines how people help produce and challenge the normative force of gender through social interaction. What people wear for clothes, which bathroom they go to, how they style their hair, how much physical space they take up as they sit or walk, and how they police the gender practices of others: All of these everyday actions add up to reflect, reproduce, and—at times—even resist gender norms in our lives and in society more broadly. A focus on gender practice shows that gender norms are neither natural nor inevitable. Because we *do* gender as active social agents, we also are capable of *undoing* gender—that is, upsetting gender binaries by refusing to perform according to gender norms.

Chapters 5–10 ask you to apply these analytical tools to various areas of social life. We include areas that appear more tightly linked to gender—such as sexuality and the family—but we also move into topics that may seem less likely sites of analysis for gender, such as violence, the economy, and social movements. Throughout, our goal is both to understand gender as social category and to use gender as a critical tool of analysis.

Chapter 5 explores gendered sexuality, tracing shifts in approaches to sexuality and identifying key ways that sexuality is intertwined with power. In keeping with the theme of the book, it describes political–economic approaches to sexuality to highlight how micro processes of intimate life are tied to macro structure of the state and the market, using global case studies to illustrate consent, domination, and resistance.

Chapter 6 considers the gendered nature of crime and justice by focusing on violent crime. It engages interpersonal violence and the complex mechanisms of social control that arise in response. It unpacks the legal institutions and socio-legal practices surrounding violent crime, particularly in the U.S. Though the U.S. is just one particular national context for violence, the analyses presented in this chapter provide concepts that can be used to make sense of gender and violence in other nations and in related contexts.

Chapter 7 examines the intimate work of caring for and maintaining human life and society: social reproduction. It explores how societies throughout history and across cultures have handled the conception and bearing of children. It also investigates who is responsible for performing reproductive labor and how that work is impacted by ideas about gendered divisions of labor either inside or outside of the household. After examining what social reproduction entails, the chapter outlines contemporary debates over changes in social reproduction and the potential consequences of those changes for society.

Chapter 8 explores the workings of gender in the economy and how gendered norms enable the exploitation of women. It also considers how relationships between work and gender are changing in the context of globalization, as women move long distances to perform factory work or to serve as part of the global care chain. It then examines how globalization affects poor men in both the United States and other parts of the world.

Chapter 9 explores how social movements have attempted to create changes in gender relations by tracing the history of feminist activism since the late 19th century. Exploring the multiple currents in feminist movements, it shows that like other social movements, feminist activism has historically been influenced by and reproduced multiple social inequalities. The chapter concludes by showing how activists around the world challenge and transform gender relations, including in ways not typically defined as *feminist*.

Chapter 10 looks at the global nature of social forces that shape gender—in particular, the history of colonialism. It also engages with feminists around the world to show that Western conceptions of gender and gender norms are not universal. The chapter ends by reflecting on what the global diversity of women's ideals means for our understanding of gender, feminism, and feminist activism.

We conclude the book with the question of feminism: What is the relationship between feminism as a political project and the sociology of gender as an intellectual project? Far from friendly bedfellows, we find that the analytical framework that emerges from a critical sociology of gender makes a unified feminist project impossible. On what terms, then, might feminist politics be based? These are the questions posed in the final chapter of this book.

NOTE

1. The gap is even wider for women of color. In comparison to white men, African American women in the U.S. earned roughly 63 cents and Latinas 54 cents on the dollar (U.S. Census Bureau 2016).

CHAPTER 1

Power

Abigail Andrews

Chapter 1 examines the relationship between gender and power. First, it shows that gender is implicated in the power arrangements of institutions such as governments, factories, and schools, and that in turn, these institutions reinforce inequalities along gender lines. Second, this chapter emphasizes how the idea of gender difference can be used as a reference point—or a signifier*—to legitimate the power of dominant groups. To understand how gender shapes politics, the chapter turns to the concept of* hegemony*: the set of ideologies that predominate in a particular place and time. In particular, predominant gender ideologies—or* gender hegemonies*—help justify relations of power. Gender hegemonies are also* dynamic*. That is, over time and in different societies, different understandings of gender may become dominant, along with different gender relationships. The last part of the chapter addresses the process by which gender hegemonies change by tracing gender relations across five historical periods:* feudalism, industrialization, colonialism, the welfare state, *and* neoliberal globalization*. Comparing the dominant gender ideologies at work in these periods challenges contemporary expectations about what is "naturally" masculine or feminine. The chapter concludes by reflecting on how, as gender hegemonies change, so do notions of freedom, liberation, and agency.*

Introduction

Gender is tied to power. A traditional understanding of gender and power points out that men can—and often do—dominate women. In the 1970s, feminists in the United States and around the world criticized the ways that men excluded women from the workplace and politics. They questioned men's status as household heads, demanded an end to rape and domestic abuse, and argued against the idea that men were naturally strong or aggressive and women were naturally weak and nurturing. Still, men continue to exercise direct power over women in much of the world. For instance, this traditional understanding of gender and power suggests that men often use their interpersonal and institutional power to make decisions about women's bodies (e.g., whether they should have babies or what they should wear) and about their labor (e.g., whether they should work outside the home or whether they should earn as much money as men).

Nevertheless, the relationship between gender and power is also broader and more complex than this traditional understanding might suggest. For one, gender relations have changed dramatically. In the 1950s, an "ideal American woman" was expected to keep her house and herself beautiful. By the 2010s, Sheryl Sandberg, the chief financial officer of Facebook and one of the country's most high-profile businesswomen, urged women to "lean in" at the workplace and embrace a new business femininity. Once excluded from higher education, U.S. women now earn more bachelor's degrees than U.S. men. The 2010 United States Census shows that 33% of women versus 32% of men have college degrees. In the labor force, even as men are losing jobs in manufacturing, women work in everything from white-collar businesses around the world to households in the United States to low-wage factories in countries such as Mexico and China. A woman is prime minister of the United Kingdom, and a woman ran for president of the United States as the Democratic Party nominee. Poor women in the Global South—once ignored by development programs or acknowledged only as dependents of men—are now held up as responsible entrepreneurs. It seems there are almost no jobs left that a woman cannot do.

Understandings of masculinity have changed as well. Though women still do a disproportionate share of household tasks, men's participation in care work is growing. In the United States, men and women do things every day that challenge the separate roles that American men and women once played. Indeed, the very idea that men and women make up two separate groups is no longer taken for granted. In today's world, people identify with a range of gender categories, from agender to cisgender to genderqueer to transgender and everywhere in between. Does it still make sense to say that, across the family, the workplace, and politics, men call the shots?

The interplay between gender and power goes deeper than the idea that one group labeled *men* dominates another labeled *women*. Early feminist scholars focused on analyzing areas considered *women's spaces*, such as the family, the home, and beauty. However, Joan Scott (1988), a feminist historian, criticized such scholars for looking for gender only in the places where it was "supposed" to appear. She argued that this focus obscured the importance of gender in areas that were not as obvious. Scott began to look at the roles gendered concepts played throughout society, even in areas that did not appear to be about gender. She argued that gender was important in institutions: places like schools, the economy, and—in particular—politics. This book looks for gender in such unexpected places. Even in arenas that appear neutral, the authors suggest, gendered ideas often reinforce unequal power dynamics. This hidden character is part of what makes gender so important.

Institutions are social arrangements that follow established rules and practices, such as the state, the legal system, and the family. Many institutions are organized around a gendered division of labor in which men and women take distinct roles. These institutions also help create the relations between men and women. They reinforce inequalities along gendered lines, limiting women's participation in spheres of power and helping produce dominance for some men (usually those who are wealthy and racially privileged). In addition, institutions shape—and reshape—gendered ideas about what is natural and desirable. For instance, welfare policies in the mid-20th-century United States enabled men but not women to earn a family wage, reinforcing the breadwinner model and the idea that women were naturally housewives. In the 2000s, meanwhile, the rise of the technology industry in Silicon Valley, California, helped inaugurate a new brand of masculinity. While images in the 1970s had portrayed "nerdy" men as soft and effeminate, corporations such as Google tied technological savvy to masculinity (Cooper 2000). The representation of technological skills as masculine now helps reinforce such workers' influence over today's growing—and increasingly important—information superhighways.

The example of the newly masculinized Google workers illustrates how ideas about gender help naturalize relations of domination. Describing individuals and actions in terms of *feminine* or *masculine* helps people represent, legitimate, and—at times—criticize political power. While these symbols may portray the dominant as masculine and the subordinate as feminine, they can also be more complex. Think back to the example of U.S. immigration enforcement described in the Introduction. On the surface, immigration control is not gendered. Nevertheless, the U.S. government has used gendered images of *both* feminine "breeders" and masculine "criminals" to justify deportation.

Analyzing how gender relates to power requires a historical understanding of the assumed differences between men and women. The history of gender reveals changing patterns that defy a linear narrative of progress that starts with men and women around the world being less equal and moves toward them being more equal. Two examples illustrate this complexity. First, as described in more detail in Chapter 10, many people today frame female genital surgeries (the cutting and shaping of the clitoris and the labia) as antiquated practices lingering only in "backward" areas of the Global South. When these surgeries are performed in places such as Sudan, U.S. feminists often denounce the practice as *genital mutilation*. At the same time, growing numbers of women in the United States, especially young women, are also seeking out plastic surgery called *labioplasty* to "improve" the appearance of their labia (Rabin 2016).

A second example is the issue of gender identity: Even though many people in the U.S. look at the acceptance of multiple gender identities (e.g., trans men) as unprecedented progress toward gender equality, nonconforming gender identities have been a long-standing practice in many parts of the world, from indigenous Zapotec communities in Southern Mexico to the *hijras* (or *third gender*) of India. In such areas, Spanish and British colonial officials objected to non-binary expressions of gender and pushed them underground, moving in a direction that people in the U.S. today might see as backward.

These two examples indicate how gendered logics of power can shift over time and across place in ways that do not always increase equality. Rather, the meanings people make of *masculinity* and *femininity* are tied to broader social relations through processes including capitalism, colonialism, and globalization. Specific relations of power shape the predominant gender norms in each historical period. In turn, the ways people talk and think about gender often help legitimate the power of those who are in charge. But power is never simply fixed. At any given historical moment, people contest the rule of those in power. Relations of domination change, and the changes introduce new ideas and arrangements of gender.

Therefore, as this chapter will show, gender is political. The chapter starts by examining the relationship between gender and institutions. It then considers the gendered arrangements that have predominated in five periods in recent history: preindustrialism, industrialization, colonialism, the welfare state, and neoliberal globalization. The chapter concludes by exploring how dominant notions of masculinity and femininity change, both in the U.S. and across the globe.

The Gender Orders of Institutions

To understand how gender works in areas such as politics or the economy, scholars analyze institutions. Every institution has its own particular set of gender practices and norms that govern its operation. For example, in workplaces, gender shapes recruitment, social divisions, and job mobility (Connell 2009). Take industrial agriculture: Farm workers who are men often do heavy lifting, while farm workers who are women (and racially subordinated groups) are expected to bend down low to the ground to pick or sort produce for packing. Similarly, in white-collar offices in the United States, the majority of managers and technological workers are men, while women tend to work in marketing, sales, human service, or clerical jobs. Gender not only shapes who does what, but it also affects how people understand the character of different occupations. For example, managers are expected to act "masculine"—tough, decisive, and sometimes ruthless—regardless of whether they are men or not. By contrast, clerical workers are expected to act "feminine"—deferential and caring, no matter their gender identities. Treating some jobs as masculine and others as feminine establishes gendered expectations for workers' behaviors. These arrangements also separate those who identify as men and women into different positions. You will learn more about gender and work in Chapter 8.

Gender also operates differently across different institutions. For example, policing and public school teaching share many similarities. Both are interactive jobs managed by government agencies. Yet police are expected to be masculine (tough, physical, and assertive), while elementary school teachers are thought of as more feminine (nurturing and concerned).

The gender arrangements across different institutions are also related to each other. For example, the gendering of paid jobs, which determine people's wages and working hours, affects people's gendered responsibilities at home. In the United States, the institution of the family relies on long-standing expectations that women make childrearing their primary responsibility, while men focus on providing resources for the family to consume. Chapter 7 will explore the family in more detail. For now, suffice it to say that even though many families vary from this model, shared gender practices and expectations shape the institution as a whole.

In a given society, the predominant pattern of gender arrangements—that is, the combination of institutional norms and practices—is called the **gender order**. Thus, while individual jobs may be marked feminine or masculine, the gender order sorts the relationship between jobs, such as by marking physical and high-status work as masculine while marking emotional or service work as feminine. Different gender orders entail distinct combinations of household production, paid work, and cultural ways of talking and thinking about gender.

Since understandings of masculinity and femininity are historically constructed and specific to particular places, gender orders change over time (Connell 1987). In the 1950s United States, the gender order positioned "good" middle and upper-class women to refrain from working outside the home, though many poor women and women of color worked for wages to support their families. A half-century later, it was considered normal for women to find paid jobs. Many white and middle- to upper-class women occupied professional jobs. During that same half-century, industrial jobs long considered to be male declined, the feminized position of *secretary* began to disappear, and the principle of equal opportunity grew increasingly important in the workplace.

These changes do not mean that there is no longer a gender order; they only mean that the gender order has changed. For instance, even as most women work for pay, the expectation remains that schoolteachers will act feminine and that police officers will act masculine—regardless of the gender identity of the individual worker. Women still predominate in jobs in the service sector and education, while men remain predominant in work such as construction and information technology. The gender order shifted to absorb women into the workforce while maintaining the gendering of jobs.

How Institutions Reinforce Inequalities

Institutions not only rely on gendered terms; they also have gendered effects. For instance, sociologist Joan Acker (1990) has shown that male power is built into corporate workplaces. Corporations often treat workers as if their jobs are their only concerns, assuming that workers are breadwinning men whose wives take care of family responsibilities. This expectation that workers will show dedication to employers by spending a substantial amount of time at work makes it difficult for people with caregiving responsibilities—particularly women—to succeed. The effects are gendered: For example, in the 2000s, women quit their jobs at Google at much higher rates than men, creating a workforce that was 70% male.

The government is also an institution with gendered effects. In the 1970s, many feminists looked to the state to protect them from men's discrimination, violence, and oppressions within the nuclear family, the workplace, and elsewhere. However, in the 1980s and 1990s, scholars pointed out that the state could also reinforce gender inequities, at times even co-opting feminist discourse as it did so. They argued that far from being neutral, the government and laws described the world from a masculine perspective and distributed greater influence to men than to women. Thus, the state reproduced the power of elite men and the subordination of women.

Feminist legal scholar Catharine MacKinnon was one of these critics. In 1982 and 1983, in a series of essays called "Feminism, Marxism, Method, and the State," MacKinnon questioned the supposed neutrality of the government by scrutinizing laws regarding rape and sexual consent. She showed that these laws defined rape in relation to men, framing the violation of women as the transgression of a man's property by another man. Rather than treating women as persons with independent rights over their own bodies, these laws reflected women's value only as wives and mothers to men. These laws reinforced women's status as the property of men while silencing women's perspectives. The *claim* to be neutral hid the fact that such laws were made from men's points of view and designed to reinforce certain men's access to women's bodies. The issues MacKinnon raised over 35 years ago echo in contemporary controversies over rape on college campuses. Rape is still framed from men's point of view—even by judges—some of whom consider it a "natural" inclination for "unruly" young men that women should take responsibility to prevent. You will learn more about the relationship between gender and violence in Chapter 6.

In addition to reinforcing individual men's power, the state exercises its own power over women. In an essay called "Finding the Man in the State" (1995), Wendy Brown argued that the state was gendered in multiple ways: It was staffed by men; it used gendered ideologies in its laws and policies; and its institutions helped produce masculine dominance. The state limited women's participation in the highest realms of politics (at the time that Brown wrote her essay, only six out of the total 100 U.S. senators were women; in 2017, only 21 of 100 senators are women, although this is the largest number of women senators in U.S. history). It also exercised control over women's sexual and reproductive health. Extending MacKinnon's insight that the state ensured men's access to women, Brown showed that the state reinforced men's power to run the world and justified their prerogative to do so.

Even after the feminist movement of the 1970s relieved some women from some of their subordination to individual men in the household, women remained subject to masculinist state institutions. For example, state policies explicitly control women's bodies. Many conservative politicians in the U.S. promote laws that limit women's decisions regarding their own reproductive health. Several candidates for the 2016 Republican nomination for the U.S. presidency strongly argued for outlawing abortions, even in cases of rape. In terms of foreign policy, each Republican administration since the early 1980s has instituted a "Global Gag Rule" to prohibit funding to foreign aid organizations that provide abortion services. Through such laws, the U.S. government exerts power over the bodies of women around the world.

Another example of how state institutions can reinforce some men's economic and political power is the U.S. Social Security Act of 1935. The Act created the U.S. welfare system of the 20th century, but it separated welfare into two tiers. First, Aid to Families with Dependent Children (AFDC) provided moderate economic support to poor single mothers on the premise that these women were "missing" a male provider. Second, the same legislation instituted Social Security to provide more generous old age entitlements to retired workers, who were almost all men. The act excluded farm workers and domestic workers, who were largely African Americans, immigrants from Asia and Latin America, and women. This welfare system reinforced men's higher-status roles as breadwinners, naturalized women's unpaid caretaking work for their families, and tied these gender inequalities to other inequities of race and immigration status. White men sustained both a predominant role in the workplace and access to more economic resources than either women or people of color. The state, meanwhile, acted as the "protective father" in laws directed at women and children.

Gender Hegemonies

Hegemony refers to dominant ideologies that make the status quo appear beneficial for everyone while making inequalities appear natural and inevitable. This concept was initially developed by the Italian Marxist Antonio Gramsci (1971) and English cultural theorist Raymond Williams (1977), both of whom used the term to analyze power relationships around social class. In many societies, they argued, the dominant did not rule by force alone. Rather, the dominant classes also reinforced their position through ideological efforts at cultivating *consent* to domination. Gramsci and Williams referred to the combination of force and consent as *hegemony*. For example, in the U.S., the belief that success comes from hard work is hegemonic. This belief both encourages people to work hard and makes it appear that poor people do not have a lot of money because they do not work hard. Circulated through schools, churches, and media, this widespread ideology generates consent for class inequality by framing wealth as an expression of merit rather than domination. To reproduce their hegemony, the dominant use these kinds of norms and symbols along with more overt forms of coercion and domination. According to Gramsci and Williams, much of this ideological work takes place in civic institutions, such as schools, churches, and government agencies.

But there are always alternative ways of thinking, and the legitimating ideology of any particular group is subject to opposition from those who do not buy into the present order. To the extent that the working classes question elites' right to rule, Gramsci and Williams argued, elites' hegemony loses sway, and their power comes into question. Opposing groups can also build support within civic institutions, including nongovernmental organizations (NGOs), churches, and so forth. When opposing groups are successful in persuading people that the current arrangements are not fair or legitimate, new ideologies gain leverage, overthrow previously dominant logics of power, and install new hegemonies in place of the old. The contested nature of hegemony means that any hegemony is *dynamic*: It is open to change.

Although the idea of hegemony was developed to understand class relations, it is also a useful concept for understanding gender because it emphasizes how norms and ideas help reproduce gender orders as well as enabling resistance to them. In *The Social Life of Gender*, we use the term **gender hegemony** to refer to a period's dominant ideology about gender relations, which in turn justify inequality. Like class hegemonies, gender hegemonies are located within a particular place and time, and like class power, they are *dynamic*.

Masculine and Feminine as Signifiers of Power

As mentioned above, Joan Scott (1988) argues that gender is "a primary way of signifying relations of power" (42). In other words, gender provides norms and symbols—known as **signifiers**—that alert people to what kinds of positions are powerful and that make power relations appear natural. Gender is an ideal signifier of political power because, for many people, gender binaries seem to be sure and fixed, as if they are outside human construction. By linking power hierarchies to the supposedly innate differences between men and women, those in power make their control seem natural. Because gender is such a ready reference point, Scott argues, political history "gets enacted on the field of gender" (49).

For example, the term *Founding Fathers* links the writers and ratifiers of the U.S. Constitution to gendered ideals of fatherhood, implying that—like fathers—these individuals acted in the best interests of the nation. More generally, the president of a nation may be portrayed as a father figure, suggesting not only that is he a powerful decision maker but also that he has a legitimate right to tell citizens of that nation what to do. Other times, people use references to gender to express a ruler's fitness to rule. For instance, as former *Terminator* actor and bodybuilder Republican Arnold Schwarzenegger campaigned for George H.W. Bush's candidacy for president, and later in his own bid for California governor, he belittled his opponents by calling them "girly men." This quip was not simply meant to refer to Democrats' personal characteristics; it also described their political actions. When Schwarzenegger proclaimed in 2004 that Democrats were "economic girly men," he was using gendered language to express his support for American capitalism. Implying that masculine men support the free market, Schwarzenegger asserted the superiority of a free-market approach to economic policy and bolstered his claim to political power.

In his recent presidential campaign, Donald Trump also presented himself as hyper-masculine. *The Atlantic* magazine (Hamblin 2016) described him in this way:

> Trump is in many other ways a caricature of a man's man. He shouts and bullies and berates people. He speaks mostly in superlatives and mentions himself in most sentences. He plays golf and has a head full of hair, as men are supposed to. He hasn't gone full Putin and hunted shirtless on horseback with his press pool, but he has alluded to the size of his penis from the stage of a presidential primary debate.

While masculinity should have nothing to do with a person's ability to be president, people often use such masculine images to help define who is suited to lead. Gendering presidential power in this manner also makes it more difficult to imagine a woman in that role.

People also use gendered language more abstractly, such as to justify going to war. For example, when the United States invaded Iraq in 2003, members of the United States armed forces were framed as the masculine rescuers of the victims of the tyrant leader Saddam Hussein. At the time, many Americans felt that the United States should not risk the human costs of military intervention in the Middle East. Yet President George W. Bush justified his actions by describing himself as a protective father figure (Young 2003). He argued that the United States should invade Iraq and Afghanistan because its army was the masculine protector of two groups of victims: innocent civilians at risk of terrorism in the United States and "oppressed"

Muslim women under the thumb of terrorists abroad (Young 2003). These gendered framings not only legitimated U.S. intervention in the Middle East but also enabled President Bush to centralize his power at home. As another example, George Kennan, one of the architects of the Cold War between the Soviet Union and the United States, imagined the Cold War as an "emotional, sexually charged struggle between a man and a woman" (Costigliola 1997). In a famous "long telegram" to the State Department in 1946, he portrayed Russians as a feminine people at the mercy of a despotic, predatory government that was applying an "unceasing pressure for penetration" into Western society. Such images are impactful insofar as they mobilize male/female oppositions as a reference point to understand and legitimate military power—and at other times, to break it down.

A History of Gender Hegemonies

Both gender orders and gender hegemonies are dynamic. There is no single, stable femininity or masculinity. Dominant arrangements and ideas are always subject to contestation and redefinition. Therefore, the shared meanings of gender—of what is masculine and feminine—change across place and time. As power gets contested, ideas about the "natural" predilections of men or women get remade. The history and examples that follow flesh out pivotal changes in gender hegemonies that have occurred in recent history in the United States and around the world.

This section traces gender hegemonies in five key periods: feudalism, industrialization, colonialism, the welfare state, and neoliberal globalization. Each subsection presents the gender hegemony that predominated at a given moment, the implications of that hegemony for who did what and who governed, and the ways that hegemony changed as political and economic circumstances undermined prior modes of control. The chapter focuses on the United States and Western Europe while also noting how the global dominance of those countries imposed Western gender hegemonies and intertwined Western ideas with gender orders in other parts of the world.

Feudalism and Dependency

Before the industrial revolution, the vast majority of both men and women in Europe worked under the feudal system as peasant farmers, sharecroppers, or serfs. Nearly everyone was economically dependent on the lords who owned the land where they worked. Politically, they were also considered *dependents* and were denied a voice in public affairs (Fraser and Gordon 1994). In the gender hegemony of the era, the nobility legitimated their power by describing themselves as father figures while treating the poor as dependent children.

Within poor families, relationships between men and women often echoed the arrangement between lords and peasants: Women were considered the property of their husbands' households and typically worked, without pay, for the benefit of the household (Kandiyoti 1988). While economic dependence was not necessarily considered masculine or feminine, women were expected to stay in the household and dutifully serve their husbands and mothers-in-law. Nevertheless, both women and men helped with farming and occasionally other work, such as artisanship and crafts.

Likewise, noble families also considered women to be the property of their husbands. In fact, the term *family* comes from the Latin *familia*, which defined members of a household (including the estate, servants, and family members) as the property of a man. This patriarchal family organization provided a basic justification for early modern state formation: Modeled after a head of household, the king subordinated men and women alike in the family cum nation. However, the gender hegemony changed with the onset of capitalism.

Industrialization and the Independent Male Worker-Citizen

By the mid-19th century, with the growth of capitalism and the Industrial Revolution, a crisis took root in the economic foundations of the feudal system. This crisis transformed gender norms, reconstructing ideas about masculinity and femininity to support the emerging capitalist political economy. Industrialization eroded farm incomes, driving the lower classes to seek wage labor in the cities. As the poor urbanized, the model in which both men and women worked in the peasant economy was replaced by what Joan Scott and Louise Tilly (1978) call a **family wage economy**, that is, an economy in which one wage—the father's—was expected to maintain a family.

Both young men and women left the countryside and poured into towns and cities in search of jobs in factories. With so many people competing for jobs, workers faced miserable wages and working conditions. As a result, economist Heidi Hartmann (1976) argued, male workers—particularly in trades undergoing rapid technological changes or where women and men worked side by side—worried that they might lose control over the most desirable, skilled jobs in the labor force and that competition might drive their wages down. In the context of this struggle, men workers began to develop new gendered signifiers to support their demands for higher pay. Unions of male workers organized to exclude women from certain job sectors, such as manufacturing, and instead crowd them into less desirable sectors. To access the higher-status, higher-paying jobs, men pushed out their women competitors with the idea that women belonged in the home. In the wage economy, they argued, "real, responsible" men were providers charged with earning income to feed their families. That is, they were breadwinners. By tying the breadwinning role to masculinity while portraying women as dependents of men, male labor activists were able to demand a family wage sufficient to support a wife and children. At the same time, such divisions between men and women workers prevented them from unifying against employers.

Taking account of these changes, gender scholars Heidi Hartmann (1976) and Joan Scott (1988) argue that a new gender hegemony emerged in the industrial period. This hegemony centered not on the image of a family in which the nobility were fathers but instead on the breadwinning role of the male citizen. The male breadwinner model emerged as formerly disenfranchised men sought citizenship. Along with better wages, men began demanding a greater say in political affairs. They supported these claims by highlighting their masculine status as responsible breadwinners and spokespeople for their families. By invoking and naturalizing the breadwinner model, men gained independence as workers and citizens, while women continued to be seen as dependent (on their husbands). Unable to speak for herself in public affairs, the female dependent became the opposite of the independent male citizen. Women went from being seen as partners in agricultural labor to being seen as "parasites" in the home, which hid the care and domestic labor they did to keep men alive. As men gained economic and political independence, dependence became stigmatized, taking on a new, feminized significance (as well as a racialized significance, as detailed below) that it had not held before.

The rise of the family wage helped nurture the ideology of the nuclear family, emphasizing women's duties in all areas related to the home, including children's education. Along with men's labor unions, various civil society institutions promoted idealized notions of the family and maternity. They demanded that women withdraw from paid work to fulfill their "appropriate" feminine duties in the domestic sphere. These norms helped stabilize the concept of the nuclear family with a man as the sole breadwinner and put women in a new kind of subordinated position.

Meanwhile, families who could not follow these ideals were considered deviant or less developed. While industrialization inaugurated new gender expectations, in reality, most working-class families were not able to subsist off only one wage. Among African Americans in the U.S. after the end of slavery, for instance, neither women nor children were exempt from labor. Women who did work outside the home in the 19th century were often disparaged using masculine terms. In a famous series of portraits, for instance, British diarist Arthur Munby sketched working-class women such as farmers, mine workers, and domestic workers as ferociously large, tough, and masculine. The implication was that these women had failed to achieve the ideal femininity of the time.

As the male breadwinner family became hegemonic in Europe and the United States, these ideals were exported in complex forms through colonialism abroad.

Colonialism and the Family of Man

The expansion of capitalism beyond Europe from the 18th century onward was fueled by European colonial intervention in countries across Africa, Asia, and Latin America. Colonialism exported European and American ideas about gender to the rest of the world, interrupting the existing gender hegemonies in those places and imposing new ones. Colonialism helped intertwine ideologies of gender and race, which is explored further in Chapter 2. While we discuss colonialism more in Chapter 10, here, we describe how it reconstituted gender hegemonies as part of a global historical process.

As European countries and the United States sought to conquer other nations, they extended the gender hegemony that depicted white middle-class European men as father figures of their own families to the level of international relations. They did so by describing European nations and the U.S. as "fathers" of a global **family of man**—a socially constructed hierarchy of human beings. To legitimate violent domination around the world, European nations described themselves as the "protectors" of a broad racial hierarchy in which people of other races were both behind historically and subordinate within the family, almost like children. According to this gendered, racialized logic, European nations were obligated to intervene abroad to teach "underdeveloped" peoples a more "modern" way of life.

As these racial ideologies became more dominant, framing white people as masculine fathers and Black and brown people as children, they also circulated back into European centers, especially as slave trades forcibly moved Black and brown bodies from the colonies to the metropolis. European upper- and middle-class people reinforced their economic privilege by symbolically distancing themselves from disenfranchised and marginalized people. They did this by denigrating the lower classes in gendered and racial terms. As historian Ann Stoler explains in her book *Race and the Education of Desire* (1995), colonialism reinforced the "cult of bourgeois domesticity" by creating boundaries between "good" bourgeois families—who supposedly had moral upbringing, order, and economic accumulation—and "bad" working-class and poor families. In the process, middle-class white women gained a new role as the protectors of the domestic sphere and the nurturers of boys who would one day become the new "fathers" of the family of man. This elevation of motherhood had important implications for white women, reinforcing the understanding that proper femininity was tied to motherhood and the home.

Meanwhile, in colonial contexts, imperialists mounted an assault on local gender traditions, demanding that people behave more like Europeans. In India, for example, British colonists claimed to be saving women from the traditional practice of immolating themselves on their husbands' funeral pyres (known as *sati*). They argued that, in the interest of more modern gender relations, Britain had a duty to intervene in and reshape Indian laws and cultural practices. Yet the imperial powers did such saving primarily through violent intervention, often doing great harm to the women they were ostensibly there to help.

While aspects of this colonial gender hegemony still persist today, it has not gone unchallenged. In many instances, people of colonized countries resisted the gendered terms used to legitimate intervention. As capitalism and colonialism spread, men and women also sought to assert other gender hegemonies. For instance, as we discuss further in Chapter 10, some women of Muslim countries actively choose to wear veils or avoid working outside of the home to practice what they see as a proper femininity and resist the imposition of Western norms. Some non-Western governments have also taken similar stances. In the past several decades, Iran has repeatedly expressed its difference from the United States by insisting that women wear veils in public, instituting gender segregation in parks and buses, and framing itself as a moral Islamic nation in contrast to what it depicts as the socially degenerate Western world.

The Welfare State: From Private to Public Patriarchy

In the latter years of global colonialism, a new gender hegemony also began to emerge in the United States. Starting in the aftermath of the American Civil War in the form of pensions for disabled veterans and war widows and then developing with the New Deal, the United States established the **welfare state,** a set of social assistance and insurance programs, universal citizenship entitlements, and public services intended to ameliorate class inequalities (Orloff 1996). At first, the welfare state upheld women's role as homemakers and men's role as breadwinners by treating men as the primary recipients of unemployment and retirement assistance and single women as recipients of aid for children and families. Reinforcing the image of men as independent, deserving breadwinners, state support provided to men tended to be greater than that provided to women.

Over time, however, government aid to families became increasingly stigmatized. Instead of being considered downtrodden widows, single mothers who received aid became marked as immoral because they did not have husbands and as lazy because they were unemployed. Thus, the welfare state promoted a gender hegemony that reinforced the norm of the nuclear family with the breadwinner father as its head. These programs protected the male breadwinner by making dependence on a man (private dependence) seem preferable to the vilified version of dependence on the state (public dependence).

At the same time, accepting aid from (or depending on) the state entailed its own form of subordination. For women who relied on public assistance, the welfare state itself acted as a "father figure." For instance, when women requested Aid for Families with Dependent Children (financial support for poor families with children), they had to submit to state assessment, which judged the quality of their homes and even their capacity as mothers. Social workers would come into women's homes and review their belongings and their parenting. Thereby, the government not only took on a more intimate presence in poor women's lives; it also put forth the idea that women who were not monitored by men needed to be monitored by public institutions. State welfare programs thus expanded the surveillance of poor, Black, and single women and stigmatized the recipients. While the shift from private to public patriarchy enabled some women to avoid depending on individual men, it also made them more susceptible to government control.

Neoliberal Globalization and the Responsible Woman Worker

Worldwide gender hegemonies shifted again with the rise of neoliberal globalization. **Neoliberalism** refers to ideas and policies that withdraw the state from public support and seek to replace it with market institutions. Starting in the 1980s and accelerating in the 1990s, governments around the world (led by Britain and the United States) embraced ideas of liberalization and free markets and withdrew many of the entitlements and services that had been associated with the welfare state. The privatization of welfare provisions in the U.S. also coincided with the dramatic rise of international free trade agreements, the offshoring of production to nations with low labor costs, and the worldwide privatization of public goods ranging from health-care to land to water. Market institutions gained power worldwide, vastly expanding the influence of multinational corporations and increasing the globalization of trade (Pyle and Ward 2003). Throughout the postcolonial world, meanwhile, institutions such as the World Bank and International Monetary Fund also promoted fiscal austerity and the withdrawal of public support for the poor.

As in prior historical periods, these shifts relied on and promoted new ideas about femininity and masculinity. This time, however, the gender hegemony emphasized women's role as self-sufficient producers. Many governments shifted from portraying women as mothers who should stay at home and look after their children to framing them as responsible workers and micro-entrepreneurs. This image of women as dependable and hardworking reinforced their growing role as wage labor for transnational corporations. On the one hand, women gained new opportunities as wage earners outside the home and more power within families. On the other hand, governments justified their withdrawal of support by referencing the self-sufficiency of these new "responsible" women, even as transnational corporations, global media, and market institutions remained dominated by men. The new femininity also suggested that women, not governments or corporations, were accountable for their own well-being. Across the globe, women faced a catch-22: States had abandoned them as self-sufficient wage earners, while corporations did not pay women the family wages that men had earned in the past because they did not consider women solely financially responsible for their families.

During the neoliberal period, being a good mother also became less and less linked to staying in the home. Worldwide, many women went out to earn money, with poor women often working in the informal sector or through migrant labor. In nations such as Mexico, Bangladesh, and China, women came to dominate sectors including export manufacturing and micro-entrepreneurship. Increasingly, women from such countries also moved to other places in search of income, often finding jobs as domestic workers and leaving their children behind (Dreby 2010; Hochschild 2005; Parreñas 2001). While these women earned more income and became more mobile than their predecessors, they still remained subject to multinational corporations, foreign states, employers, and trafficking networks.

In the United States, neoliberalism reinforced the idea that welfare dependency was pathological, especially for women of color. In 1996, the Personal Responsibility and Work Opportunity Reconciliation Act (PRWORA), otherwise known as "welfare reform," ended welfare as an entitlement, requiring recipients to begin working after two years of receiving benefits. It also dismantled AFDC and placed a lifetime limit on benefits paid by federal funds. Whereas AFDC was initially designed to help single mothers avoid having to work, by the 1990s, the dominant political rhetoric argued that these same women should get "off welfare and into work." PRWORA also penetrated the private sphere by explicitly encouraging two-parent families and discouraging unmarried women from having children. With the ideological power and economic feasibility of the male breadwinning model on the wane, the *worker* became the universal social subject for both men and women. In turn, those who did not work faced punitive sanctions.

Mothers who received welfare were stereotyped as Black, unmarried teenagers who did not take care of themselves. Though women with such characteristics faced significant barriers to entering the job market, their economic struggles were portrayed as their own fault and not that of the state, the economy, or racial exclusion (Fraser and Gordon 1994: 327). Yet as Kathryn Edin and Laura Lein (1997) show in a study of mothers receiving welfare assistance, the prescribed transition from welfare to work was not, in fact, economically feasible. Rather, most people used governmental assistance because the kinds of low-wage work available to women did not provide sufficient income to support a family. In the neoliberal market economy, women needed *multiple* means of income to survive. In sum, the notion of welfare dependency came to describe women unable to make ends meet in the neoliberal economy, making their problems appear individual and moral rather than structural and economic.

The Ambiguities of "Progress"

Gender does not stand on its own but is intertwined with the state, the economy, and social movements. In this chapter, we showed how gender hegemonies reflect and reinforce power relations, generating consent for unequal relations between men and women, among men, and among women. Because these hegemonies are unstable and incomplete, they can always be contested, and they can change dynamically over time. The sections above traced key moments of gender change in feudalism, industrialization, colonialism, the welfare state, and neoliberalism. These five historical periods illustrate the need to account for how gendered ideas inform power relationships across time and geographic locations, often in intersection with race and class. To challenge existing ideas about gender, feminists must question the notion that differences between men and women are natural and instead historicize and locate specific understandings of gender difference.

Examining transformations in gender hegemonies over the last few centuries, some may be tempted to ask whether neoliberal gender relations have benefited women. By some measures, they have. Paid work has helped millions of women escape political disenfranchisement, exclusion from the workplace, and domestic abuse. Women have gained new access to income and new voices in politics, both as activists and as leaders.

But Nancy Fraser (2009) reminds us that corporations have also appropriated the idea that working can help liberate women and have used this idea to incorporate women into the low-wage global workforce. The more people expect corporations to liberate women, the more they may let governments withdraw from the responsibility to promote greater gender equality. As Sylvia Walby (1997) shows in her book *Gender Transformations,* increased economic opportunities for women in the United States and Europe have been accompanied by new forms of inequality. As upper- and middle-class white women gained new income, positions in the labor market, and political sway, poorer women and those in postcolonial countries came to work at jobs that were more uncertain, lower paid, and had fewer benefits than those once enjoyed by working-class men. As we discuss in more detail in Chapter 8, women are now subject to abuse within the workplace, often working long hours at factories or in housecleaning without basic labor protections such as rest breaks or access to clean water and air. As control over the global economy and politics increasingly shifts into the hands of ultra-rich elites, even women who are active in politics may have less influence over the kinds of policies that matter for their lives.

In sum, new gender hegemonies represent both opportunities and constraints. As in each of the other historical periods we described, neoliberalism has shifted the ways people understand masculinity and femininity, with repercussions for who does what and who gets what. Like previous political–economic systems, neoliberalism recreates gender differences to legitimate power inequalities. While new ways of thinking about femininity and masculinity can be freeing for some men and women, references to gender still rely on gender binaries that can reinforce inequalities between the people and activities that are marked as feminine and those that are marked as masculine. Before proclaiming that changes in gender relations are a step toward justice, one must consider how gender continues to be redefined in potentially pernicious ways.

KEYWORDS

Family of man 12
Gender hegemony 7
Gender order 4
Hegemony 7
Institutions 2
Neoliberalism 13
Signifiers 7
Welfare state 13

QUESTIONS

1. What kinds of gender arrangements are at work in contemporary universities? How is labor divided, and who in the university is expected to act in feminine ways? In masculine ways? Reflect on how gender terms shape universities and power relations within them.

2. Give examples of gender terms you see at work in U.S. policies and politics today. Which groups are portrayed in masculine terms and which in feminine terms? How do these representations legitimate power relationships between these groups?

3. What does a comparison of the welfare state and neoliberalism reveal about the state as a gendered institution as well as the possibilities for feminist critique?

4. To what extent do you believe there is gender justice in the 21st-century United States? How about in the world? What has gotten better for men and women, and what has gotten worse since the 1970s and the welfare state period? What remains problematic about the ways we understand masculinity and femininity and the ways we use these norms in the political sphere? Why?

ASSOCIATED READINGS

- Acker, Joan. 1990. "Hierarchies, Jobs, Bodies: A Theory of Gendered Organizations." *Gender & Society* 4 (2): 139–158.
- Brown, Wendy. 1995. *States of Injury: Power and Freedom in Late Modernity*. Princeton: Princeton University Press.
- Fraser, Nancy, and Linda Gordon. 1994. "A Genealogy of Dependency: Tracing a Keyword of the U.S. Welfare State." *Signs: Journal of Women in Culture and Society* 19 (2): 309–336.
- MacKinnon, Catharine A. 1982. "Feminism, Marxism, Method and the State: An Agenda for Theory." *Signs: Journal of Women in Culture and Society* 7 (3): 515–544.
- MacKinnon, Catharine A. 1983. "Feminism, Marxism, Method and the State: Toward Feminist Jurisprudence." *Signs: Journal of Women in Culture and Society* 8 (4): 635–658.
- McClintock, Ann. 1995. *Imperial Leather: Race, Gender and Sexuality in the Colonial Context*. New York: Routledge.
- Scott, Joan. 1986. "Gender: A Useful Category of Historical Analysis." *American Historical Review* 91 (5): 1053–1075.
- Young, Iris Marion. 2003. "The Logic of Masculinist Protection: Reflections on the Current Security State." *Signs: Journal of Women in Culture and Society* 29 (1): 1–25.

CHAPTER

2 Position

Abigail Andrews

How does social position shape a person's knowledge of the world? This chapter begins from the recognition that there is a vast array of gender identities and a wide range of points of view on the social world. This chapter highlights how standpoint*—the social position from which a person views the world—shapes that person's knowledge. Whereas some sociologists aspired to create knowledge that was* universal*—that is, that applied to all—feminists questioned the idea that all people shared a universal experience. They argued that women had a different way of understanding the world from men and challenged the claims made by men in positions of power that their knowledge was* objective *or unbiased. Feminists showed that the multifaceted nature of gender—as well as differences of race, class, age, ability, and so on—gave people of different gender identities distinct ways of knowing. In particular, they argued that the standpoints of women, people of color, and others who occupied historically subordinated positions could reveal the limitations of supposedly objective ways of thinking. This chapter uses these standpoints as a starting point for examining the relationship between power and knowledge. It concludes by proposing a sociology of gender approach to knowledge, urging thinkers to recognize their own positions, treat all knowledge as partial, and emphasize multiple perspectives and forms of knowing.*

Introduction

In 2009, U.S. Second Circuit Judge Sonia Sotomayor was nominated to be the first Latina and the third woman ever named to the U.S. Supreme Court. Her confirmation process was marked by controversy over a remark she had repeatedly made in speeches, beginning with a 2001 address at Berkeley Law School: "I would hope that a wise Latina woman with the richness of her experiences would more often than not reach a better conclusion than a white male who hasn't lived that life." While her predecessors Sandra Day O'Connor and Ruth Bader Ginsberg had argued that the judgment of a woman would be no different from that of a man, Sotomayor disagreed. The notion that a "wise Latina" might bring a needed perspective to the Court was criticized by Republican senators and conservative media, who vilified Sotomayor as biased by her Puerto Rican ancestry and thus lacking objectivity. However, many sociologists of gender agreed with Sotomayor that social position shapes what people know and how they come to know it. In doing so, they questioned the idea that knowledge about the social world can be objective.

This chapter begins with the premise that each person's social position provides a special perspective on the social world. This idea traces back to the 1960s, when feminist women sociologists recognized that the "facts" asserted by men sociologists did not resonate with their experiences. At the time, sociology had no framework for understanding the kinds of things many women experienced on a daily basis: child care, housework, or work in feminized occupations. Furthermore, they found that scholars and U.S. law alike defined harms that tended to affect women, such as domestic violence and rape, in terms of their relevance to men. These feminist scholars concluded that supposedly neutral scientific observers actually spoke from a masculine perspective. In fields dominated by men, men decided what topics were worthy of inquiry and how they should be understood. By contrast, women were left out of "objective" and "neutral" science. When women presented their views of the world, they were (and still are) marked as emotional, irrational, and subjective. Therefore, women sociologists raised fundamental questions about *whose* perspective was represented in supposedly objective knowledge. These scholars then asked how sociology might look different if it were made by women instead of by men.

Such scholars argued that instead of being objective, people had different **standpoints**, perspectives that stem from one's social position. In particular, they highlighted how contrasting categories of *masculine* and *feminine* shape how people view the world. This is not to say that gender relations or identities are fixed or that people's experiences of gender are uniform. Yet, because gender hegemonies structure society (see Chapter 1), all people—even in their diversity—have a relationship to gender categories. This relationship shapes the positions from which people come to know things. These insights have since helped fuel a field of critical inquiry that examines how gender—as well as race, class, and other categories of difference—shape what we know and how we know it.

The feminist critique described in this chapter is an epistemological critique. **Epistemology** refers to the study of knowledge, and **epistemological questions** focus on how knowledge is produced and evaluated. In other words, what counts as true? And how do we know what we know? A scientific approach to knowledge production is often considered to be the gold standard. Scientific knowledge is believed to be **objective**—that is, neutral and unbiased. Taking a controlled experiment conducted in a laboratory as its model, this approach embraces the idea that if science is done properly, the results will be the same no matter who the experimenter is. Thus, this approach seeks to produce knowledge that is **universal**, in other words, that holds true no matter where you are or who you are. In the study of the social world, this approach implies that the researcher has no effect on the people under study and vice versa, separating the *knower* (scientist) from the *known* (the people being studied).

Early gender sociologists upended this understanding by suggesting that knowledge is not objective and universal but, rather, is dependent on our particular positions as knowers. Elite white men created the fields of sociology and other social sciences, and they historically had a monopoly on knowledge production (see Connell 1997). Not surprisingly, these sociologists tended to pay more attention to questions surrounding *men's* existence, especially men's lives in the public spheres of work and politics, while ignoring women's work in the private sphere of the home. The activities of childbearing, childcare, housework, and work in feminized occupations were easily dismissed by sociologists. Indeed, early male sociologists' freedom to study the social world *depended* on other people—mostly women—who took care of their day-to-day needs. By contrast, as women entered sociology, they recognized that work within the home was no less strenuous, difficult, or socially significant than men's jobs outside the household. These women introduced new subjects of study and a new epistemology (or way of thinking), asserting that rather than being objective and universal, knowledge was partial, situated, and linked to social position. Like Sotomayor, they suggested that members of subordinated groups had critical insights into power relations that dominant groups did not.

This chapter illustrates how sociologists of gender use experience as a starting point to reflect on both the source of their knowledge and their positions as knowers. It does so by following a brief history of feminist thought within social science. First, it investigates how the claim of objectivity reinforces the power of dominant groups. Second, the chapter reflects on how people are situated and how positions of power or marginality affect people's understandings of the world. Throughout, the chapter considers the multifaceted nature of power relationships and explores how various social differences are intertwined. After all, gender represents one of many lines of difference through which knowledge is produced. Similar categorizations of *self* and *other* and similar claims to objectivity and universality exist in racial categories and colonial relationships. They also exist across class, age, sexuality, nationality, and other social positions. Thus, the meanings of masculine and feminine take shape differently for different people and gain further meaning in relation to other categories of domination. The acknowledgment of these relationships (which scholars refer to as *intersectionality*) reveals how binary categories commonly undergird the link between knowledge and power as well as how individuals can challenge that link by naming the standpoints involved in the production of knowledge.

Thinking through Difference: Beyond Universality and Objectivity

The field of sociology was established by elite white men. Although the American Sociological Association was founded in 1879, it did not admit women until 1937. While women—most of whom were also elite and white—began to enter the field in larger numbers in the 1960s, even as of 1970, only 9% of graduate faculty in American sociology were women (Roby 1992). These women began to notice that the ideas that men sociologists claimed were objective often excluded women's perspectives and devalued their analyses.

Since its founding, sociology has defined itself as the scientific study of society. This definition implies that sociological methods are objective and conjures up the image of a researcher—usually, a man—who observes, measures, and analyzes something called *data*. *Data* could refer to the number of murders in a particular year, the number of religious institutions in a city, or the proportion of Americans who feel that immigration is a major problem. Given the right data on a particular place or population, the objective approach suggests, any researcher should be able to arrive at the same conclusions about what explains the murder rate, predicts the number of religious institutions, or explains why some Americans think immigration is a problem but others do not. According to this approach, a researcher's feelings about immigration should play no part in his observations, the way he generates questions, or his analysis; such subjective biases would tarnish the scientific process. Thus, an immigrant's involvement in the question of immigration might make him biased, while a researcher who set himself outside of the phenomenon could glean objective knowledge. This approach frames researchers as detached outsiders whose lack of involvement in the phenomenon makes them objective.

Instead, feminist scholars located knowledge about society *within* relationships of power. Dorothy Smith was among the first women sociologists to raise the question of how including women's perspectives might make sociology look different from the status quo. Smith came to the University of California, Berkeley as a graduate student in the late 1950s, and in 1964, she became the only female lecturer on Berkeley's faculty of 44 men. In 1987, looking back on her training as a sociologist, Smith wrote,

> The forms of thought, the means of expression that we had available to us to formulate our experience were made or controlled by men. From that center, women appeared as objects. In relation to men (or the ruling class), women's consciousness did not, and most probably generally still does not, appear as an autonomous source of knowledge, experience, relevance, and imagination. Women's experience did not appear as the source of an authoritative general expression about the world. (51)

Smith faced a contradiction between her identity as a sociologist and her identity as a woman, which she called **bifurcated consciousness**. As a sociologist, she was asked to master the practice of treating the social world as an object of knowledge, "objectifying" the world. But even as she developed these skills, she remained acutely aware that despite its claims to universality, sociology did not account for her experiences as a woman. Thus, her understanding was *bifurcated*, or divided. As she wrote in 1974 in an article entitled "Women's Perspective as a Radical Critique of Sociology,"

> The relationship between ourselves as practicing sociologists and ourselves as working women is continually visible to us, a central feature of experience of the world, so that the bifurcation of consciousness becomes for us a daily chasm which is to be crossed, on the one side of which is this special conceptual activity of thought, research, teaching, administration, and on the other the world of concrete practical activities in keeping things clean, managing somehow the house and household and the children a world in

> which the particularities of persons in their full organic immediacy (cleaning up the vomit, changing the diapers, as well as feeding) are inescapable. (10)

To gain legitimacy as knowers, Smith explained, "We [women] were constrained to treat ourselves as looked at from the outside, as other" (1987: 52). Unlike men sociologists, who could pass off the messy necessities of cleaning, cooking, feeding, and reproducing to the women in their lives, women sociologists of the 1960s and 1970s had to confront the labor of social reproduction alongside the labor of knowledge production. Yet sociology did not treat the "concrete femininity" demanded by these everyday exigencies as a basis for knowledge. Instead, professional sociology asked women sociologists to fit themselves into what Smith called *abstract masculinity*: the idea that experts' detachment from the social worlds they studied gave them objectivity. Unable to reconcile these two demands, women sociologists faced bifurcated consciousness.

This experience prompted Smith to challenge the assumption that people could understand society from the outside as disengaged, unbiased knowers. She argued that the people who knew particular social worlds from the inside and were most engaged in the social realities under study provided a crucial standpoint for understanding those realities. Smith illustrated the problem with outsider knowledge by referencing a seemingly inconsequential experience:

> Riding a train not long ago in Ontario I saw a family of Indians, woman, man, and three children, standing together on a spur above a river watching the train go by. There was (for me) that moment—the train, those five people seen on the other side of the glass. I saw first that I could tell this incident as it was, but that telling as a description built in my position and my interpretations. I have called them a family; I have said they were watching the train. My understanding has already subsumed theirs. Everything may have been quite other for them. My description is privileged to stand as what actually happened, because theirs is not heard in the contexts in which I may speak. (1974: 12)

Smith highlighted that when she looked at others from afar—such as the people she passed in the train—even *she* read their lives through a set of assumptions. The people she saw as an Indian family may have been unrelated, and they may have understood their nationality in some other term than "Indians." Likewise, they may not have been watching the train. But as a sociologist, Smith was in a privileged position to write about the people she saw and to represent them through the lens of her assumptions. She argued that far from an isolated incident, this experience "epitomizes the sociological relation" (12).

Smith critiqued the sociology she had learned as a graduate student for assuming a particular relationship between the *knower* (subject) and the *known* (object). This sociology insisted that legitimate knowledge production required the sociologist to maintain a disengaged stance toward the social world under study. The participants in those social worlds could not produce legitimate knowledge but instead were treated as objects of research. In objectifying the world in this manner, Smith argued, sociologists in fact create partial views of the world, similar to the view from the window of a train. In particular, Smith realized that men sociologists could provide only a partial view of women, which privileged their experiences as men in relation to women.

Smith's critique provided a basis for making sociology by emphasizing how people's social positions shape whether they get to produce knowledge at all as well as what kinds of knowledge they produce. She argued that, for one, sociologists must acknowledge the systematic gaps in their knowledge. In addition to her critique of sociology itself, Smith was also concerned with how knowledge reproduces gender difference. Similar to other social relations, she pointed out, the sociological relationship is one of power. Smith hoped to challenge gender inequalities by legitimating women's standpoints. She felt that women sociologists had a duty to call attention to men's monopoly on legitimate knowledge, which reproduced masculine domination.

Standpoint Theory: A Sociology for Women

As an alternative to the "scientific" masculine sociology that predominated until the 1970s, Smith and several other feminist theorists, including Nancy Hartsock (1983) and Sandra Harding (1986), argued that their experiences as part of a subordinated group (women) gave them critical insight into the social world. Smith explained, "The only way of knowing a socially constructed world is knowing it from within. We can never stand outside it" (1). Smith advocated what she called a "sociology for women" (she later changed it to "a sociology for people") that would take experience as the starting point for sociological inquiry. This emphasis on experience was reflected in a famous slogan of the feminist movement: *The personal is political*. Feminist scholars expanded on Smith's emphasis on experience to argue that women's experiences of marginalization offered them special insight into power relations. Because men stood in a privileged position in relation to gender, their position made it difficult for them to recognize these power relations.

Social theory has long recognized that those who are disempowered, marginalized, oppressed, or dominated can have unique insights into hegemonic power relations. Perhaps one of the most famous elaborations of this idea is the Marxist argument that members of the working class have a clearer and more holistic understanding of capitalism than members of the ruling capitalist class. Capitalists might believe that the market demand for an object, say a vase, determines its profit. When they see only the market, however, capitalists underplay the role of labor and their own exploitation of workers. It is in their economic interest not to see this exploitation. Workers, however, understand that it is their labor that creates the vase that capitalists can sell for profit in the market. Labor, rather than the alchemy of the market, produces wealth under capitalism. This more holistic knowledge reflects workers' interests as a class. In turn, as workers collectively organize themselves, they come to understand both the process of production and the role of their exploitation in creating the capitalist's profit. The workers' standpoint stems from both their social position within production and their collective struggles. This analysis suggests an explanation for how hegemonies—as defined in Chapter 1—can be challenged and changed.

Feminist scholars applied this reasoning to argue that women's experiences as child bearers, caretakers, cooks, cleaners, and housewives provide critical insight into social reproduction (that is, the physical maintenance of workers, including researchers)—and the gender hegemonies that sustain it. In the 1980s, Nancy Hartsock (1983) and Sandra Harding (1986) argued that a sexual division of labor in which men served as breadwinners and women as mothers made it possible for women to see social relations more fully and honestly than men, who benefited from the exploitation of women. Hartsock noted that men's and women's different activities under the sexual division of labor and their unequal positions within the gender order gave them very different perceptions of social reality. Insofar as these perceptions were tied to social relations of power, they could be diametrically opposed. Men, however, controlled (and still control) institutions such as the media, the church, and educational institutions that generated hegemonic ideas about the social world. Therefore, men's understanding of the social world predominated. As a result, many women perceived their own subordination individually as a personal trouble. However, Hartsock, Harding, and others argued, once women started to share their experiences with one another, they realized that these seemingly personal troubles added up to striking patterns: Their experiences reflected their position as *women* in relation to *men*. This realization in itself was an act of knowledge production. Thus, feminist theorists reasoned that just like the workers in Marxist theory, women too must struggle together and strive to make their knowledge known and recognized as valid. A standpoint was the perspective achieved in the struggle to question these ruling ideas.

A scholar named Donna Haraway took this critique a step further by proposing that scholars pursue what she called **situated knowledges**, meaning research that accounts for the social positions of both the researcher and the object of study. In a 1988 essay called "Situated Knowledges: The Science Question in Feminism and the Privilege of Partial Perspective," Haraway critiqued what she called the "god trick," in which men scholars claimed an impossible (objective) perspective where they could "see everything from nowhere." To reveal this trick, she suggested that feminists create a new kind of objectivity, emphasizing that while people could *know* from their own positions, all *knowledge* was partial and contingent. Haraway insisted that all claims to truth must be located in a particular standpoint. She explained,

> I am arguing for politics and epistemologies of location, positioning, and situating, where partiality and not universality is the condition of being heard to make rational knowledge claims. I am arguing for the view from a body, always a complex, contradictory, structuring, and structured body, versus the view from above, from nowhere, from simplicity. Only the god trick is forbidden. (589)

In other words, Haraway contended, all knowledge should be located and recognized as partial. Instead of universality, partiality should be the yardstick for recognizing something as true. Situated knowledge thus entailed perceiving information from the body (one's own perspective) rather than from nowhere (the "unbiased" outside).

From Thinking Gender to Thinking Difference

As social science shifted to include women, feminists of color began to question whether the women's standpoint advocated by white, elite women scholars obscured other standpoints, reproducing the same problems of male knowledge production. Feminists of color noted that the women included in knowledge production tended to be white, middle- or upper-class, and straight. As a social group, women are heterogeneous: There are many different kinds of women with very different experiences of the social world. The standpoints of women of color, lower-class women, lesbian women, queer women, and trans women were not reflected in "women's" scholarship. These critics called for attention to the ways in which other axes of difference, such as race, class, age, and sexuality, informed people's experiences and standpoints.

In particular, feminists of color such as Audre Lorde, bell hooks, Gloria Anzaldúa, Patricia Hill Collins, and Kimberlé Crenshaw, along with feminists from postcolonial countries, such as Chandra Mohanty, challenged the assumption that women had a shared experience of gender. Instead, they foregrounded the difference between white, middle-class, straight women's experiences in the Global North and those of groups that had been subjugated in multiple ways, such as African American women in the United States. They argued that rather than an isolated social phenomenon, gender emerged in relation to other categories of difference.

Just as Hartsock applied Marxist insights to gender, these feminists used standpoint theory to particularize the white, class-privileged experience of being exploited as housewives. They argued that Hartsock's and Smith's understandings of women's experiences were embedded in their own race and class positions. Recall that Smith's entrance into the workplace produced a contradiction—between her scholarship and her position in the household—that led her to question masculine sociological knowledge. But this experience of juggling work and family was novel only for white middle- and upper-class women who, by virtue of their privileged race and class position, had been able to afford lives of domesticity.

By contrast, most poor and African American women had a different relationship to domesticity. In an article titled "The Social Construction of Black Feminist Thought," Black feminist scholar Patricia Hill Collins (1989) suggested that the kind of bifurcated consciousness Smith described with respect to white women's entry into the workforce had long been experienced by women of color. In that article, Collins quoted an elderly African American domestic worker named Rosa Wakefield, who explained,

> Since I have to work, I don't really have to worry about most of the things that most of the white women I have worked for are worrying

about. And if these women did their own work, they would think just like I do. (748)

Here, Rosa Wakefield understood that her labor as a domestic worker gave her certain insights not only into her own life but also into the lives of the women for whom she worked. Because the white women for whom she worked did not have access to her home, Ms. Wakefield could understand the social structure of both white and Black homes, but her employers could not.

Collins (1986) introduced the term **outsider within** to describe how African American women were historically privy to the secrets of racialized and gendered power relations by virtue of their work in white homes as cooks, cleaners, and caretakers, first through enslavement and then as domestic workers. As participants in the reproduction of the white nuclear family, African American women who worked in white homes witnessed the labor required to sustain and reproduce the sexual division of labor in white families. These lived contradictions, Collins argued, gave African American women a basis for developing a critical standpoint regarding how race, class, and gender produce relations of inequality. More than simply bifurcated, African American women were situated at a crossroads of power, enabling Black feminists in the U.S. to critique not only masculine knowledge production but also feminist narratives that obscured race and class as axes of power, domination, and inequality for women.

By emphasizing the standpoints of poor women of color, Collins and other Black feminists sought to move beyond **binary thinking**. Collins noted that the binary terms used to describe social relations—whether masculine/feminine, white/Black, or rich/poor—hid a complex interplay of relationships. Binary thinking tended to reduce subordination to a single axis of marginalization, such as gender subordination (implicitly of white middle-class women), racial discrimination (against African American men), and class subjugation (of lower-class white men). Reducing complex social realities to single axes of oppression (i.e., gender *or* race *or* class) hid how subordination operated through multiple lines of difference. Binary thinking thus obscured, for example, that housewives could be *both* subordinated in terms of gender and privileged in terms of race and class. It also flattened, if not silenced, the experiences of people who confronted multiple forms of oppression, particularly poor women of color.

To capture the relationships between gender and other lines of difference, Kimberlé Crenshaw (1991) proposed the concept of **intersectionality**. She defined *intersectionality* as the ways "race and gender interact to shape the multiple dimensions of Black women's [or anyone's] experiences" (1244). Crenshaw argued that African American women's experiences of subordination could not be reduced to either gender or race but instead reflected the mutual reinforcement of multiple lines of oppression. In this regard, race, gender, and other lines of difference were similar to intersecting streets. Crenshaw illustrated her argument using the example of the confirmation hearings of Justice Clarence Thomas, an African American judge nominated to the Supreme Court by President George Bush in 1991. During the hearings, news leaked that Thomas had been accused of sexually harassing Anita

Hill, an African American woman who had worked as his assistant. The U.S. Congress asked Anita Hill to testify about the sexual harassment in the confirmation hearings, which she did. However, Crenshaw argued, because Americans tended to understand sexual harassment as a white woman's issue, people did not know what to make of an African American woman victim. Meanwhile, then-Judge Thomas dismissed Hill's testimony as "a high-tech lynching." So doing, he tapped into a propensity among Americans to view issues of race primarily in terms of the oppression of African American men, with lynching standing out as an example of the very worst racist offence. Thomas's claim resonated throughout the country, while Hill's did not. Justice Thomas now sits on the Supreme Court. Crenshaw argued that understanding why Thomas's words carried so much more weight than Hill's requires unraveling the interlocking oppressions of race and gender. Hill's story was intersectional, and Americans did not have much language for such interrelated forms of oppression. By contrast, Thomas could frame Hill's accusations in binary racial terms (as a lynching), ultimately enhancing his perceived fitness as a Justice of the Supreme Court.

This analysis of intersectionality did not simply lengthen the list of categories of difference to be included in standpoint theory. Instead, it revealed power relations between women, particularly between white women and women of color. For example, Black feminists such as Audre Lorde and bell hooks challenged white feminists to confront questions of difference among women. In her essay "The Master's Tools Will Never Dismantle the Master's House," Lorde (1984) condemned the exclusion of Black thinkers from feminism. She argued that white feminists reproduced racism by marginalizing Black women thinkers except when their stories were helpful to white women. Far from overthrowing the "master" (i.e., men), white women embraced what Lorde called "the Master's tools"—the mechanisms of power that supported sexual subordination alongside racial privilege. Lorde explained that by excluding voices marginalized by race, age, and sexuality, white feminists were just as evasive of difference as the masculine narrative they hoped to critique. She reflected,

> Poor women and women of Color know there is a difference between the daily manifestations of marital slavery and prostitution because it is our daughters who line 42nd Street. If white American feminist theory need not deal with the differences between us, and the resulting difference in our oppressions, then how do you deal with the fact that the women who clean your houses and tend your children while you attend conferences on feminist theory are, for the most part, poor women and women of Color? What is the theory behind racist feminism? (Lorde [1992] 2012: 112)

As Lorde made clear, not only was it inaccurate to conflate white women's experiences as housewives with African American women's experiences as sex workers and domestic servants, but doing so also obscured white women's reliance on poor women of color. Lorde contended that acknowledging and embracing difference was the only way to avoid the power dynamics inherent in the claim that one kind of experience—even that of women—was universal.

Feminist scholars of color also insisted on attending to the alternative forms of knowledge that Black women (and others) developed in their everyday lives. Patricia Hill Collins, in particular, argued that the definition of *thought* should be expanded to include music, speech, and literature. Citing writers such as Zora Neale Hurston and singers such as Billie Holiday, she suggested that people who wrote and sang about their lived experiences contributed to knowledge in a vital way. While poetry, song, and dance could engage emotions and the body, they could also convey knowledge. She argued that whereas typical academic studies portrayed knowledge as disengaged and therefore objective, these forms of expression allowed the producer of information to be part of their social world. Resisting the disciplinary boundaries of sociology, she demanded that these types of expression count as legitimate, alongside more traditional academic work.

Beyond Binary Thinking

Just as Black feminists critiqued binary thinking, other feminists of color questioned categories altogether. For example, in "La Conciencia de la Mestiza," Gloria Anzaldúa (1990) used her position as *mestiza*, or a person with mixed racial or ethnic ancestry, to show how a Black feminist standpoint such as that proposed by Patricia Hill Collins could reify the categories used by those in power. Rather than an additional category, Anzaldúa understood **mestizaje** (racial mixing) as a social position that spanned multiple racial and ethnic categories yet could be captured by none of them. She explained,

> The work of the *mestiza* consciousness is to break down the subject–object duality that keeps her a prisoner and to show in the flesh and through the images in her work how duality is transcended . . . [and results in] a massive uprooting of dualistic thinking. (379)

Mestizaje, she suggested, expressed radical inclusivity by melding the Mexican, indigenous, and Anglo worlds. In using the feminization of the word "*mestizo*," Anzaldúa reappropriated a negative word that had implied bastardization and transformed it into a hybrid she saw as liberating.

Anzaldúa also argued that mestizaje compelled people to tolerate contradictions. *Mestizas* had histories across multiple cultures, which could make them confused. Therefore, a *mestiza* learned to think in pluralities, not binaries. In this way, Anzaldúa argued, *mestizas* symbolized a future when divisions would be broken down. They embodied, and therefore bridged, the Anglo/Mexican and Indian/Hispanic divides. In so doing, they broke down the binaries through which many people lived their lives. Through her writing, Anzaldúa imagined a future where there was no one way of being masculine or feminine, Indian or Hispanic. It was possible to be both one *and* the other—a synthesis—through the creation of a new, hybrid culture.

Anzaldúa, among others, also noted that the power divisions across binary categories such as masculine/feminine or Black/white may not be as clear as they first appeared. For example, the question of who is subjugated by gender is complicated when one considers that men are sometimes more fettered by gender expectations than women. Anzaldúa suggested that among *mestizo* men, poverty and low self-esteem sometimes enforced *machismo*—that is, an attitude that puts down and brutalizes women. She argued that *machismo* emerged from a "loss of dignity and respect" that "overlays a deep sense of racial shame" (1990: 105). Therefore, understanding the effects of binary categories also required understanding how they were used in relation to each other.

An Epistemology of Difference

Critical thinkers question knowledge wherever they find it: in classrooms, on the news, on social media, or in books. They ask how the knowledge they encounter is produced, who produces this knowledge, and what alternative kinds of knowledge might look like. Standpoint theory questions claims of objectivity or universality and calls attention to the power relationships that shape knowledge production. Though standpoint theory originated with the examination of gender by white, middle-class feminists, feminists of color extended their insights to show how knowledge reflects an array of social relationships, including race, class, and sexuality.

Sociologists can use insights gleaned from standpoint theory and intersectionality to rethink the production of "legitimate" knowledge. Feminist theory demands that scholars take the insights of oppressed groups (the margins) seriously in order to rethink the ideas of privileged researchers (the center), as in the title of bell hooks's 1984 book, *Feminist Theory: From Margin to Center*. Feminist theory also highlights that people do not necessarily share experiences and that people's personal experiences are significant for their development as sociological thinkers. Sociologists of gender have done important work to acknowledge differences. They have also highlighted how certain approaches to difference can reinforce binary thinking—and with it, as Chapter 1 showed, gender (and other) hegemonies. By calling attention to how difference, power, and privilege are embedded in social relations, they expand the practice of sociology.

In particular, feminist epistemology teaches the following practices:

Situate knowledge within relations of power and categories of difference. Recognizing one's position in relations of power continues the feminist tradition of questioning claims to universality and objectivity. Sociologists of gender must reflect on their own experiences in order to see their knowledge as situated and account for their engagement in a variety of power relationships. These relationships can also place scholars in conflicting positions of privilege and marginalization, power and oppression. Scholars can draw on such positions to reflect on the power dynamics that underlie different interpretations of the world and expand sociological thought.

Emphasize multiple dimensions of difference and demand a variety of viewpoints. To understand the world, sociologists of gender seek multiple perspectives. They celebrate subjugated and alternative forms of knowledge rather than leaving them on the margins or treating them as token examples of difference. While dominant narratives tend to standardize and homogenize the social world, sociologists of gender use the experiences of oppressed groups to rethink the canon and develop more nuanced accounts of social reality. They consider how gender is fractured along lines of race, class, and sexuality and pay attention to the connections between gender experiences in different parts of the world. Instead of ignoring or even eradicating difference, gender sociologists treat difference as what bell hooks (1990) calls "the necessary polarities from which our creativity can spark" (111).

Practice the exchange and affirmation of their distinct struggles. To include the voices of the marginalized, oppressed, and excluded, each of the scholars discussed in this chapter insisted that social scientists bring an open heart and mind to critical analysis. Donna Haraway suggested that seeing faithfully from another's point of view required "loving care" (1988: 583), while Patricia Hill Collins said that only a humanist *we* could overcome the multiple *I*'s of Western social science. Gloria Anzaldúa also advocated collective affirmation of people's distinct struggles as intertwined and interdependent. Each of these scholars re-centered the production of sociological knowledge on the recognition of the diversity of social experience, the realities of social privilege and power, and the productive tensions that make people better thinkers. Regardless of whether the focus is gender or not, this is the goal of critical sociology: listening not only to people's experiences but also to the interplay between experiences—and then abstracting and analyzing from there.

KEYWORDS

Bifurcated consciousness 22
Binary thinking 27
Epistemological questions 20
Epistemology 20
Intersectionality 27
Mestizaje 29
Objective 20
Outsider within 27
Situated knowledges 25
Standpoints 20
Universal 20

QUESTIONS

- In a university setting, which words and language do people tend to listen to? Which groups of knowers and which forms of knowledge are dismissed?
- Should oppressed groups reframe their ideas in language familiar to the dominant group in order to be heard? Why or why not?
- How do people's positions shape what they know? Can one draw directly on experience to understand the world? Do all people in the same category (e.g., all African American women) share experiences?
- Do some positions reveal more about the world than others? For instance, are subjugated groups better able to see both their own experiences and those of more dominant groups? What about outsiders within? What about those in hybrid

positions, such as Anzaldua's *mestiza*? Explain.

- Can people in positions of power see their own power? Why or why not?
- Scholars often argue that objectivity and universality make knowledge believable. How convincing are these criteria? What criteria would you propose for believable knowledge?

ASSOCIATED READINGS

- Anzaldúa, Gloria. 1990. "La Conciencia de la Mestiza: Towards a New Consciousness." In *Making Face, Making Soul: Creative and Critical Perspectives by Feminists of Color*, edited by G. Anzaldúa, 337–389. San Francisco: Aunt Lute Books.
- Collins, Patricia Hill. 1990. *Black Feminist Thought: Knowledge, Consciousness, and the Politics of Empowerment*. Boston: Routledge Classics.
- Crenshaw, Kimberlé W. 1991. "Mapping the Margins: Intersectionality, Identity Politics, and Violence against Women of Color." *Stanford Law Review* 43, no. 6 (July): 1241–1299.
- Haraway, Donna. 1988. "Situated Knowledges: The Science Question in Feminism as a Site of Discourse on the Privilege of Partial Perspective." *Feminist Studies* 14, no. 3 (Autumn): 575–599.
- Hartsock, Nancy. 1987. "The Feminist Standpoint." In *Feminism and Methodology*, edited by S.G. Harding, 157–180. Bloomington: Indiana University Press.
- Lorde, Audre. 1984. "The Master's Tools Will Never Dismantle the Master's House." In *Sister Outsider*, edited by Audre Lorde, 110–114. Berkeley: Crossing Press.
- Nakano Glenn, Evelyn. 1992. "From Servitude to Service Work." *Signs: Journal of Women in Culture and Society* 18 (1): 1–43.
- Smith, Dorothy. 1987. "A Sociology for Women." In *The Everyday World as Problematic: A Feminist Sociology*, edited by Dorothy Smith, 49–104. Boston: Northeastern University Press.

CHAPTER

3

Representation

Jennifer Carlson

This chapter considers how representations of gender establish standards of behavior, often revolving around sets of dominant norms referred to as emphasized femininity *and* hegemonic masculinity. *To illuminate how norms work as vectors of social control and inequality, the chapter highlights examples from historical and contemporary advertising. Starting with emphasized femininity, the chapter considers how such images affect social life by setting unattainable standards. Linking emphasized femininity to privileges of race, class, age, nation, and heterosexuality and highlighting its shifting relationship to the needs of capital, the chapter traces images of femininity from the age of 19th-century imperialism through the mid-20th century in the United States and into the present period. The chapter then moves on to masculinity, looking at how representations of masculinity work in ways similar to and different from those of femininity to establish and reinforce norms, especially in times of social anxiety and crisis. By approaching gender as normative, the chapter reminds students of sociology to question the naturalization of particular gender arrangements and to pay attention to how images and discourses shape gendered ways of seeing and being seen in the world.*

Introduction

In 2014, Meghan Trainor, a white, self-described "curvy" cisgender woman singer in her early 20s from Nashville, Tennessee, rose to the top of the Billboard charts with her song "All About That Bass." The song captured an explicitly body-positive message and called out the mocked-up images and unhealthy messages that circulate about girls' and women's bodies:

Yeah it's pretty clear, I ain't no size two

But I can shake it, shake it

Like I'm supposed to do

'Cause I got that boom boom

That all the boys chase

All the right junk in all the right places

I see the magazines working that Photoshop

We know that shit ain't real

...

I'm bringing booty back

Go 'head and tell them skinny bitches that

No, I'm just playing, I know you think you're fat

But I'm here to tell you that

Every inch of you is perfect

From the bottom to the top

The song reads as a loud refusal of **fat shaming**, according to which people who are judged to be fat or overweight are mocked, degraded, or bullied. As the song suggests, fat shaming is based on a distorted view of bodies: Women and girls are so embedded in the culture of fat shaming that even thin women "think [they're] fat."

Despite the song's success and its apparent positive message, it sparked fast and fierce backlash. Some vehemently resisted Trainor's attempt to counter "fat shaming" and accused her of instead shaming thin women with the words "skinny bitches." Some claimed that she promoted unhealthy bodies by celebrating larger-than-skinny bodies. Others saw her as playing into the very ideologies she was trying to critique. After all, the song still defines a woman's worth by her desirability to men. In other words, Trainor is still exploiting body image, though with the twist of prioritizing women with "all the right junk" over "skinny" women. And in doing so, she did what many white artists have done throughout U.S. cultural history: appropriated Black culture for profit. In the video for the song, Trainor primarily features Black back-up dancers flaunting large bodies; indeed, they appear in the video to validate large white women's beauty and desirability to men.

Trainor's song and the backlash it sparked highlight both the power and resilience of **gender norms**, which are popular representations of femininity and masculinity that define and set expectations for men and women.

Gender is normative because it establishes standards about what it means to be a man or a woman, naturalizes certain attributes, and punishes and polices those who do not or cannot achieve them. On the one hand, this set of expectations (or norms) portrays a narrow collection of attributes as natural and desirable, making the categories of *masculine* and *feminine* appear fixed and universal. On the other hand, these expectations rely on the refusal of alternatives and ambiguities, and they come with social sanctions for those who fail to achieve them. In their dominant forms, these gender norms intersect with race, class, nation, and other lines of difference such that whiteness and middle- to upper-class status become intertwined with feminine beauty or masculine authority. Young, thin, white, heterosexual women tend to set the benchmark for the ideal woman, while negative representations work to subordinate other women, such as poor women, women of color, women who are not thin enough, or, perhaps, women who don't have "all the right junk in all the right places."

In any given time or place, gendered images and discourses shape the ways people understand beauty, love, and happiness—and who can achieve them. Contemporary U.S. representations of femininity suggest that women who can fulfill the standards set by photoshopped models will be happier in their careers, love lives, and family lives. This chapter traces gender norms across historical time and social space. It examines how norms work to assert the moral legitimacy of broader projects such as economic expansion, nation building, and imperialism as well as how technologies that emerge from these broader projects (such as the photograph, the television, or the internet) shape the reach of gender norms.

Emphasized Femininity

"It's called Cover Girl. Not Beautiful on the Inside Girl."

—*Anonymous*

What is beauty?

Some associate the original Barbie doll with idealized femininity, with her blond hair, blue eyes, and impossibly thin waist. But Barbie now shares the shelf with other versions of this beauty ideal: Theresa (Barbie's brunette friend), African American Barbie, and Nikki (Barbie's Latina friend), among others. Beyond Barbie, there are many representations that saturate American media with models for beauty: There is the sexy tough girl (Halle Berry in *Die Another Day* or Jennifer Lopez in *Enough*), the smart-but-cute girl (Emma Watson in *Harry Potter*), the chic career woman (Kerry Washington in *Scandal*), the bimbo (Snookie in *Jersey Shore*), the virgin (Molly Ringwald in *Sixteen Candles*), and the slut (Kirsten Dunst in *Crazy/Beautiful*). The variations in beauty are wide and striking, especially in contexts beyond the U.S. and the contemporary period. For example, during the Qajar Dynasty of 19th-century Iran, it was considered beautiful for women to have mustaches, so much that women sometimes painted their upper lips with mascara (Najmabadi 2005).

Given such variations, it is impossible to identify one single standard of universal beauty. Nevertheless, many women feel that there are strict expectations for how they should look, act, and feel. Certain kinds of femininity carry more social value than others. For example, the spectacle of the Miss America Beauty Pageant provides a theatrical setting for women to compete to be crowned most beautiful. Miss America participants are judged on talent, poise, and social activism in addition to beauty; still, the physical attributes of winners unmistakably set them apart as beauty queens. The average American woman is 5'4" and weighs 166.2 pounds; by contrast, at just over 20 years old, the average Miss America contestant is 5'6" and 121 pounds (Ogden, Fryar, Carroll, and Flegal 2004; Public Broadcasting System 2002). Far from representing one beautiful individual, Miss America serves as a "visual representation of eternal femininity" (Banet-Weiser 1999: 180). As Sarah Banet-Weiser (1999) points out, the Miss America pageant both reflects and reinforces a national feminine identity that sets a standard not only for looks but also for female respectability and civic engagement. Furthermore, the Miss World and Miss Universe competitions as well as myriad national pageants often entail the exportation of Western beauty ideals of whiteness, blondness, and thinness. And in some cases, beauty pageants are used to resist Western ideals, as in the case of the Nigerian beauty pageants discussed in Chapter 5.

To make sense of the idea that there are many ideals of femininity but not all femininities are equally esteemed, sociologist Raewyn Connell developed the term **emphasized femininity**. This term refers to a particular kind of femininity that is more socially valued—or seen as more ideal—than others.

Rather than representing timeless characteristics of beauty and desirability, emphasized femininity is contingent on the particular social, geographic, and historical context in which it emerges. Furthermore, emphasized femininity is more than just a beauty ideal. It is also a vector of power. The collection of norms that comprise emphasized femininity help reproduce men's dominance over women as well as the dominance of elite, heterosexual, cisgender women over women of subordinated races, sexualities, and classes, trans women and gender nonconformers.

To understand how emphasized femininity reproduces men's dominance over women, consider the norms of docility, politeness, and sexual availability often associated with idealized femininity. These attributes reflect and reinforce power relations between men and women by positioning women as submissive to men.

To illustrate how emphasized femininity sustains inequalities among women, consider the sheer costs of adhering to these idealized feminine attributes. In the U.S., such ideals may encourage women to stay home to cook and clean for their husbands and raise children as well as diet, exercise, and purchase beauty products to enhance their desirability to men. But such a lifestyle requires resources. These attributes reflect the social position of white middle- and upper-class women who can afford—in terms of both time and money—to cultivate these characteristics. In other contexts, however, emphasized femininity entails different kinds of norms. For instance, in some areas of the Middle East and South Asia, women's respectability is tied to *purdah*, the practice of staying concealed from men, often within the home. Interestingly, as sociologist Patricia Jeffrey (1979) has shown, this form of emphasized femininity relies on upper-class and upper-caste status; in places such as India and Pakistan, low-income or low-caste women may have no choice but to work in jobs that expose their bodies or take place outside the home. In both cases, emphasized femininity is a narrow femininity that intersects with race and class privilege while also reproducing men's dominance.

Emphasized femininity defines standards for beauty, and it also sets apart men versus women and women among women. Even for the most well-resourced women, emphasized femininity remains an ideal that is generally only fleetingly attainable.

The Power of Images

Most Americans readily recognize that the paradigms of emphasized femininity exemplified by Miss America, Barbie, or Angelina Jolie are unattainable for most women. Few women or men assume that the images of women that circulate in the media through the likes of beauty pageants, movies, fashion, and music represent the average woman. Recent exposés on the use of airbrushing[1] in women's magazines reveal that even the women who make the beauty standards in fact break them: Popular images of Gwyneth Paltrow, Britney Spears, and others are edited fabrications rather than reflections of feminine beauty. This is why supermodel Cindy Crawford famously announced, "I wish I looked like Cindy Crawford."

Even as women diet, exercise, and spend hundreds to thousands of dollars on beauty products, services, and surgeries, they are simultaneously aware that images in the media should not be confused with reality. Dawn Currie (1997: 471), a gender scholar, highlighted this paradox in her study of how teenage girls actively interpret gender representations in magazines: "Although participants freely acknowledge that magazines are 'only' texts, motivated by economic interests, the girls in this study engaged in a manner of reading that brought their construction of self, rather than magazine discourse, into question." In other words, the awareness that these images are idealizations does not diminish their power to shape social expectations for women. Rather, these images continue to operate as containers for the gender norms that make up emphasized femininity.

To understand the power of gender representation, scholars have analyzed how images construct social relations. Art historian John Berger (1992), author of *Ways of Seeing*, defines *images* as follows:

> An image is a sight, which has been recreated or reproduced. It is an appearance, or a set of appearances, which has been detached from the place and time in which it first made its appearance and preserved—for a few moments or a few centuries. Every image embodies a way of seeing. Even a photograph. For photographs are not, as is often assumed, a mechanical record. Every time we look at a photograph, we are aware, however slightly, of the photographer selecting that sight from an infinity of other possible sights. (9–10)

Berger suggests that images do not represent an objective reality; rather, images are always narrow accounts that obscure, distort, and simplify (recall the discussion of epistemology in Chapter 2). Further, images do not simply reflect; they also create. So doing, they **objectify** people, or transform them into objects. Women's **objectification** (being degraded to the status of an object or into typified images) exemplifies this narrowing of social reality into emphasized femininity.

Images provide a powerful way of thinking about norms because they imply a social relation between the *looked upon* (i.e., the woman who comprises the image) and the *viewer* (i.e., the onlooker who consumes the image). Think about images of women you have recently viewed: What assumptions do they make about the person who looks at such images? To whom do these images appeal? For whom is the idealized woman idealized?

Berger answers these questions by thinking about the **male gaze**, particularly the way that images are designed to appeal to the assumed perspective of a heterosexual man. Berger suggests that the male gaze not only constitutes contemporary representations of women but also has shaped representations of women for hundreds of years. Berger (2009) documents a divide in men's and women's visual portrayals in European nude paintings starting in the 17th century, a difference that he explains by theorizing the male gaze. In such nudes, "a man's presence suggests what he is capable of doing to you or for you" (45–46) while "a woman's presence" in an image "defines what can and cannot be done to her" (46). According to Berger, while men are free to concern themselves with doing, women concern themselves with being *seen*. The representation of women as the object of action (i.e., what can and cannot be done to her) and men as the subject of action (i.e., the doers) means that men and women inhabit images—and, by extension, their social worlds—differently.

A woman, Berger (1992) argues, is "split into two. . . . [S]he is almost continuously accompanied by her own image of herself" (46). That is, a woman experiences life both as the seer and as the object of someone else's gaze. The demand for a woman to constantly monitor herself is the internalization of the male gaze: she learns to see like a man to become the woman desired by men. As Berger writes,

> Men look at women. Women watch themselves being looked at. This determines not only most relations between men and women but also the relation of women to themselves (42).

As such, Berger's analysis is useful in understanding how a particular kind of femininity marked by race and class privilege—namely, emphasized femininity—came to hold power through the circulation of images. Although his account focuses on fine art in 17th-century Europe, his analysis helps make sense of gendered imagery of the past and present in the West and around the globe.

Imperial Advertising and Commodity Fetishism

Women's images have figured prominently as symbols of war, nation building, and economic expansion. Ironically, for instance, while women on board ships were treated as bad luck, Greeks, Romans, and others carved images of voluptuous, even bare women into the mastheads of ships as symbols of protection. Meanwhile, European and American colonizers imagined Africa, Asia, the Western frontier, and other sites of imperial expansion as "virgin" territory. For example, in her book, *Imperial Leather*, Anne McClintock (1995) examines how imperialists visually infused land with femininity by sketching mountains, mountain peaks, rivers, and trails as if they were breasts or areas to be penetrated. Imagining foreign peoples and lands in feminized terms helped frame imperial conquest as natural and give colonizers access to the resources, labor, and—later—consumers located within colonized spaces.

During the colonial era, gendered imagery thus helped expand emerging markets, promoting consumer products by connecting them to dreams of national ascendency, civilization, and higher purpose. As McClintock shows, 19th-century soap advertisements communicated and consolidated emergent middle-class values. In particular, by presenting people as brilliantly clean, they promoted the **cult of domesticity**, that is, the celebration of women's role within the household. They further tied women's domesticity to the civilizing mission, the notion that colonial powers brought civilization, hygiene, and so on to colonized people. For the first time, domestic imagery was mobilized to sell products that enhanced the cleanliness of domestic space and were therefore considered "civilizing." Women were not always the centerpieces of these advertisements, but women's private labor and households tended to be the focus of the civilizing practices they presented. In one Pears' soap advertisement (Photo 3.2), soap is presented as an expression of the "white man's burden" to teach the "virtues of cleanliness" to colonized people. In another advertisement (Photo 3.1), soap connects the colonial space of conquest to domestic, middle-class life by acting as a magical means of "whitening," and therefore civilizing, the home.

People in the 19th-century United States also imagined the cult of domesticity through racial difference. American trade cards of the late 19th century juxtaposed white women's domestic space with images of African American laborers who provided a counterpoint to—and condition of—white women's domesticity. In one advertisement for spool cotton analyzed by Mehaffy (1997: 134), a well-dressed and well-coiffed white woman is pensively engaged in a quintessential activity of white domesticity (sewing), while a Black woman hovers above her in tattered clothing, holding a basket of cotton. The advertisement depicts a clear division of labor shaped by race and class: A "visual narrative of ideal (white) consuming domesticity takes shape through her juxtaposition with a mirroring Black female figure, typically associated, in contrast, with preindustrial technologies and economies of home production" (134).

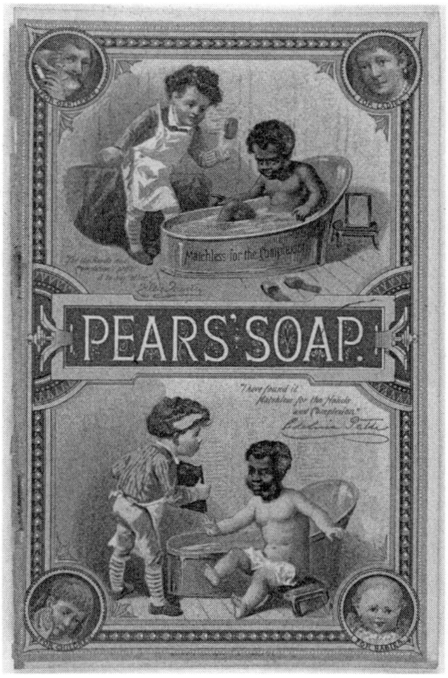

Photo 3.1

Source: Advert for Pears' Soap from Wellcome Images, https://commons.wikimedia.org/wiki/File:Advert_for_Pears%27_Soap_Wellcome_L0030380.jpg, licensed under CC BY 4.0 http://creativecommons.org/licenses/by-sa/4.0/.

Advertising from this era is striking in that it draws on gendered and racial ideologies to shape the social imagination of both feminine-marked spaces (the domestic sphere) and masculine-marked spaces (the nation and the colony). On one hand, racial hierarchy within the domestic sphere communicates messages about the overall hierarchy of civilization, placing white identity at the top of the racial order we described in Chapter 1 as the *family of man*. On the other hand, this racialized domesticity links gender to nation building, even depicting women on the front lines of civilizing development.

Such connections between women, nation, and development persist in contemporary advertising. For example, airline advertisements conflate femininity and national identity to sell consumers an exotic, luxurious flight experience. A 2014 Korean Air advertising campaign entitled "It's All About You" featured women flight attendants dressed in sharp, feminized light business suits. Promising that "our commitment to be the best will

Photo 3.2

Source: A & F Pears.

always be all about you," one commercial shows a tiny Korean woman pouring a blue martini that ends up in the hands of a blue-eyed, blond-haired woman gazing at the image of a globe on her airline television. Global travel advertising campaigns aimed at Western viewers such as this one mobilize stereotypes of Asian women as servants eager to evoke the promises of paradise, fantasy, and luxury that are predicated on the exoticization of local people and their exploitation as cheap service labor.

As this section shows, the use of intersecting images of femininity, race, and nation to sell products—whether soap or airline tickets—is not new, but it can be traced to the economic speculation and expansion of the mid-1800s. Over the next 100 years, advertising from large, multinational firms would become more powerful and more narrowly focused on white middle-class femininity as significant changes in media formats—especially the proliferation of televisions—transformed how images mediated desires and dreams.

Gendered Advertising and the Growth of Industrial Capitalism in the U.S.

By the 1950s, the U.S. economy was ripe for the advertising culture depicted in the hit television drama *Mad Men*. America's first credit card was introduced in 1950, and the economy grew by 37% over the course of the decade. World War II had provided both a moral imperative and an economic boost for American consumption. Soon, Americans embraced the dream of upward mobility as evidence of American virtue and of the strength of the American economy. While 25% of Americans lived in poverty during this period (mostly urban Blacks and rural whites), middle-class whites were able to enjoy newfound economic abundance. Furthermore, Americans in the 1950s suddenly found their social worlds mediated by a novel contraption: the television. Whereas less than 1% of American households owned a television in 1948, by 1960, 90% of households featured a television set.

Visual images, of course, had already taken over the pages of magazines: long-form photo essays, featured in magazines such as *Life* since the 1930s, told stories through photographs. By 1955, the photography of *Life* was praised "as the most vivid means of portraying our times" (Goldsby 1996: 258). Though "our times" depicted on television and in magazines mostly focused on the life experiences of middle-class white Americans, during this period, Black magazines such as *Jet* and *Ebony* also emerged as popular spaces for Black audiences to consume images of Black upward mobility and success, "giving voice to black aspirations" (Leslie 1995: 426). For their audiences, magazine images literally expanded the scope of reality. Americans came to know the world through *looking*, from the so-called New

Look in women's fashions (Marling 1992) to race relations as captured in the brutalized and disfigured face of Emmett Till (Goldsby 1996). As Karal Ann Marling (1992: 5) summarizes, "seeing is absolutely central to the meaning of the 1950s."

The golden age of 1950s advertising was made possible by both the visual novelty of magazine and television media and the postwar political economy. Domestic femininity offered a reprieve from the sacrifice and asceticism practiced during the war:

> After seven long years of wartime make-do, rationing, and stringent rules governing the amount of fabric in a given garment, after seven years of skimpy, asexual suits and silence from the great French couturiers, fashion and femininity were back at last. (Marling 1992: 9)

Accordingly, the 1950s were marked by advertisements that sold a particular kind of domestic femininity to white, middle-class women who, as housewives, now controlled a significant portion of spending power in their families.

This shift in product portrayal applied not only to fashion but also to products that were less straightforwardly gendered. Products of all kinds started to be feminized, as Penny Sparke (1995), author of *As Long as It's Pink,* argues. Awash in pink, new inventions and household products promised to make women consumers into ideal wives and mothers, suggesting that women could buy their way into domesticity and, therefore, emphasized femininity. In an analysis of ads in women's magazines of the 1950s, marketing researchers Alice Courtney and Sarah Lockeretz (1971) conclude that these images portrayed a woman's place as in the home: tending the children, cleaning the house, cooking for her husband and family, and looking peppy and cheerful while doing it all. Thus, in 1950s America, emphasized femininity entailed white women looking and behaving as housewives. As Ann Oakley (1990) writes in *Housewife*, these 1950s images posited an ideal female "self which aspires to be a good wife, a good mother, and an efficient homemaker. . . . Women's expected role in society is to strive after perfection in all three roles" (cited in Wolf [1991] 2002: 64).

It is worth noting that a related but distinct depiction of femininity appeared on the pages of 1950s outlets targeting Black audiences. As Michael Leslie (1995) notes, by the 1950s, many Black publications featured as much as 60% advertising content targeted at Black middle-class readers. Compared to ads in Black publications in the 1970s and 1980s, these 1950s ads were much more likely to feature models who looked aesthetically whiter, with straightened hair, thinner lips, and lighter skin. Leslie's analysis suggests that many of the 1950s advertisements were for beauty products that allowed Black women to conform to white standards of beauty, such as hair straightening. Meanwhile, few images of Black Americans appeared in advertisements marketed toward white, middle-class women, unless they were continuations of "mammy" stereotypes such as Aunt Jemima, who was used to sell pancakes through an image of African Americans as deferential servants. Thus, in contrast to 19th-century images of Black labor in the shadows of white domesticity, advertising of the 1950s reflected the segregated color line that organized American society.

This color line also shaped the critiques that feminists brought to bear on images of women. In 1963, Betty Friedan published *The Feminine Mystique*; the term **feminine mystique** refers to the misplaced belief that the only fulfilling role for women was as mothers and housewives. Advertisements of the 1950s, Friedan argued, compelled women to accept their own subordination, as if embracing femininity would make them happier. They promised that women's fulfillment of their duties as housewives gave them a noble purpose that could be achieved with the purchase of new vacuum cleaners, dishwashers, or instant pudding. But caught in what Friedan called "the problem that has no name," privileged women who were attempting to live up to those ideals were, in fact, incredibly unhappy.

Meanwhile, Friedan argued, such images placed sanctions on women who did not conform, particularly career women. Indeed, white women's magazines of the 1950s gave women an abysmal choice: either be happy housewives or unhappy, neurotic, dysfunctional, careerist women. As the antithesis of the housewife, the career woman was viewed scornfully as having rejected her true nature to selfishly pursue her own interests. The working woman was considered not only self-destructive; she was also antisocial, threatening to undermine the family as the basis of social life through her decision to pursue her own interests. Friedan's manifesto challenged the notion that domesticity was white women's destiny and brought into the open the ways advertisements manipulated women's hopes, aspirations, and sense of self.

Friedan's writing captures a seismic shift away from the white, middle-class feminine ideals of the 1950s, but she was not the only social critic to challenge images of femininity in advertising. A separate line of critique regarding the portrayal of women also underway by the 1960s focused on images of Black women. The **Black Is Beautiful** campaign of the 1960s, which emerged from the Civil Rights and the Black Power movements, resisted the denigration of Black beauty and the whitening of Black bodies through skin bleaching and hair straightening. The power of this movement can be seen in the pages of *Ebony* magazine's swift shift toward natural hair in the 1970s (Leslie 1995).

Norms of Neoliberalism

Today, Americans are bombarded with advertisements selling the keys to femininity; some experts estimate that the average woman sees about 400 to 600 images a day. In contrast to the 1950s, when Americans tuned into or read a narrow set of television broadcasts and magazine spreads, Americans now have an overwhelming degree of choice in terms of what they consume. Media outlets also have to contend not with the mass markets of the 1950s but rather with the niche markets that grew in the 1990s and blossomed in the 2000s.

As media scholars argue, the fractioning of media markets created new opportunities for a diverse range of voices, images, and standpoints to be seen and heard (McRobbie and Thornton 1995). The images used to sell products today no longer rely on narrow notions of white women as housewives, as they did in the 1950s. For one thing, the kinds of bodies that populate advertising space are now more diverse. Though advertisements targeting women still disproportionately feature white women, Asian, African American, and Latina women are increasingly represented. Meanwhile, the popularity of African American and Latina pop stars in the 1990s and onward, such as Jennifer Lopez (Guzman and Valdivia 2004) and Beyoncé (Durham 2012), have challenged beauty norms by emphasizing large "booties," for instance, as celebrated markers of beauty.

However, scholars interrogating this diversity in more depth find that increased representation is not necessarily an indicator of progress. For example, McLaughlin and Goulet (1999) found that Black women in magazine advertisements targeting white audiences are more likely to be in submissive poses than in magazines targeting Black audiences. Even in *Jet* and *Essence*, two magazines targeting Black audiences, "ideologies of racism and White supremacy continue to pervade advertisements" (Hazell and Clarke 2008: 5). Colorism—discrimination based on skin complexion—remains a persistent phenomenon, as Black women who appear in advertisements tend to have lighter skin and whiter facial features (Keenan 1996). Black celebrities sometimes appear whitewashed in magazines and advertisements; for example, Black singer Beyoncé appeared in a 2008 advertisement for L'Oréal with blond hair and noticeably lighter skin. L'Oréal denied any intentional whitening of the celebrity's image.

In addition to featuring more diverse bodies, advertisements today routinely disrupt the feminine mystique's emphasis on domestic virtue. Many media representations now encourage women to enter the workforce. Yet many times, women are still placed into roles that advance men's career aspirations—this time as secretaries and assistants rather than housewives (Massoni 2004). And, like the primped housewife of the 1950s, today's media images continue to portray the idealized woman as beautiful and sexually available, even as she is also career minded and ambitious.

Contemporary advertisements still sell the tools to achieve emphasized femininity, but instead of the household products of the 1950s, today's toolkit includes diet plans, cosmetics, fitness gear, and plastic surgery. Displacing the feminine mystique of the 1950s, the contemporary **beauty myth** asserts that women should aspire to particular beauty standards and that they can achieve those standards if—and only if—they are determined to work hard to get there. Whereas the feminine mystique revolved around the consumerism of industrial capitalism, the beauty myth emerges in the context of neoliberalism. As Naomi Wolf ([1991] 2002) argues in *The Beauty Myth*, beauty work encourages women to take on "an aspirational, individualist, can-do tone that says that you should be your best and nothing should get in your way" (69).

McRobbie (2004) labels this neoliberal sensibility *postfeminism* because it reduces women's agency to personal choice. In postfeminism, it is a woman's personal responsibility to be beautiful as part of being all she can be. Achieving silky, smooth hair; the perfect waistline; the smile she's always wanted; or clear skin is placed squarely on a woman's shoulders: Supposedly, with the right diet, exercise, and beauty product purchases, any woman can be beautiful. Even though an advertisement from Pantene Pro-V (a hair product company) maintains, "You don't need the sun to shine," it insists that women do need—and thus should purchase—products to have beautiful hair.

This compulsion to be beautiful takes on certain demands in the context of colorism. The marketing of skin whitening products is illustrative. The whitening of beauty is rooted in imperial understandings that connect whiteness with beauty, wealth, and success (Picton 2013). It also transcends national context: Skin-lightening products marketed throughout the globe promise beauty through lighter skin, as seen in the "Fair and Lovely" advertising campaign in India and the Whitenicious hyperpigmentation solution marketed by Cameroonian pop star, Dencia. The message from such products is that porcelain skin is beautiful. These images may encourage today's woman to empower herself as beautiful, but they mobilize empowerment in restricted and racialized ways.

As another example, consider cosmetic surgery: In 2015 alone, Americans spent more than 13.5 billion dollars on so-called aesthetic procedures (American Society for Aesthetic Plastic Surgery 2016). Women in the U.S. trim their fat with liposuction, enlarge their breasts with silicone, tuck their tummies, and modify their eyelids at unprecedented rates. While some women find cosmetic surgery an affirming route to social acceptance (as transgender icon Caitlyn Jenner has argued), others raise concerns about the pervasiveness of cosmetic surgery. *Time Magazine* columnist Joel Stein (2015) argues that cosmetic surgery has "become the new makeup," creating a compulsion for American women to engage in ever more expensive and invasive beauty rituals. We might ask, then, is cosmetic surgery an example of empowerment or the latest technology in the reproduction of gender norms? If the latter, which—or whose—gender norms are at stake?

As with skin whitening products, cosmetic surgery standardizes white, Western ideals of beauty by obliterating bodily difference. Consider cosmetic surgery in Asia. One in five South Korean women undergo plastic surgery, making South Korea the cosmetic surgery capital of the world. One of the most popular procedures is *blepharoplasty*, or double eyelid surgery. While many argue that the surgery simply opens the eyes and thus makes women more attractive, others see the procedure as importing a Western standard of beauty and injecting it into the bodies of Asian women. They point to the procedure's racist history: The doctor who introduced blepharoplasty in the 1950s justified it with racist stereotypes of Koreans, saying that "the absence of the puerperal fold produces a passive expression which seems to epitomize the stoical and unemotional manner of the oriental" (Baer 2015). One surgeon noted that his patients often were sex workers catering to American GIs; the surgery, he assumed, would make them more appealing to their johns.

Over 50 years later, however, Hoang (2014) returned to the sex industry in Asia and found a very different relationship between cosmetic surgery, national identity, and femininity. Studying sex workers in Vietnam stratified by clientele as diverse as Asian businessmen and Western expatriates, she finds that women turn to different kinds of cosmetic procedures for different reasons. Rather than adopting a standardized, Western definition of beauty, "sex workers reflect men clients' different projections of

Vietnam's place in the global economy" by embodying distinct kinds of femininity, including "pan-Asian Modernity" (for local elite businessmen) and "third world dependency" (for Western expatriates) (517). Hoang's analysis establishes that non-Western beauty projects are not necessarily used in reference to the West. Rather, beauty projects unfold in complex ways across localities, regions, and globally and are embedded in projects of political economy and national ascendance. Her analysis also complicates the relationship between cosmetic surgery, gender norms, and agency. On one hand, Vietnamese women are surely playing into the fantasies of their male clients, whether they be anticipatory fantasies of Asian ascendance or nostalgic fantasies of Western imperialism. On the other hand, Hoang finds, these women are also proactively harnessing these norms as they navigate the socioeconomic opportunities in rapidly developing countries such as Vietnam.

How Images Harm

Women who do not or cannot conform to the standards of emphasized femininity are often subject to social exclusion and denigration. As noted above, emphasized femininity is premised on racial and class privilege. It also encourages women to "buy" beauty. As described in the famous feminist health book, *Our Bodies, Ourselves* (Norsigian 2005),

> Most of the women we see in the media are young and white. Hollywood movies rarely feature women over forty, and the older women we do see represented in the media, from movie stars to news anchors and even politicians, look much younger, thanks to plastic surgery. As a result, those of us who choose to age naturally, without the aid of plastic surgery, are sometimes seen as "letting ourselves go." (10)

This passage suggests that gender norms do not constrain all women equally, nor do individual women respond to norms in uniform ways.

To explain how representations constrain women and men of color, Patricia Hill Collins introduces the notion of **controlling images**, which "are designed to make racism, sexism and poverty appear to be natural, normal and a part of everyday life" (Collins 2000: 67–68). Controlling images degrade, denigrate, and/or pathologize Black women by marking them as matriarchs, mammies, welfare queens, or jezebels. Controlling images thus may be used to mark some women's practices as honorable or naturally feminine and others' practices as vulgar, indecent, or degrading, even for the same activity. Consider child care: When carried out by a wealthy, stay-at-home mother, child care may be represented as dignified, whereas when Latina immigrants do child care for pay, it is no longer seen as nobly feminine.

Women whose bodies do not conform to gender ideals because of size, age, or other physical attributes are also subject to bullying and harassment, which can take both subtle and overt forms. For example, the Stop Childhood Obesity campaign considers itself a public health campaign, but it has released campaigns that convey their message in the form of fat shaming, whereby people—especially girls and women, but also boys and men—are disparaged, belittled, and taunted for having fat bodies.

Fat shaming can take a variety of forms, including the policing of clothing; bullying and name-calling; and the circulation of messages that certain bodies are not only unwanted but also unhealthy and even immoral. In her book *Killer Fat*, sociologist Natalie Boero (2012) questions the framing of obesity as an "epidemic," arguing that considering fat bodies a public health concern has legitimated bullying based on body fat. Fat shaming also intersects with policing class-based boundaries of respectability. As Abigail Saguy and Kjersten Gruys (2010) found in their review of media coverage of obesity and eating disorders, thin bodies are presented as higher-status bodies, associated with moral virtues of self-control, while large bodies are presented as lower-status bodies, associated with laziness, uncouth personal habits, and unhealthy lifestyle choices. In this way, body size becomes a vehicle for communicating class privilege alongside moral virtue: Success, wealth, and thinness come together as a package deal of emphasized femininity.

Fat shaming shows the power of images not only to distort the social world but also to impact inequality. Katherine Mason (2012) shows that obesity interacts with gender: Due to body discrimination, women seen as obese experience a loss of income over their lifetimes. Meanwhile, obesity is associated with criminal guilt. Using mock criminal vignettes, scholars have found that men in particular are more likely to attribute guilt to women defendants who are obese as compared to those who are thin (Schvey, Puhl, Levandoski, and Brownell 2013). Many women also internalize bullying and shaming: Obesity is associated with increased risk of suicide (Heneghan, Heinberg, Windover, Rogula, and Schauer 2012). (You will learn more about these dynamics in Chapter 4.)

Further, fat shaming—and normative images more broadly—have different effects on women and men based on their social locations. Consider eating disorders: Researchers trace eating disorders among women to the circulation of normative images of women. Numerous studies have found that media images contribute to girls' and women's dissatisfaction with their bodies and the prevalence of eating disorders among girls and women (Groesz, Levine, and Murnen 2002; Harrison and Cantor 1997). Despite stereotypes that eating disorders are especially prevalent among young, white, class-privileged girls and women, scholars document what Story and colleagues (Story, French, Resnick, and Blum 1995: 173) call "unhealthy weight control habits" across racial and ethnic divides. Nevertheless, Black girls and women tend to report higher levels of satisfaction with their bodies. Some scholars suggest that while advertising campaigns have focused on white middle-class femininity, Black girls and women in the U.S. have alternative beauty standards that may protect them from the harmful effects of mainstream advertisements, thanks to cultural movements such as the Black is Beautiful campaign. At the same time, as more diverse bodies appear in advertisements, a broader spectrum of women may feel themselves constrained by normative images.

These racial dynamics help illuminate Tyra Banks's electrifying 2007 indictment of gender images and bullying. Though Banks was formerly a highly successful model, tabloids and social media users mocked her as appearing "fat" in photographs of her swimming after she had stopped modeling. Banks returned to *The Tyra Banks Show* in the same bathing suit and explained,

> Luckily, I'm a strong woman and I have a good support network . . . so I can overcome these attacks. But if I had lower self-esteem, I would probably be starving myself *right now.* But that's exactly what happening to women all over this country. So I have something to say. To all of you who have something nasty to say about me or other women who are built like me. Women that sometimes or all the times look like this [juts out her stomach], women whose names you know, women whose names you don't, women who have been picked on, women whose husbands put them down, women at work, or girls in school. I have one thing to say to you: KISS MY FAT ASS.

The clip makes explicit what girls and women from a variety of social backgrounds know firsthand to be true: the pain of unrealistic body expectations. This pain may be experienced differently for different women and in different places, but it nevertheless wields a disproportionate effect on girls and women. Suggesting its powerful impact, the video clip went viral: Millions of viewers have watched Banks's indictment of gender images since it aired in 2007. Banks was rightly applauded for her strength in calling out gender norms and their harmful effects.

However, some scholars also note a troubling dynamic when women applaud Black girls and women for their strength in standing up to gender norms. Tamara Beauboeuf-Lafontant (2003) suggests that attributing strength to larger Black women oversimplifies Black femininity. Reflecting cultural pressures on Black girls and women to appear strong and cultural biases that discount Black pain and suffering, the problem of eating disorders among African American girls and women is often overlooked or obscured, while the eating disorders of white girls and women are more heavily discussed and dissected in the media.

Nevertheless, even as women in different social positions bear the burdens of harmful images differently, these burdens are distinctly *gendered.* Because these images assume a male gaze, women share an experience of objectification that men do not. Indeed, this is why gender is so powerful: Gender celebrates a particular set of norms, pushing women to aspire to them and penalizing them when they do not.

Representing Hegemonic Masculinity

Often, discussions of gendered images focus on women because women are overwhelmingly the objects of these images and the targets of the social harm they cause. That is not to say, however, that men are free from the constraints and consequences of gender norms. Though perhaps less visibly, men also bear the burdens of gender ideals. Representations of masculinity create expectations about how men should act, how they should feel, and how they should deal with conflict or crisis. These expectations have real-world consequences for men, just as they do for women. Understanding gender as normative helps make sense of how gender constrains not only women but also men.

While a significant body of research has analyzed normative representation of women in the media, fewer scholars have analyzed how the media represents men. One reason is that men are often presumed to be unique individuals. After all, the male gaze presupposes women as objects and men as subjects. This means that while women are reduced to images of femininity, part of achieving masculinity is becoming an individual who acts on others rather than being acted upon. Thus, rather than being represented by generic "masculine" images, men—particularly white middle- and upper-class cismen—are often represented as individuals who are more than their masculinity. Indeed, the very irreducibility of men to their gender is one marker of masculine privilege.

The expectations associated with masculinity are reflected in the Dos Equis beer commercials that ran for nine years between 2009 and 2017, presenting the "Most Interesting Man in the World." The advertising campaign focused on the mystique of a gray-haired, weather-worn white man, often surrounded by younger, beautiful women and always accompanied by Dos Equis beer. The commercials follow a formula: A voice-over delivers three to four clever one-liners that reveal the grit, bravado, and sheer prowess of the "Most Interesting Man in the World":

> When in Rome, they do as he does.
>
> In a past life, he was himself.
>
> If opportunity knocks and he's not home, opportunity waits.
>
> Mosquitoes refuse to bite him purely out of respect.

The advertisements typically end with the gray-haired man sipping a beer and delivering the dual taglines "I don't always drink beer, but when I do, I prefer Dos Equis" and "Stay thirsty, my friends." In commenting on the success of the ads, one marketing expert noted that they are both "unexpected and aspirational" (Malcolm 2016). Though the one-liners are exaggerated, they instruct people on the qualities that they should use to judge men.

Sociologist Raewyn Connell (2005) calls the dominant collection of norms associated with masculine prowess **hegemonic masculinity**, which she defines as "the configuration of gender practice which embodies the currently accepted answer to the problem of the legitimacy of patriarchy, which guarantees (or is taken to guarantee) the dominant position of men and the subordination of women" (77). As described in Chapter 1, *hegemonic* refers to how domination is primarily sustained by consent. Like emphasized femininity, hegemonic masculinity entails a collection of norms that constitute the ideal man at a particular time and place, marking the top of the gender hierarchy. Representations of hegemonic masculinity are generally associated with white, middle- to upper-class, heterosexual, cisgender men who ostensibly enjoy fame, fortune, and respect, and, of course, always get the girl.

Like emphasized femininity, hegemonic masculinity is defined both against femininity and against other masculinities marked by class, race, and other forms of marginality.

As in the case of femininity, the terms of hegemonic masculinity vary with time and place. Practices considered emasculating in U.S. society, such as men holding each other's hands, are perfectly accepted in other locales across the globe. In Japan, hegemonic masculinity is embodied by "the salaryman," a well-educated worker whose life is governed by the needs of his corporation and who has little or nothing to do with the home. In the contemporary U.S., hegemonic masculinity is associated with independence, physical strength, mental agility, respect, power, and control—qualities that tend to be socially valued over their opposites such as dependency or weakness.

One powerful historical source for the American understanding of hegemonic masculinity is what scholars have called "the frontier myth," a belief that Americans—particularly Anglo-Saxon men—were uniquely defined through their experience on the Western frontier (Slotkin 1992). This made them distinct from both Native peoples (whom Americans denigrated as "savages") and Europeans (whom they belittled as effete aristocrats). Instead, Americans celebrated a version of hegemonic masculinity that was distinctly individualist, self-reliant, and gritty. A stylized version of the Wild West, which featured this brand of masculinity, was popularized first in traveling shows such as Buffalo Bill's Wild West Show and Western dime novels and later in Hollywood film. Through the frontier myth, this masculinity became linked to both national identity and imperial imperative. As historian Richard Slotkin (1992) shows, this myth always represented a dramatic rewriting of history in the service of American national identity.

Ironically, the frontier myth gained substantial steam after the frontier was officially closed in 1890. The myth's ascendancy accelerated in the early 20th century, as urbanization unleashed a crisis of confidence in the individualistic, heroic image of white American men. This crisis in American masculinity produced an opportunity for gun manufacturers at the time. Contrary to popular wisdom, guns were not in high demand at the end of the 19th century through the turn of the 20th century (Haag 2016; see also Slotkin 1992). Rather, gun manufacturers harnessed the frontier myth to expand their markets. Though American men could no longer prove themselves on the frontier, they could purchase a gun and—as gun advertisements promised—participate in a mythologized version of the American history of heroic conquest. One Winchester advertisement that circulated after the frontier was closed showed a Western scene and promised consumers that they, too, could own a "version of the gun that won the West." Another Winchester advertisement depicted a man in a suit—a businessman—gifting a firearm to his son; the man, presumably, understands that raising an American boy requires a firearm to "start him right." These advertisements and others thus depicted the association between white American men and firearms as heroic and rejuvenating.

Today's advertisements continue to use violence—or its means—to appeal to men. In the contemporary U.S., the **angry white man** has become a new dominant trope—or motif—to commodify masculinity and market products. As Jackson Katz (2003) writes,

> Men's magazines and mainstream newsweeklies are rife with ads featuring violent male icons, such as uniformed football players, big-fisted boxers, and leather-clad bikers. . . . [T]he appeal of violent behavior for men, including its rewards, is coded into mainstream advertising in numerous ways: from violent male icons (such as particularly aggressive athletes or superheroes) overtly threatening consumers to buy products to ads that exploit men's feelings of not being big, strong, or violent enough by promising to provide them with products that will enhance those qualities. (351–352)

For example, the 1999 film *Fight Club* portrays masculine rejuvenation through violence: White men are depicted as "slaves with white collars" who have been emasculated through "the Ikea nesting instinct" as "a generation raised by women." The solution in the film is for men to learn to be men again by starting a "fight club," which glorifies violence for the sake of violence. The film ends in a dramatic display of violence against the consumerism depicted as a castrating force in men's lives: The protagonist blows up a credit card company. Paralleling the Winchester advertisements of the early 20th century, *Fight Club* dramatizes a contemporary crisis of white masculinity by appealing to violent masculinity (Boon 2003).

Similar imagery is at work with Walter White, the protagonist of the TV show *Breaking Bad*. The series depicts a man (White) who walks away from the risk and reward of entrepreneurship early on in his life and instead settles for a career as a chemistry teacher. Upon learning he has terminal lung cancer and will likely leave his family in financial shambles, White turns to drug manufacturing. Ultimately, though, the series reveals that his willingness to break the law has less to do with his concern about his family's well-being and more to do with his masculine redemption through a hyperviolent alter-ego named Heisenberg. The series is littered with one-liners that assert White's dominance (Hudson 2013): "Say my name." "I am the danger." "I am the one who knocks." "I won." This pursuit of masculinity ends in tragedy (Trudell 2013): To win is ultimately to "die like a man." At the end of the series (spoiler alert!), Walt orchestrates his own death before law enforcement agents entrap him.

Marginalized Masculinities

Not all men are represented equally in images of masculinity. Consider the following: Most references to guns or violence (e.g., *heater*, *Glock*, *AK*, *piece*) in hip-hop songs by Black and Latino artists are censored on mainstream radio stations. Nevertheless, country music singers, most of whom are white, are permitted to sing lines such as, "I got a shotgun, rifle, and a four-wheel drive" and "I'd love to spit some beechnut [tobacco] into that dude's [a mugger] eye, and shoot him with my old .45 [a large-caliber handgun]" (Williams 1982). While violence associated with white men is permissible and even applauded, violence associated with Black men is treated as taboo and criminal.

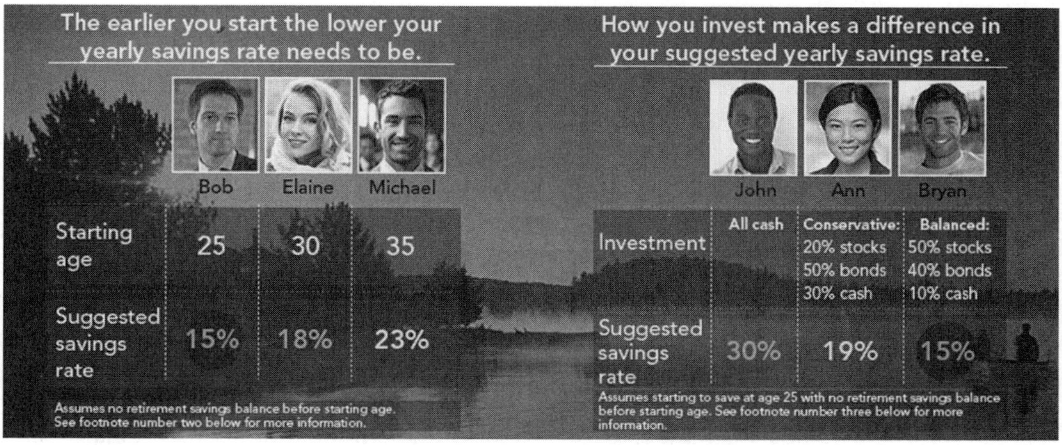

Photo 3.3

Source: Fidelity Brokerage Services LLC.

Representations of Black men in the media illustrate what Raewyn Connell (2001) calls **marginalized masculinity**, that is, "gender forms produced in exploited or oppressed groups such as ethnic minorities, which may share many features with hegemonic masculinity but are socially de-authorized" (30–31). Because of their race or class status, such men are often blocked from hegemonic masculinity. This concept reminds us that hegemonic masculinity is defined not only against femininity but also against other, more marginal masculinities that may intersect with lines of race, class, and social position. For a visual depiction of this hierarchy, consider Photo 3.3 above, taken from the website of Fidelity, an investment and retirement company, in 2015. Who is making the most sensible investment choices? How are these choices portrayed?

Photo 3.3 shows gender hierarchies in action: In both panels, the investor who gets it right is a white man (Bob and Bryan). Both maximize their returns by saving early and by having the right balance to their portfolio. Examining hegemonic masculinity reveals that there is a gendered and racialized pattern to the financial "winners" in society. But there is also a gendered pattern to the "losers." Consider John, a Black man, and Ann, an Asian American woman. Both have less-than-ideal retirement plans: John because he's dealing in all cash, and Ann because she's too conservative. Perhaps the graphic would have been just as instructive if their retirement plans had been switched. The way it stands, John's all-cash approach evokes stereotypes of Black people as having bad credit, poor investment acumen, and a preference for cash, perhaps because of the popular association between African Americans and drug dealing. Meanwhile, Ann's conservative portfolio resonates with stereotypes of Asian women as uptight. On the surface, this Fidelity spread is just an infographic about retirement strategies, but when viewed through the intersectional lens of gender, race, and class, it is also so much more.

Marginalized masculinities have been historically mobilized in the service of economic expansion, colonialism, and racial domination. Consider historical representations of Black men in America. While enslaved, Black men were infantilized by their white masters as "Sambos" (Boskin 1988): simpleminded, overgrown children, happy to be slaves. Rules forbidding slaves from learning to read, write, or even practice Christianity reinforced this stereotype. Ignorant by design, the "good" slave was one who was content to serve. This depiction of slaves as happy and docile created an expectation for how they should behave.

Like the Sambo, the stereotype of Black men as predators is long-standing. As slavery came to an end and Southern whites lost some of the legal and economic means to enforce their supremacy, they turned to more informal and cultural means to enforce segregation. Segregation was formalized in the Jim Crow system in the South from the late 1880s until the mid-1960s. During this period, a new controlling image of Black men emerged: Black men as criminals, especially rapists. While the historical record reveals scant accusations of Black men raping white women under slavery, starting in the late 1800s, whites used allegations of rape of white women as a pretext to pursue, torture, and murder thousands of Black men, as will be discussed in detail in Chapter 6.

Contemporary news coverage in the United States and beyond continues to depict Black and Latino men, in particular, as criminals. Blacks and Latinos are overrepresented as criminal suspects in news broadcasts, and they are often depicted in threatening contexts, for example, by being associated with gang-related violence. At the same time, whites are overrepresented as victims (Carlson and Cobb 2017; Chiricos and Eschholz 2002; Dixon and Linz 2000; Parham-Payne 2014). These popular images create a vicious cycle: Black boys and men suffer discrimination from people of all racial identifications, including even other African Americans who have internalized media representation of Black males as dangerous, aggressive, or hypersexual. As a report from The Opportunity Agenda (2011) summarizes, the effects "include everything from less attention from doctors to harsher sentencing by judges, lower likelihood of being hired for a job or admitted to school, lower odds of getting loans, and a higher likelihood of being shot by police" (14).

Even media portrayals that celebrate Black masculinity may do so by reducing them to bodies, such as in sports. Ben Carrington, a sociologist of race and sports, notes that "This idolization of the black athletic form produces a black athlete as post-human. . . . Strange creatures [who] possess [the] alien-like and certainly subhuman abilities to jump higher, hang in the air longer, punch harder and run faster" (Munir 2011). As Patricia Hill Collins (2004) notes,

> In some cases, the physical strength, aggression, and sexuality thought to reside in Black men's bodies generates admiration, whereas in others, these qualities garner fear. While the Black athlete might be praised despite being reduced to his physicality and aggression, other Black tropes receive far fewer popular adulations: represented as criminals, gangstas, rappers, and hip hop stars, Black men are marked as criminally violent and excessively sexual. (153)

Thus, dominant images of Black masculinity are marginalizing in divergent ways: at times criminalizing and at other times patronizing.

Conclusion: Shifting Gendered Norms

Gender is normative not simply because it celebrates men at the expense of women; it is normative because it creates narrow expectations for everyone, including men, along varying lines of race, class, sexuality, ability, and other forms of difference. These expectations may benefit some, but for many, they are dehumanizing and materially harmful.

Nevertheless, representations and popular culture may open space for subversion. From *Ru Paul's Drag Race* to Laverne Cox, the transgender star of *Orange Is the New Black,* representations of nonnormative gender identities are becoming more common in mass media. Even in advertising, some companies have moved away from using emphasized femininity to sell products that entrench and reproduce old feminine norms, such as submissiveness or modesty. For example, Lynn Comella (2010) argues that "sex positive feminist retailers in the U.S. have used consumer culture as an instrument for sexual consciousness-raising and social change by imbuing sex toys and sex toy stores with new kinds of cultural and political possibilities" (13).

Moreover, consumers are not simply passive receptors of gender representations. With the advent of social media such as Twitter, Facebook, Instagram, and blogs, everyday people more actively produce, use, and consume gender images. Some scholars argue that social media may begin to undermine gender, race, and even class difference by giving users equal standing (Danet 1998). Others highlight how avatars and nicknames allow social media users to proactively construct alternative identities that resist gender normativity (Andrejevic 2008; Turkle 1995). These new media forms hold possibilities for allowing people to carve out alternative ways of representing themselves and their worlds. As Dawn Dow (2016b) shows, for instance, Black mommy blogs allow Black mothers to broaden what it means to be Black, what it means to be a mother, and what it means to be both at the same time. Meanwhile, the use of Twitter has spawned its own distinct brand of social movement politics: the hashtag. Black Lives Matter, which started as a hashtag and became a social movement, has combined this new media form with the visual politics of Black bodies killed at the hands of law enforcement not only to galvanize the public but also to contest images of Black men as criminals (see Chapter 6).

However, gender scholars have also found that social media can reproduce gender norms. Men are more likely to use social media than women, giving men greater control over the content that is produced (Schradie 2011). In one ethnography of an online forum called BlueSky, Lori Kendall (2000) found that users also tend to reproduce their offline lives: The predominantly white male participants in her study negotiated their identities as "nerds" along the lines of masculinity, whiteness, and heterosexuality, which reflected their offline interests in computer-related work. Meanwhile, Sanja Kapidzic and Susan Herring (2011) studied teen chat sites to evaluate the claim that normative gender self-presentation was on the wane among teenage online users; far from debunking stereotypes, they found that teens' speech acts, message tones, and profile pictures conformed to traditional gender images. These studies suggest that those rushing to celebrate the promise of social media may miss the persistence influence of gender norms;

at least, this is how Kapidzic and Herring interpret their findings. Indeed, the persistent pull of gender—and of sex—is what we will explore further in Chapter 4.

Overall, normative representations of gender are embedded in gender hegemonies (see Chapter 1), which themselves are often driven by projects of capitalism, colonialism, and racial domination. To the extent that such norms are linked to broader social anxieties, one must also interrogate how gendered images are linked to inequalities of race, class, nation, and beyond. With this broader context in mind, scholars can more rigorously question the portrayal of certain gender arrangements as natural, inevitable, or rightful—and imagine how these arrangements can change.

KEYWORDS

Angry white man 49
Beauty myth 43
Black Is Beautiful 42
Controlling images 45
Cult of domesticity 39
Emphasized femininity 36
Fat shaming 34
Feminine mystique 42
Gender norms 34
Hegemonic masculinity 48
Male gaze 37
Marginalized masculinity 51
Objectification 37
Objectify 37

QUESTIONS

- What kinds of images or words are used to describe girls and women in the community where you grew up? To what extent do these terms echo emphasized femininity and to what extent do they act as controlling images? How do the girls and women you know navigate these images?
- Scholars discussing the male gaze suggest that *seeing* is as important an act as *doing*. Take a day to reflect on how gender shapes how you see the everyday world around you. How do you find yourself seeing differently as you bring gender into focus?
- Advertisements today are rich spaces for examining gender. Sometimes, they reinforce gender norms in remarkably predictable ways. Other times, they push and play with gender norms. Find an example of an advertisement that seems to subvert gender norms. For whom are gender norms subverted? In what ways does it also sustain or subvert norms surrounding age, class, race, nation, or other lines of difference?
- Thinking about your own online engagement, how does social media impact how gender norms circulate? From your own experiences, do you think gender norms have lost or gained strength in the context of social media?

ASSOCIATED READINGS

- Banet-Weiser, Sarah. 1999. *The Most Beautiful Girl in the World: Beauty Pageants and National Identity*. Berkeley: University of California Press.
- Berger, John. 1992. *Ways of Seeing*. New York: Penguin Modern Classics.
- Collins, Patricia Hill. 2002. *Black Feminist Thought: Knowledge, Consciousness, and the Politics of Empowerment*. Abingdon, UK: Routledge.
- Connell, Raewyn. 2005. *Masculinities*. Berkeley: University of California Press.
- Friedan, Betty. 1963. *The Feminine Mystique*. New York: W. W. Norton & Company.
- Halberstam, J. Jack. 2012. *Gaga Feminism: Sex, Gender, and the End of Normal*. New York: Beacon Press.
- Katz, Jackson. 2003. "Advertising and the Construction of Violent White Masculinity: From Eminem to Clinique for Men." In *Gender, Race, and Class in Media: A Text-Reader*, edited by G. Dines and J. M. Humez, 349–358. Thousand Oaks: SAGE.
- McClintock, Anne. 2013. *Imperial Leather: Race, Gender, and Sexuality in the Colonial Contest*. Abingdon, UK: Routledge.

NOTE

1. In the summer of 2012, a 14-year-old American named Julia Bluhm protested *Seventeen Magazine*'s use of airbrushing by starting a petition demanding that the magazine include at least one unaltered photograph in every issue. The petition received over 84,000 signatures. The magazine's editor responded by offering a "Body Peace Treaty" and agreed to never change girls' body or face shapes, although the magazine reserved the use of Photoshop for hair, clothing wrinkles, and wayward bra straps (Botelho 2012).

CHAPTER 4

Practice

Jennifer Carlson

Gender is enacted through practice. *This chapter suggests that through behaviors, interactions, and activities, people participate in defining and producing the normative force of gender. What people wear, which bathroom they use, how they style their hair, how much physical space they take up, their body language, their workout regimes at the gym: all of these practices work to make people recognizable, or not, as feminine or masculine and—especially as people evaluate and police the behaviors, interactions, and activities of others—fortify the constraining force of gender. But because people do gender as active social agents, they also are capable of undoing gender, upsetting gender binaries by refusing to appropriately perform gender norms—and by refusing to enforce gender norms on others.*

Introduction

Broad generalizations abound about women and men. Many of these norms are easily recognized as socially constructed; after all, the idealized woman—with her particular weight, bust line, and aesthetic—is a figment of our collective imagination sustained by pervasive popular representations of men and women (as discussed in Chapter 3). However, as pervasive as they may be, such representations—acting on us from the outside—cannot alone explain the power of gender norms in shaping our social lives.

Another widely cited explanation for gender norms appeals to biology and focuses on gender difference from *within*. Consider these supposedly biological distinctions between men and women:

Men don't menstruate; women do.

Men are strong; women are flexible.

Men excel at competition; women excel at cooperation.

Men have gross motor skills; women have fine motor skills.

Men are good at "hard" skills, such as math and science; women are good at "soft" skills, such as communication.

Men have penises; women have vaginas.

Men have more testosterone; women have more estrogen.

Men have XY chromosomes; women have XX chromosomes.

These differences are implicitly or explicitly used to justify a variety of social practices and institutions. For example, some support the military's barring women from combat because they believe—in the 1995 words of Newt Gingrich—that "females have biological problems staying in a ditch for 30 days because they get infections, and they don't have upper body strength" (Seelye 1995). Likewise, male and female athletes usually play in sex-segregated teams because men's muscular superiority, ostensibly, gives them an inherent advantage relative to women. Meanwhile, women predominate in paid care work occupations such as nursing, domestic labor, and child care as well as in other jobs involving communication skills; many people assume such skill sets reflect women's biological predisposition to being mothers and caregivers. As indicated by controversies over transgender people in the military, in sports, and even in bathrooms, these institutional arrangements do not just separate men and women and reify gender differences, but they also assert these binary gender categories as "naturally" mapping onto sexed bodies, thereby reproducing cisgender privilege.

But biology alone cannot explain gender difference. Renowned feminist Gloria Steinem ([1978] 1995) notes, "the truth is that, if men could menstruate, the power justifications would go on and on" (369). In other words, it is not menstruation *per se* that renders women vulnerable or incapacitated. Rather, menstruation is seen in this way because it is attached to a socially devalued group—women. If men, as Steinem suggests, menstruated, then menstruation would be seen as a symbol of power. Rather than revealing the foundation of gender differences, biology provides "just so" explanations (i.e., it's "just so" that boys are naturally stronger than girls) that conceal the origin of gender norms.

This chapter thus raises two sets of interrelated questions: First, where do norms come from, and how do people—as gendered social beings—reproduce them? Second, what is the relationship between gender and sex?

In considering these questions, this chapter lays out what it means to "do" gender. The chapter begins by showing how gender is a social practice in which people both perform gender norms and police others' gendered practices. It introduces two terms developed by gender scholars, **doing gender** and **gender performativity**, which together refer to how widespread engagement in patterned gendered practices *create*, rather than merely *reflect*, the binding power of gender norms. Though many people feel constrained by norms, believing them to exist outside of the individual, norms are instead the effect of people's collective engagement in gendered practices. After examining how everyday practices produce gender norms, the chapter turns to the question of biology to examine where gender ends and sex begins—and ultimately asks whether it makes sense to draw this line at all. This chapter challenges the widespread idea that gender is merely the cultural counterpart to the biological reality of sex, instead entertaining the possibility that gender norms shape which biological differences are sexed and thus seen as socially significant. The chapter introduces two additional terms, **embodiment** and the **materiality of sex**, which jointly refer to the ways in which gender norms and ideologies provide the lens through which people understand and engage with the body as a physical object. These terms make sense of how even bodies are socially constructed. The chapter ends by more generally considering the promise and price of "undoing" gender.

From Gender Identities to Gender Practices

Achieving brawns and beauty takes work, as reality TV shows such as *Extreme Makeover* or *Queer Eye for the Straight Guy* demonstrate and as the examples of dieting, skin-whitening, and cosmetic surgery discussed in Chapter 3 reveal. Yet, oftentimes, we overlook subtler ways in which gender structures our actions: After all, how one sits, how one greets others, or how one grooms herself or himself may require little thought. Such small, seemingly inconsequential activities are, in fact, the stuff of gender practice.

The notion of gender as a practice is rooted in a broader sociological perspective that treats social interaction as involving performance. Erving Goffman ([1959] 2008) is credited with the idea that society can be examined in terms of its dramaturgical elements. Goffman notes that people are socialized into roles: doctor/patient, waitress/customer, student/teacher. Each role has a set of expectations as to how it should be acted out; for example, a waitress is supposed to be cheerful and deferential to customers, while students expect teachers to enact expertise in the classroom. Individuals go through daily life moving through different roles in different social spaces. To capture this movement, Goffman argues that people treat some social spaces as a "backstage," where they prepare with other performers, and they treat other spaces as a "frontstage," where they enact their performance with an audience. For example, a waitress treats her tables as her frontstage and the kitchen as her backstage.

With the help of Goffman's theoretical framework, scholars began to see gender less as biological destiny and more as social performance. In a famous early analysis, Harold Garfinkel ([1967] 2006) used the story of Agnes to theorize gender as a social achievement. Garfinkel met Agnes after she came to University of California, Los Angeles (where Garfinkel was a sociology professor) to undergo sex transition surgery. Over the course of hours of interviews, she insisted to Garfinkel that she was 100% female, save for the inconvenience of her penis; Garfinkel, for his part, came to see Agnes's everyday gender performance, such as deference to men by appearing demure and soft-spoken, as situating her as social female, for all intents and purposes. Gender was not about having a particular body; it was about convincingly pulling off a performance of oneself as a particular gender.

A study such as Garfinkel's would not be conducted today; whereas Agnes's condition was treated as a medical abnormality, today transgender identity is recognized as a personal identity rather than a mental illness. Though homosexuality was removed from the *Diagnostic and Statistical Manual of Mental Disorders* (DSM) in 1973, it was not until 2013 that *gender identity disorder* was renamed *gender dysphoria* and removed from the list of sexual dysfunctions and paraphilic disorders (see American Psychiatric

Association 2013). The DSM ultimately retained the condition because insurance coverage for treatments such as counseling, cross-sex hormones, gender reassignment surgery and other medical treatments "need a diagnosis." Nevertheless, the American Psychiatric Association recognized that "it is important to note that gender nonconformity is not in itself a mental disorder." This modified terminology reflects a profound acknowledgment that the physical or mental health issues that transgender people experience have less to do with their psyche and more to do with the social stigma they face, an issue to which we return at the end of this section.

The social phenomenon of drag is another example where Goffman's dramaturgical take on the social world has helped illuminate gender as a performance. Drag queens and kings modify their appearance and body language to exemplify—and even dramatize—feminine and masculine self-presentation. Similar to the other social roles Goffman identifies, this gendered performance has a clear frontstage (the drag ball or drag show) and backstage (including the places where performers prepare as well as their daily lives outside the ball). Drag thus highlights how much of the work that people do to enact gender is a performance: from wearing or not wearing makeup to holding our bodies in particular ways to enacting deference or authority, our everyday lives are cut through with performances that establish us as gendered beings.

The world of drag balls was famously depicted in the 1990 film *Paris Is Burning*, which documented the vibrant drag culture of New York in the mid- to late 1980s. The film's featured protagonists—Venus Xtravaganza, Willi Ninja, Pepper LaBeija—contrasted with the kinds of celebrities who usually populate the silver screen. Almost all were poor, young, queer people of color, but they aspired to the lives of glamour and luxury. The film depicts drag balls as a mix of dance-off and beauty pageant: Participants, organized into "houses," created costumes, routines, and personas to display in a competition format. Performances were judged on their "realness" in a range of categories that required them to present themselves as rich women, college girls, or Wall Street executives, among others.

The drag balls of New York City served as a stage for artistic expression and social survival for a community marginalized by racism, sexism, heteronormativity, and economic inequality. From their *outsider within* position (see Chapter 2), the participants in drag balls understood that gender, race, and class were performances, not destinies. As Dorian Corey, one of the film's stars, stated, "The fact the you are not an executive is merely because of the social standing of life. . . . [I]n a ballroom, you can be anything you want—you say to the straight world that you could be an executive if only they [would] let you." Successfully navigating drag balls meant flawlessly performing the very social identities from which participants were excluded "merely because of the social standing of life." Another of the film's stars, Pepper LaBeija, described the process of presenting herself as a woman: "You've erased all the flaws, all the giveaways to make your illusion perfect."

The film—and drag culture more broadly—has given rise to critical analyses that interrogate gender as a social achievement. In particular, feminist theorist Judith Butler used the film as an illustration of the "illegitimacy of the law of sex" (2011: xxiii). Drag raises questions about the naturalness of categories such as emphasized femininity and hegemonic masculinity (see Chapter 3) by suggesting, first, that gender can be read as a performance and, second, that the capacity to engage in a particular brand of gender performance is not biologically determined. Waging a damning critique of gender as natural, drag exposes gender as something radically constructed (an "illusion" according to Pepper LaBeija) and thus, open for reconstruction.

If gender is a performance, then, how are gender norms so binding and inescapable? To explain this seeming paradox, Judith Butler refers to the "congealing," or fixing, of gender through constant performance as *gender performativity*. Calling gender *performative* has a slightly different connotation than saying that gender is a *performance*. Butler argues that when people engage in gender practice, they are doing much more than simply responding to preexisting gender norms. In fact, they are creating those norms through everyday practice. Collectively, people's individual gender performances create the expectation that human beings are divided into two neat, mutually exclusive biological groups of male and females and that this biology is reflected in the binary social categories of men and women.

Gender Accountability

The social construction of gender relies not just on "doing gender." Such performances are also accountable to others. In an influential article entitled "Doing Gender," Candace West and Don Zimmerman (1987) suggest that while Goffman's analysis of gender as performed (or *done*, in their terms) offers a key point of departure for understanding how gender structures our everyday social interactions, *doing* gender is different from other types of social performance because gender is not merely a role that can be put on or taken off at will. A waitress can leave the restaurant; a doctor can leave the hospital; a student can leave the classroom. But the roles of mother, wife, girlfriend, daughter, and so forth cannot be divided into backstage and frontstage performances. Furthermore, *how* one performs the role of waitress, doctor, or student reflects not only that role but also one's gender. All people carry gender throughout their daily performances as they move through different social roles.

Thus, gender is not merely a set of social roles that are enacted differently in a frontstage and backstage but rather a master identity. As West and Zimmerman (1987) write,

> Roles are *situated* identities—assumed and relinquished as the situation demands—rather than master identities, such as sex category, that cut across situations. Unlike most roles, such as "nurse," "doctor," and "patient" or "professor" and "student," gender has no specific site or organizational context. (128)

As with Butler's analysis, West and Zimmerman (1987) emphasize that people perform gender as an ongoing achievement, and as people perform social activities, they "may be held accountable for performance of that activity as a *woman* or a *man*" (136). Gender is thus not about playing a certain role; it is about establishing oneself as a socially recognizable person. This is why gender is always achieved in relation to others who can discredit or delegitimize one's gender and, therefore, one's credibility as a social being: "To 'do' gender is not always to live up to normative conceptions of femininity or masculinity; it is to engage in behavior *at the risk of gender assessment*" (136).

People put pressure on both themselves and others to perform gender appropriately. This means that, in addition to affirming their own gender identities through practice, people police the gender practices of others. An excellent example of gender policing comes from C.J. Pascoe's *Dude, You're a Fag!* (2011), a study of how boys achieve masculinity in an American high school setting. Pascoe observed that boys used a homophobic slur—*fag*—to sanction the behavior of other boys. Instead of referring to homosexuality, the *fag* epithet was often used by boys to police each other's masculine identities. As one of the boys in her study explained, the term could be used to discredit almost any type of behavior as non-masculine: "Anything . . . literally anything. Like you were trying to turn a wrench the wrong way, 'Dude, you're a fag.' Even if a piece of meat drops out of your sandwich, 'You fag!'" (57). As anticipated by West and Zimmerman's (1987) analysis, doing masculinity in this way appeared across all kinds of social interactions and social contexts: In shop class, in the hallway, in the cafeteria, and on the athletic field, boys were constantly reading—and reviewing—each other's performances of masculinity.

This policing of masculinity illustrates how people participate in gender not only by doing gender but also by *determining gender*, a term developed by Laurel Westbrook and Kristin Schilt. **Determining gender**, as they note, involves more than the evaluation of a particular gender of self. Rather, determining gender involves differentially drawing on identity and biological criteria to assert "who counts as a man and who counts as a woman" (Westbrook and Schilt 2014: 32). Their inclusion of ascribed sex as an axis of accountability helps shed light on how gender policing disadvantages differently gendered and sexed people differently: While the boys in Pascoe's study experienced anxiety over their achievement of masculinity, they generally enjoyed a privileged status as "real"—that is, apparently biological—boys. This privilege is known as **cisgender privilege**, which describes the advantages accrued by virtue of identifying with one's ascribed birth sex.

Gender policing is especially acute where ascribed biological sex and gender identity neither correspond to each other nor exist as neat, binary categories. Consider **transgender** people, whose identity does not correspond to their ascribed birth sex. As sociologist Tey Meadow (2010) writes,

> Transgender people create a profound category crisis for social institutions built on the idea that biological sex is both immutable and dichotomous. . . . [C]ultural anxieties about reproduction and the heterosexual, conjugal family underscore institutional efforts to manage the uncertainty of postmodern gender identities. (814)

The "bathroom panic" (Stone 2016) that erupted in 2016 is a prime example of the cultural anxieties and institutional crises that emerged in response to gender nonconforming identities that challenged the binary construction of sex and gender. In early summer of that year, the U.S. Department of Education issued guidelines that public education institutions should allow transgender students to use the gender-segregated bathroom associated with their chosen gender identity. The directive, grounded in the principles of equality enshrined in Title IX, drew massive backlash from conservative states. Advocates of anti-trans bills in states such as North Carolina rallied around the issue of safety, maintaining that the bathroom directive would allow men disguised as women to penetrate the safe space of women's bathrooms, putting ciswomen at risk. This focus on safety for ciswomen elided more commonplace experiences of vulnerability in bathroom stalls: While some ciswomen pledged to carry guns into bathrooms in response to fears of transwomen entering ciswomen's space, it is transwomen, as Stone notes, who are particularly likely to experience discrimination, harassment, and assault when they use bathrooms. Such negative treatment of transgender people—ranging from stereotyping to discrimination to hate speech to violence—is known as **transphobia**.

Whether taking place in legislative halls or bathroom stalls, these transphobic panics and anxieties about gender categories can have catastrophic consequences for those who fail to conform to gender norms. The price of failing to legibly perform gender is social, and sometimes physical, death. While failure to perform the role of doctor, teacher, or waitress may lead to expulsion from the clinic, the classroom, or the restaurant, the failure to perform gender can lead to expulsion from society altogether. Indeed, although high-profile, class-privileged trans women such as Caitlyn Jenner and Laverne Cox have brought increased visibility and awareness to transphobia and cisgender privilege alike, transgender people experience a variety of heightened vulnerabilities to discrimination, assault, and death. For example, Venus Xtravaganza, one of the drag queens in *Paris Is Burning* who worked as an escort, was murdered when one of her clients apparently found out the "secret" between her legs. Likewise, the film *Boys Don't Cry* depicts the true story of a teenage trans boy named Brandon Teena who was raped and murdered by two men in Nebraska after they forcibly assaulted him and discovered his genitalia. The title *Boys Don't Cry* most directly interrogates the silencing of Brandon Teena, but it also highlights the broader cultural code in which men like his attackers learn to deal with their anxieties using violence, anger, and hatred. Self-righteous in their crime, they felt no remorse for Teena's death.

Statistics confirm that despite increased visibility and awareness for some, the experiences of Xtravaganza and Teena are all too common. A fact sheet released by the National Coalition of Anti-Violence Program (2017) reports that transgender women are vastly overrepresented among hate crime victims, and they are also more likely to experience sexual violence. Meanwhile, transgender people were 3.7 times as likely as cisgender people to experience police violence. Finally, amid experiences of physical abuse, bullying, and harassment, transgender people are at exceptionally high risk of lifetime suicide attempts, according to a joint report from the American Foundation for Suicide Prevention and the Williams Institute at UCLA Law (Haas, Rodgers, and Herman 2014). In light of such troubling figures, Laverne Cox (2015) notes,

> Most trans folks don't have the privileges Caitlyn [Jenner] and I have now. . . . It is those trans folks we must continue to lift up, get them access to healthcare, jobs, housing, safe streets, safe schools

> and homes for our young people. We must lift up the stories of those most at risk, statistically trans people of color who are poor and working class.

The experiences of transgender people, thus, highlight the limits of gender analyses that treat gender merely as an "illusion" or a "performance"; while this is an illuminating angle through which to understand the reproduction of gender norms, it misses the ways in which gender comprises a core part of a person's identity, on the one hand, and the ways in which certain bodies are able to socially achieve gender norms as compared to other bodies, on the other hand. Rather than suggesting a person's gender identity is fake, wrong, or superficial, theorizing gender as something that is "done" provides a mechanism for understanding *how* gender norms come to be, for imagining *what kinds* of gendered worlds we want to live in, and for sketching out *how* we make such worlds possible.

Interrogating the Science of Sexual Difference

Thanks to massive societal shifts such as large-scale increases in women's workforce participation and the permeation of feminist critique into mainstream society, the idea that gender is socially constructed is now part of mainstream consciousness. As television, magazines, and social media dramatize doing gender, it becomes easier to see how everyday actions and activities help construct gender differences.

Yet the acceptance of the notion that gender is a social construction has not done away with the assumption that gender is somehow linked to sex and that sex is biological rather than social. What is the relationship between sex and gender? Do people do gender as a means of expressing sex (perhaps because sex markers, such as genitalia, remain concealed in public view)? Are gender and sex wholly unrelated? Or, perhaps, is sex the *effect* of gender, much as gender is the *effect* of repeated social practices?

Today's gender scholars question the dichotomy between gender as socially constructed and sex as innate. Some argue that ideas about gender in fact distort the biological reality that the term *sex* is intended to capture. Scientists "see" gender in biological processes, and then they reproduce these gendered interpretations as fundamental differences in what they treat as sex (see Chapter 3 on seeing as a gendered process). To put it a different way, gender scholars argue that binary thinking (see Chapter 2) is imposed on sex, creating rather than reflecting "natural" sexual difference.

To illustrate, consider Emily Martin's (1991) study of scientific textbooks that narrate sexual reproduction. She found that these textbooks used the language of gender to explain seemingly innate biological processes. The textbooks treated eggs and sperm not as biological cells but as gendered actors in a heterosexual romance, with corresponding gendered characteristics, desires, and capacities. These textbooks described eggs as passively waiting for the sperm in a cave-like environment, evoking the "sleeping beauty" narrative of the slumbering princess who awaits the prince who will awaken her.

Meanwhile, they portrayed the sperm that ultimately unites with the egg as the heroic rescuer who must outperform the other sperm—and thus prove his physical superiority—in the race for reproduction. The textbooks also described female reproductive systems as wasteful: women shed reproductive debris, "slowly degenerating and aging like overstocked inventory" of eggs (487). By contrast, the textbooks treat the millions of sperm that a human male produces every day not as waste but as an indication of male virility.

Despite their resonance with widespread social assumptions about men and women, these gendered descriptions do not effectively capture the biological processes they are meant to describe. Martin notes that the sperm's dominant action is back and forth, not forward propulsion, which means that the egg must catch the sperm in its sticky outer layer to keep the sperm from flying off once it makes contact with the egg. Such a mismatch between reproductive process and gender imaginaries, of course, opens up the possibilities for alternative metaphors for the drama of reproduction. Nevertheless, the textbooks' narratives explaining how the sperm attaches emphasize the *sperm's* activeness: In one scientific report, the sperm is said to fire a harpoon into the egg, which is described as a "sperm receptor." Thus, Martin's study demonstrates that the language used to explain biological processes is deeply gendered, which in turn influences how people imagine those biological processes.

Beyond eggs and sperm, gender scholars also point out that scientists see sex in a vast array of biological phenomena and processes, including genitalia, chromosomes, brains, and other parts of the body. For example, the so-called sex hormones, estrogen and testosterone, provide mechanisms by which entire bodies—well beyond reproductive processes—become sexed in scientific discourse. Ann Fausto-Sterling (2000) notes that scientific studies of estrogen and testosterone follow the binary thinking uncovered by Martin in textbooks on sperm and eggs. Scientists, for example, often treat these two hormones as antagonistic, such that the domination of one hormone or the other produced sexed bodies. Thus, bodies with high levels of estrogen are categorized as female; bodies with high levels of testosterone are male. This association between hormones and bodies means that scientists no longer see sex difference as limited to primary sex characteristics (e.g., the reproductive organs) and secondary sex characteristics (e.g., visible differences such as pubic hair, breasts, or the Adam's apple). As Ann Fausto-Sterling (2000: 179) explains,

> Even more astonishing than the number of articles [on sex hormones] was the diversity of topics. Articles on estrogen covered subjects ranging from heart disease, Alzheimer's, nutrition, pain tolerance, immunity and birth control to bone growth and cancer. Articles on testosterone covered behaviors such as asking directions . . . cooperation, aggression, hugging, and "female road rage," as well as a diverse range of medical topics including cancer, bone growth, heart disease, female impotence, contraception and fertility.

As Fausto-Sterling notes, however, the two so-called sex hormones actually regulate many other activities such as "brain and blood cell formation, the circulatory system, the liver, lip and carbohydrate metabolism, gastrointestinal function, and gall bladder, muscle, and kidney activities" that do not resonate with presumed gender differences between men and women. Nevertheless, both research and media seem fixated on findings that situate estrogen as the female and testosterone as the male hormone.

Binary thinking, when imposed on sex, can powerfully frame how scientists see basic biological processes. Furthermore, binary thinking obscures the diversity inherent in human biology. From person to person, there is a wide range of differences in hormones and physiology. This includes significant variation in people's genitalia and variation in how genitalia, chromosomes, hormones, and secondary sex characteristics appear together in a particular body. For example, **intersexuality** describes a circumstance when a person's sex does not correspond with scientifically stipulated criteria for biological sex, which can include hormones, genitals, and/or chromosomes. Fausto-Sterling estimates that about 1.7 out of 100 births are, to some extent, sex ambiguous or intersex.

Despite its high frequency, Fausto-Sterling argues that intersexuality is largely hidden because it upsets the binary thinking that structures common wisdom about bodies. As with transgender persons until recently, medical professionals have adopted a variety of practices to "cure" intersex people. Specifically, Fausto-Sterling describes three dominant approaches to "fixing" intersexed children:

1. The prenatal fix: The intersexed fetus is treated with hormones, or it is aborted.
2. The surgical fix: Doctors reconstruct children's ambiguous genitalia to fit the aesthetic image of either a vagina or a penis.
3. The psychological fix: Experts urge parents to raise intersex children without any gender ambiguity so that they will socialize into the sex/gender combination they are assigned at or soon after birth.

Each of these "fixes" demonstrates how medical science reproduces binary thinking by pathologizing different bodies as deviant. Such "cures," which can be administered during infancy or early childhood, force intersex individuals into binary categories of sex, often without their consent or comprehension. Further, these "cures" reinforce the notion that the female/male binary is a meaningful, useful, and appropriate way of organizing the world. Not unlike everyday people who read and police gender in everyday life, scientists, medical doctors, and other experts read and enforce sex onto the body.

However, this may be changing: In 2017, three former U.S. Surgeons General coauthored a paper condemning the surgical fix, noting that

> our review of the available evidence has persuaded us that cosmetic infant genitoplasty is not justified absent a need to ensure physical functioning, and we hope that professionals and parents who face this difficult decision will heed the growing consensus that the practice should stop. (Elders, Satcher, and Carmona 2017: 2)

Such a shift is a reminder that coercive practices for enforcing gender/sex binaries can, and do, change.

Embodiment: Bodies as the Effect of Gender

Critical of taken-for-granted knowledge (see Chapter 2), gender scholars reveal that widely accepted ideas about gender binaries can shape the science of the sexed body. But bodies are not only the effects of gendered knowledge; they are also the effects of gender practice in a different sense.

To start, consider how the feminist scholar Iris Marion Young (1980) analyzes *embodiment*, which refers to the physical aspects of subjective experiences that locate individuals within and through space. Young starts her examination of gendered embodiment with a well-known example of gender difference from the sports world: "**throwing like a girl**," a throw that comes not from the entire force of the body but from the hand or the forearm. Though differences in throwing styles and skill are often taken as evidence of biological difference between boys and girls, she suggests that these differences are instead evidence of how socialization shapes understandings of physical difference. The term *throwing like a girl*, after all, is meant to both disparage athletic girls and women and also to discourage them from participating in sports in the first place. Historically, women were barred from sports because of widespread beliefs that women's athletic participation was unnatural. Pierre de Coubertin, founder of the modern Olympic Games, said, "Women's sports are against the laws of nature," and throughout much of the 20th century and into the 21st century, female athletes have been labeled as lesbians or accused of being men, following the assumption that women's natural inferiority made them unfit for athletics.

Broadening out from the stereotypically feminine action of throwing like a girl, Young focuses on body movement aimed at a particular task. In other words, she is interested in how comfortable girls and women are in using their bodies as instruments for getting things done. She notes that girls and women face a contradiction: They are treated as objects by the male gaze in the sense that they *are* bodies (see Chapter 3), but they are also subjects in the sense that they *have* bodies. Young argues that as a result, girls and women feel uncomfortable in their own bodies and in using their own bodies. Girls and women hesitate to use their full bodies, and they tend to move in constricted spaces. Internalizing this ascribed inefficacy and frailty, girls and women may worry that they are unable to perform tasks that boys and men can, and that if they do, they may get hurt, look awkward, or look too strong. Writing more than four decades ago, Young (1980: 153) concludes that femininity physically limits women:

> We are physically inhibited, confined, positioned, and objectified. . . . The more a girl assumes her status as feminine, the more she takes herself to be fragile and immobile, and the more she actively enacts her own body inhibition.

In highlighting embodiment as socially constructed, sociologists of gender do not mean to imply that bodies are somehow not real or figments of our social imaginations. Bodies are real, concrete, material entities that exist. But Young's early analysis opens up questions about *how* this existence is shaped—which bodies matter, what about these bodies matters, and what bodies that matter can do—and suggests that these questions are as much about society as they are about biology.

This idea of bodies mattering leads us to the concept of the *materiality of sex*, a concept developed decades later by Judith Butler. Taking seriously the notion that bodies are both objects to be manipulated and subjects within social space (as Young suggests and as discussed also in Chapter 3), Butler understands the materiality of sex as achieved through the repeated actions that shape the body as a material object.

To illustrate this concept, consider a study of female weightlifters by Shari Dworkin (2001), a sociologist who wanted to understand the gendered line between biology and society. Her intention was to examine a contradiction faced by women fitness participants: Although women are told that their biology will keep them from gaining muscle, weight training increases muscle mass in women and men alike. Rather than being physically unable to increase muscle size, Dworkin found that many women *chose* not to lift too much weight to avoid getting big. One participant told her, "I don't want to look like a female bodybuilder. . . . I don't ever want to be non-feminine" (338). Another woman said she didn't lift weights because

> I gain muscle really fast. . . . [I] don't want to look masculine. They say lift light and with lots of reps and you won't gain mass, but *not me!* I gain mass so fast! I should have been a man! (339)

Among women who continued with weights as part of their fitness routine, Dworkin found that they tended to keep a constant weight while increasing repetitions (instead of increasing weight) as a strategy for avoiding muscle gain. One woman said she backed off because "I like strength, and I like maintaining my physical structure with muscles, but I don't like the look of being too buff. . . . I like lean, fit, a little buff, feminine" (342).

Interestingly, the women in Dworkin's study tended to believe that their ability to gain muscle through weight lifting made them biologically unusual or aberrant women. Yet Dworkin reaches a different conclusion:

> [The limitation on] muscular size is not simply imposed on women. Rather, they actively define it, wrestle with it, nudge it up and down, and shape its current and future placement. Women in fitness sites are immersed in an arena of continual negotiation as to the placement of the [glass] ceiling [on muscular strength], which is in part influenced by historically shifting definitions of emphasized femininity. (346)

In this context, Dworkin uses the term *glass ceiling* on muscular strength in the same way that the term has been used to describe women's blocked opportunities in the workforce, as will be discussed in Chapter 8. Though common wisdom states that men are naturally stronger than women, the women in Dworkin's study helped create this difference by limiting their bodies' capacities.

Illustrating the materiality of sex, Dworkin's analysis shows how bodies are the physical repository of the actions people take. It suggests that many of the attributes people associate with maleness or femaleness are the result of repeated actions, not biological destiny. And if embodied difference is, at least in part, a product of social practice rather than biological destiny, then nature can also be changed. One scholar who explores how women transform their embodiment is Martha McCaughey (1998), who studies women involved in self-defense training. She argues that participation in self-defense classes creates a new experience of embodiment for women. McCaughey argues that men may be marked as violent and aggressive, and women may be deemed weak and passive not because of biological destiny but because they rehearse particular kinds of bodily practices, noting that "gender is an embodied belief" that is repeated as we literally move through our lives.

McCaughey argues that women's self-defense classes interrupt feminine embodiment by providing women with a different relationship to their bodies and to space. When women in her study started self-defense courses, McCaughey observes, they were concerned about exhibiting their physical power and worried about looking stupid, which resonated with the feminine hesitancy and physical incompetence described by Young. But with time, the self-defense classes forced them to feel new possibilities for action. Through what McCaughey calls the **fighting spirit**, self-defense reversed the feminine embodiment described by Young in which the female body is perceived to be reflective of and affected by patriarchal beliefs. Women began to feel in control of their bodies. They learned to "stay in their bodies" to work their bodily capacity concretely to their advantage. They even learned that they can take a punch without falling apart or giving up. As one self-defense instructor told McCaughey, "When I get a woman in her body for 40 hours and she has a kinesthetic experience of her power, that's a major difference" (291).

How people inhabit their bodies matters: On one hand, the repeated actions people undertake through their bodies give their bodies their materiality; on the other hand, people's embodiment affects their ways of thinking about the world. McCaughey argues that while consciousness-raising groups—in which women often discuss personal experiences of gender-based inequality, harassment, and violence—raise women's awareness, changes in embodiment transform their lives in a practical manner because it transforms how women experience space. McCaughey explains,

> Self-defensers do not just think about assertiveness; they practice it. That the practice engages the body, the mind, and the emotions is critical. Femininity is embodied, sensual, and habitual; this is how it gets disembodied and replaced with the fighting spirit. The fighting spirit is simultaneously a new body, a new idea, and a new feeling. (291)

Thus, according to McCaughey, self-defense has embodied benefits: Increased confidence increases one's chances of physical survival and enhances women's social survival by giving them a new entitlement to stand up to the men in their lives.

Not all body projects, however, are equally valued. While the women whom McCaughey worked with accrued empowerment by virtue of experiencing their bodies as powerful tools, there is no indication that they drastically disrupted the expectations of women's bodies by, for example, breaking the glass ceiling on women's muscular strength described by Dworkin.

In contrast, consider South African runner Caster Semenya. Semenya was the center of controversy in 2009 and again in the 2016 Olympic Games in Brazil due to her remarkable performance, and significant improvements, as a runner. She soon caught the attention of the International Association of Athletic Federations (IAAF), which required Semenya to take a number of tests to verify her eligibility for the 2009 World Championships. Just three hours before her event, news leaked that one of these tests was a sex test. Although the results were not disclosed, rumors about her medical reports suggested that she had higher levels of testosterone than most women.

Despite the scrutiny she endured so close to her race, Semenya still excelled at her event, winning the 800-meter by over two seconds. In the aftermath of the race, the news about the sex test led to a flurry of media attention. Some of the most hostile responses came from other competitors who questioned whether Semenya was biologically qualified to compete, that is, whether she was "really" a woman. Elisa Cusma, an Italian runner who finished sixth, said, "These kind of people should not run with us. . . . For me, she's not a woman. She's a man"; Russian runner Mariya Savinova, who finished 15th, bluntly stated, "Just look at her" (Clarey 2009). Commenting on Semenya's running career, *Sports Illustrated*'s David Epstein explained that Semenya was caught in a double bind with regard to her running:

> If Semenya wins the gold, she is likely to be accused of having an unfair advantage. If she runs poorly, she is likely to be accused of sandbagging the race so as not to be accused of having an unfair advantage. (Thomas 2012)

Illustrating how embodiment reveals the line between sex and gender can be a hazy one, Semenya responded to these harsh critiques by feminizing her self-presentation. Soon after her 2009 race, Semenya appeared on the cover of South Africa's *YOU* magazine with the caption, "WE TURN SA'S [South Africa's] POWER GIRL INTO A GLAMOUR GIRL—AND SHE LOVES IT!" In the accompanying article, Semenya explained that she simply lacks the time, rather than the willingness, to appropriately perform femininity: "I'd like to dress up more often and wear dresses but I never get the chance." Semenya thus illustrated how deeply accountable people are to how their bodies both look and perform. Her story shows the work that must go into confirming not only one's gender but also its presumed biological basis in one's sex.

Furthermore, Semenya's story suggests a gendered double standard in embodiment. Her story contrasts sharply with that of Michael Phelps, who won over 28 Olympic medals between 2004 and 2016, making him the most decorated Olympian of all time. His winning achievements, too, have been biologized; one UK Telegraph story featured an anatomical analysis of Phelps's unusual physique (e.g., his "wingspan" of 6'7") that was "made to swim" (Siebert 2014). Yet rather than treated as a biological freak with an unfair advantage, Phelps's body is treated as a marvel that enhances, rather than undermines, his appeal as an accomplished swimmer. Whereas Semenya's body suggests that her wins may be fraudulent, Phelps's body reinforces his tenacity to win.

Semenya fell out of public view for several years, but by the 2016 Olympics, other athletes had taken up her cause. Indian sprinter Dutee Chand, who was disqualified from competition because of testosterone levels that exceeded the guidelines set by the IAAF, refused to take hormone-suppressing drugs and instead contested the guidelines as arbitrary and unscientific (Branch 2015). She won her appeal, opening the door not only for herself to compete, but for Caster Semenya, too. On the eve of Semenya's participation in the 2016 Olympics, commentators anticipated that "Semenya's full ability has now been unleashed" (Engber 2016). Her gold medal victory in the 800-meter unleashed another wave of resentment, but this time around, there were many vocal supporters as well. Though debates continue about sex testing in sports, Semenya nevertheless has awed many onlookers with the sheer prowess of her athletic performance—inspiring them to question and, for some, to set aside binary thinking about sex and gender.

Doing/Undoing Gender and Sex

Both sex and gender are enacted through a range of practices: people's dress, the ways they move their bodies, and even how they see biological sex. Instead of thinking about sex and gender as separate and demarcated, Ann Fausto-Sterling suggests thinking of the two as a Mobius strip. A mathematical conundrum, the Mobius strip appears to be a two-sided figure, but this is an illusion. In fact, the Mobius strip is a three-dimensional, but one-sided, object. In the same sense, sex and gender appear to be separate parts of the same whole. This is useful for mapping out, for example, how cisgender privilege may operate separately from, but intersect with, masculine privilege. Yet from a different angle, sex and gender appear inseparable. This is not to say that sex is *only* gender but rather that sex and gender are *co-constitutive*: Understandings of sex and gender are inextricably bound together. Part of the reason that gender and sex are inextricably bound together is that they are enacted in similar ways. Both refer to how difference is naturalized through repeated practices that create the force of gender and sex as stable categories, independent of society.

If gender and sex are done (or accomplished) through practice, might they also be undone? After all, this chapter shows that people actively participate in creating gender normativity. Therefore, they might be able to undo gender by consciously transforming their everyday practices. Such projects may be ambitious and consuming—for example, the body projects that competitive athletes undergo—but they may be subtler and less noticeable. As another example, recent campaigns to include pronoun designations on lapel pins, office doors, and in email signatures quietly—but profoundly—remind people that biology is not destiny. Furthermore, the proliferation of pronoun language such as they/them/theirs and zhe/zher/zhim not only provides space to re-gender everyday language but also questions how cisgender binaries (i.e., he/his/him, she/hers/her) are built into the most quotidian social interactions through language. Such everyday destabilization has led critical theorists such as Judith Jack Halberstam (2011, 2012) to go so far as to question whether the norm itself is dead and to call for a "queer art of failure" (2011), that is, an embrace of one's sex and gender "failures" in order to expose sex and gender as illusory.

It is important to remember that today's terrain of gender identities and sexed bodies is complex and nuanced and that, therefore, undoing gender can take multiple forms: scrambling the categories of masculinity and femininity; forging new gender categories; disentangling bodies from identities; and attempting to dissolve gender categories altogether. Indeed, even the distinction between doing gender and undoing gender may become increasingly blurred. These many potentials for disrupting gender suggest that categories themselves are not necessarily problematic; rather, what matters is how they translate into static, binding statuses that allocate resources and life chances.

As this chapter showed, there are real costs to failing to perform sex and gender in a binary sex–gender system, and these costs are not equally distributed. Especially for people marginalized along multiple lines of difference, there is tremendous fallout—from ridicule, harassment, and bullying to assault and death—to defying gender norms because people also actively police each other as gendered and sexed beings. Thus, to transform gender hegemonies, we must not simply note that gender is a practice in which we engage so that we are legible to ourselves and to one another; we must also recognize how gender compels us to compel *others* to be legible to us.

KEYWORDS

Cisgender privilege 62
Determining gender 62
Doing gender 58
Embodiment 58
Fighting spirit 69
Gender performativity 58
Intersexuality 66
Materiality of sex 58
Throwing like a girl 67
Transgender 62
Transphobia 63

QUESTIONS

- Doing and undoing gender is fraught social practice: It can be pleasurable, fun, and exhilarating, but it also can be tedious, anxiety producing, and exhausting. How do your everyday practices of doing and undoing gender impact you? Where do they bring you up versus bring you down? Do you ever hold back—whether at the gym, in classrooms, or elsewhere—because of gendered expectations? Alternatively, when do you feel emboldened because of gendered expectations?
- While people engage in an array of practices that mark us as masculine or feminine, our sexed bodies are almost always concealed behind clothing. Why are people compelled to publicly display our gender when our sex—the supposed explanation for gender difference—remains hidden?
- Gender-segregated sports level the playing field for female athletes by reinforcing the gender binary between biological maleness

and femaleness. Can—and should—competitive sports be organized differently? What would a feminist approach to competitive athletics look like?

- The costs and benefits of performing—or failing to perform—gender are not distributed equally. How do race, class, sexuality, embodiment, and other lines of difference shape who pays for and who profits from gender performativity?
- Why are people's gender identities so important in organizing their social lives? Thinking about gender as embedded in practices of performing and policing, is a gender-neutral world possible—or even desirable?
- Some bodies are sick, some are healthy; some are weak, some are strong; some produce more testosterone, others produce less; some bodies can become pregnant, others cannot. In other words, the body—and differences across bodies—is not merely a figment of our social imaginations. How can this observation be squared with the claim that sex is socially constructed alongside—and through—gender?
- Some scholars argue that transgender identity is transgressive in that it upsets widely held assumptions about biological sex and gender identity; others argue that reducing transgender identity to its transgressive potential is, itself, an example of transphobia that reproduces its non-normativity as a social identity. In your view, how does the emergence of transgender identity impact the binary gender/sex system? In the long run, will the binary gender/sex system absorb transgender identity? Or will this binary system be replaced by some other normative way of thinking about gender and bodies?

ASSOCIATED READINGS

- Butler, Judith. 2011. *Bodies That Matter: On the Discursive Limits of Sex*. New York: Taylor & Francis.
- Dworkin, Shari L. 2001. "'Holding Back': Negotiating a Glass Ceiling on Women's Muscular Strength." *Sociological Perspectives* 44 (3): 333–350.
- Faust-Sterling, Anne. 2000. *Sexing the Body: Gender Politics and the Construction of Sexuality*. New York: Basic Books.
- Garfinkel, Harold. (1967) 2006. "Passing and the Managed Achievement of Sex Status in an 'Intersexed' Person." In *The Transgender Studies Reader*, edited by Susan Stryker and Stephen Whittle, 58–93. New York: Routledge.
- McCaughey, Martha. 1998. "The Fighting Spirit: Women's Self-Defense Training and the Discourse of Sexed Embodiment." *Gender & Society*, 12 (3): 277–300.
- Meadow, Tey. 2010. "'A Rose is a Rose': On Producing Legal Gender Classifications." *Gender & Society* 24 (6): 814–837.
- Pascoe, C. J. 2011. *Dude, You're a Fag: Masculinity and Sexuality in High School, With a New Preface*. Berkeley: University of California Press.
- West, Candace, and Don H. Zimmerman. 1987. "Doing Gender." *Gender & Society* 1 (2): 125–151.
- Westbrook, Laurel, and Kristen Schilt. 2014. "Doing Gender, Determining Gender Transgender People, Gender Panics, and the Maintenance of the Sex/Gender/Sexuality System." *Gender & Society* 28 (1): 32–57.
- Young, Iris Marion. 1980. "Throwing Like a Girl: A Phenomenology of Feminine Body Comportment Motility and Spatiality." *Human Studies* 3 (1): 137–156.

CHAPTER 5

Gendering Sexuality

Oluwakemi M. Balogun and Kimberly Kay Hoang

This chapter explores gendered sexuality. It begins with early scholarship that focused on sexuality as a biological, psychological, and individual phenomenon and traces a shift toward scholarship that stressed social construction. This shift opened up the possibility for feminist interventions into domination and control in the realm of sexuality. The chapter then turns to scholars who adopted postmodern, queer, and intersectional theories to better understand inequality and identity by identifying key ways that sexuality is intertwined with power. Finally, the chapter describes political–economic approaches to gendered sexuality to highlight how the microprocesses of intimate life are tied to macro structures of the state and market. In doing so, the chapter uses case studies on the global sex industry to explore questions related to consent, domination, and resistance. Taken together, a critical examination of gender, sexuality, and other lines of difference highlight the complex dynamics of inequality in social life.

Introduction

In the summer of 2014, rumors swirled that Hank Baskett, a former professional football player, had cheated on his wife of five years. His wife, Kendra Wilkinson, was an ex-Playboy playmate and star of reality shows such as *The Girls Next Door* and *Kendra on Top*. As the gossip swelled, celebrity blogs repeatedly highlighted two details about the alleged affair: Wilkinson was eight months pregnant, and Baskett was sexually involved with transgender model Ava Sabrina London. The media sensationalized London's transgender identity and alleged that Baskett paid London $500 after their encounter. Many of these media accounts questioned Baskett's sexual identity as a straight man and fetishized London's identity as a transgender woman.

In this example, a private and intimate moment was pushed into a public discussion about the boundaries of gender and sexual identity. The media accounts relied on simplified understandings of sex and gender that have been challenged by queer theorists who focus on the links among sex, sexuality, and gender. In presenting sex with a transgender person as salacious, not straight, and transactional in nature, the media normalized particular forms of sexuality and sexual practices while pathologizing others. Indeed, it used its institutional power to reproduce certain categories and practices as conventional.

This chapter brings sexuality to the fore of studies on gender by outlining the development of human sexuality as a mode of research inquiry. Initial studies that incorporated sexuality used the term *homosexual* as a variable in quantitative analysis (see Chapter 2 on objectivity); feminists later intervened in the literature by highlighting subjective social relations. These later theories of sexuality emphasized the social construction of gender and the oppressive structures that render women vulnerable to sexual exploitation by men. Yet feminists are not a monolithic group of women. Anti-pornography feminist activists soon found themselves in a heated battle with sex-positive feminist scholars who pursued new ways of thinking about issues of consent and agency in sexual relations. Sex-positive feminists asserted that anti-pornography movements were repressive to women and inhibited them from exploring their own desires. Taking seriously issues of labor, they argued that sex workers should have the same legal rights and protections as any other worker in civil society.

Around the same time, queer theory emerged to theorize the relationship between pleasure and power. Scholars of queer theory moved away from sexual repression to theorize desire as a force of production. These scholars also broke free from boundaries of **heteronormativity** (the ideology that treats heterosexuality as normal and normative), opening up the possibility to imagine gendered and sexual relations beyond the belief that men and women fall into distinct and complementary genders. Their theorization represented a rupture with traditional beliefs that tied sex and sexuality to monogamy, marriage, and procreation. Wider social movements also challenged heteronormativity as lesbian, gay, bisexual, transgender, and queer groups began to organize to fight for equal protection under the law.

And finally, gender and sexuality do not operate in isolation from other intersecting relations of race, class, and nation. Intersectional feminists subsequently advanced studies of sexuality by integrating theories that highlight race, class, and gender inequalities. These intersectional approaches reshaped gender scholars' understanding of social relationships in an increasingly globalized world economy.

Throughout these feminist, queer, and intersectional interventions, the themes of desire, consent, and agency have been central to the study of sexuality. Although **desire** generally refers to individual longings, aspirations, and pleasure, scholars analyze desire as a social phenomenon that is linked to the intimate domains of sex, love, attraction, aesthetics, and the erotic but also transcends the individual. Next, feminist scholars think about **consent** as voluntary participation in sexual activities, which includes both informed understanding about one's bodily autonomy and freedom from force, harm, or fear. **Agency** refers to the ability people have to make decisions about, or to act on, their preferences, and it usually implies the ability to resist social structure. (Chapter 10 takes a deeper look at the complex notion of agency.) These organizing concepts help make sense of the links between gender and sexuality.

The Development of Human Sexuality as a Field of Inquiry

Second-wave feminist scholarship (the women's movements of the sixties and seventies, discussed in Chapter 9) developed through the political struggles experienced in the lives of women and sought to explain the oppression of women in multiple spaces around the world. In contrast, the subfield of sexuality developed internal to the social science disciplines as scholars turned their attention to sex as an object of empirical knowledge production.

Early scholars of human sexuality grounded their research in the tools and theories of biology. In the 19th century, the emerging field of sexology formulated sex as an **overpowering instinctual drive**—a basic biological mandate that must be neutralized through social control and appropriate cultural norms (Gagnon and Simon [1973] 2017; Weeks 1985). With the emergence of psychoanalysis at the turn of the 20th century, Sigmund Freud further popularized the notion that people had a fixed, biologically innate sex drive independent of social structure (Freud 1995). Freud's major contribution was to bring about a deeper understanding of desire by theorizing sexuality at the level of the subconscious. According to him, three parts of our subconscious mind are activated in the realm of desire. The *id* consists of our uncontrollable instincts that are driven by pleasure, instant self-gratification, and impulse. The id remains attuned to our basic bodily needs, including sexual desire. The *super-ego* internalizes the dominant cultural norms from society, for example, through parental and peer influence in order to repress the id. The *ego* mediates between the id and the super-ego, seeking to bring balance between the two. Through the interaction of these three elements of the psyche, Freud saw social constraints as repressing people's strong, and presumably natural, sexual instincts.

In the mid-20th century, the study of human sexuality began to incorporate empirical methods from the social sciences. Alfred Kinsey (1948, 1953) famously used interviewing methods to produce the **Kinsey reports**. These reports, which described a person's sexual history or sexual episodes during a given period, used a quantitative scale known as the Kinsey scale, where 0 referred to those deemed exclusively heterosexual and 6 to those categorized as exclusively homosexual. This study represented the first attempt at a large-scale study of human sexuality (the reports were based on 2,700 cases), and it treated sexuality as an individual psychological and biological phenomenon.

Scholars and activists toward the end of the 20th century critically engaged Kinsey's research, raising both academic concerns and serious moral and ethical objections. For example, Kinsey participated in sexual activity with research volunteers and members of his research team that may well have involved elements of coercion. Kinsey's findings were also likely skewed by self-selection and other sampling biases that favored male prostitutes and prison populations. In other words, those who volunteered to be in the study, as well as those who were ultimately included in the sample, were not likely to be representative of the general population.

These critiques, which followed from the assumption that different groups had different sexual practices, led to a new way of thinking about sexuality as a social phenomenon. Sociologists shifted from a "nature" model focused on the biological and psychological foundations of sex to a "nurture" model that emphasized the social construction of sex and sexuality. This second model made possible new kinds of questions: How is sexuality related to the gender order? Given the inequalities in power and representation, do sexual practices reproduce masculine domination and feminine acquiescence? Is pornography—by teaching boys and men that women are theirs to objectify—by definition misogynistic?

Early Feminist Interventions: Force versus Consent

In the late 1970s and early 1980s, feminists began a debate around issues of prostitution, sex work, and pornography. Viewing women's sexual objectification as central to women's oppression, second-wave feminists argued that they could not afford to overlook the ways in which pornography, prostitution, and rape sustain gender inequality. Feminist theorist and legal scholar Catharine MacKinnon made this clear when she wrote, "Sexuality is to feminism what work is to Marxism." Her point was that just as Marxists who seek to transform capitalism focused on work as the central organizing factor of class inequality, feminists who seek to transform patriarchy must focus on sexuality as the central organizing factor of gender inequality. Scholars such as MacKinnon did not see sexuality as separate from gender but rather understood sexuality as the means through which gender—especially gender inequality—was achieved.

This insight led second-wave feminists to theorize how men's access to women's bodies both expressed and reproduced broader systems of masculine domination. MacKinnon saw sexuality not only as structuring relationships between men and women but also as shaping how the state reproduces gender inequality (as mentioned in Chapter 1). Developing a feminist theory of the state, MacKinnon argued that the state preserves a false division between the private and public to protect the private sphere as a zone free from state intervention, allowing men to retain unmitigated access to women and their bodies. This, for example, explains the absence of marital rape as a crime until relatively recently: The state recognized men as free to do as they please in the privacy of their own homes with their wives, even if that involved force. Carole Pateman (1988) further theorized human sexuality by examining the relationship between the state and sex. She argued while philosophers such as Jean-Jacques Rousseau and John Locke asserted that a social contract or agreement among all individuals who lived in a society was essential to its functioning, at the heart of this civil society lies an unspoken sexual contract that implies the subordination of women to men. The law, rather than offering everyone equal protection, serves to subordinate women as a group to men as a group in both civil and political spheres. In arguing that a "sexual contract" must be considered as separate from the social contract, Pateman emphasized that the social contract used by political theorists is an incomplete concept—one that privileges men's rights while obscuring gender inequality.

In addition to theorizing how sexuality reinforced gender inequality, second-wave feminists were concerned with challenging sexuality, especially in the realms of pornography, prostitution, and sex work.

Can anyone ever consent to their own domination? This question was central to the "**Sex Wars**," an intense debate among feminists in the 1970s and 1980s around issues of pornography, prostitution, and rape. Many second-wave feminists, including anti-prostitution/anti-pornography feminists such as Andrea Dworkin (1981), Catharine MacKinnon (1989), Carole Pateman (1988), and Kathleen Barry (1995), were intensely concerned with questions of force and consent in the realms of sexuality. Arlene Stein (1989) captured the tenor of their arguments when she wrote that discourses of choice "fail to appreciate the extent to which power relations in a heterosexual, male-dominated culture continue to constrain sexual options, privileging heterosexuality over homosexuality and male sexuality over female sexuality" (8).

Emphasizing the sexual dangers and degradation of women in patriarchal and capitalist societies, these feminists argued that prostitution legitimizes relations of social inequality between men and women. If men's sexual dominance is the root of women's oppression, then allowing men the power to purchase women's bodies only reinforces notions of masculine supremacy and feminine subordination. For Catharine MacKinnon (1989), prostitution was not a matter of a woman's choice to perform this work but rather, like rape (see Chapter 6), was an institution where the subordinate actor's decisions could not be considered a true choice or a legitimate act of agency. Elaborating a similar point, Kathleen Barry (1995) argued that women working as prostitutes do not have a choice because prostitution, like pornography, is a sexually explicit form of subordination for women, something akin to sexual exploitation and slavery. She boldly asserted that sex work, regardless of whether it is consensual or not, remains a form of oppression. She argued that prostitution is not different from rape because prostitution defines sex on men's terms to sustain women's subordination and men's domination. Finally, in her book *Prostitution, Power, and Freedom,* Julia O'Connell Davidson (1998) similarly asserted that prostitution is an institution that enables clients to temporarily secure certain powers of sexual command over prostitutes. She argued that regardless of whether they are highly compensated for their work, women involved in the sale of their sexuality are subject to materialistic forms of domination. Thus, women who engage in prostitution are, by definition, victims, forced into the sex trade because they have no other options.

Even as they critiqued the state for maintaining these sexual inequalities between men and women, anti-prostitution/anti-pornography feminists turned to the state to protect women, whom they saw as victims. Dworkin and MacKinnon drafted a law that would have banned pornography, but it was ultimately struck down by the U.S. Supreme Court. The Antipornography Civil Rights Ordinance of 1983 would have let women seek monetary damages from pornography distributors and producers in civil court on the grounds of sex discrimination.

Not all feminists felt that banning pornography was the answer, nor did they see sexuality and gender as neatly tied together. As the pornography industry grew, its proponents argued that it was an expression of free speech.

Rather than seeing women's sexual activity as repressive, they argued, feminists should embrace women's desires. Indeed, some feminists argued, as long as the women involved had consented to their participation and were not forced against their will, feminists should support their participation in various forms of sex work.

This side of the debate included sex-positive feminists such as Gayle Rubin (2000), Lynn Chancer (1993), and Wendy Chapkis (1997). Reflecting a different understanding of the relationship between gender and sexuality, sex-positive feminists fought against anti-prostitution and anti-pornography movements, asserting that anti-prostitution/anti-pornography feminists reinforced female sexual repression—this time via censorship. For sex-positive feminists, the anti-prostitution/anti-pornography movements were repressive because they reinstated notions of traditional morality and heterosexual monogamy linked to marriage. Furthermore, sex-positive feminists aligned themselves with sex worker rights activists, who argued that sex workers are like any other worker. The exchange of sex for money may not be inherently degrading if it happens under conditions of informed consent. While sex-positive feminists recognized the dangers sex workers faced in their work, they believed that women should have the right to choose sexual liberation, explore their own desires, and choose to engage in sex work. Contrary to viewing women as victims, they saw sex workers as subverting structures of patriarchy. This called for a different kind of state intervention. Instead of banning pornography and prostitution, they believed the decriminalization of prostitution would better serve women who participated in sex work by providing them with legal protections and better access to health care and safety.

In addition to informing different kinds of political action as compared to anti-prostitution/anti-pornography feminism, sex-positive feminism gave rise to a distinct theoretical framework for analyzing, and raising questions of, the relationship between gender and sexuality. Gayle Rubin's (1997) landmark article, entitled "Thinking Sex," was a groundbreaking manifesto of sex-positive feminism. Rubin examined sexuality within the context of politics, inequality, and oppression. Arguing for a radical theory of sex that should "identify, describe, explain and denounce erotic injustice and sexual oppression," she interrogated both conservative and liberal attitudes that labeled some behaviors as good/positive sex and others as bad/negative sex. Rubin portrayed sexuality as governed by a sex hierarchy in which socially accepted sexual acts, such as sex between a man and a woman in a monogamous relationship that takes place in the bedroom, are in a **charmed circle**. In contrast, those deemed abnormal, such as games of bondage and domination or sexual acts between men, are part of the **outer limits**. Those who are in the charmed circle are rewarded with approval and status, while those in the outer limits may be considered immoral, mentally ill, or criminal. Rubin, who is often credited with being one of the first queer theorists, also explicitly developed sex and sexuality as politically and conceptually different from gender, arguing that while feminism informs a theory of gender oppression, this does not automatically include a theory of *sexual* oppression. In speaking to feminist theorists who developed a theory of gender based on the oppression of women, Rubin boldly claimed that sexual oppression has different consequences from gender oppression. Accordingly, she asserted that scholars need to develop an autonomous theory and politics specific to sexuality. At the same time, she argued, sexual liberation must be and "is a feminist goal" (29). Rubin's theorizing laid the groundwork for understanding sex, gender, and sexuality as separate but related concepts. It also raised core questions surrounding the relationship among power, practices, and sexuality, particularly how these varied from context to context.

Contemporary Debates around Sex Trafficking

While feminists no longer speak in the terms of the Sex Wars that took place between anti-pornography/prostitution feminists and sex-positive feminists in the late 1970s and early 1980s, new debates have arisen around the issue of sex trafficking that evoke questions of consent and agency. Contemporary debates revolve around the topic of sex trafficking on a global scale and can be roughly divided into two camps: abolitionists who seek to completely eradicate the sex trade as an example of human trafficking and sex worker rights advocates who focus on the autonomy of adult sex workers and the place of their sexual labor in the global economy.

Abolitionists such as Kevin Bales (2000), Kara Siddharth (2009), Kathryn Farr (2005), and Laura Lederer (2012) followed the logic of Catharine MacKinnon in arguing that no woman could ever consent to prostitution. Using the language of slavery to mobilize a social movement around sex trafficking, these scholars have argued that the global community should criminalize human trafficking and eradicate all forms of sexual slavery. An increasing number of abolitionist organizations have mobilized religious organizations (Farrag, Flory, and Loskota 2014), private companies such as Google and Microsoft (Musto 2014), and celebrities (Haynes 2014) to engage in public relations campaigns and fundraising around these issues. Secular and Christian organizations also have aligned to offer tours of sex trafficking and rescue in the Southeast Asian context (Bernstein and Shih 2014) to draw public awareness to the issue. This work fueled a worldwide moral agenda that framed women working in the sex industry as victims who are bought and sold to fulfill men's sexual desires and are in desperate need of rescue (for a more thorough analysis of trafficking as economic exploitation, see Chapter 8 on gendering exploitation). Drawing from these moral framings, abolitionists advocate for legal protections by pressuring the state to criminalize traffickers and rescue trafficked women (Chuang 2013).

But is the story as simple as that? Through on-the-ground advocacy, scholars critical of these anti-trafficking initiatives have accumulated substantial evidence to demonstrate that the moral and legal agendas around criminalizing sex work have caused greater harm than good to women working in the global sex industry (Brennan 2001; Chin 2013; Kempadoo 2005). Sex worker rights advocates such as Denise Brennan (2004), Laura Agustín (2007), and Kimberly Hoang and Rhacel Parreñas (2014) caution against sweeping generalizations of human trafficking. Returning to the issue of consent, they assert that not all women are trafficked or forced into sex work.

In fact, many women willingly enter the sex trade because it provides them with more opportunities for mobility than other types of work.

Several empirical investigations on workers in sexual labor markets in Asia (Cheng 2010; Chin 2013; Chin and Finckenauer 2012; Hoang 2010), Latin America (Brennan 2005; Cabezas 2009; Schaeffer 2012), and Europe (Agathangelou and Ling 2003; Andrijasevic 2010; Hoigard and Finstad 1992) demonstrate that most sex workers are often misidentified as trafficked persons. Ann Jordan (2009) accuses abolitionists of harming the very victims of trafficking they intend to be advocates for by criminalizing prostitution, which has resulted in arrest, prison, violence, and forced rehabilitation for women who have no alternative means of earning an adequate livelihood. Likewise, in her study of migrant Filipina hostess workers in Japan, Rhacel Parreñas (2011) describes how the women in her study—dubbed as "trafficked" victims by the U.S. State Department—never saw themselves as victims in need of aid.

The criminalization of prostitution also has unintended and unequal consequences for male clients. Annie Fukushima (2014) shows that the U.S. government's attempt to crack down on the demand side through Dear John Campaigns disproportionality targets Black and Latino men compared with white men. Sex worker rights advocates point out that the criminalization of sex work, whether targeting clients or workers, seeks to draw clear legal lines between clients as criminals and sex workers as victims (Brennan 2014), but these legal lines often fail to capture the intersecting lines of difference that complicate the on-the-ground dynamics of sex work.

Ann Jordan (2009) thus argues that abolitionist solutions are dangerous, unworkable, and unrealistic because they do not address the needs and concerns either of actually trafficked persons or of adult sex workers. Jordan asserts that abolitionists ignore the fact that women will continue to migrate and sell sex, no matter how many men are imprisoned. Instead of stigmatizing and harassing women in the sex sector, Jordan suggests that governments and civil society should recognize their value and their accomplishments and reject ideology-driven policies, practices, and programs that are not derived from objective evidence.

The Politics of Sexual Rights: LGBTQ Rights Movement

The movement for gay rights has revolutionized popular understandings of sexuality, transforming homosexuality from a sin into another form of desire, from a disease to the essence of a person's identity, and from a secret to a right. According to Pew surveys of lesbian, gay, bisexual, and transgender (LGBT) Americans, the number of Americans identifying as LGBT has risen from 8.3 million to 10.1 million from 2012 to 2016 alone, with younger Americans (18–36 years of age) much more likely to identify as such (Brown 2017). Meanwhile, American public opinion has undergone a striking reversal: In 2017, more Americans supported same-sex marriage (67%) than opposed it (57%) in 2001 (see Pew 2017).

The first gay rights demonstrations in the United States were influenced by the civil rights movement of the sixties. Grassroots organizations proliferated as lesbians and gay men were inspired by the political movements of this time to engage in more visible and daring tactics (Armstrong 2002; Epstein 1999). Sociologist Mary Bernstein argues that

> for the lesbian and gay movement . . . cultural goals include (but are not limited to) challenging dominant constructions of masculinity and femininity, homophobia, and the primacy of the gendered heterosexual nuclear family. Political goals include changing laws and policies in order to gain new rights, benefits, and protections from harm. . . . Activists seek both types of goals in both the civil and political spheres. (Bernstein 2002: 536)

One of the most iconic events in this period of lesbian, gay, bisexual, transgender, and queer (LGBTQ) activism was a six-day uprising in late June of 1969. On the 27th of June, patrons of the popular Stonewall Inn in New York's Greenwich Village, tired of ongoing police raids in their neighborhood bar, fought back. Drag performers, gay men of color, and transgender patrons led this movement against police brutality. As Garance Franke-Ruta (2013) wrote in *the Atlantic* magazine, these six days saw

> fire hoses turned on people in the street, thrown barricades, gay cheerleaders chanting bawdy variants of New York City schoolgirl songs, Rockette-style kick lines in front of the police, the throwing of a firebomb into the bar, a police officer throwing his gun at the mob, cries of "Occupy—take over, take over," "Fag power," "Liberate the bar!" and "We're the pink panthers!", smashed windows, uprooted parking meters, thrown pennies, frightened policemen, angry policemen, arrested mafiosi, thrown cobblestones, thrown bottles, the singing of "We Shall Overcome" in high camp fashion, and a drag queen hitting a police officer on the head with her purse.

Those who participated in these raids did so not simply to protect a place to drink but also to protect one of the few places in which LGBTQ people felt safe. The uprising publicly ignited the gay liberation movement of the 1970s, and political organizations emerged to be advocates for the rights of LGBTQ people in society, which is discussed in more detail in Chapter 9. These groups worked toward equality by protecting LGBTQ communities from homophobia, biphobia, and transphobia, at times turning to the state for legal remedies. For example, student groups sued their universities for official recognition and funding (see *Gay Lib v. University of Missouri*, 558 F. 2d 848 [8th Cir. 1977]) (Armstrong 2002). At the same time, one court case, *Doe v. Commonwealth's Attorney for City of Richmond* (403 F. Supp. 1199 [E.D. Va. 1975]), named the district attorney of Richmond as the defendant in a class action suit by lesbian and gay activists that challenged Virginia's punitive sodomy laws. The district court ruled that the sodomy law was constitutional, and on appeal, the U.S. Supreme Court affirmed that ruling (Armstrong 2002). These court cases highlighted the uphill battle that LGBTQ activists faced but also showcased their collective agency to resist in the face of hostile circumstances.

In the 1980s, the HIV/AIDS epidemic devastated LGBTQ communities, radically shifting the face of lesbian and gay politics. At a time when the religious right mounted a movement against LGBTQ rights that helped normalize pervasive anti-LGBTQ discrimination, harassment, and violence, few government resources were allocated to fight the epidemic. AIDS facilitated political cooperation between lesbians and gay men fighting for the equal rights to health care given to heterosexual couples (Armstrong 2002). People were dying, making the devastating consequences of discrimination against LGBTQ groups all too apparent.

In the 1986 *Bowers v. Hardwick* (478 U.S. 186 [1986]) case, the U.S. Supreme Court upheld a Georgia anti-sodomy law that was used to prosecute homosexual oral and anal sex between consenting adults in the home, even though the Court had previously held in *Griswold v. Connecticut* (381 U.S. 479 [1965]) that the marital bedroom was a "zone of privacy" in a case regarding anti-contraception laws (Armstrong 2002). This decision further spurred a national movement. Several thousand people made their way to the U.S. capital to protest, sparking a resurgence of grassroots activism.

Recognizing that sexuality is codified into categories through concrete policies such as marriage laws, welfare policies, and health care, one consequence of this period was to refocus LGBTQ activism toward marriage equality. Reflecting these efforts, same-sex civil unions were first recognized under Vermont law in 2000, and Massachusetts was the first state to perform same-sex marriages in 2003, freeing gay and lesbian couples from criminal classifications. In 2015, a landmark decision was reached by the United States Supreme Court in *Obergefell v. Hodges* (576 U.S. ___ [2015]), which gave same-sex couples the constitutional right to marry in the United States and to have their unions recognized in all states. While much of the focus of the LGBTQ movement has been on efforts to gain civil rights such as the right to marriage, many trans and queer activists reject this as a politics of assimilation that acquiesces to a new regime of regulation (after all, it is the state that regulates marriage). These activists look to alternative forms of politics based not on fixed sexual identities but on the idea that sexuality is fluid.

From Sexuality to Sexualities: Power and Play

As feminists debated the relationship across sex, sexuality, and gender and LGBTQ activists challenged traditional understandings of sexuality, postmodern and queer theorists, including Michel Foucault (1976) and Judith Butler (1993), began to interrogate sexuality on its own terms. They soon developed a theory of power that does not draw a stark line between pleasure and empowerment on the one hand and repression and subordination on the other. Foucault saw power not as merely possessed by some people at the top of a hierarchy but as plural, fragmentary, differentiated, and everywhere. He focused on power as it is generated through discourses, knowledge, and language. *The History of Sexuality*, which he published in 1976, starts with a small but powerful observation about the way people talked about sexuality in the 19th and 20th centuries (and today as well): Despite constantly insisting they are "sexually repressed" (an idea popularized by Freud), Foucault observed that people talked about sex more than ever. He uses the term **repressive hypothesis** to refer to the taken-for-granted idea that people are repressed in their sexuality. Challenging the repressive hypothesis, Foucault saw the pleasure of sexuality as revolving around creating a false sense of liberation—a false sense that, in fact, binds people to a particular way of being. In other words, while people might talk about their desires as free and liberated, that is exactly the moment at which they are being constrained. Foucault uses these insights to trace how people talk about and regulate sex in early modern Western societies to the present.

Judith Butler brings Foucault's ideas about power and sexuality to bear on gender, bodies, and sex (see also Chapter 4). She is particularly concerned with how desires and identities are constrained by, and reproduce, heteronormativity. Heteronormativity assumes the normalcy of heterosexuality, and refers to social norms that presume that all people fit into two separate and complementary genders of *men* and *women*, who are attracted to each other. According to this ideology, biological sex, gender identity, and heterosexual orientation are thought to be neatly aligned and to govern the organization of social life. Heteronormativity organizes society by permeating expectations and constraints in various social situations, and it shapes social institutions such as families, politics, religion, medicine, media, and law.

Recall from Chapter 4 that Butler maintains that bodies are not given but rather are produced through repeated practice. Linking the body to heteronormativity, Butler likewise argues that bodies are produced through the training of desire. They are made material through discourses surrounding desire and sexuality. A body is *intelligible*, that is, understandable and acceptable, if it can be situated within this matrix of heteronormativity; *unintelligible* bodies—butch, queer, or transgender—disrupt normative identities (as discussed in Chapter 4) as well as normative desires. Accordingly, bodies are an effect of the dominant discourses and practices that privilege heteronormativity.

Together, Butler's and Foucault's work provide examples of **queer theory.** This body of theory sees sexuality as a lens (just as this book sees gender) through which to view a world that reflects and privileges heteronormativity. Sociologists Arlene Stein and Ken Plummer define queer theory according to the following ideas:

a. Sexual power can be found in many levels of social life, and it is maintained and enforced through the policing of boundaries,

b. but sexualized identities are always open to change and thus inherently unstable;

c. thus, possibilities of change lie not in conventional rights-based politics but in acts of "carnival, transgression, and parody" that challenge the policed boundaries in various ways;

d. and, finally, because the world can be viewed through the lens of sexuality, everything from films to politics and economics can be subjected to a sexual analysis.

In short, queer theorists call for a questioning of all sexual categories, a move toward more dynamic ways of understanding sexuality, and the recognition of how sexualities pervade all social life (Stein and Plummer 1994).

Queer theorists compel sociologists of gender to move beyond the liberation/repression binary (from Foucault) and to think about sexualities as rooted in discourse and practice (from Butler). Applying these two insights, contemporary sociologists of gender and sexuality now emphasize fluidity and hybridity to make sense of how sexuality shapes social life in conjunction with gender, all the while maintaining a focus on how gender and sexuality interact to buttress heteronormativity. This approach is helpful to understanding the *margins* or the *outer limits* of sexuality, in Rubin's terms. It is critical for understanding mainstream, heteronormative sexuality as well.

Doing Gender, Doing Sexuality

The late 2000s saw the emergence of public debate about sexual cultures due to the so-called hook-up culture on college campuses. *Hook-ups* refer to casual sexual activity between two people who are not in a committed relationship. Some argue that hook-ups are on the rise as part of a new, highly sexualized college culture; others insist that this is just a new name for an old phenomenon (Hamilton and Armstrong 2009; Rupp, Taylor, Regev-Messalem, Fogarty, and England 2014).

Sociologists of gender and sexuality take a slightly different approach. After all, sociologists of gender are interested in how gender and sexuality work together to reinforce dominant ideas about masculinity and femininity and how gender and sexuality scripts come together to produce normative identities (e.g., hegemonic masculinity and emphasized femininity; see Chapter 3) and sexual ideals (e.g., heterosexuality). Instead of debating whether so-called hook-ups are increasing or decreasing (a strategy akin to Kinsey's style of research), they ask different questions: Why do college students participate in "hook-up culture"? Do men and women accrue the same benefits from participating? What kinds of values are reflected in hook-up culture?

Sociologist Danielle Currier showed that it is hard to talk about hook-ups in quantitative terms (e.g., to measure an increase or decrease) because college students purposely use the vague language of *hook-ups* to allow them to avoid divulging details about their sexual activities while simultaneously presenting themselves in gender-appropriate terms. Heldman and Wade (2010) argue that despite women being empowered to initiate hook-ups, they are seldom able to shape the trajectory of the sexual encounter, and Hamilton and Armstrong (2009) find that many women ultimately find the experience coercive or unpleasurable. Hook-up culture thus illustrates how sexuality and gender operate as separate but mutually constitutive lines of difference. It works at the micro level to allow men and women the agency to navigate their social identities, even as it reproduces the existing gender order.

Hook-up culture is only one example of how dominant gendered categories legitimate and are reinforced by sexual boundaries. Sexuality remains embedded in gendered relationships and persisting ideologies about masculinity and femininity. As another example, consider homophobia: Much of gender theorizing on masculinity focuses on how homophobia (that is, negative feelings and behaviors motivated by a dislike or disgust of homosexuality) remains central to performances of masculinity. Sociologists such as Michael Kimmel (1994) and Raewyn Connell (1992) highlight **gendered homophobia** as a type of gender policing that allows men to distance themselves from other men to establish themselves as properly embodying hegemonic masculinity, the dominant cultural expectations of manhood. Chapter 3 argued that hegemonic masculinity existed alongside marginalized masculinity, which is the masculinity of men who belong to less-dominant classes and ethnic groups. But hegemonic masculinity is also distinguished from another denigrated masculinity: **subordinated masculinity** (Connell 1995), which is associated with effeminacy or homosexuality. As introduced in Chapter 4, C.J. Pascoe (2011) discusses the use of homophobic slurs among high school boys to demonstrate how masculine behaviors are sustained. High school boys attempt to prove their masculinity through lobbing the "fag" epithet at each other and sexually harassing their female classmates, tactics that use homophobia to reinforce normative gender arrangements.

But the relationship between sexuality and gender may also provide people, especially privileged people, with more flexibility and ambiguity with respect to their social identities. Hybrid masculinities, for example, describe the selective incorporation of marginalized and subordinated masculine and feminine identities into the gendered performances of mostly privileged, young, white, cisgender, and heterosexual men (Bridges 2014; Bridges and Pascoe 2014; Schippers 2000; Wilkins 2009). Sociologist Tristan Bridges (2014) highlights how groups of young straight men identify with aspects of gay culture while still constructing heterosexual masculine identities. Examining father's rights activists, pro-feminist men, and bar regulars, Bridges argues that these men distance themselves from stereotypes about men as always tough and emotionally detached and instead position themselves as socially progressive.

Another example of the flexibility of gender and sexual boundaries is the term *metrosexual* that emerged in the 1990s. The term captures the sexualization of gendered identities. *Metrosexual* refers to well-groomed, typically heterosexual men who buy expensive clothing, hair products, and skincare. The reference is meant to counter the stereotype that only women or gay men care about their looks. Kristin Barber (2008) studied white, middle-class, heterosexual men who preferred high-end hair salons to barbershops. Barber argues that these men avoid feminization and assumptions about their sexuality by creating distance between themselves and working-class men to assert their identity as straight, economically privileged, stylish men. Her work highlights how gendered norms are often built on sexualized expectations.

These examples show that although gender and sexual identities have become increasingly flexible, these blurred boundaries still reproduce and mask existing social inequalities and maintain the prevailing hierarchies of hegemonic masculinity.

Sexualized Intersections: Sexuality, Race, Class, and Nation

Feminist, postmodern, and queer theorists have emphasized the multiple ways of embodying sexual identities and the many conflicts that exist within and across sexual and gender categories. Yet sexuality is not only connected to gender; sociologists of gender must remain attuned to how other social categories such as race, ethnicity, class, and nationalism matter for the performance and experience of sexual identities. Building on the work of intersectional scholars (see Chapter 2), scholars must analyze how sexuality interacts with other systems of oppression and ways of identifying beyond gender.

Patricia Hill Collins's (2000, 2004) work on Black sexual politics documents how racial categories are built in part through sexualized assumptions. She discusses how sexual tropes serve to naturalize racial oppression. For example, controlling images (see Chapter 3), which portray Black women as sexually promiscuous jezebels or Black men as sexually violent (see Chapter 6), sustain racist ideologies. Such racialized representations are built through images that pathologize certain groups through assumptions about—and expectations for—their sexuality (Collins 2000). These sexualized labels are not restricted to Black men and women. Asian American women are often constructed as either sexually docile ("Lotus Blossom") or as cunning ("Dragon Lady"), while Asian American men are viewed as asexual and effeminate (Chou 2012). These sexualized representations shape how people understand the intersections between gender, sexuality, and race.

An intersectional perspective further highlights how central the management of sexuality is to personal and collective identity. Sociologist Lorena Garcia (2012) examines the complex lives of Latina girls, arguing that they understand their emerging sexual identities as tied to their experiences with sexism, racism, homophobia, and economic marginality. They approach their sexuality through a lens that emphasizes respect, safety, pleasure, and agency. Anthony Ocampo's (2012) work on U.S.-born Filipino and Latino gay men in Los Angeles looks at the negotiation of masculinity within gay racial minority groups. According to his research, their racialization as Asians and Latinos, their gender socialization in immigrant families, and their feelings of exclusion in mainstream gay spaces shape their social interactions and enactments of masculinity. In turn, their sexual identities play an important role in shaping their adaptation and integration as children of immigrants in the United States. As these studies illuminate, it is not possible to understand identities without a deep examination of how race, immigration status, class, gender, and sexuality together impact our self-understandings within specific contexts.

The examples cited above are part of what Joanne Nagel (2000) terms **ethnosexualization**: the construction of categories of race, ethnicity, nation, and gender through sexual definitions. Racial domination can be justified in part through attempts to police sexual morality and purity. Drawing from historical and contemporary examples of conquest, intermarriage, rape, and war, Nagel contends that sexual desire and power construct racial categories and vice versa. Similarly, in an exploration of urban middle-class sexuality in India, Jyoti Puri (1999) argues that ideas about sexuality are linked to questions of modernity, development, and globalization. Women's bodies and sexualities are controlled to reinforce and naturalize gendered boundaries between men and women and preserve social mandates as India projects a particular image of itself in the world. Meanwhile, in Singapore, the state uses housing incentives to encourage the heteronormative reproduction of families by allocating housing to young couples under the age of 35 who form a "family nucleus" (Teo 2009).

Some scholars have considered these relationships within the context of colonialism, as described in Chapter 7 and Chapter 10. Ann Stoler (2002) maintains that sex has been a powerful marker of race, class, and gender that has sustained distinctions between categories of people in the colonial encounter. These distinctions, often based on supposed differences in morals, were meant to secure European superiority over the colonized. Stoler points out that colonialism, a public enterprise, brought the intimate (i.e., domestic arrangements, the family, sexual relations, the body, and so forth) within its purview to organize domination and secure power. Asymmetric gender relations were an integral element in the maintenance of colonial racism, and sexual regulations were central tropes that shored up ethnoracial boundaries, setting the colonizers apart from the colonized (see also Chapters 1 and 3).

In the Dutch Indies, colonialists encouraged extramarital relationships through concubinage between European colonial men and indigenous colonized women to acclimatize European men to a new environment. Yet colonial powers restricted marriage to unions between European men and European women, and European women were brought to the colonies to serve as suitable wives. Thus, colonized women were marked for sexual relationships, while European women were marked for marriage to create domestic worlds for colonial men. This organization of sexual relationships along lines of race was intended to stabilize the colonial enterprise. Categories of race, class, and gender were given meaning in relation to one another, sometimes in contradictory ways.

Sexualized politics also help organize contemporary nations. Oluwakemi Balogun's (2012) research on Nigerian beauty queens illustrates how women's bodies represent the nation to the world. Beauty pageants are controversial: Some believe that they objectify women (see Chapter 3) as they glorify emphasized femininity in the societies where they take place. Others see them as a platform for upward mobility through the opportunity to win cash prizes, scholarships, or celebrity status. In Nigeria, beauty pageant contestants are expected to act as role models of class and sexual respectability for other Nigerian girls and women. Thus, throughout the course of the competition and during their subsequent reign, they must maintain an image of wholesomeness.

The demand for sexual respectability emerged most explicitly with respect to the bikini segments of the competition. Balogun studied two national beauty competitions, and one of these, the Queen Nigeria competition, banned bikinis. The organizers of Queen Nigeria believed that bikinis were too overtly sexual because they showed too much of the contestants' skin in public. These organizers also inspected contestants' costumes and attire prior to the final show to make sure they were not too revealing, and during excursions to visit public officials and sponsors (mostly men), contestants were instructed to cover up with a shawl if their clothes were deemed too tight-fitting or skimpy to avoid arousing onlookers' sexual desires. By banning bikinis and regulating contestants' attire, organizers sought to establish a national brand for the pageant and to attract a broad audience reflecting the country's ethnic and religious diversity. As one organizer put it, "We want to celebrate our culture, without celebrity bikinis" (372).

By contrast, women who auditioned to be a contestant on The Most Beautiful Girl in Nigeria were almost immediately instructed to change into a bikini and five-inch high heels. The would-be contestants then stepped forward one by one in their bikinis to introduce themselves before standing in a lineup to take a "Barbie turn" (a slow, 360-degree spin) so that screeners could inspect their bodies. These organizers stressed that this audition process allowed them to select the most confident women for the pageant. They believed that women's confidence was key to portraying Nigeria as a cosmopolitan nation. Organizers brushed off concerns about including bikinis in the competition with matter-of-fact statements such as, "When you go to the beach what do you wear? A bathing suit" (373).

In fact, bathing suits of any type are uncommon at the beach in Nigeria, a culturally conservative and highly religious West African country whose population is almost evenly split between Christians and Muslims. But the controversy over bikini segments—and the two pageants' different approaches to dealing with that controversy—reflects broader social discourse regarding Nigeria's national identity. While some Nigerians would like to see the nation become more modern and forward-looking, others wish to affirm the nation's traditions, including modesty. Balogun's research on the Nigerian beauty pageant industry illustrates how gender, sexuality, and other lines of difference are implicated in disagreements over the trajectory of a nation.

Globalizing Sexualities

The meanings attached to gender and sexuality take shape not only within national boundaries but also across them through the global circulation of ideas. In *Global Sex*, Dennis Altman (2001) asserts that attitudes toward sexuality reflect social changes across the globe. He argues that the global political economy creates the conditions for sexual acts and identities. A political economy perspective means recognizing how national and global systems have both distinct and shared economics and politics that are co-constitutive with class, gender, and race. That is, intersectionality inheres in structures as well as identities. These factors include the economic, as growing affluence allows new ways of organizing private life, and the cultural, as images of different sexualities are rapidly diffused across the world. Thus, he asserts,

> the pleasures of the body cannot be separated from the world outside . . . [since] sexuality is an area of human behavior, emotion and understanding long associated with the "natural" and the "private" is also an arena of life with the most surveillance and control." (2)

In *Temporarily Yours,* Elizabeth Bernstein (2007) locates sex work in the burgeoning global service economy. Her study takes place in the cities of San Francisco, Stockholm, and Amsterdam, where sex workers and their clients were targeted as symbols of global economic distress and urban decay. Bernstein examines intimate interactions between male clients and female sex workers in these cities as they reflect expectations of service work in globalizing economies. Stepping beyond the framework of the Sex Wars, her book situates sex work as a type of labor that is located within economically stratified urban spaces and that is regulated by local, state, and national laws.

Building on Bernstein's efforts, Kimberly Hoang's (2015) book *Dealing in Desire* examines the mutually reinforcing connection between intimacy and the political economy. Hoang shows how changes in the global economy structure relations of intimacy between clients and sex workers in Ho Chi Minh City (HCMC), a fast-growing city central to Vietnam's global sex industry; in turn, intimacy operates as a vital form of currency that shapes economic and political relations. Vietnam is a rapidly developing Southeast Asian nation whose economic and political leaders are seeking to replicate the exponential growth of Asian powers such as China; the nation's sex industry plays a vital role in this growth.

Hoang spent 22 months conducting ethnography (2006–2010) as a bartender and hostess in HCMC's stratified sex industry. She shows that in the highest tier of the industry, sex workers help their businessmen clients "sell" Vietnam as a dynamic place to potential Asian investors from other nations. In another tier of the sex industry catering to white Western backpacker clients, Vietnamese sex workers showcase Vietnam as a poverty-stricken nation dependent on Western capital by seeking charity donations and additional monetary gifts. Thus, HCMC's sex industry is not only a microcosm of the global economy but also a vector shaping financial globalization.

Like Balogun (2012), Hoang illustrates how women's bodies come to represent the nation. For example, HCMC sex workers' surgical and cosmetic bodily projects represent competing desires for Vietnam's trajectory in the global economy, as mentioned in Chapter 3. In a high-end niche market that caters to local elite Vietnamese businessmen, sex workers project emergent pan-Asian beauty ideals such as light skin, double eyelid folds, and narrow nose bridges, which symbolically signal the rise of Asia through surgical body transformations. In contrast, sex workers who cater to *Viet Kieu* (Vietnamese who live overseas) men construct themselves as nostalgic cosmopolitan subjects, altering their bodies to make themselves more desirable than white Western and *Viet Kieu* women. They cater to their clients' desires to relive a nostalgic past where women served men and buttressed male superiority (Hoang 2015). To appeal to Western clients, sex workers in the sector catering to Western backpackers darken their skin by tanning and apply makeup to portray a more exotic look; they also enhance their breasts. By comparing multiple markets, Hoang shows how individual agents in the developing world actively reimagine their nation's place in the global economy through their embodied practices (Hoang 2014, 2015).

As Hoang, Bernstein, and others show, sex work provides a unique realm for examining not only how transformations in the global economy reshape intimate life but also how the emotional intimacy (and not merely sex) provided by sex workers serves as an important currency in transnational dealings. Their work follows in the tradition of studies on the global sex trade and intimate life that recognize the importance of gendered sexualities. These studies thus situate sex work squarely in the context of **globalization**: the economic, cultural, and political processes that connect and integrate people, capital, and ideas around the world. In doing so, this body of scholarship moves beyond the questions of force and choice that characterized the Sex Wars to focus on the global forces that shape the production and consumption of sexual services and that facilitate the commodification of men's desire and women's bodies in global capitalist orders.

Conclusion

This chapter explored a wide range of theoretical concepts and empirical research in the area of gendered sexuality. The chapter discussed a key shift within the field from conceptualizing sexuality as a biological, psychological, and individual phenomenon to a perspective that stressed social construction. This shift toward social construction allowed for an analysis of social conditions, opening up the study of sexuality for feminist interventions related to domination, consent, and control. Later scholars adopted postmodern, queer, and intersectional theories to discuss the multiple and conflicting ways that sexuality remains important to our understanding of inequality and identity. Postmodern and queer theorists focus on identifying the key ways that sexuality is intertwined with power, deconstructing many taken-for-granted assumptions about the significance and consequences of sexuality in society. Intersectional theorists focus on sexuality as an integral category of difference that intersects with other identity categories such as race, class, and immigration. Lastly, political–economic approaches to sexuality highlight how the micro processes of intimate life are tied to macro structures of state and market. Taken together, a critical examination of sexuality, alongside gender and other lines of difference, highlights the complex domains of inequality in social life.

KEYWORDS

Agency 76
Charmed circle 80
Consent 76
Desire 76
Ethnosexualization 88
Gendered homophobia 87
Globalization 92
Heteronormativity 76
Kinsey reports 77
Outer limits 80
Overpowering instinctual drive 77
Queer theory 85
Repressive hypothesis 85
Sex wars 79
Subordinated masculinity 87

QUESTIONS

- What does the study of gender have to gain from considering sexuality?
- How are both everyday practices in intimate life and the larger structures of the political economy shaped by desire, consent, and agency?
- In what ways does a focus on power enhance our understanding of the connections between gender and sexuality?

ASSOCIATED READINGS

- Bernstein, Elizabeth. 2007. *Temporarily Yours: Intimacy, Authenticity, and the Commerce of Sex*. Chicago: University of Chicago Press.
- Collins, Patricia Hill. 2005. *Black Sexual Politics: African Americans, Gender, and the New Racism*. New York: Routledge.
- Connell, Raewyn W. 1995. *Masculinities*. Berkeley: University of California Press.
- Foucault, Michel. 1988. *The History of Sexuality*. 1st ed. New York: Vintage Books.
- Hoang, Kimberly Kay. 2015. *Dealing in Desire: Asian Ascendancy, Western Decline, and the Hidden Currencies of Global Sex Work*. Oakland, CA: University of California Press.
- McClintock, Anne. 1995. *Imperial Leather*. New York: Routledge.
- MacKinnon, Catharine. 1989. *Toward a Feminist Theory of the State*. Cambridge: Harvard University Press.
- Pascoe, C.J. 2007. *"Dude You're a Fag": Sexuality and Masculinity in High School*. Berkeley: University of California Press.
- Rubin, Gayle. 1993. "Thinking Sex: Notes for a Radical Theory of the Politics of Sexuality." In *The Lesbian and Gay Studies Reader*, edited by Henry Abelove and Michèle Aina Barale, 3–44. New York: Routledge.
- Stoler, Ann. 1995. *Race and the Education of Desire*. Durham: Duke University Press.

CHAPTER 6

Gendering Crime and Justice

Jennifer Carlson

How are boys' and men's acts of violence examples of doing gender? How does women's violence challenge gender ideologies and with what consequences? How does gender shape the social control of violent offenders by police, courts, and prisons? This chapter considers the gendered nature of crime and justice by focusing on violence: It engages interpersonal violence and the complex mechanisms of social control that arise in response. In doing so, it unpacks the legal institutions and socio-legal practices surrounding violent crime, particularly in the U.S. Though the U.S. is one particular national context for violence, the analyses presented in this chapter provide concepts that can be used to make sense of gender and violence in other nations and in related contexts.

Introduction

In the United States in 2015, there were 1,197,704 violent crimes reported to the Federal Bureau of Investigation (FBI): According to the FBI's "2015 Crime Clock," one murder occurred every 33.5 minutes, one rape every 4.2 minutes, and one aggravated assault every 41.3 seconds.

Each of these thousands of acts of physical violence takes place as an interaction between two or more people, usually in relatively close contact. Rapes, muggings, assaults, and murders do not happen from afar; rather, they represent intimate, embodied acts. Gender ideologies facilitate violence by creating certain possibilities for contact and by imbuing violent encounters with gendered meanings. For example, Michael Kimmel (2012) argues that masculine ideology asserts that "real men" can—and should—use violence to get even with others. In this sense, violence accomplishes gender at an interactional level.

Violence, in turn, reinforces and produces gendered expectations about who should be feared (cisgender men) and who should be fearful (cisgender women, members of the lesbian, gay, bisexual, transgender, and queer [LGBTQ] community, and gender-nonconforming people). Dominant narratives construct men as powerful, strong, and capable of violence while constructing women (and feminized men) as weak, vulnerable, and incapable of violence (Hollander 2001). Because they are victimized in gender-specific ways, women are more likely to fear crime as women's fear of sexual assault comes to shadow concerns about crime more generally (Ferraro 1996).

This chapter locates *doing violence* as a means of *doing gender*, which was defined in Chapter 4 as the everyday practices through which people account for, and achieve, socially recognizable gendered selves. The first half of this chapter "genders" violence by showing that experiences and acts of violence and victimization are embedded in gender ideologies that define strength, power, and physical domination as masculine attributes, and in doing so, the chapter explores how gender ideologies intersect with racial ideologies. The second half of the chapter considers the forms of social control applied to people marked as criminals, showing that gender, alongside race, shapes the forms of power that criminal justice institutions—including police, courts, and prisons—exert over criminals marked as "failed men" and "failed women." The chapter ends with reconsidering the relationship between gender and violence by examining how efforts to challenge violence relate to efforts to challenge gender.

From Violence against Women to Sexual Violence and Intimate Partner Violence

Women face particular kinds of threats: stalking, intimate partner violence, stranger sexual assault, date rape, and other kinds of violent acts. Such acts are often grouped under the broad heading of *violence against women*, *gender violence*, or, more recently, *sexual violence*.

The Rape, Abuse and Incest National Network (RAINN, 2017a) estimates that every 98 seconds, a person is raped in the United States. Nearly 1 in 5 American women have been raped, compared to 1 in 59 men, according to the 2014 National Intimate Partner and Sexual Violence Survey (Centers for Disease Control and Prevention 2014). Most (78.7%) victimized girls and women experienced their first rape by the age of 25. Women are also more likely to be stalked: 1 in 6 women have been stalked, as compared to 1 in 19 men. Women are more likely than men to experience the most severe forms of intimate partner violence, and they are also more likely to report short- and long-term impacts of violence on their lives, from injury to post-traumatic stress disorder. Finally, women comprise 70% of those killed by intimate partners, meaning that they are roughly twice as likely to be killed by an intimate partner as men. African American women are two to four times more likely than white women to be murdered by an intimate partner (Catalano, Smith, Snyder, and Rand 2009). Many of these crimes are never reported to police and become what criminologists call the "dark figure of crime": RAINN (2017c) estimates that two-thirds of sexual assaults never make it to the police logbooks.

These numbers paint a stark picture: Women suffer disproportionately at the hands of intimate partners and are much more likely to be the victims of sexual coercion than men. However, early criminologists did not feel that these trends were worth pursuing in their own right. As feminist criminologist Meda Chesney-Lind (2006: 7) writes, "Turning back the clock, one can recall that prior to path-breaking feminist works on sexual assault, sexual harassment, and wife abuse, these forms of gender violence were ignored, minimized, and trivialized."

Taking account of these disparities, second-wave feminists such as Catharine MacKinnon (1982) and Susan Brownmiller ([1975] 2013) theorized rape as central to gender domination between men and women and to gender hierarchies among men. Defining *rape* in her 1975 text *Against Our Will* as "nothing more or less than a conscious process of intimidation by which all men keep all women in a state of fear" (15), Brownmiller called attention to how rape serves not only as the means for individual men to dominate individual women but also as a mechanism through which broader gender hierarchies are enforced. She noted that even as rape has been criminalized for hundreds of years, its early formulation as a crime defined it *not* as a crime against persons (women, after all, were not considered persons in early legal codes) but as a crime against property—men's property.

Second-wave feminists thus placed power at the center of efforts to recognize domestic violence as a social problem. Reflecting the notion that men use domestic violence to enact power and control over women in a cyclical manner, the Power and Control Wheel was a popular diagram that visually called attention to the multifaceted and oftentimes violent abuse that disproportionately pervaded women's intimate lives (Kolb 2014; see also Figure 6.1). The wheel showed the totalizing impact of the abuse many women experience, and it demonstrated that this abuse takes a different form than the kinds of violence that men experience. The wheel continues to be displayed in organizations and shelters that aid and assist abuse victims.

Second-wave feminists were critical in calling public attention to rape, sexual assault, domestic violence, and other kinds of violence that particularly and uniquely affects women. At the same time, intersectional feminists, queer feminists, and others began to add nuance regarding which women experience abuse, how they experience abuse, and in what contexts. They rightly noted that certain women are more vulnerable to such violence, particularly women of color, class-marginalized women, and members of the LGBTQ community. Furthermore, moving from identities to institutions revealed that certain settings are particularly hostile with respect to sexual coercion, intimate partner violence, and other forms of gendered violence.

Consider the contemporary U.S. university campus. RAINN's (2017b) factsheet on campus sexual violence shows that whereas national statistics suggest that robberies outnumber sexual assaults by a ratio of 5 to 4, on campus, this ratio reverses to 2 to 1. Nearly 1 in 4 women students have experienced rape or sexual assault; women's victimization outnumbers men's by a ratio greater than 4 to 1. Meanwhile, 21% of transgender, genderqueer and gender nonconforming students have experienced rape or sexual assault. Finally, as compared to their non-student counterparts, college students are 50% less likely to report a rape or sexual assault to law enforcement, even though the vast majority of campus police have the legal authority to arrest both on and off campus.

As another example, consider the U.S. military. The nonprofit Protect Our Defenders (2017), aimed at addressing military sexual assault, reports that 1 in 4 women and 1 in 15 men faced "severe and persistent sexual harassment or gender discrimination in 2016." Women returning from military service are particularly likely to experience ongoing trauma as a result of sexual violence. Out of the women who seek healthcare through

Figure 6.1 Power and Control Wheel

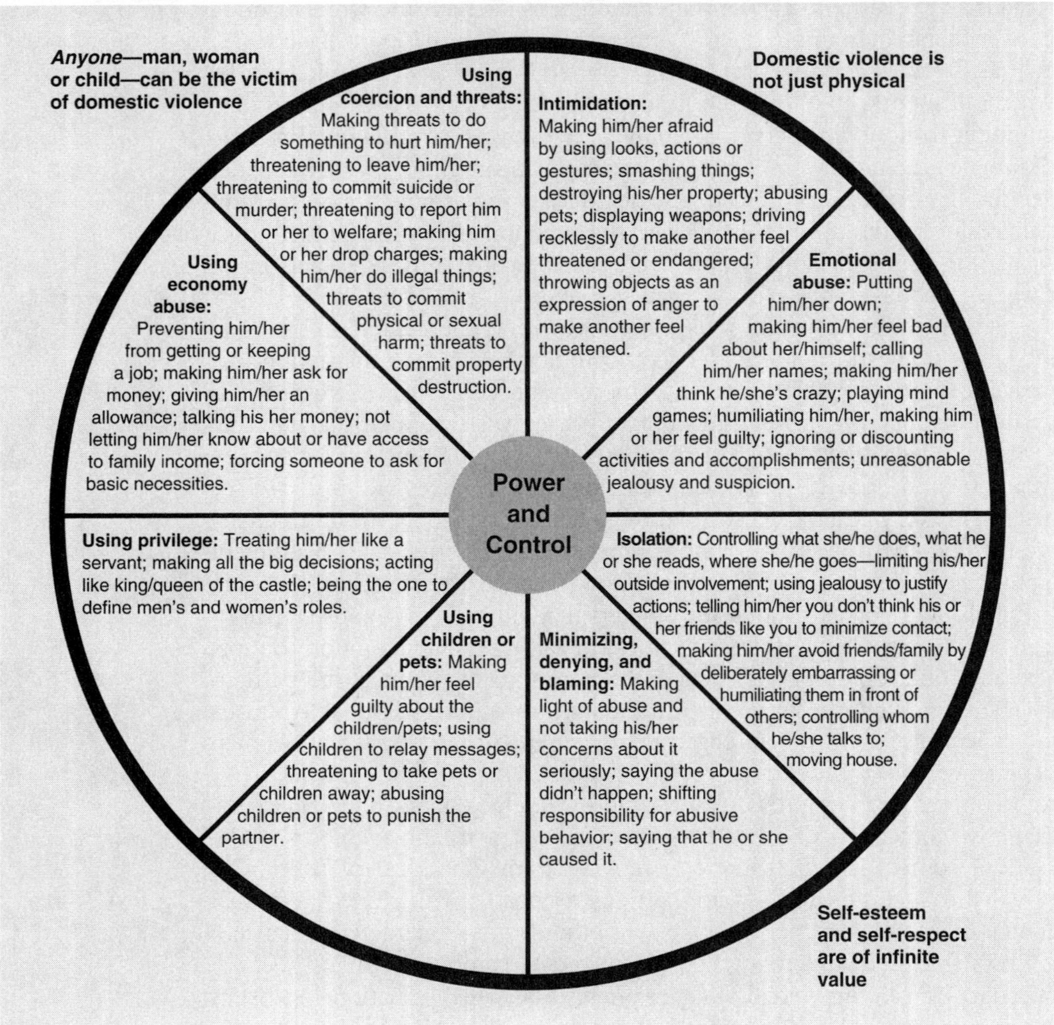

Source: Cycle of abuse, power, and control issues in domestic abuse situations from Flickr, https://commons.wikimedia.org/wiki/File:(2)_Cycle_of_abuse,_power_%26_control_issues_in_domestic_abuse_situations.gif, licensed under CC BY 2.0, https://creativecommons.org/licenses/by/2.0/deed.en.

the Department of Veteran Affairs, around 1 in 5 show symptoms of military sexual trauma (U.S. Department of Veteran Affairs 2012). The vast majority of victims choose not to report these crimes. One reason reporting is so low is that reporting entails the threat of shame and retaliation. According to Protect Our Defenders (2017), a third of those who report sexual violence face retaliation in the form of discharges, while relatively few military sexual assault cases are prosecuted (13%) and even fewer result in a conviction (4%). As Cynthia Enloe (2000: 276) suggests, such statistics illustrate the "deeply masculinized, even misogynist, institutional culture" that sustains the military as masculine space despite women's increasing representation.

But in terms of their absolute numbers, sexual assaults in the military reverse a trend found in other realms: Specifically, most victims of sexual assault in the military are men (Childress 2013). This suggests another reason why underreporting of sexual assault may occur: Men who experience sexual assault resist the victim label, instead seeing themselves as the *targets* rather than the *victims* of violence (Durfee 2011). Nevertheless, this is still gendered violence: Men's sexual assault of other men carries the same dehumanizing—and feminizing—message as men's sexual assault of women.

Thus, an emphasis on heterosexual, cisgender women's victimhood may paint an incomplete picture of gendered violence: Members of the LGBTQ community as well as men are also the victims of sexual assault and intimate partner violence, and not all women are equally impacted by gendered violence. To reflect this nuanced focus, the term **sexual violence** refers to violent acts of sexual coercion. In contrast to *violence against women*, this term destabilizes the notion that this kind of victimization necessarily follows the pattern of man-on-woman violence while also maintaining a clear focus on the role of gender relations in structuring this violence. Likewise, **intimate partner violence** refers to physical, verbal, emotional, sexual, and economic coercion between partners; such partners may be domestic spouses (as suggested by the common term *domestic violence*) but can include non-live-in partners as well. Together, the terms *sexual violence* and *intimate partner violence* emphasize both how gender and sexuality work together as mechanisms of violent domination and how intimacy is used as a vector of gendered and sexualized violence, disproportionately, but not exclusively so, against women and against transgender, genderqueer and gender-non-conforming people.

Rape Myths

In 2010, Daisy Coleman, a 14-year-old white teenager, moved with her family to the town of Marysville, Missouri, after her father died in a car crash. Adjusting to life in her new town and coping with family loss, Coleman joined the cheerleading squad at Maryville High School as a freshman and met Matthew Barnett, a popular white football player. Though her older brother warned Coleman not to become too close to Barnett, she befriended him via text message exchanges. On January 8, 2012, she went to a party at Barnett's house. The events that followed are murky: According to Coleman, she had two clear alcoholic drinks and blacked out. Witnesses said she was so inebriated she could not speak coherently. When she woke up hours later, she was lying on her mother's front lawn, badly bruised, freezing cold, and barely conscious. She had been left in front of her own house in below-30-degree temperature, her hair frozen. She dragged herself to the door and scratched it loudly enough to wake her mother, who took her to the hospital. The doctors found evidence that she had been raped, as her mother suspected.

When Coleman came back to school, she was taunted by students who called her a slut for "asking for it" from the popular football star. Some students ridiculed Coleman by wearing T-shirts that read, "Matthew 1, Daisy 0."

Coleman's mother pressed charges against Barnett, but the charges were later dropped. Eventually, Coleman's family decided to leave town. Six months after they left, their house mysteriously burnt to the ground. Meanwhile, Coleman suffered mental health crises, including suicidality. Although prosecutors attempted to reopen her case in 2013, Barnett's parents refused to cooperate, saying, "My son is the victim here" (Payne 2013). Often focusing on the text messages that Coleman sent rather than the actions that took place in Barnett's house, many people in the town of Marysville blamed Coleman for her own victimization—and even for the victimization of her alleged rapist.

Girls and women who share Coleman's experiences can find themselves in the impossible position of being both vulnerable to rape (as a physical act of violence) but also un-rapeable (in the perceptions of others, including the justice system). Advocates and scholars use the term *rape myth* to describe the narratives that produce this position. **Rape myths** are beliefs that trivialize rape or maintain that certain women cannot be raped or that a sexual assault was not "really" rape.

Rape myths take different forms:

- Under the **blame the victim myth**, women and girls are blamed for their own victimization. This myth suggests that assaulted girls and women desired the act of sexual violence that was perpetrated against them or that they were too half-hearted in convincing their rapist that they did not consent. A woman's sexual history can be used against her to label her a "slut." Suggesting the power of this myth even to those looking to advocate on behalf of victims, some jurisdictions in the U.S. have frowned upon including sexually transmitted disease tests in rape kits; if a victim's test comes back positive without evidence that it was transmitted as part of the assault, she might be deemed promiscuous—and thus more easily blamed for the rape.

- Closely related to the blame the victim myth, the **ideal victim myth** places strict boundaries on how victims should look and behave. It treats certain reactions to the trauma of victimization as evidence that the victim could not have been raped. Erroneous details or inconsistent details cast doubt on the trustworthiness of the victim. Initial attempts at concealing or downplaying the assault are used to suggest that the victim is rewriting or exaggerating events. Excessive emotion or hysteria are seen as evidence of an unstable victim—one perhaps prone to overstatement.

- Just as the blame the victim and ideal victim myths minimize women's and girls' experiences of victimization, the **boys will be boys myth** exonerates boys and men: It perpetuates the notion that rapists are not really violent perpetrators but merely boys and men who got carried away having a good time. Consider the 2016 case of Brock Turner, a Stanford swimmer who was found guilty of three counts of felony assault, including sexually penetrating an unconscious, intoxicated woman behind a dumpster, and assault with attempt to commit rape. In appealing for leniency, Turner's father pleaded with the judge to view his son's deeds as merely a mistake; jail time, his father insisted, "is a steep price to pay for 20 minutes of action" (Miller 2016). The judge sentenced Turner to only six months in prison for the crime.

Rape myths are embedded in cultural beliefs and codified within the legal system. Laws regarding violence against women are relatively new in the U.S.: As mentioned in Chapter 5, it was not until 1993 that all 50 U.S. states recognized marital rape as a crime. Indeed, before the 1970s, state-level statutes often included a "marital rape exemption" to prevent one marital partner from prosecuting the other for rape (RAINN, 2009). Men in the U.S. have also historically had the legal right to commit other forms of violence against their wives. After Alabama became the first state to rescind the legal right of men to beat their wives in 1871 and Maryland made wife-beating a crime in 1882, it took another century for the U.S. federal government to put in place systematic protections for abused women through the 1984 Family Violence Prevention Services Act and the 1994 Violence Against Women Act (SafeNetwork 1999). Meanwhile, stalking was not a criminal offense in any jurisdiction until California criminalized it in 1991 in response to the murder of five Orange County women in a six-week period by former husbands or boyfriends under court restraining orders.

Rape myths translate into high costs for those coming forward to report one's rape to police, college administrators, or even to one's trusted friends and family. Karen Weiss (2010: 288) argues that the "shame of sexual victimization is mediated by the ways in which the culture defines appropriate gender behaviors and sexual practices for men and women." Further, victims often describe the turmoil of bringing their perpetrators to justice as the **second rape** because of the demand to repeatedly recount the sexual assault and to assert one's virtue as a victim. In the courtroom, women who have been raped are often accused of giving inconsistent testimony, of appearing hysterically emotional, and of seeming vindictive. When their rapists, however, come to the stand, a different performance often unfolds: Their straightforward, unemotional curtness seems to enhance their credibility. (We will discuss witness credibility in more detail below.) Of course, there is an alternative reading of these affective differences: She is emotional because she is traumatized by her experience of victimization while his calmness may simply reflect his confidence that he did nothing wrong. A rape trial thus becomes an adjudication on both the perpetrator *and* the victim.

In addition to the formal criminal justice system, other institutions have systematically minimized sexual assault. As the 2015 film *The Hunting Ground* details, university administrators often echo rape myths and diminish the experiences of victims. In some cases, university administrators have silenced victims by encouraging them to drop their complaints; in other cases, universities have addressed sexual assault through nominal punishments for the perpetrators, such as writing an essay, paying a small fine, or expulsion upon graduation. In response to university apathy over sexual assault, two students at University of North Carolina at Charlotte, Annie Clark and Andrea Pino, filed a Title IX complaint with the U.S. Department of Justice against the university in 2013. By innovatively applying

Title IX to sexual assault, these students sparked unprecedented attention to the culture of sexual assault on many U.S. campuses as well as federal action. By May 2014, the U.S. Department of Education released a list of colleges and universities with open Title IX sexual violence investigations as well as updated reporting guidelines for schools receiving federal funds (U.S. Department of Education 2014).

The Social Construction of Victims and Criminals

Rape myths shape how allegations of sexual assault fare in legal courts and the courts of public opinion. But peeling back further to look at how rape myths implicate men and women and boys and girls differently along the lines of race suggests a broader context in which sexual violence comes to matter. This broader context is shaped by gendered and racialized understandings of who constitutes sympathetic victims versus blameworthy criminals.

Even though victims of sexual violence are often doubted, some fare better than others. For example, white, heterosexual, cisgender girls and women are more likely to be understood as **ideal victims** because they are more likely to viewed as innocent and undeserving of the violence they may experience. According to sociologist Esther Madriz, women of diverse racial background share an understanding that the most sympathetic victim is white, a girl, and naïve, or as one respondent put it:

> I imagine a blond girl, like . . . from the Midwest, with a ponytail, naïve, unaware, walking down the street in New York City, singing laralaralara. (Madriz 1997: 349)

As Kristin Bumiller (2008: 9) notes, high-profile rape cases often reinforce "iconic representations of victims (as innocent, white, and/or angelic)" at the same time as they "sacrifice the actual victims for their failure to live up to this idealization."

Pervasive representations of criminality, including perpetrators of sexual violence, are likewise informed by race and gender. As sociologist Dawn Dow (2016d: 175) explains, **the Thug** represents a controlling image of "African American masculinity associated with criminality and poverty." Recall from Chapter 3 that controlling images are tropes used to explain and justify social inequalities as individual pathologies. The controlling image of the Thug is reflected in crime coverage, which disproportionately features Black and brown boys and men as compared to whites; in phenomena such as the weapons bias, whereby ambiguous objects are more likely to be seen as guns when associated with Black and brown faces as compared to white faces; and in widespread patterns of policing practices that disproportionately target African American boys and men (Dixon and Linz 2000; Epp, Maynard-Moody, and Haider-Markel 2014; Payne 2006). As Dow summarizes, such imagery legitimates "attacks on African American boys' and men's bodies and minds" (2016d: 182).

The infamous 1989 Central Park jogger rape illustrates these intersecting dynamics of gender and race in shaping the allocation of victimhood and criminality in cases of sexual violence. In that case, a young white professional woman was sexually assaulted to the point of losing consciousness. When she awoke from a coma nearly two weeks later, she remembered nothing of the events that transpired the night of her rape. Her inability to bear witness to her own rape exonerated her of the kind of moral culpability often demanded of victims. As Kristin Bumiller describes it, "This, ironically, turned her into an unassailable woman because her amnesia made it impossible to accuse her of lying about her willful participation in the sexual act" (2008: 99).

Many feminist activists joined in demanding justice in the case, and soon, prosecutors Linda Fairstein and Elizabeth Lederer filed charges against five African American boys, four of whom appeared to have confessed to the crime after extensive police interrogations. Consensus grew among an outraged public that these boys were guilty of the rape, and by 1991, all five defendants were convicted. In 2002, however, a man named Matias Reyes, who was serving a life sentence, heard about the convictions and confessed to the rape. After subsequent DNA testing, the verdict was clear: Each of the "Central Park Five," as they came to be called, had spent over a decade in prison for a crime they did not commit. Twenty-five years after the trial, the film *The Central Park Five* documented how the prosecutors were able to win the trial despite shoddy evidence and coerced confessions because the story they told—a group of savage young boys of color raping a white woman—fit a widely accepted social narrative.

Indeed, this is a social narrative that dates back more than 100 years in U.S. history. As Angela Davis (1983) cautions, in the U.S., the history of the criminalization of sexual violence was racist before it became feminist. After all, controlling images of African American boys and men as aggressive and violent are not recent; they began to circulate in the decades that followed the Civil War in the second half of the 19th century. White Southerners in particular popularized the threat of Black rapists as a justification for engaging in **lynchings** that terrorized African Americans after the abolition of slavery. Lynchings were public executions, usually of men of color, orchestrated by white mobs and often with the approval of local law enforcement; these mobs enacted gruesome torture on the victim, ranging from mutilation with knives or blunt objects (lynchers were known to take home body parts as souvenirs) to immolation and hanging. From the 1880s to the 1950s, nearly 4,000 people, the vast majority of whom were African American men, were lynched (Robertson 2015). The alleged assault of a white woman was a popular galvanizer for these lynchings; white mobs, mostly but not exclusively men, mobilized as protectors of feminine virtue. But far from a feminist defense of women's bodily integrity (after all, the sexual assault of Black women was not treated as a crime), lynchings often used the white women victim as a prop for instilling racial terror. After all, lynchings were even perpetrated against African American men in consenting interracial relationships to provide a horrific lesson to both African Americans and whites on the unacceptability of intimacy that crossed the color line.

This racial history helps further clarify the ambiguous legal responses to sexual violence and intimate partner violence across U.S. history. While intimate partner violence, marital rape, and stalking were not considered crimes until recently, rape by a stranger was considered a *capital offense*—deserving of the death penalty—until the Supreme Court ruled that this constituted cruel and unusual punishment in 1977. Court records reveal that only certain men received capital sentences for rape; in addition to extralegal punishment in the form of lynching, African American boys and men were disproportionately subject to state-sanctioned executions. Using data on rape cases from 1945 to 1965, sociologists Marvin Wolfgang and Marc Riedel (1973) found that "Black defendants whose victims were white were sentenced to death approximately eighteen times more frequently than defendants in any other racial category" (130). By contrast, white men were rarely brought to court on rape charges. From 1930 to 1972, "not a single white man was executed for rape . . . in Louisiana, Mississippi, Oklahoma, Virginia, West Virginia, and the District of Columbia" as compared to 66 executions of African Americans (Wolfgang and Riedel 1973: 125). Finally, cases where victims were African American girls and women, who were often presumed to be promiscuous, were often treated with leniency—regardless of the race of the perpetrator (Wolfgang and Riedel 1973: 125). Though rape is no longer punishable by death, executions in the U.S. still reflect these racial and gender disparities for other violent crimes.

Thus, contemporary American politics often continues to reflect U.S. history that has designated white women as ideal victims, white men as ideal protectors, men of color as criminals, and women of color as invisible. And race, of course, is not the only line along which the victimization is trivialized and criminalization is sanctioned; as discussed in Chapter 4, the heightened rates of violence facing LGBTQ people, particularly LGBTQ people of color, both reflects and reproduces marginalization within the gender hierarchy.

The Paradox of Women's Violence: Blurring Victimhood and Criminality

In 1982, Deborah Peagler, an African American woman in her early 20s who lived in Compton, California, was charged with first-degree murder. Her story parallels that of many women accused of homicide: She suffered years of abuse at the hands of her partner, an African American man named Oliver Wilson. Wilson forced her into prostitution, beat her repeatedly, and eventually sexually abused their daughter. She went to the police, but they refused to help her. Finally, her mother reached out to a group of local gang members for help. Believing that they would simply give Oliver a swift beating, Peagler led Wilson to an agreed-upon location where the attack would take place. But instead of giving him a physical warning, the gang members beat and strangled him to death. The case was picked up by the local police gang unit and vigorously pursued. Threatened with the death penalty if the case went to trial, Peagler pled guilty and received 25 years to life in prison, as the film *Crime After Crime* documents.

Peagler's case reveals a gender pattern that distinguishes women violent offenders from men offenders: Histories of abuse tend to play a more prominent role in women's violence, with women offenders more likely than men offenders to report experiences of childhood abuse and repeated victimization (Belknap and Holsinger 2006). Jennifer Wesely (2006) uses the term **cumulative violence** to explain the experiences of women who assault or kill: Their violence accumulates from experiences of child abuse, sexual objectification, and adult sexual, physical and emotional abuse. Summarizing the experiences of the women in her study, Wesely (2006: 314) notes,

> They were . . . revictimized by intermittent and ongoing feelings of being unsafe, unprotected, and silenced by both individuals and society at large; by perpetrators who experienced few consequences for their actions; and by the message that their value as human beings was minimized as violence against them was condoned and justified. These lived experiences, along with the lack of support and the lack of options for the women, maintained these grim realities. Therefore, the violent victimizations they experienced were not just isolated events but a pervasive atmosphere of cumulative violence.

Wesely (2006: 320) argues that the women in her study employed violence as a reaction "to years of cumulative abuses and exclusions" that "creates a kind of pressure-cooker situation for these women—with more degradation and victimization heaped on without intervention, relief, or healing, they are moved closer to a tipping point. For the women in this study, that resulted in violence."

Embedding women's criminality and violent offending in intersecting power structures helps explain why women who are marginalized by class and race are more likely to engage in violence (Bernard 2013). As Nikki Jones (2008) reveals, girls and women living in violent contexts navigate violence in complex ways, sometimes mustering the toughness associated with the "code of the street" (described below) while at other times emphasizing their femininity. This deliberate deployment of different "street codes" blurs the line between violence as a survival strategy and violence as a criminal offense.

Taking note of how histories of abuse shape women's and girls' offending is thus an important step in understanding violence as gendered. Nevertheless, treating women's violence as merely a reaction to abusive situations risks reproducing feminine stereotypes by robbing these women of their agency: They are merely acting out as victims. Yet criminologists Candace Kruttschnitt and Kristin Carbone-Lopez (2006) note that women violent offenders often voice the same motivations as men: money, power, respect. Similarly, Jody Miller (2001) finds in her study of gender and gangs that while the significance of gender varies by context, girl gang members are motivated by similar dynamics and embrace similarly stereotypical attitudes about gender differences as do boys. While feminist criminologists continue these debates surrounding whether and how girls' and women's violence should be treated as different or the same as boys' and men's, their efforts have had an impact on understanding the perpetration of violence more broadly. By bringing girls and women into the conversation, they have compelled criminologists and sociologists to make gender an explicit consideration when explaining violence and violent crime.

The Gender Gap in Violence: Men and Masculinity

Though explicit conversations about gender and violence oftentimes focus on women's experiences, most violence involves men, not women. There is a **gender gap in violence** such that women are much less likely than men to be violently victimized by strangers, and women are also much less likely to perpetrate violence. For example, American men are more than three times as likely as women to be murdered with a firearm, and they are almost six times more likely to murder with a firearm. Darrell Steffensmeier and Emilie Allan (1996: 459) describe this gender gap in violence as universal, saying that "women are always and everywhere less likely to commit criminal acts" than men.

Given this consistent and clear gender disparity, gender scholars have put a discussion of masculinity at the center of conversations about why people—mostly men—commit violence. Consider the American phenomenon of school shootings. In a study that analyzed school shootings from 1982 to 2001, Michael Kimmel and Matthew Mahler (2003) found that most of the rural and suburban white boys who engaged in school shootings were regularly subject to homophobic bullying and that their willingness to open random fire could be interpreted as a way to vindicate their masculinity (recall the discussion of homophobic slurs as gender policing in Chapter 4). In other words, school shootings—for the shooter—are about (re)establishing one's position at the top of the gender hierarchy. As Kimmel (2012) writes in an Op-Ed in response to the 2012 Newtown, Connecticut, shootings, in which Adam Lanza, a white 20-year-old, killed more than two dozen children and teachers,

> From an early age, boys learn that violence is not only an acceptable form of conflict resolution, but one that is admired. . . . In a sense, they [school shooters] weren't deviants, but over-conformists to norms of masculinity that prescribe violence as a solution. Like real men, they didn't just get mad, they got even. Until we transform that definition of manhood, this terrible equation of masculinity and violence will continue to produce such horrific sums.

In making this argument, Kimmel notes that

> The belief that violence is an inherently male characteristic is a fallacy . . . boys learn it. They learn it from their fathers. They learn it from a media that glorifies it, from sports heroes who commit felonies and get big contracts, from a culture saturated in images of heroic and redemptive violence. They learn it from each other.

Here, Kimmel and others point to how men's violence is celebrated throughout contemporary U.S. culture, even if such expressions are oftentimes symbolic and subtle. For example, scholars (Dill and Thill 2007) show that video games shape how children understand the use of violence against others. In such games, violence is used as a legitimate means to win a game against other boy and men players; girl and women characters tend to appear in video games as sex objects rather than competitors.

While Kimmel focuses on white men's encounters with violence, others have analyzed violence and victimization with respect to men marginalized along the lines of race. Black men are disproportionately likely to be the victims of gun violence as compared to their white counterparts, and they are disproportionately killed by other Black men. Indeed, African American men are eight times as likely as white men to die of homicide. Criminologists and sociologists have come up with a variety of explanations for this disparity; one body of thought emphasizes what Elijah Anderson (1999) has called the *street code*, which links men's self-presentations to their participation in violence within contexts of underfunded public institutions, rampant poverty, and bleak opportunities for upward mobility. The street code operates as an adaptive, informal mechanism of social control within these contexts; those adhering to the street code present themselves in public space with a tough demeanor that communicates their willingness to engage in violence. This practice can be understood as an embodied version of *target hardening*, whereby the security of a person or place is strengthened to mitigate attack relative to other possible targets. The objective of these hypermasculine displays is to *avoid* violence by persuading would-be attackers to look for a different victim. However, this adaptive strategy can backfire, leading to more street violence: If tested, adherents to the street code must follow through on their threats, lest they be branded easy targets.

Both Kimmel and Anderson reveal profound ways in which *doing violence* is also *doing gender*—in this case, *doing masculinity*. Furthermore, those who perpetrate violence can consciously use gender—both masculinity and femininity—as a tool to accomplish violence in even more nuanced ways. Consider this example from *The Stickup Kids* (2012) by Randol Contreras. The book chronicles the story of Gus and Pablo, two Puerto Rican crack dealers from the Bronx who strike it rich before experiencing rapid downward mobility. Contreras situates the feelings of domination that these men experience during drug robberies within their broader biographies, detailing the blocked labor opportunities these men experienced that led to their involvement in the drug market as well as the subsequent masculine esteem these men held in their neighborhoods when the drug market was flush. During the height of the drug market, Gus and Pablo were the guys who got the girls and who had the jewelry and nice cars. They were also the guys who could help out others on the block. The crash of the crack market meant that their esteemed status as men came crashing down as well. After the crack market dried up, they turn to drug robberies to make ends meet. The two began to call themselves the "stickup kids" for the coordinated acts of violence they orchestrated to rob drug dealers of their cash and stash. To accomplish these crimes, they made strategic use of masculinity and femininity. As Contreras reveals, they often lured unsuspecting their victims using "the girl," a woman decoy who approaches the drug dealer and seduces him, often through dancing and alcohol. Once he is in a state of vulnerability, she suggests that they go back to her apartment for the night. Instead of leading him to her apartment, however, she sets him up for a brutal drug robbery, leading him to Gus and Pablo. Calling attention to how Gus and

Pablo played on the gendered vulnerabilities of men targeted for drug robberies, Contreras reveals that not only masculinity but also femininity can be a tool used to accomplish violence.

Taken together, Kimmel, Anderson, and Contreras show that gender, race, and class intersect to shape both men's willingness and capacity for violence and their vulnerability to violence as well. They show that the relationship between gender and violence is as central to men's experiences of violence as to women's. Indeed, a full understanding of the gendered dimensions of violence requires a consideration of how masculinity is achieved through violence, how masculinity shapes violence, and how the relationship between violence and masculinity is shaped by race, class, and other lines of difference.

Gendering Justice

Sociological accounts of punishment have long acknowledged that the social importance of punishment far exceeds the individual recipient of this punishment. As Durkheim provocatively argued over 100 years ago, without punishment, society would fall apart. This is because punishment affirms the collective consciousness (e.g., mutual understandings of right and wrong) that holds society together. When people violate social norms or codes, the state steps in not simply to punish the criminal (i.e., retribution), not only to take the criminal off the streets (i.e., incapacitation), and not necessarily even to prevent future wrongdoing (i.e., deterrence), but rather to uphold to the very social norms that have been violated by the criminal act (i.e., to maintain social cohesion).

This collective consciousness, however, is not gender neutral nor colorblind. Society's intolerance for certain criminal acts can depend heavily on the offender's and victim's gender and race, as discussed earlier. Furthermore, since the 1970s, the pursuit of "tough on crime" measures at local, state, and federal levels and the subsequent expansion of the criminal justice system has resulted in the mass incarceration of boys and men of color, especially African American boys and men, while white offenders continue to receive relative leniency at every stage of criminal justice contact, from initial police contact to parole. Today, prisoners, probationers, and parolees are disproportionately men of color. One in three Black men in the U.S. will go to prison in their lifetime (Lyons and Pettit 2011). Further, race, gender, and age all affect whether an offender will be sentenced to incarceration, interacting "to produce substantially harsher sentences for one category of offenders—young black males" (Spohn and Holleran 2000: 281).

But spikes in incarceration have not been confined to men: As Chesney-Lind (2006: 17) notes,

> few considered the impact that this correctional course change would have on women. Yet the number of women in jail and prison continues to soar (outstripping male increases for most of the past decade), completely untethered from women's crime rate, which has not increased by nearly the same amount.

Because crime often entails "unladylike" behavior, women offenders—especially those who break from gender respectability by being unmarried, having a history of violence, or are sexually promiscuous—are at risk of receiving harsher sentences than men for the same crimes (Carlen 2010; Chesney-Lind 1987). Further, the racial disparities that render boys and men of color more vulnerable to incarceration than white boys and men also affect girls and women: Lori Moore and Irene Padavic (2010) looked at juvenile offenders in Florida and found that Black girls receive harsher punishments than white and Hispanic girls.

These facts and figures confirm an intersectional approach that gender, race, and class matter for understanding *who* is implicated in the criminal justice system. But gender, race, and class also matter for understanding *how* they are implicated in the criminal justice system, including not only the severity but also the style of justice. Each stop in the contemporary criminal justice pipeline—from the police car to the courtroom to the prison cell—draws on and reproduces gender norms and practices.

The Police

Cop dramas such as *Law & Order* feature depictions of policing as an exciting, high-action profession that requires courage, resolve, and the willingness to use violence. They show police heroically risking their lives to protect victims and track down criminals. Criminologist and geographer Steven Herbert (1997) uses the term *hard-charger* to capture this popular, and popularized, masculine ethos of policing, but he cautions that in reality, police work is more about filling out paperwork than catching bad guys in high-speed chases.

Still, police can, and do, engage in violence, and gender ideologies lie at the core of how such violence is transformed from an ugly but perhaps necessary social duty to a prized social act. Indeed, police work symbolically centers on **masculine protectionism**, a logic that Iris Marion Young (2003: 4) summarizes as follows:

> the "good" man is one who keeps vigilant watch over the safety of his family and readily risks himself in the face of threats from the outside world in order to protect the subordinate members of his household. . . . [T]he gallantly masculine man is loving and self-sacrificing, especially in relation to women. He faces the world's difficulties and dangers in order to shield women from harm. . . . [T]he role of this courageous, responsible, and virtuous man is that of a protector.

With women representing only 12% of police officers, such an emphasis on masculine protectionism can make policing a hostile environment for women. Anastasia Prokos and Irene Padavic (2002) reveal how masculinity shapes law enforcement in their study of a police academy. Though there was no overt distinction between men and women police officers, they found a "hidden curriculum" that communicated to officers that women were outsiders, that gender differences were not only large but also consequential for police work, and that men officers had permission to denigrate and objectify women—as well as resist women in positions of authority. But by celebrating a cult of masculinity within police work, this hidden curriculum endangered both men and women officers. It bred distrust and lowered morale, especially for men officers partnered with women officers. According to a 2016 report by Pew, 43% of women cops said that "men are treated better than women" with respect to assignments and promotions; only 6% of men police officers agreed (Stepler 2017).

Given these dynamics, it is perhaps not surprising that police have historically minimized crimes that disproportionately affect women. Prior to the 1980s, intimate partner violence incidents were considered low-priority calls involving private matters rather than acute public safety concerns. That changed, however, with the **Minneapolis Domestic Violence Experiment**, which took place in Minneapolis, Minnesota, from 1981 to 1982. The experiment tested three different approaches to address misdemeanor intimate partner violence calls: separate the abuser and victim for eight hours, provide mediation, or make an arrest. The results revealed that abusers who were arrested had lower rates of reoffending than abusers subject to mediation or separation (Sherman and Berk 1984).

Paradoxically, this experiment had the effect of transforming the historic underpolicing of intimate partner violence into overpolicing: Police agencies across the United States adopted mandatory arrest policies that increased arrests, including dual arrests of both partners when officers are unable to distinguish between abuser and victim. A police saying developed to describe this situation: *The only bad arrest is no arrest*. In response, women became more reluctant to call the police because they feared mandatory arrests. A follow-up study by Lawrence Sherman and Heather Harris (2015) found decades later that "partner arrests for domestic common assault apparently increased premature death for their victims, especially African Americans" (1). This latter finding suggests a complex relationship between arrest, domestic abuse, and health, as the causes of death were mostly heart disease and other internal morbidity.

Thus, although law enforcement prioritization of intimate partner violence was initially read as a feminist victory, the decades that followed revealed that the masculine ethos of policing prevailed: Instead of developing policing approaches appropriate to the problem of intimate partner violence, police applied the tactics of arrest they were already accustomed to. After all, the prioritization of intimate partner violence took place during the same period as when police were increasingly turning to militarized tactics and equipment more generally (Kraska 1996). The policing of intimate partner violence provided an opportunity for police to engage in masculine protectionism while mobilizing the hard-charger (to use Herbert's [1997] terminology) tactics familiar to law enforcement.

Further, as Herbert's (1997) analysis shows, the gendering of police work also shapes police interactions with civilians well beyond contexts that immediately involve women as victims. No doubt, some suggest that men and women officers do policing differently: Studies show that women cops are less likely to resort to force on duty. Whereas 30% of men officers have fired their weapons at some point in their careers, only 11% of women police officers have (Stepler 2017). Nevertheless, with men comprising the vast majority of law enforcement, legal scholar Frank Rudy Cooper (2009) argues that officers strategically deploy masculinity to achieve compliance during police stops. Likewise, policing scholar Susan Martin (1999) explains that to establish masculine dominance over presumed criminals—often racialized men, class-marginalized men or other men of lower status—an officer may "draw . . . on his age superiority and treat . . . the challenger as too young to merit a response," "dispense so-called street justice," or even appeal to a civilian's masculine pride to "pull yourself together [and] act like a man" by "drawing on shared manhood" (118). As she summarizes, "Since a key element of policing—gaining and maintaining control of situations—remains associated with manhood, [men] officers do gender along with doing domination" (118).

This gendered insight on police interactions with civilians emerged in Supreme Court Justice Sonia Sotomayor's dissent in the 2016 *Utah v. Strieff* case, which revolved around whether the police could legally search a detainee who had been stopped for a traffic violation warrant. While the majority of U.S. Supreme Court agreed that the police have a broad prerogative to search civilians they detained, Sotomayor disagreed:

> Although many Americans have been stopped for speeding or jaywalking, few may realize how degrading a stop can be when the officer is looking for more. The indignity of the stop is not limited to an officer telling you that you look like a criminal. . . . If the officer thinks you might be dangerous, he may then "frisk" you for weapons. This involves more than just a pat down. As onlookers pass by, the officer may "feel with sensitive fingers every portion of [your] body. A thorough search [may] be made of [your] arms and armpits, waistline and back, the groin and area about the testicles, and entire surface of the legs down to the feet."

What Justice Sotomayor describes here is gendered degradation: The violation of one's bodily integrity, including one's groin, puts the officer in the position of masculine dominator and effeminizes the civilian. With African American men disproportionately detained by police for investigatory police stops (Epp et al. 2014), police stops can dramatize the achievement of hegemonic masculinity (that is, of the cop) in relation to marginalized masculinity (that is, of the racialized detainee).

The Courts

Gender shapes courtroom dynamics. Courts are often based on an **adversarial model of justice** in which the courtroom resembles a duel: "The traditional adversary system puts defense and prosecuting attorneys on opposite sides, so to speak, with the idea that truth will emerge through confrontation" (Mirchandani 2006: 784, 795). Mirchandani (2006: 784) argues that this privileges a "masculine mode of argumentation that may inhibit women's ability to speak or be heard." Especially within the context of intimate partner violence, the winner-take-all approach encourages domination by opposing sides, but it fosters neither responsibility in the abuser nor a restoration of the relationship between the abuser and the victim.

For an alternative, Mirchandani (2006) looks to domestic violence courts in Salt Lake City, Utah. Instead of a typical trial, these courts modelled a different kind of **consensus-based justice**: the victim's responsibility in the abuse is explicitly rejected as a term of any plea deal; pleas include counseling and community service requirements for the perpetrator; the victim is supportively included in the process; and follow-up reviews, often with the same personnel, occur at different intervals to ensure continued compliance.

Although these alternative courts have gained popularity, the vast majority of courts continue to follow an adversarial model of meting out justice and often use gender norms in deciding case outcomes. Even evidence—whether or not it is included and how it is considered if it is admitted into court proceedings—is gendered. To illustrate, consider two kinds of evidence: witness testimony and expert testimony.

Witness testimony is often the most important form of evidence in criminal cases, despite advances in technologies such as DNA testing or surveillance. This is because forensic evidence often tells an incomplete story. A rape kit may reveal that sexual intercourse happened, but it cannot decisively show whether it was consensual. Hence, witnesses are often brought to the stand to provide the backstory that renders this evidence meaningful. To do so, witnesses must provide a believable or reasonable account of the facts of the case. This believability depends not only on the story the witness tells but also on judges' and jurors' assessment of the witness's own credibility. This assessment in part depends on how witnesses comport with widely held gender norms and other social norms, which may determine the extent to which jurors and judges find witnesses relatable and trustworthy.

Doing gender, alongside race, class, and other lines of difference, leads some witnesses to be more credible than others. For example, in 2013, Rachel Jeantel, an African American teenager, took the stand to testify on behalf of her friend Trayvon Martin, an African American teenager, who was shot dead by George Zimmerman, a white Hispanic man, over a year earlier. While Zimmerman's defense was that he had shot the teenager in self-defense, Jeantel's testimony maintained that Martin was the one who was in fear of his life and who was trying to escape from Zimmerman (Cadet 2013). Her recounting of the final phone call she had with Martin minutes before he would be fatally shot is the closest the court could come to hearing Martin's perspective.

Yet commentators were quick to condemn Jeantel's testimony as uncredible and inconsistent. Their criticisms focused on Jeantel's self-presentation: She spoke in curt, sometimes one-word responses; she used slang that was incomprehensible to many of the white viewers of the trial; and one commentator stated that she came across as "raw, emotional, aggressive and hostile" (Samara 2013). When Jeantel testified that she refused to attend the funeral or meet with Martin's mother because she did not want to "see somebody cry," she was read as a cold and uncaring friend rather than an emotionally traumatized confidante who was grieving the loss of Martin. Portrayed as uncooperative and belligerent, Jeantel was framed through the controlling image of the "angry Black woman"—even though she was only 19 years old.

While this case provided an acute rendering of how race, violence, victimization, and impunity intersect in the contemporary American context, the case thus also revealed the relevance of gender in structuring court outcomes: On the one hand, the defense use the gendered and racial imagery of the Thug (described above) to present Martin as a threat, while on the other hand, the devaluation of Jeantel as a trustworthy witness further helped undermine the prosecution's case that Trayvon Martin, rather than George Zimmerman, was the victim. Martin's only chance to speak for himself—through Rachel Jeantel—was discredited. Zimmerman was acquitted of both manslaughter and second-degree murder because jurors found that he had acted "reasonably" in response to Martin by shooting him dead.

Expert testimony is another place where gender dynamics become acute in the courtroom, specifically with respect to intimate partner violence. Deborah Peagler, described earlier in this Chapter, received 25 years to life in prison for her involvement in the murder of her abusive partner. When her case unfolded in the early 1980s, her abuse at the hands of her partner was deemed inadmissible in court. Nevertheless, at that time, scholars and practitioners were beginning to circulate a theory that explained why some abused women wielded violence against their aggressors. **Intimate partner battering and its effects** (formerly *battered women's syndrome*) explained that not unlike Stockholm syndrome, victims of prolonged intimate partner violence experience profound psychological trauma that distorts their understanding of the abuse. Because abusers tend to use physical and psychological abuse alongside social isolation, victims may justify the abuse as deserved and tolerate it for prolonged periods. They may also view any attempt to reach out for support—through friends, coworkers, or police—as futile and risky, as it may provoke retaliation from their abusers. Accordingly, women may stay in relationships with their abusers only to later violently lash out at them.

Courts, however, have historically resisted including expert testimony on this syndrome because it lacked scientific consensus (see Chapter 2 on knowledge production). California, where Peagler's case took place, only admitted such evidence into trial in 1992, a decade too late for Peagler. In 2002, however, a new law allowed incarcerated inmates such as Peagler to submit a writ of habeas corpus challenging their original conviction on the basis of evidence of their abuse having been deemed inadmissible. After a protracted fight for justice, Peagler was eventually freed in 2009. California's law, however, remains unique within the U.S.

The stories of Deborah Peagler and Rachel Jeantel suggest the real effect of gender, alongside race, in the courtroom. With this insight in mind, some lawyers deliberately use gender as a tool, particularly during sentencing. Gathings and Parrotta (2013) studied courts in North Carolina and found that defense attorneys used gender narratives to present defendants as worthy of leniency in sentencing. They described accused men as good workers and good providers, and they described accused women as good caretakers and mothers. While individual defendants may benefit from these narratives, they risk reproducing the gender binaries that further justify harsh treatment of women and men who are marked as criminals.

The Prison

Like the courts and the police, the prison is a gendered organization. The gendering of prisons is facilitated by a core feature of incarceration: Prisons are, by law, gender segregated. This is justified by security concerns for inmates and guards. But this separation is not only about safety but also about responding to gendered norms about why men versus women engage in criminal activity and what constitutes appropriate punishment when they do.

Scholarship on prisons reveals that men and women are subject to different technologies of social control within prison. Men's prisons tend to follow a **custodial model** centered on retribution or incapacitation. The prison authority structure is dominated by men, from the warden to the guards, and prisons are architecturally designed to enhance security. Such prisons are often panoptic in the sense that they enhance the capacity of guards to observe prisoners. The **panopticon**, developed by Jeremy Bentham (1791) and later theorized by Michel Foucault (1975) as a metaphor for disciplinary power, works by compelling inmates to internalize the gaze of the prison guard: Because prisoners never know when they are being watched, they must assume—and act as if—they are under constant surveillance. As feminist criminologists such as Jill McCorkel (2003) point out, the panopticon provides a masculine model of punishment in line with a hierarchical, authoritative ethos of control. Furthermore, within men's prisons, reformative elements typically emphasize hard labor. This carceral emphasis on work fits with broader social expectations regarding masculinity (see Chapter 1).

A different set of technologies and norms has shaped women's prisons. As punishment scholar Kelly Hannah-Moffat shows in *Punishment in Disguise* (2001), women's prisons have historically integrated a maternal logic into their operations. Under the **maternal model**, women's prisons are explicitly motivated by reform and rehabilitation rather than retribution or incapacitation. Wardens historically used maternal authority both as a mechanism for organizing control within prisons (i.e., wardens are "prison mothers"; prisoners are children) and as a means of modeling womanhood to wayward inmates. In this way, feminine caretaking supplants masculine authority in women's prisons. Unlike men's prisons' emphasis on hard labor, women's prisons have historically emphasized women's work, especially domestic labor; and whereas incarcerated men are presumed to be irresponsible, women offenders are assumed to be excessively dependent and needy (Haney 2010; Wyse 2013).

The historical efforts, led by reformers such as Elizabeth Frye, to separate women into specific prisons that would champion this maternal model were targeted at the kinds of women deemed reformable. Similar to early welfare regimes (see Chapter 1), this generally meant white women. Yet, as noted above, women of color, not white women, disproportionately populate prison cells in the U.S. To historically consider how race has shaped gendered punishment, Sarah Haley (2013) examined Georgia's prison reform of 1908, showing that by excluding white women from harsh punishment, reformers created a bifurcated system that reproduced the gender and racial politics of slavery. While in prison, the reforms treated African American women no differently than men, subjecting them to the harsh punishment of the chain gang. At the same time, Georgia implemented what Haley calls "domestic carceral spheres":

> Under parole, black women were forced to labor as domestic workers for white families, giving new meaning to the concept of the prison of the home. They were subject to constant surveillance and

the threat of return to the prison camp for any transgression; private individuals served as police and warders. (Haley 2013: 54)

In this way, "the dual mandate of hard road labor and domestic labor" (Haley 2013: 55) repurposed the mechanisms that underpinned Black women's subordination under U.S. slavery as a means of punishment for Black women under Jim Crow.

Sterilization illustrates another example of how gender and race have historically intersected to shape the social control of incarcerated women: Women, particularly poor women of color, have been forced to undergo sterilization for decades in the U.S. as part of medical care within prison facilities. In 1907, Indiana enacted one of the first mandatory sterilization laws for inmates in state custody under the belief that "criminality, mental problems, and pauperism were hereditary" (Laws of Indiana 1907). Soon, roughly thirty states joined Indiana. North Carolina was one of the one of the worst cases: African American women were disproportionately represented among the 7,600 people sterilized under the state's eugenics board from 1929 to 1974 (Carmon 2014). Although formal eugenics boards were dismantled in the 1970s, the practice of involuntary sterilization continued well into the 21st century: A report from the California state auditor revealed that from 2005 to 2011, 39 incarcerated women were sterilized without consent.

Alongside and sometimes in place of these overt, harsh punishments, more softened social control has more recently emerged within facilities that house girls and women of color. Lynne Haney's book, *Offending Women* (2010), for example, examines centers for incarcerated mothers, finding that contemporary forms of social control center on controlling and reshaping incarcerated mothers' *desires*, especially material or sexual desires and dependencies that prison officials blamed for their crimes. Jill McCorkel (2003) likewise shows how therapy and punishment intertwine for incarcerated women. As she notes,

> The gendered character of punishment results in a distinct system of social control within women's prisons that merges key features of punishment (in the form of surveillance) and therapy (in the form of diagnosis) to advance institutional claims about the deviant self and to engineer a shift in behavior. (43)

In her work, McCorkel shows how women inmates are incorporated into the power structure of the women's facility she studied through a mechanism she calls **embodied surveillance**. Unlike the panopticon, in which the watched neither personally knows nor is aware of whether he is under surveillance by the watcher, in embodied surveillance, the watched understands in real-time that she is under surveillance and personally knows her watchers. In the women's facility she studied, McCorkel found that women were encouraged to take responsibility for their criminal behavior; repudiate dependency (whether on men or on substance abuse); and to confess their failings in group meetings with staff and inmates. Inmates were watched by guards, and they were also encouraged to watch and report on other inmates. Sometimes, inmates were subjected to a ritual that staff called the "hot seat": One inmate would sit on a chair in the middle of a circle of her other inmates, who were encouraged by staff to collectively confront and expose the hot seat inmate with prying questions, provocative disclosures, and hurtful accusations. In this way, intimates' intimate relationships were exploited, with inmates pitted against one another to enhance the staff's punitive therapeutic goals.

The gendering of punishment thus goes far beyond the sex-segregated nature of prisons. Gender informs the justification for punishment, the technologies of punishment, and the ideologies surrounding inmates. Staff and prisons do not only do punishment, they also do gender by proactively attempting to punish bad, harmful, inappropriate, or deviant versions of femininity and masculinity.

Undoing Violence, Recognizing Gender

This chapter has demonstrated that violence, or the threat of violence, is one means by which gender difference is achieved and sustained. This chapter has focused on violent crime and its control in the U.S., but the kinds of analyses presented here can and should be applied well beyond the U.S. After all, the World Health Organization estimates that 30% of women worldwide have experienced intimate partner violence (Chaib, Orton, Ratsela, and Steels 2013). Violence against women is a public health issue worldwide, and no region is immune (see, e.g., Roychowdhury 2013; Chapters 9 and 10).

In highlighting how doing gender is connected to doing violence, this chapter points to how *undoing* violence must also involve recognizing gender. This chapter concludes by considering two examples that illustrate how gender may inform movements against violence: men's involvement in the movement to end violence against women and the Say Her Name campaign that emerged out of the Black Lives Matter movement.

First, efforts to challenge sexual violence are often speared-headed by members of the groups who are the disproportionate targets of sexual violence, including cisgender women and the LGBTQ community. But because violence is embedded in gender relations, heterosexual, cisgender men's involvement is crucial to problematize the intersection of gender and violence. Michael Messner, Max Greenberg, and Tal Peretz make this point in their 2015 book, *Some Men*, which examines the history of men's involvement as allies in the movement to end violence against women. Men's involvement is required to ensure that sexual violence and intimate partner violence are addressed not only "downstream" (i.e., in the moment of crisis, where rape crisis centers and domestic violence shelters focus their efforts) but also "upstream" (i.e., in the broader culture that sanctions sexual violence). One "upstream" strategy is known as the **bystander approach**. Because the reproduction of rape myths often occurs in semiprivate men- or boy-only spaces, this approach calls on boys and men to intervene to stop friends, classmates, and teammates not only from perpetrating sexual violence but also from participating in rape culture. As a related strategy, the "My Strength Is Not For Hurting" campaign from Men Can Stop Rape uses hegemonic masculinity as a means to call men to do gender differently: Posters from the campaign include phrases such as "My strength is not for hurting . . . so when she changed her mind, I stopped" and " . . . So when she said No, I said Ok."

While encouraging, these approaches have also been subjected to feminist critique. As C.J. Pascoe and Jocelyn Hollander (2016: 67, 68) caution, mobilizing hegemonic masculinity as a means of countering rape culture does not necessarily "call into question assumptions about the central role of sexual assault in enforcing gender inequality" but instead may merely redefine the boundaries of hegemonic masculinity, such that "*real* [men are defined to] be so sexually desirable as to render force unnecessary." Others, like Jill Cermele and Martha McCaughey (2016), note that the bystander approach likewise undermines women's agency by erasing women's own capacity for self-defense. And finally, because feminists are often eager to embrace men who fight gender inequality, men who join the movement against violence against women often experience a "glass elevator" within feminist organizations, as Ken Kolb (2014) describes in his book, *Moral Wages*, which has the effect of reproducing gender disparities in the very organizations meant to dismantle them.

Second, because violence is shaped at the intersection of gender and race (and other lines of difference), attention to gender can enhance efforts to dismantle racialized violence. Since the acquittal of armed civilian George Zimmerman for the killing of unarmed teenager Trayvon Martin in 2013 (discussed above), the Black Lives Matter movement has sought to reverse the long-standing discrimination and denigration of African Americans, particularly their vulnerability to state- or socially sanctioned violence. Though official figures on people killed by police are woefully inadequate (itself a reflection of sustained disregard), existing data suggest that unarmed African American men are several times more likely to die by police gunfire than whites (e.g., see Lowery 2016; Somashekhar, Lowery, Alexander, Kindy, and Tate 2015; Zimring 2017). Black Lives Matter activists have succeeded in calling attention to the disparate vulnerability of Black boys and Black men to police violence by marching in the streets, mobilizing social media, and demanding justice in the courts, even as legal victories remain elusive. Because of this movement, Michael Brown, along with Eric Garner, Alton Sterling, Philando Castile, Oscar Grant, and others killed by public law enforcement have been mobilized as potent symbols of the deadly costs of being a Black boy or man in America.

Yet, as Kimberlé Crenshaw has highlighted (African American Policy Forum [AAPF] 2017), there has been a noticeable silence in this movement. Despite heightened awareness regarding anti-Black violence, the names of African American girls and women killed or assaulted (including sexual assault) by police, such as Korryn Gaines, Jessica Williams, Aiyana Jones, and others, rarely capture headlines or arouse sustained public concern. The AAPF reports that African American women and girls are represented among 33% of police shooting fatalities of women, even though they are only 13% of American women. As Crenshaw (AAPF 2017) notes, "Although Black women are routinely killed, raped, and beaten by the police, their experiences are rarely foregrounded in popular understandings of police brutality." Thus, a campaign to **Say Her Name**—originating as a social media hashtag similar to the original incarnation of Black Lives Matter—has emerged in order to render visible the often-invisible victimization of Black girls and women.

This chapter ends with these two contemporary movements not only to challenge the gendered and racial contours of violence but also to push us to expand our social imaginations about how we imagine appropriate responses to violence. Expanding our social imagination is critical because criminal justice institutions often address the problem of violence by doubling down on gender difference in ways that exacerbate racial inequalities—and vice versa. Attention to how gender (alongside race, class, and other lines of difference) shapes violence does not simply illuminate the dynamics of violence per se—it also cautions us to resist the temptation to address violence with yet more violence.

KEYWORDS

Adversarial model of justice 111
Blame the victim myth 100
Boys will be boys 100
Bystander approach 116
Consensus-based justice 112
Cumulative violence 105
Custodial model 114
Embodied surveillance 115
Gender gap in violence 106
Ideal victim myth 100
Ideal victims 102
Intimate partner battering and its effects 113
Intimate partner violence 99
Lynchings 103
Masculine protectionism 109
Maternal model 114
Minneapolis Domestic Violence Experiment 110
Panopticon 114
Rape myths 100
Say Her Name 117
Second rape 101
Sexual violence 99
The Thug 102

QUESTIONS

- Despite a significant gender gap in violent offending, gender has often been overlooked in criminological theories. Should women's offending be theorized separately from men's, particularly as offending intersects with race and class?
- In a variety of ways, hegemonic masculinity—especially masculine protectionism—has been mobilized to compel men to intervene on behalf of women who are victimized or at risk of being victimized. What form have these campaigns taken, and how do they shake—or not—the foundations of sexual violence? How do such campaigns intersect with racial and class projects?
- Feminist scholars reveal that gender-specific technologies of punishment have long worked to deepen punitive control over women and men; consensus-based models of justice, however, suggest that punishment can be done differently. Considering the pitfalls that have beset projects to reform women's prisons, what should feminist punishment look like? Is punishment antithetical to feminist projects?
- In what ways do social forms of policing and punishment reflect gender dynamics (alongside race and class) in terms of the form control takes and who is targeted?

ASSOCIATED READINGS

- Brownmiller, Susan. (1975) 2013. *Against Our Will: Men, Women and Rape*. New York: Open Road Media.
- Chesney-Lind, Meda, and Lisa Pasko. 2013. *The Female Offender: Girls, Women, and Crime*. Thousand Oaks: SAGE.
- Haney, Lynne. 2010. *Offending Women: Power, Punishment, and the Regulation of Desire*. Berkeley: University of California Press.
- Madriz, Esther I. 1997. *Nothing Bad Happens to Good Girls: Fear of Crime in Women's Lives*. Berkeley: University of California Press.
- McCorkel, Jill A. 2003. "Embodied Surveillance and the Gendering of Punishment." *Journal of Contemporary Ethnography* 32 (1): 41–76.
- Messner, Michael A., Max A. Greenberg, and Tal Peretz. 2015. *Some Men: Feminist Allies and the Movement to End Violence against Women*. Oxford: Oxford University Press.
- Roychowdhury, Poulami. 2013. "'The Delhi Gang Rape': The Making of International Causes." *Feminist Studies* 39 (1): 282–292.

CHAPTER 7

Gendering Social Reproduction

Dawn Dow and Katherine Mason[1]

This chapter examines the intimate work of caring for and maintaining human life and society: social reproduction. The chapter is organized around a series of questions focusing on the how, who, *and* what *of social reproduction. The chapter begins by examining the case that is probably most familiar to the reader—the U.S.—but then expands to include other contexts. The chapter explores how societies throughout history and across cultures have handled the conception and bearing of children: the social organization of biological reproduction. It then investigates who is responsible for performing reproductive labor and how that work is impacted by ideas about gendered divisions of labor either inside or outside of the household. The chapter examines what social reproduction entails (i.e., which tasks or commitments it includes). Next, it outlines contemporary debates over changes in the* how, who, *and* what *of social reproduction and the potential consequences of those changes for society. The chapter concludes by encouraging readers to think critically about the assumptions they may have made about the characteristics of social reproduction in their own societies.*

Introduction

Within feminist sociology, *social reproduction* refers to the intimate work of caring for and maintaining human life and society (Glenn 1992; Hartmann 1981; Laslett and Brenner 1989). Social reproduction involves a wide range of tasks and responsibilities, and as most feminist scholars agree, it is both an everyday, microsocial practice and an intergenerational, macrosocial phenomenon. Social reproduction occurs through individuals, groups, and institutions. This chapter will treat **social reproduction** and **reproductive labor** as similar—but not identical—terms, pointing (respectively) to the phenomenon of how human beings and society are maintained and to the practical work this phenomenon entails.

Everyday reproductive labor includes the various tasks done to ensure people's physical and emotional well-being from one day to the next. These tasks include preparing and cleaning up after meals; making, cleaning, and/or purchasing clothing; scheduling medical appointments; caring for a sick child or adult; and helping people feel happy, fulfilled, and included within their families and communities. While every person needs these things—and no one person can fulfill these needs entirely on their own—the labor connected to social reproduction is especially critical for people who need more help in meeting these needs: children, the elderly, and people with certain disabilities and/or chronic illnesses. Intergenerational reproductive labor ensures the health and functioning of human society, particularly by creating and sustaining new life—babies—and by socializing children and caring for ill or aging family members. Without these activities, people would not be able to participate in productive labor. Thus, social reproduction acts as the glue that holds society together from one generation to the next.

Through these activities, society is reproduced at the microsocial level by sustaining individual human lives on a daily basis and at the macrosocial level by engaging in generational reproduction: sustaining the species, its knowledge, and its institutions. Just as the concept of human reproduction points to the fact that the human species continues—even as individual humans are born and then die—social reproduction refers to active process through which human society is sustained: not by remaining static and unchanging, but through the ongoing work of individuals and communities. And similar to human reproduction, the fact that society must be reproduced over time opens up the possibility that—as with human life—societies can change and evolve.

Social reproduction is necessary and inevitable if humans are to continue as a species. How people organize the work of social reproduction, however, is not inevitable. As the next sections show, the West—and other societies—provide individuals and communities with a range of guidelines, societal norms, and taken-for-granted assumptions about how social reproduction should be performed and by whom. These norms vary from one society to another and during different historical eras. Norms are also reinforced through cultural images and expectations (see Chapter 3) as well as through legal and material incentives that reward some arrangements of reproductive labor and penalize others.

The remainder of this chapter is organized around a series of questions that focuses on the how, who, and what of social reproduction. First, the chapter asks *how* societies throughout history and across cultures have handled the conception and bearing of children: the social organization of biological reproduction. From there, the chapter explores *who* is held responsible for performing reproductive labor and *what* social reproduction entails (i.e., which tasks or commitments it includes). Finally, the chapter examines contemporary debates over changes in the *how*, *who*, and *what* of social reproduction and the potential consequences of those changes for society. In answering each of these questions, the chapter will begin by examining the area that is probably most familiar to the reader—the U.S.—but will expand to include other contexts.

The Social Organization of Biological Reproduction: Historical and Global Perspectives

Human sexual reproduction involves, at its origin, the meeting of egg and sperm to form a zygote. Yet this process is simultaneously biological and social. Whose sperm and eggs are meeting? Where are they meeting—in a fallopian tube or a test tube? How are they meeting—through traditional heterosexual intercourse involving a penis and vagina or through medical interventions such as artificial insemination or other assisted reproductive technologies? And are the people who contributed genetic material considered parents? As societies around the globe and in different historical eras offer different answers to these questions, they contribute to the **social organization of biological reproduction**: the social arrangements for conception, pregnancy, childbirth, and breastfeeding. This section asks *how* these social arrangements determine *who* will perform these tasks and *what* they typically entail.

In most times and places, women have been held responsible for pregnancy and breastfeeding by virtue of their biology. Indeed, one common argument is that women's and men's different roles in sexual reproduction are the basis for all other sex differences: Most adult women's bodies are capable of conceiving and bearing children, and most men's are not. The "just-so" story of the gendered division of labor within families follows this logic: Women's reproductive capacities make them well-suited to caring for children and other family members, and men must take on the remaining work of protecting and providing for the family (e.g., Luker 1985; Ortner 1972; Parsons and Bales 1955). This perspective also holds that biological motherhood and the subsequent work of caring for one's own genetic descendants is an essential, defining feature of womanhood.

In contrast, fatherhood ideologies often define fathers as men who take financial and legal responsibility for a child, placing less emphasis on genetic ties. As Rene Almeling and Miranda Waggoner (2013) point out, most scholarship on reproduction focuses on women. After all, "it is within [women's] bodies that conception, gestation, and birth occur" (822). Under English common law—which contributed significantly to the U.S. legal system—the "presumption of paternity" means that children born to a married woman are automatically presumed to be her husband's offspring. By default, a husband is listed as the legal father on a child's birth certificate even if the mother was impregnated by a man other than her husband (assuming no one requests a genetic paternity test), and even when the couple used donor sperm to conceive. Thus, whereas the existence of a genetic tie between mother and child remains critical to many contemporary understandings of motherhood, the same is not equally true for fathers.

As with caregiving, biological reproduction is necessary on both an individual level (every person began life as an embryo that developed during a pregnancy and was born) and a societal level (without it, the species would end). Yet, as with caregiving, it is social arrangements—not simple biology—that determine who will perform this work and what it will entail.

Adoption and Fosterage: Decoupling Biological Reproduction from Child-Rearing

Despite the popular expectation—particularly in the U.S.—that women will share a maternal bond with their biological children, social arrangements across many societies and eras separate the biological process of creating a child from the identity of mother. This distinction becomes clear when examining the case of adoption. When a woman surrenders her child for formal adoption, the state generally terminates her social and legal status as mother to that child, even as her biological ties to the child remain. Many adoptive families and children use special language to denote this relationship, distinguishing between "adoptive parents" (who assume legal and financial responsibility for a child) and "birth parents."

Furthermore, not every woman with an unplanned or unwanted pregnancy is equally likely to put a baby up for adoption (and thus to become a "birth mother"). In the mid-20th century, before abortion was legalized in the U.S., Rickie Solinger (1994) found significant racial differences in adoption: White teens who became pregnant were encouraged to give up their children for adoption, while Black teens were steered toward keeping their children. The reason, Solinger found, was that U.S. society had racialized views of motherhood and children. White children were comparatively easy to find adoptive homes for; social workers often urged young white women to give up their children for adoption in order to avoid the stigma of having a child outside of marriage. In contrast, Black babies had a harder time getting adopted, and their biological mothers were stereotyped as sexually promiscuous but also as natural, loving mothers. Thus, it was seen as pointless for social workers to try to intervene and remove Black children from their mothers. The result was a racially differentiated view of motherhood: For white women, pregnancy and childbirth could now be separated from the social status of *mother*; for Black women, the two remained connected.

In addition to legal adoption, many communities in the U.S. and in other countries arrange for the care of children by extended family or other adults when biological parents are unable or unwilling to do this work themselves. These arrangements are often informal, as in the case of "**othermothers**" in African American communities—aunts, grandmothers, and community matriarchs who look after children in their neighborhoods (Collins 2000).

Outside of the U.S. context, in several African societies that have traditionally practiced polygyny (one husband with multiple wives)—for example, Nigeria (Ware 1979), Cote d'Ivoire (Jacoby 1995), and Sierra Leone (Bledsoe 1993)—biological mothers regularly send their children to be fostered by other households. Caroline Bledsoe (1993) found that among the mothers in polygynous relationships she studied, 34% of their children were currently living in another home, and 39% of the children in the women's households were not their own offspring (179). Women engage in this practice for multiple reasons: to protect a favored child from jealous co-wives and/or to secure educational and financial advantages for their children.

Outsourcing Reproduction and Reproducing Inequality

In the cases above, a biological mother gives the care of her offspring to another because she is unwilling or unable to care for the child herself or because she believes the child will have better opportunities in another household. In other cases, people may be the biological and/or social parents of their children but depend on others to perform some of the biological elements of reproduction for them.

One of the oldest variants of this "outsourced reproductive labor" is wet nursing, the practice of breastfeeding by a woman who is not a child's biological parent. Wet nurses, women actively lactating after having a child of their own, were critical—particularly before the invention of commercial infant formula—for feeding infants whose mothers had died or who had insufficient milk supply. These women tend to be drawn from lower social and economic strata than those of the children they nourish: poor women (Apple 1987; Scheper-Hughes 1987), slaves (Roberts 1997), and colonial subjects (Stoler 2002). Like other forms of caregiving, wet nursing is both necessary to life (in the absence of modern infant formula) and treated as unskilled, low-status labor.

As noted above, when elements of human reproduction are outsourced, those who take on the labor tend to come from lower social and economic strata. For example, it was not uncommon for wealthy European and colonial families to hire poor or colonized women as wet nurses and nursemaids. Yet such families also worried about the possible contaminating influences of these women. Commercial infant formula makers drew on these fears when marketing their product in the 19th century, claiming that "wet nurses are not selected from the highly-intelligent classes" (Apple 1987: 15). In the Dutch East Indies and colonial Hawaii, native nurses were told to hold children away from their bodies to prevent children from smelling like the women's sweat (Stoler 2002). Meanwhile,

> Virtually every medical and household handbook in the Dutch, French, and British colonies warned against leaving small children in the unsupervised care of local servants. . . . Precautions had to be taken against "sexual danger," against the uncleanly habits of domestics, against a "stupid negress" who might leave a child exposed to the sun. Even in colonies where the climate was not considered unhealthy, European children supposedly thrived well "only up to the age of six," when native cultural influences came into stronger play. Thus in late-nineteenth-century Hawaii, native nursemaids commonly looked after American children until the age of five. (Stoler 2002: 74)

Throughout history and across cultures, a common theme is that biological parents of unequal social status have had unequal rights over their children. In Europe, from ancient Rome up to the mid-19th century, children were considered the legal property of their fathers. In the case of parental separation or divorce, fathers—not mothers—were given preference in custody arrangements (Kelly 1994). This reflected the fact that women lacked full citizenship rights, with legal restrictions on their ability to own property or participate in politics. Even more restricted were the parental rights of slaves who bore children in the pre-Civil War United States. American laws dating back to the 17th century decreed that any child born to a slave—regardless of who the father was—would be a slave as well, the legal property of the mother's owner. This is also why sexual relationships between free white women and enslaved Africans were so heavily policed. In other words, social status, not mere biological parentage, often determined one's ability to be recognized as a parent to a child.

The biological elements of human reproduction—including conception, gestation/pregnancy, childbirth, and breastfeeding/infant feeding—are objective and necessary aspects of reproduction. Yet the *meanings* of these biological processes (and the social roles and status of the people who perform them) vary considerably across cultures and historical eras.

Who Is Responsible for Social Reproduction? Historical and Global Perspectives

The social institution most commonly associated with reproductive labor is the *family*, typically made up of people who have blood and/or legal ties to one another and who share a household. In the U.S., popular images of the "traditional family" further specify what that family will look like: a married heterosexual couple, with 2.5 children, and perhaps a dog or cat as the family pet. In this version of the family, fathers work outside of the home as breadwinners, and mothers stay at home to care for their children and the household, even if assisted by (typically female, non-white and/or working class) household staff.

Most Americans believe that this family form of parents and their immediate children, often referred to as the **nuclear family** (Parsons and Bales 1955), has existed for a long period of time, but it is actually a modern creation (Coontz 1993). In the premodern United States and Europe, households worked collectively to provide for the physical, emotional, and material needs of their members, as described in Chapter 1. These family units were larger in size and often stretched beyond the nuclear family to include extended kin: grandparents, adult siblings, cousins, and so on. As Laura Ingalls Wilder (1935) depicts in her *Little House on the Prairie* series of novels, farming families in the preindustrial U.S. relied on the labor of women, men, adults, and children working together to harvest food, produce garments to wear in their day-to-day lives, and craft household sundry items. Economic labor also occurred in small shops. Although men and women often engaged in different tasks, the home was a site of both reproductive and economic labor. These social arrangements were reinforced by laws and policies. For example, women and children were not only viewed as loved ones but were legally defined as the chattel of the family patriarch because of their material contributions to the family's well-being. Indeed, people were encouraged to have large families to increase their wealth and guard against infant mortality.

During the onset of the Industrial Revolution in the mid-19th century, economic labor moved out of the household and into factories. Yet women and children alike continued to be valued for their economic contributions, and they worked alongside men in factories and mills. The nursery rhyme "The Girls and Boys Come Out to Play" depicts a different version of childhood than the one commonly imagined in the contemporary U.S.

> Girls and boys, come out to play,
>
> The moon doth shine as bright as day;

Leave your supper, and leave your sleep,

And come with your playfellows into the street. (Halliwell 1844: 203)

As this rhyme illustrates, during the Industrial Revolution, it was common for children to work at home or in factories during the day and to have only a brief period of playtime in the evening. It was not until the Great Depression that legal restrictions were placed on child labor in the form of the Fair Labor Standards Act. During this period, social norms about the form and characteristics of childhood and adolescence were created and transformed into something that more closely resembles the norms that are present today.

As explained in Chapter 1, industrialization led to changes not only in the role of children but also in the meanings of family and the relationships between women and men. During this time, the work of producing necessary goods and services moved out of the household and into the public workplace, where it was labeled *productive labor*. This new economy was organized around large-scale economic activities such as factory work, mining, and industrial agriculture. These workers did not own the things they produced but were instead compensated for their labor with a wage that they could use to purchase the goods and services they needed. At the same time, private households remained responsible for meeting the immediate needs of their members through the provision of emotional support, maintenance of clothing, and preparation of nutritious food, all of which sustained family members from day to day and from one generation to the next. This work is known as *reproductive labor* and results in social reproduction.

This new division of labor had significant consequences for gender relations both within and outside the family, as two new, highly gendered, raced, and classed ideologies emerged: the *cult of domesticity* and *separate spheres*. The **separate spheres ideology** held that men should specialize in being breadwinners—the primary economic providers for the household—by earning a family wage in the "public" sphere of paid work. Women, meanwhile, were consigned to the "private" sphere as mothers and homemakers, which rendered their labor invisible within the home (Hays 1996; Landry 2000; Williams 2001). Within the household, the cult of domesticity emphasized that women should exemplify four key virtues: piety, purity, submissiveness, and domesticity (Landry 2000; Welter 1966; Williams 2001).

With this ideological backdrop in place, mid-20th-century academic work and popular culture such as *Leave It to Beaver* and *Father Knows Best* depicted the stay-at-home mother and breadwinning father as the ideal. The term *nuclear family* was coined by sociologists Talcott Parsons and Robert Bales in 1955 to describe a new family form that emerged following the end of World War II, when the United States experienced enormous economic prosperity. During this period, many men's salaries increased, enabling them to earn what is often referred to as a **family wage** (as described in Chapter 1): a wage large enough to permit a man's spouse to stay at home without contributing to their home through any form of market activity. Simultaneously, family size continued to decrease; lower infant mortality rates meant that women need not bear so many children as insurance against child death, and married women's increasing access to birth control offered them the ability to manage their fertility.

The ideal of the nuclear family was not uniformly accepted by all women, and many wrote sharply against what it implied for women's lives. In addition to Betty Friedan, discussed in Chapter 3, who described the life of a 1950s housewife (a life devoted to social reproduction) as "the problem without a name," French philosopher Simone de Beauvoir insisted that true happiness arises through one's participation in "exploits or projects that serve as a mode of transcendence" ([1949] 1989: xxxiv) rather than by navigating the "brutish life of subjection to given conditions" (xxxv). In other words, a rich, meaningful life can be achieved only through an active life of the mind; the mundane, repetitive work of attending to human bodies and their needs offers no such fulfillment.

However, it is important to note that the nuclear family, even as it was contested and critiqued by emerging feminist scholars and activists, was primarily attainable by middle- and upper-middle class white families. Recall from Chapter 1 that it was not the reality for many working-class white families and families of color (Coontz 1993). Many African American men and other men of color were prevented from earning a family wage because of various forms of employment discrimination. Thus, many women from working-class families and families of color continued to engage in paid labor inside and outside of the family, often in the households of other women, to contribute economically to their households (Glenn 1992).

Although the nuclear family is often presented as the ideal in the U.S., many families have deviated from it for a range of reasons. Some people belong to cultural traditions that value extended family and community ties, while others idealize the nuclear family but face material conditions that prevent them from embodying it. For example, African American families have a long history of multigenerational households and extended family networks. This extended family tradition existed in the West African countries from which enslaved Africans were transported and continued to be a necessity during the period of American chattel slavery. During the antebellum period, slaves' family ties were not recognized—spouses were separated and children were sold from their families to other slaveholders and raised by other women.

Today, legal slavery no longer exists, but other structural and economic factors affect the forms that African American families take. In the U.S., employment discrimination—combined with mass incarceration in the nation with the largest prison population in the world, where as many as 1 in 3 Black men will be incarcerated at some point in their lives—often prevents African American men from earning a family wage and providing for their families (The Sentencing Project 2013). Working women often rely on female relatives and community members to care for children during men's absences. Indeed, Patricia Hill Collins (2000) argues in *Black Feminist Thought* that relying on the nuclear family form could be problematic, underscoring that African American women have

> recognized that vesting one person with full responsibility for mothering a child may not be wise or possible. As a result, othermothers—women who assist bloodmothers by sharing mothering responsibilities—traditionally have been central to the institution of Black motherhood. (178)

Dorothy Roberts (2002) adds,

> In the early part of the [20th] century, Black people relied primarily on extended family networks and community resources such as churches, women's clubs, and benevolent societies to take care of children whose parents were unable to meet their needs. (7)

In addition, within families of color, a clear-cut gendered division of labor does not exist; women and girls often share the tasks of reproductive labor with men and boys.

Some social scientists have pointed out that families that utilize extended family networks often fare better economically than their nuclear family counterparts (Sennett 1970). However, the dominant perspective among American social scientists in the 1960s, most notably from Oscar Lewis (1959) and Daniel Patrick Moynihan (1965), suggested that racial and ethnic minorities' use of kin networks for reproductive labor, which challenged the dominance of the nuclear family, was a maladaptive strategy, calling such networks part of the culture of poverty and the result of a tangle of pathology. Many of these same social scientists viewed practices such as pooling resources to provide a social safety net as normal or desirable within nuclear families—when husbands and wives share a bank account, for example, or when one partner goes back to school and is financially supported by their spouse. Yet when they took place within extended minority families and communities, these same activities were deemed pathological. While Moynihan's infamous report—*The Negro Family: The Case for National Action*—is most often read as an expression of racist views toward Black families and communities, it may also signal a deep American discomfort with the possibility of communal, public responsibility for reproductive labor. Indeed, the nationwide legalization of same-sex marriage may represent a relatively conservative impulse toward compromise: While legalized same-sex marriage does allow for greater diversity in the gender composition of married couples, it may also steer queer families toward a nuclear, rather than extended, notion of kinship and reproductive labor.

Even as there is this conservative push to encourage families to conform to the nuclear family form, scholars have noted that the extended family continues to play a key role in helping many families manage work and family duties (Higginbotham and Weber 1992; Kamo 2000; Lee and Aytac 1998; Meyer 2014; Sarkisian, Gerena, and Gerstel 2007). Grandparents are increasingly taking on the role of primary caregiver for their grandchildren (Gibson 2005; Taylor, Livingston, Parker, Wang, and Dockterman 2010). Indeed, in recent years, more than 1 in 10 grandparents in the U.S. have become primary caregivers for grandchildren for six months or more and many for much longer periods (Fuller-Thomson, Minkler, and Driver 1997).

Overwhelmingly, in the U.S. context, the family members that are expected to take on the work of social reproduction and caregiving are women: sometimes grandmothers, sisters, and aunts, but primarily wives and mothers (and in the case of caring for elderly relatives, daughters). And most people believe this is as it should be. Data from the 2012 General Social Survey (GSS) show that, when asked about how families should arrange for the care of children too young to attend school, the majority of U.S.

respondents (57.3%) said that families should be the ones to provide childcare. Also, when asked how such care should be organized, nearly 42% of respondents said that a father should work full time and the mother part time; almost as many people (39.7%) said mothers should stay at home (GSS 2012).

Yet, fewer mothers stay home today than in the past. Accordingly, public views on working mothers have become somewhat more permissive, shifting away from a preference for full-time stay-at-home mothering to an expectation that mothers will work part time. In 1985, more than half of Americans believed that young children would suffer if they had a mother who worked outside of the home; by 2012, only about a third of survey respondents agreed with this statement, and almost 60% described the ideal situation as one in which mothers worked part time or full time (Cohn, Livingston, and Wang 2014). According to research from the Pew Research Center, 6 out of 10 working moms, if given the choice, would prefer to work part time. Some scholars suggest that women were largely pushed into the public sphere of work because of a shifting economic structure and wage deflation in the 1970s and 1980s that demanded dual-earner families to maintain middle-class living standards (*Inequality for All* 2013). Others point to ideological shifts produced by the U.S. Women's Rights Movement of the 1960s that encouraged new groups of women to pursue paid employment outside of the home. Still others would point to a combination of factors, including the lack of paid parental leave in the U.S. or job protection when taking a leave of absence to care for children.

These shifting beliefs and patterns of paid work matter for the question of who does reproductive labor. In 1965, married men spent approximately 4.7 hours on weekly household chores while married women spent 33.9 hours on housework every week (7.2 times the work that men did) (Bianchi, Sayer, Milkie, and Robinson 2012). Over the next several decades, women increasingly began to work for pay—demanding equal pay in the workplace and equal partnership in the home—and time spent on housework changed: In 2010, married women spent 17.8 hours per week on housework and married men spent 10.3 hours (Bianchi et al. 2012). Thus, although the gap has decreased, women continue to spend significantly more time on household chores than men. Arlie Hochschild ([1989] 2003, 1997) also points out that this decrease in women's household labor has coincided with both an increase in convenience items that make meal preparation easier and the increasing ability to outsource tasks once completed in the home. Thus, although men are doing more than in the past, Hochschild finds that women continue to be more engaged in the activities associated with social reproduction either by directly doing them or by coordinating their completion. This remains true even in dual-earner couples and in heterosexual married couples in which the wife earns more than the husband.

Until this point, this section has primarily focused on social reproduction in the U.S., but there is substantial variation in how the tasks of social reproduction are carried out in different countries and during different time frames. Some countries enact social reproduction in ways that align with the United States; others, where there is more inequality (such as Bolivia or India), rely on paid domestic workers to do the bulk of this work (Ray and Qayum 2009); and yet others embrace a more communal approach because children are thought to belong not only to parents but also to the community.

A division of household labor similar to that in the U.S. exists in other Western countries. Jonas Edlund and Ida Öun (2016) studied five European countries and found that while the exact proportions varied, "women do a majority of the unpaid labor in all of the countries," including Poland, Germany, Denmark, Finland, and Sweden (154). Even more than in the U.S., respondents in these countries favored what Edlund and Öun call a "one-and-a-half earner model," (158) with one parent working full time and one working part time—and the general expectation is that women will be the ones working part time.

Some countries encourage a different gendered division of social reproduction by mandating paid paternity leave through laws and policies. Indeed, compared to other modern Western societies, the U.S. appears to be an anomaly—some might even term U.S. parental leave policies draconian. In 1993, the U.S. passed the Family and Medical Leave Act (FMLA) to provide some job security and unpaid leave to people caring for children and sick family members. However, people's ability to take such leave is limited both by the characteristics of their employer (small businesses and the staff of elected officials are exempt from the law) and by financial pressures. Although they are permitted to take this leave with some degree of job security, unless they live in one of the few states with paid family leave through disability insurance or other programs, they may not be able to afford to live without their income.

At the time of this chapter's publication, the United States was the only member of the Organization for Economic Cooperation and Development (OECD)—a group of 35 of the most highly developed capitalist democracies in the world—that did not mandate paid parental leave for its citizens at the national level following the birth of a child (OECD Family Database 2016).[2]

Cultural beliefs and laws affect how childcare is divided within nuclear families in different nations. As mentioned above, some cultures prioritize other family forms besides the nuclear family, which expands the range of childcare arrangements that families might make. Several African nations, including Nigeria (Ware 1979), Sierra Leone (Bledsoe 1993), and Cote d'Ivoire (Jacoby 1995), have a cultural history of polygyny: polygamous marriages composed of one man and multiple wives. Under these arrangements, women tend to engage in economic activity and receive only limited financial support from their husbands, which is usually reserved for their children. While these women may occasionally share child-rearing duties with their co-wives, it is more common for them to send school-aged children to be fostered by their sisters and other female relatives and to care for those relatives' children in turn (Bledsoe 1993: 179). In contemporary China, meanwhile, dominant cultural ideologies of filial piety—children's duty to respect and care for their parents—contribute to high numbers of households where three or more generations are present. Indeed, as Chen, Liu, and Mair (2011) find, not only do aging parents continue to live with their adult children, but these grandparents also now play a key role in caring for and socializing their grandchildren, freeing the parents to work full time.

Given these examples, it is clear that societies have answered the question of who is responsible for social reproduction in different ways.

What Does Reproductive Labor Entail?

A 2008 commercial for Electrolux appliances begins on the set of talk show host Kelly Ripa's television program with Ripa dashing offstage to head home and spend time with her family. As the theme song of the 1960s show *Bewitched* plays in the background, the petite, blonde Ripa begins to prepare dinner for her family with a voiceover narration:

> How do I entertain a packed house? With my Electrolux appliances! Now I can cook the roast for the dinner party *and* the mac and cheese for the sleepover, simmer the chocolate sauce, toss Chuck [the dog] his toy, serve the Gummy Bears and the apple juice—at the perfect temperature—be the charming co-host, clean the stemware perfectly, and end the night looking for monsters under the bed! . . . With [these appliances], you can be even more amazing! ("Kelly Ripa's Electrolux Commercial" 2008)

With an annual salary estimated at $20 million in 2016 (not counting additional income from her work in television commercial advertisements), Kelly Ripa is the primary breadwinner in her household. Yet this commercial shows her single-handedly (with the help of her appliances) feeding, entertaining, and cleaning up after her three children and guests. Not only is she doing these tasks, but she is doing them on time and with attention to guests' preferences (apple juice at the perfect temperature). In other words, she is doing reproductive labor.

Ripa's actions—attentive care to the needs of her children and guests, providing food, and offering emotional reassurance ("looking for monsters under the bed")—fit within the framework of what Sharon Hays calls *intensive mothering*. The **intensive mothering ideology**, which Hays describes as the dominant vision of contemporary 20th-century U.S. motherhood, "tells us that children are innocent and priceless, that their rearing should be carried out primarily by individual mothers and that it should be centered on [the] children's needs, with methods that are informed by experts, [and are] labor-intensive, and costly" (Hays 1996: 21). This notion that child-rearing requires an intense, constant focus on cultivating a child is not a universal truth but rather a relatively recent ideological development in the West. With significant proportions of mothers now working part or full time, it is an ideal that is out of reach for most. Yet even when children are well provided for and safe, the intensive mothering ideology insists that they are best served by having a mother who will stay home and attend to their needs and development. A father, another family member, or a paid caregiver simply will not do.

Intensive mothering takes place within the context of what Dorothy Smith (1993) calls the "standard North American family," which—like Parsons and Bales' earlier formulation of the idealized nuclear family—features a heterosexual couple legally bound in marriage where the husband earns a family wage and the wife's financial contributions are supplemental at best; her primary duties are to care for the husband, household, and children. As Smith points out, other institutions such as workplaces and schools are structured based on the assumption that workers and children will live in such families. This assumption leads to the paradox that surfaces in the advertisement mentioned above: Despite her demanding, successful career, Kelly Ripa is shown as still responsible for the household labor of feeding and caring for the family, a burden Arlie Hochschild and Anne Machung ([1989] 2003) have famously termed the "second shift."

The intensive mothering ideology that dominates mainstream American culture prescribes not only *who* should do this work but also *what* should be done and *how*. This ideology puts children's needs before those of other family members and suggests that no price—financial, emotional, or otherwise—is too high to pay to ensure children's optimal development.

In the past, different ideologies of motherhood—as well as changing economic and technological conditions—shaped the varying contents of reproductive labor. As Susan Strasser ([1982] 2000) describes, reproductive labor in the preindustrial era tended to involve a great deal of hard, physical labor in the form of housework: fetching water for cooking and washing, doing laundry by hand, growing and preserving food, sewing and mending clothing, and cleaning kerosene lamps for reuse (p. 3). The Industrial Revolution brought many labor-saving devices—including 1950s-era washing machines and vacuums and, eventually, the shiny appliances that Kelly Ripa advertises. Interestingly, as time spent on some household tasks decreased, expectations for mothers' work in other areas increased. Strasser cites the text of one electric company advertisement for its labor-saving products: "This is the test of a successful mother—she puts first things first. She does not give to sweeping the time that belongs to her children" (p. 78). As this advertisement shows, so-called labor-saving technologies of the industrial era served less to *reduce* reproductive labor and more to *redirect* it, shifting women's energies from physical care of the household to the emotional care of their children.

Indeed, as the physical demands of basic provision for the family decreased—particularly for households with sufficient wealth to afford these new technologies—a legion of experts began generating additional guidelines for how women should care for their children and households. And so, the standard of care was raised. With the advent of indoor plumbing, standards for cleanliness and hygiene increased; home economists urged women to practice "scientific housekeeping" by eliminating germs from their households; and the once-simple, repetitive meals of the preindustrial era were replaced by demands that housewives produce varied and nutritious meals tailored to the tastes of their families (Ehrenreich and English [1978] 2005).

These heightened standards for housekeeping were joined by similarly heightened expectations for child-rearing. As in the field of home economics, formally trained experts—often physicians or government health workers—developed curricula designed to replace maternal instinct with scientifically validated child-rearing procedures (Apple 1987; Ehrenreich and English [1978] 2005). These new standards intensified the demands of motherhood and reproductive labor, laying the groundwork for the contemporary ideology of intensive mothering that Sharon Hays describes.

Given the many increasingly burdensome demands of reproductive labor, it was hard for many women to live up to these ideological standards. Carolyn Kay Steedman, writing about her working-class childhood in England, recalls the shaming words of a welfare caseworker who visited their threadbare home: "This house isn't fit for a baby" (Steedman 1986: 2). For women of means, however, there was another way: hired help (Glenn 1992; Rollins 1987). White middle-class women often sought to meet their household responsibilities by hiring women of color or white working-class women as domestic servants, who were often also mothers. The practice of employing domestic help allowed these women to perform the more enjoyable aspects of social reproduction or even, in some cases, to work outside the home. In this case, the contents of reproductive labor shifted again. Even as these women no longer performed the physical tasks themselves, they remained responsible for making sure that those jobs were done—and done well—by someone else. For more on paid domestic labor, see Chapter 8.

Motherhood ideologies shifted once again during World War II, when the U.S. government called on women to take up men's places in factories. In various propaganda films, the state asserted that good womanhood—specifically, being a good wife and mother—meant supporting men through engagement in industrial production (Field 1980). Mothers who answered that call often enlisted the help of other relatives (usually their own mothers) or paid help, delegating some of the work of reproductive labor in the process. Ladies' magazines published recipes that emphasized speed and ease of cooking to free up women's time to help out with the war effort. As Connie Field's 1980 documentary, *The Life and Times of Rosie the Riveter*, shows, those messages abruptly changed once the war reached its end. Postwar propaganda advertising framed working women as irresponsible mothers who were failing to fulfill their social reproduction duties—some such films included images of unsupervised children playing in traffic or smoking. Of course, women had remained responsible for reproductive labor throughout the war years; what changed was the intensity and the amount of time they were expected to devote to that work.

Today, the intensive mothering ideology continues to shape the contents of reproductive labor in ways that make this work take more of women's time, resources, or both. Examples of these intensive mothering practices include homeschooling children (Lois 2006); devising frugal but time-intensive cooking and crafting projects (Davis 2014; Lois 2006); and eschewing vaccinations in favor of breastfeeding and eating organic foods (Reich 2014). Indeed, scholars such as Norah MacKendrick (2014) and Katherine Mason (2016) each find that these practices begin before and during pregnancy. MacKendrick (2014) examines women's precautionary use of natural cosmetics and cleaning products during pregnancy to minimize fetal exposure to synthetic chemicals. Mason (2016) finds that women adopt pregnant body care practices that include stress management, consumption of the "right" diet and vitamins, and attending prenatal exercise and birth classes. In these ways and more, contemporary intensive mothering ideologies frame motherhood—and even the months leading up to motherhood—as requiring significant time investment and expertise.

In sum, the point of intensive mothering as an ideology is that it is time-intensive and child-focused and often appears incompatible with mothers' paid work (or, at least, it creates a great deal of potential conflict between mothers' work roles and their roles as mothers at home—what Hays calls the *cultural contradictions of motherhood*). Yet this notion of mothering and reproductive labor is not universal—views of sufficient or morally correct child care and reproductive labor vary tremendously across historical eras and cultures.

Dawn Marie Dow (2016c) uncovered an alternative ideology of motherhood among middle- and upper-middle class African American mothers who did not feel accountable to the intensive mothering ideology. These mothers embraced what Dow labeled **integrated motherhood**: an ideology of motherhood that assumed mothers should work outside of the home, be financially self-reliant, and have support in raising their children from spouses and other family and community members. This research underscored that African American middle-class mothers often confront different cultural expectations from within their communities and from mainstream white society about the place of work and family in their lives. These expectations prompt them to view paid employment as a key duty of motherhood.

Dow (2016d) found that the reproductive labor that African American middle- and upper-middle-class mothers perform includes elements not found in white mothering ideologies: protecting sons and daughters, often in different ways, from racism. Even though these mothers often could afford nannies or daycare centers, they instead preferred childcare provided by extended kin or community members out of a desire to protect their children from earlier experiences of racism (Dow 2016a; Uttal 1996). Similarly, African American homeschoolers often decide to educate their children at home because they are prompted by different concerns than those of white homeschoolers, such as a desire to protect their children from school-related experiences of racism (Mazama and Lundy 2012). This research demonstrates that the tasks associated with social reproduction vary based upon the social location of families and their perceptions of the challenges they and their children will confront in the broader society.

Outside of the U.S., there exists even more variation in the meanings and content of reproductive labor. One account of this variation appears in anthropologist Nancy Scheper-Hughes' account of motherhood in rural Northeast Brazil in the 1960s. While living in a poverty-stricken shantytown, Scheper-Hughes met a mother named Lourdes, whose son, Ze, was dying from acute malnutrition. Frustrated with Lourdes' indifference to Ze's declining health, Scheper-Hughes brought him to a local daycare center run by community women. There, however, she encountered a similar attitude: The women at the center "agree[d] with Lourdes that here was a baby with a ghost of a chance. Leave him alone, they cautioned. It makes no sense to fight with death" (Scheper-Hughes 1989: 10). To Scheper-Hughes, an American scholar, this response seemed to be the opposite of reproductive labor: Instead of care, mothers in this community treated Ze with neglect. Upon reflection, however, she argues that the strategy of "benign neglect" she observed may be practical: Among women in desperate poverty, who experienced an average of 9.5 pregnancies over a lifetime, reproductive labor demanded that women prioritize caring for their children who stood the best chance of survival while neglecting those who were likely to die anyway (and who consumed valuable resources in the meantime).

In response to the question that began this section—What does reproductive labor entail?—a few key points emerge. First and foremost, the contents of reproductive labor are not static. Social reproduction generally involves caring for individuals and families to meet their daily physical and emotional needs, and it is also concerned with child-rearing and the maintenance of human beings and communities from one generation to the next. Within that broad mandate, however, specific tasks—and the meanings and intensity with which they are performed—vary considerably.

On one hand, reproductive labor varies in relation to the specific material conditions of a given household and society; just as Brazilian mothers' benign neglect of their children is a tactic necessitated by the desperately poor life circumstances within which they reside, so too did industrial-era mothers begin intensifying their child-rearing strategies as the strains of basic material provision began to subside.

On the other hand, the contents and meaning of reproductive labor also respond to political and cultural conditions, as anticipated by Chapter 1. Some authors (Bordo 1993; Faludi [1991] 2006; Wolf [1991] 2002) have suggested that standards for acceptable femininity—including beauty regimens and mothering responsibilities—become stricter when women begin to gain economic and political power. If meeting one's responsibilities at home is the precondition for women's entry into public life, then, these authors suggest, raising the bar for those responsibilities makes it harder for women to pursue careers or seek leadership positions (and diminishes their political and economic power as a result). Women for whom staying home is not an option—or who believe that reproductive labor and paid labor are not mutually exclusive—challenge intensive mothering ideals, but they may also face societal judgment for failing to embody those ideals. In addition to challenging dominant ideals of mothering, some mothers may feel accountable to different cultural ideals of motherhood (Dow 2016d) and view additional tasks as falling within the realm of reproductive labor (Dow 2016c; Mazama and Lundy 2012; Uttal 1996). In this way, the answer to the question of "What does reproductive labor entail?" is determined both by material conditions and by the prevailing political and social climate.

Debating Reproductive Labor

Thus far, the chapter has shown that reproductive labor in the U.S.—both currently and in the recent past—has been viewed as a responsibility of women more than men and of private families rather than of public institutions and government. The demands of that labor vary in relation to prevailing conditions, sometimes expanding the scope of women's responsibilities and, at other times, diminishing them to make room for other work and responsibilities. Given the constancy of women's ties to social reproduction, feminist debates about women's place in society at large have often been linked to discussions of women's family roles and reproductive labor. The following section explores some of those debates in the recent history of the U.S. and ends by looking ahead to the future of reproductive labor.

The Stalled Revolution: Persisting Gender Differences in Reproductive Labor

Feminist critiques of the separate spheres ideology and women's disproportionate responsibility for reproductive labor in the 1960s and 1970s led to significant changes in men's and women's roles in the family, as described above. Even as most women's roles and responsibilities expanded beyond reproductive labor and the work of meeting family members' day-to-day needs, those needs did not cease to exist. The questions then changed: How would women's increasing presence and permanence in the workplace impact the division of labor in the home? Who, if not women, would meet those needs? Were men ready to step up and perform half (or more) of the work of reproductive labor? And would employers adapt to a new type of worker who did not have a stay-at-home wife but who, instead, had responsibilities to family as well as to work?

Just as popular media from the 1980s and early 1990s reflect trends in women's work patterns, they also reflect slower-to-change societal views on men's reproductive labor. Films such as *3 Men and a Baby* (1987) and the TV shows such as *Full House* (1987–1995) and *My Two Dads* (1987–1990) featured men living together (but not romantically involved with one another) while acting as primary caregivers to their children, whether due to a mother's abandonment or to her death. This "bumbling dad" genre showed men to be loving, if often comically inept, caregivers for children. Even more tellingly, films such as *Mr. Mom* (1983) and *Mrs. Doubtfire* (1993) suggested that men must symbolically—or, in the case of Mrs. Doubtfire, practically—*become* women in order to be good parents to their children. These mixed messages about men's ability to parent continue into the present; describing young men's models for adulthood, Michael Kimmel (2008) writes, "Shows like *Everybody Loves Raymond* and *According to Jim* feature grown men being infantilized by their wives, unable to do the simplest things for themselves, clueless about their kids' lives" (26).

Taken as a snapshot of cultural attitudes, these popular media suggest that although people were beginning to consider the possibility of men taking on more responsibility for reproductive labor, they were not yet completely comfortable with the idea. Data from the 1980s suggest that men did start performing more home and childcare work, but that progress was uneven: Men did not take up as much housework as women dropped, and women still did more work at home than men. By 1995, women spent, on average, twice as many hours per week on housework as men did (Bianchi, Milkie, Sayer, and Robinson 2000). This led to a situation that Arlie Hochschild and Anne Machung ([1989] 2003) call "the second shift": Women were going to work for a "first shift," then spending nearly as much time at home (a "second shift") attending to reproductive labor and the needs of their families. Thus, while women's widespread entry into paid work constituted the first stage of a revolution in U.S. gender relations and family ideology, the persistent gender imbalance of responsibility in the home—and the failure of social institutions to adapt to women's paid work—led Hochschild to term it the *stalled revolution*.

Workplace policies in the 1980s made it difficult for couples to share parenting and household tasks equally. Prior to the FMLA, there was no federal right to parental leave. The 1978 Pregnancy Discrimination Act made it illegal to make employment decisions based on pregnancy or childbirth, but specific provisions for leave remained up to individual employers and states. The availability of employer-provided leave—whether paid or unpaid—increased throughout the 1980s, but women with higher levels of education were more likely to have the option of paid maternity leave (Smith, Downs, and O'Connell 2001). Some women, unable to figure out leave and childcare arrangements, quit their jobs after having their first child: Nearly 36% of working mothers did so in the first half of the 1980s, but that figure decreased in the second half of the decade to 27% (Smith et al. 2001). This pattern made men's breadwinning activities all the more necessary to the family.

Thus, the 1980s saw significant increases in women's participation in paid work, and popular culture seemed willing to consider—even if only in comedy for the time being—the possibility of men performing reproductive labor. Nevertheless, workplace and government policies slowed progress, pushing even egalitarian-minded couples to adopt more traditional roles once they had children.

The Mommy Wars and the "Opt-Out Revolution"

Despite changing gender demographics in the workplace and the reality that women and mothers of young children regularly work full time, scholars have identified a "stalled revolution." Shifts in government and employer policies to support working parents remain slow to adapt and often presume women will bear the brunt of child-rearing responsibilities. In 1993, Congress passed the FMLA, a federal law described earlier in this chapter that provides qualified workers with up to 12 weeks of *unpaid* leave to care for an ailing family member or to welcome the birth or adoption of a child.

However, policies such as the FMLA assume a family structure that increasingly does not match the reality for a growing number of American families that are headed by a single parent. The fact that FMLA leave is unpaid suggests that most households will have two working partners, one of whom—usually a man—will keep working while the other takes temporary leave to care for members of the family. Yet by 1995, 70% of married mothers were in the workforce in some capacity (U.S. Bureau of Labor Statistics 2014b), and their earnings were often critical to maintaining their family's economic stability.

Meanwhile, decisions about balancing work and family look different when households deviate from the nuclear family model. In 1980, only 18.6% of children were born to unmarried women; today, more than 40%

of all U.S. children are born to unmarried mothers. Though some of those women live with a partner or other family members, many are single parents who must act as both breadwinner *and* caregiver. Additionally, the divorce rate has increased from 2.6 divorces per 1,000 people in 1950 to 3.4 per 1,000 in 2012 (Centers for Disease Control and Prevention 2015), leading to an increase in divorced parents and stepfamilies raising children. Multigenerational households are also on the rise, making up 18.1% of U.S. households in 2008 (Livingston and Cohn 2015). Yet as family forms and configurations continue to change, sociological research suggests that having two incomes is critical to reproducing and maintaining middle-class households (*Inequality for All* 2013; Warren and Tyagi 2003). Arrangements for the work of social reproduction are intimately connected to the reproduction of status and inequality.

Given these competing devotions of work and family, productive and reproductive labor (Blair-Loy 2003) remain hot-button political issues in the 21st century. In 2006, Leslie Morgan Steiner published the bestselling anthology *Mommy Wars*, which chronicled contemporary debates over the contents of "good motherhood." These debates touched on the physical, emotional, political, economic, social, legal, and cultural elements of "good motherhood," highlighting in particular the divisions between two camps of mothers: stay-at-home and career moms. Women in each of these two camps—both made up primarily of middle-class and white mothers—defended their own lifestyles while critically evaluating the work and family choices of women in the other camp. On one hand, many women who bought into the Mommy Wars debates came to feel that no choice was above reproach and that to be a mother was inevitably to be judged as coming up short. On the other hand, non-white mothers, single mothers, and mothers of limited financial means perceived many of the choices of their more advantaged peers—the choice to hire a nanny, for example, or to leave the labor force—to be undesirable or impossible.

In recent years, a recurrent story has focused on the experiences of high-profile working mothers who step forward to describe the "real deal" of work and family balance. In 2003, Lisa Belkin published a now-infamous article, "The Opt-Out Revolution," which argued that women were not reaching the top ranks of corporations because they were choosing motherhood instead, "opting out" of power and opting in to reproductive labor. In 2012, Anne-Marie Slaughter, a former State Department policy director for the Obama administration, argued that the inflexible schedules and expectations of the typical workplace make it difficult, if not impossible, for mothers to balance work and family demands. As the title of her essay explained, these incompatibilities are "Why Women Still Can't Have It All."

These regular—even predictable—calls to arms about work/family balance continue because workplace norms still value the ideal of an unencumbered male worker and because existing policy remedies are insufficient. Although Slaughter may be right that women can't "have it all"—that is, they cannot satisfy mainstream expectations for good mothers and good workers at the same time—many women nevertheless "do it all," caring for children while working full time. This is particularly true for African American mothers, a greater percentage of whom work full time than women of any other racial/ethnic group, and it is also true for working-class and single mothers.

Such women often turn to extended kin networks for help with caregiving as a matter of preference, not only necessity (Dow 2015), and they will not benefit from solutions premised on having (or desiring) a nuclear family. Universal, high-quality childcare (as well as care for dependent adults) would alleviate the burdens of reproductive labor for those who need or wish to spend more time at work; on the other hand, paid parental leave for mothers, fathers, and other caregivers, along with flexible work schedules, would help make paid work more compatible with caregiving.

New Family Forms, New Forms of Social Reproduction? Legal and Technological Innovations

In recent years, a variety of legal and technological developments have contributed to further changes in the diversity of family forms and relationships. From assisted reproductive technologies to expanded legal recognition for nontraditional partnerships, these developments offer the possibility of changing the meanings and content of reproductive labor—but, in many cases, they may also mirror long-standing beliefs about who should do reproductive labor and what it should entail.

One of the most significant developments in contemporary definitions of *family* has been the gradual recognition of same-sex couples and their children (*Obergefell v. Hodges*, 576 U.S. ___ [2015]; see Chapter 5). According to estimates from the Williams Institute at the University of California, Los Angeles, 37% of lesbian, gay, bisexual, and transgender (LGBT)-identified Americans have had a child at some point in their adult lives, and—among single and partnered LGBT people under 50—35% are currently raising at least one child under 18. Nearly half (48%) of lesbians under age 50 are raising children (Gates 2013).

These changing family forms have potentially significant consequences for gender and reproductive labor. Among same-sex couples, sex alone cannot serve as the basis for dividing up household and child-rearing tasks. In many cases, this may lead to a more egalitarian or thoughtful strategies for dividing and allocating reproductive labor. However, Mignon Moore (2008) points out that, similar to heterosexual couples, gay and lesbian couples who adopt egalitarian strategies for housework and childcare usually do so because they have egalitarian ideologies; such couples tend to be college-educated and middle-class. Same-sex couples who do not prioritize a 50/50 division of household labor find criteria other than sex to determine who should be responsible for reproductive labor. Christopher Carrington (1999) found that many gay male couples in California assigned "kinwork" tasks such as keeping house, making social plans, and maintaining family ties through phone calls and holiday cards on the basis of income: When one partner earned less or worked only part time, he was more likely to take on the work historically associated with women and homemakers.

Moore (2008), who studied Black lesbian couples in New York, found that biological motherhood and gender identity/presentation were important determinants of the division of household labor. Women who had given birth to the couple's children handled more of the child-rearing, cooking, and cleaning. Furthermore, in lesbian couples where one partner identified more strongly as masculine or "butch," she was more likely to adopt stereotypically masculine household tasks, such as taking out the trash or doing household repairs. And Carla Pfeffer (2010) finds that in relationships between cisgender women and transgender men—even when both partners self-identify as feminist—women partners more frequently reported doing the bulk of household labor and caring for their partner's emotional needs. In other words, while queer couples challenge, through their very existence, the notion that reproductive labor is distinctively *female*, in many cases, they reproduce the association of reproductive labor with *femininity*. These couples often assign reproductive labor to partners who are not the primary breadwinner, who identify as feminine, or who have given birth to a child, thereby reproducing a version of a traditional gendered division of labor.

A second way in which gay, lesbian, and queer families challenge traditional norms of reproductive labor is by pursuing non-biolegal family relationships/fictive kin (people who are not related by blood nor legally recognized as family through marriage or adoption). Queer families were not the first to develop alternatives to the nuclear family norm of family and reproductive labor; many others, most notably lower-income Black communities (Chatters, Taylor, and Jayakody 1994), have also developed an expanded sense of family and community to counterbalance their social marginalization and the ramifications of families divided during slavery. As Terry Boggis (2001), director of New York's Lesbian and Gay Services Center's family program, writes, queer people have a long history of creating chosen families with or without children, often as a result of being cast out of their biolegal families. Christopher Carrington (1999) adds that these relationships nevertheless fulfill many of the traditional reproductive functions of family—hosting holiday celebrations, caring for members who fall ill, and providing financial support and security—even as their family forms are anything but traditional. In this way, queer families not only challenge gendered norms about who should be doing reproductive labor; they also challenge social norms about who should be the beneficiaries of reproductive labor. Specifically, queer kin networks provide a model for thinking about reproductive labor as a wider community responsibility.

Recent years have seen legal recognition of unconventional families in more ways than one. In addition to the legalization of same-sex marriage, local governments in a handful of places have begun recognizing the possibility of a child who has more than two parents. In late 2013, California passed a bill that would allow children born under special circumstances to have more than two legally recognized parents. This law was formulated in response to a case involving a biological mother, her lesbian partner, and the man with whom she had conceived a child who were involved in a series of custody disputes as the parents' relationships crumbled. One could easily imagine other scenarios where three (or more) adults decide to jointly raise a child, sharing parenting rights and responsibilities equally. In the Netherlands, one fivesome comprising a lesbian couple and a gay triad (three romantically involved men) is planning to raise a child together (Spanjer 2015). The law in the Netherlands does not allow all five to claim legal parenthood, but the group has decided on an informal, legally nonbinding plan to parent their child together. As this latter case shows, most alternative family forms remain extralegal and informal in nature, relying on community norms and good faith, rather than legal guarantees, for their stability.

In addition to changing social and legal developments affecting families, new reproductive technologies—which are social forms in the sense that they are the product of human societies—have the potential to influence the contents and allocation of reproductive labor. Some of these technologies offer prospective parents—particularly those dealing with infertility—the chance to outsource some or all of the labor of producing a child. Sperm banks and artificial insemination are available to women who wish to become pregnant without a fertile male partner; the resulting child often has no social connection to its biological father (though recent years have seen the rising popularity of "open" sperm donors, whom offspring can choose to contact once they turn 18 years old).

Similarly, gestational surrogates are women who agree to carry a pregnancy for an individual or couple, usually with financial compensation; the surrogate lacks the legal status of *mother*, and extensive legal contracts are designed to ensure the contracting parents' "ownership" of the child. In some cases, individuals and couples choose to pursue parenthood through a surrogate because they wish to have a child who is biologically related to one or both partners, but they lack the ability to carry a pregnancy (whether due to infertility or to being a gay couple). In other cases, the contracting parent may be able to become pregnant but chooses not to do so. These recent advances in reproductive technology allow for both greater social distance between biological/gestational parents and the people who will raise children—such that the parties may come from different social locations and need never meet—and greater geographic distance, such that the work of gestational surrogacy and sperm/egg donation may be outsourced to people in distant parts of the world.

Still other social and technological arrangements in the U.S. and around the world determine the status of *mother* or *father*. Among lesbian couples who raise children, both women are mothers in the social and/or legal sense, yet only one (or neither) is the biological parent of the child. Additionally, a small number of transgender men (individuals assigned female at birth but who identify and live legally and/or socially as men) have become pregnant and given birth. Trans men who have given birth, such as Thomas Beatie, tend to eschew the gendered term *mother*, often preferring to be called *gestational parents* or, more simply, *fathers* (Trebay 2008). Other transgender individuals who undergo hormone therapy or gender confirmation surgery as part of their transition now have the option to have their eggs or sperm extracted and frozen for use in the future, should they wish to have a child biologically related to them.

These new legal and technological innovations offer more choices—particularly to people who can afford them—in the ways people form and grow their families. Such innovations may push people to expand their understandings of what a family looks like or how reproductive labor should be distributed; on the other hand, as in the case of same-sex couples who continue to associate care work with femininity or in reproductive technologies that stress the importance of biological parenthood, these developments may simply present a reformulated version of older ideologies of family and reproductive labor.

Conclusion

Reproductive labor is the glue that holds societies together. It is the often-invisible work that may be performed as an unpaid family duty or a paid service. This labor is undertaken within private households or in the public sphere by mothers, fathers, grandparents, or others. In the United States, reproductive labor has tended to be seen as "women's work," performed primarily within the private sphere of the home. The exact contents of reproductive labor vary based on political ideologies and material realities, but its basic requirements remain the same: Human beings require food, clothing, and shelter that must be acquired and prepared for human use/consumption, and people require love, community, and attention to the things that bring them happiness. People especially require care when they are young, old, sick, or disabled. The reproductive labor that provides this care sustains human life and culture over time and from one generation to the next.

People in different historic eras and global societies arrange for these needs to be met in different ways. In the contemporary period, the division of productive and reproductive labor into separate spheres risks devaluing reproductive labor, treating it as a private, rather than as a public, good. Yet just as whole communities and societies benefit by sharing the work of production (by dividing up, specializing, and increasing the productivity of labor), there are a range of ways that the task of social reproduction can be organized. For example, while social reproduction can be viewed and structured as the responsibility of individual families, one might also view social reproduction as a social good to be maximized, which requires sharing the work communally and valuing those who do it.

Past and present contestations over reproductive labor in the U.S. support this latter view. Women wishing to expand their roles beyond the household and participate in paid labor can do so only by devoting proportionally less of their time to social reproduction. Individual men and public policy have not responded by increasing their contributions to social reproduction in an equal amount, with two results: (1) On the whole, families perform less reproductive labor (childcare, housework, etc.) than in the past, and (2) women remain ideologically and temporally torn between home and work, laboring more hours per day than men. Thus, women in the contemporary U.S. often feel pulled—or pushed—back into the home to perform much-needed reproductive labor.

Most proposed policy solutions to this "time bind" (Hochschild 1997) have focused on private arrangements within the home, usually depending on compromises between spouses and/or on individual determination and hard work. Even recent expansions in the legal definition of *family*, most notably the legalization of same-sex marriage, retain a focus on nuclear family forms and the belief that caregiving is most suitably performed by private individuals and families. An expanded vision of reproductive labor—one that recognizes the critical importance of that labor and the people who do it—might reimagine social reproduction as a community need and responsibility. It would look at the particular needs of children, people with illness and disabilities, and the elderly to design better laws, better public institutions and accommodations, and better support systems for people who need care and for the people who provide it.

KEYWORDS

Family wage 127
Integrated motherhood 135
Intensive mothering ideology 132
Nuclear family 126
Othermothers 124
Reproductive labor 121
Separate spheres ideology 127
Social organization of biological reproduction 123
Social reproduction 121
Stalled revolution 138

QUESTIONS

- What is social reproduction? And why does it matter for society?
- Who was responsible for reproductive labor in the household you grew up in? What kinds of tasks did that include? How did you decide who would do what, and how did you feel about that division of labor?
- In your own household as an adult, how do you expect to divide up household labor (i.e., cleaning, caring for children, etc.)?
- In societies and time periods where the bulk of reproductive labor is done by women (most of them!), what beliefs, social institutions, and policies make it likely that women will do more reproductive labor than men? What kinds of changes would need to happen to facilitate more equal sharing of this work?
- How do social inequalities affect who performs reproductive labor? Think not only about gender inequalities but also about inequalities due to race, immigration status, socioeconomic class, and colonization.

ASSOCIATED READINGS

- Blair-Loy, Mary. 2003. *Competing Devotions: Career and Family among Women Executives*. Cambridge: Harvard University Press.
- Carrington, Christopher. 1999. *No Place Like Home: Relationships and Family Life among Lesbians and Gay Men*. Chicago: University of Chicago Press.
- Christopher, Karen. 2012. "Extensive Mothering: Employed Mothers' Constructions of the Good Mother." *Gender & Society* 26 (1): 73–96.
- Collins, Patricia Hill. 2000. *Black Feminist Thought: Knowledge, Consciousness, and the Politics of Empowerment*. 2nd edition. New York: Routledge.
- Coontz, Stephanie. 1993. *The Way We Never Were: American Families and the Nostalgia Trap*. New York: Basic Books.
- Dow, Dawn Marie. 2016. "Integrated Motherhood: Beyond Traditional Ideologies of Motherhood." *Journal of Marriage and Family* 78 (1): 180–196.
- Hays, Sharon. 1996. *The Cultural Contradictions of Motherhood*. New Haven: Yale University Press.
- Hochschild, Arlie. (1989) 2003. *The Second Shift*. New York: Penguin Books.
- Meyer, Madonna H. 2014. *Grandmothers at Work: Juggling Families and Jobs*. New York: New York University Press.

- Moore, Mignon. 2008. "Gendered Power Relations among Women: A Study of Household Decision Making in Black, Lesbian Stepfamilies." *American Sociological Review* 73: 335–356.
- Roberts, Dorothy. 1997. *Killing the Black Body: Race, Reproduction, and the Meaning of Liberty*. New York: Random House.

NOTES

1. Authors are listed alphabetically; both authors contributed equally to writing this chapter.
2. Parental leave in the U.S. is both more and less expansive than the guidelines of the FMLA might suggest. It is *less* expansive in that the federal guidelines cover all public employees but only apply to larger private employers (companies with more than 50 employees); to be eligible, moreover, employees must have worked for their employer for all of the preceding year and worked at least 1,250 hours during that period. However, leave policies in the U.S. are also sometimes *more* expansive than the FMLA rules because individual states (such as California) and companies are free to provide more generous leave policies. Thus, some people in the U.S. have access to longer or paid parental leave because of where they live or work, while other people do not.

CHAPTER

8

Gendering Exploitation

Abigail Andrews and Raka Ray

This chapter uses the analysis of power, position, representation, and practice to uncover how gender works in the economy, the market, and the workplace. It examines how gendered norms have enabled exploitation*—the unjust extraction of a person's labor—and have created economic inequities between and among women and men. The chapter begins by examining the ways organizations use* gendered tropes *(recurring symbols) to keep workers in line. It then looks at how work is sex segregated, both within workplaces and along a public/private divide. The chapter considers how gendered norms have created inequities in pay and authority, including the* gender wage gap, *the* glass ceiling, *and the* motherhood penalty. *Nevertheless, since the 1970s, women in the U.S. and around the world have increasingly worked outside the home. The chapter looks at how women's increasing involvement in the workplace has led to new forms of interdependence among women by race and class, particularly in the domestic sphere. Finally, the chapter considers how relationships between work and gender are changing in the context of globalization, as women move long distances to perform factory work or to serve as part of the* global care chain. *The chapter concludes by examining whether changes in gender and the economy spell the "end of men" and for which men. In a capitalist system that relies on gender norms and sex segregation to perpetuate economic inequity, we ask, can women—or men—ever "have it all"?*

Introduction

From 1979 until her retirement in 1998, Lilly Ledbetter was a supervisor at the Goodyear Tire and Rubber plant in Gadsden, Alabama. For most of those years, she worked as an area manager, a position largely occupied by men. In 1996, Goodyear gave Ms. Ledbetter a "Top Performance Award" for her work. When Ledbetter started at the plant, her salary was in line with the salaries of men performing similar work. Over time, however, her pay slipped in comparison to the pay of men managers with equal or less seniority. Yet because employees were strictly forbidden from discussing compensation, Ledbetter did not know she was paid less than her men peers.

Shortly before Ledbetter was due to retire in 1998, an anonymous coworker slipped a note into her mailbox comparing her pay to that of three of her men counterparts. The note revealed that while men in her position were paid $4,286 to $5,236 per month, Ledbetter was making only $3,727 for the same job—that is, somewhere between 71% and 86% of the men's pay. In response, Ledbetter filed a complaint with the U.S. Equal Employment Opportunity Commission (EEOC). Shortly after the complaint, Goodyear reassigned her to lift heavy tires. For Ledbetter, the transfer felt like retribution.

Lilly Ledbetter responded by suing Goodyear, which claimed it had paid her less than her men peers because she was not a good worker. However, the jury sided with Ledbetter, awarding her about $3.3 million in damages. Later, the amount was reduced to only $300,000, and then the Supreme Court ruled that Ledbetter was not entitled to any compensation at all because she had filed her claim more than 180 days after receiving her first discriminatory paycheck. Nevertheless, Ledbetter became an icon of the ways gender inequalities can bolster **exploitation,** that is, employers' unfair treatment of workers in order to benefit from their work.

In 2009, the 111th United States Congress passed the Lilly Ledbetter Fair Pay Act, amending previous laws on equal rights to clarify that not only an initial wage decision but also every single discriminatory paycheck is considered unlawful. President Barack Obama signed the Ledbetter Act into law on January 29, 2009.

***

Often, when scholars and the media discuss questions such as jobs, corporations, and financial markets, they frame the economic sphere as gender neutral. Common assumptions hold that the economy is separate from the household and therefore removed from questions of gender.

This chapter challenges such assumptions by examining how gendered norms and relations of power shape social life at the level of institutions, including the capitalist system. For one, men have long maintained positions of economic domination and workplace control. At the same time, masculine and feminine norms shape the nature of work, even in today's changing world. Personal relationships, such as those in the home, also interact with people's gendered roles in institutions.

Gender works in the economy in several ways. First, gender norms organize the division of labor across society (see Chapters 3 and 4), that is, how all of the work people do (from raising children to paid labor) is divvied up and assigned meanings. Under 20th-century capitalism, as Chapters 1 and 7 show, the division of labor meant separating the formal economy from household work and men's production in the public sphere from women's work in the private sphere. The public/private separation made it appear that the public was naturally men's domain. While this division was not true for all people, it still structures people's assumptions about who should work for wages and who should be paid more. The **sex segregation of work** means that men and women do different kinds of jobs. As discussed briefly in Chapter 1, jobs such as farm work and office management are often considered masculine and dominated by men, while jobs such as service and secretarial work tend to be seen as feminine and dominated by women. Even within a single corporation, men and women are often segregated by sex.

Second, gender norms prescribe certain forms of behavior at work. **Gendered tropes**—recurring, gendered images of certain types of workers—provide workers with subjective identities that encourage them to submit to management and help facilitate labor control. Examples of such tropes include the male breadwinner and the male boss as well as the image of the docile third world woman worker, who is taught to behave submissively in today's global factories. Such gendered tropes help naturalize relationships of domination between labor and capital.

As the case of Lilly Ledbetter illustrates, gender norms, segregation, and tropes often perpetuate unacknowledged (or even explicit) inequities between men and women. In particular, they reinforce a gender wage gap, that is, a difference in earnings between women and men. To this day, the average woman in the United States makes only 80 cents per dollar made by a man. Similarly, women continue to face harassment at work and limits to workplace promotions that men do not.

Yet, do these gender norms, public/private divisions, instances of sex segregation, and gendered tropes *still* shape inequities among capital and labor to the same degree as they did historically? As Chapter 1 showed, the global economy has transformed since the 1970s, reconfiguring the relationship between gender and work. Women are a growing presence in the sphere of paid labor around the world.

However, rather than decreasing the importance of gender altogether, economic changes have reconfigured the relationship between gender and work, transforming public/private divisions. Increasingly, in the U.S., multiple adults must work to support a family. The new social division of labor has also produced new gender norms and forms of subjugation. As Chapter 7 described, middle- and upper-class women's desire to work for wages created conflicts between work and family. Many well-off families have passed such conflicts on to poorer women and women of color by hiring them to do domestic work. In turn, women across the globe have come to play a fundamental role as service workers. At the same time, many corporations now treat women as an ideal workforce for global factories, ostensibly due to their nimble fingers and responsible character. Today, women workers make everything ranging from clothing to iPhones and iPads.

Some pundits suggest that women's economic rise will spell the "end of men," consigning men to ever more economically and socially marginal positions. Nevertheless, the effects of economic change on men are shaped by race and class. As working-class men fight to sustain their masculinity, elite men still control corporations, technology, and finance; that is, the dominant positions of economic power across the world.

Gender Norms and Inequities in Today's Workplace

Today, while a large percentage of women around the world work outside the home, norms of male breadwinning and female domesticity continue to create gendered inequities in work practices, income, and economic power. This section considers how workplaces are gendered before examining three key issues related to gender and work: (1) job segregation by sex, (2) the gender wage gap, and (3) other forms of gender discrimination. The section focuses on the United States while also taking note of how similar issues reverberate elsewhere.

In 1990, sociologist Joan Acker argued that even though people often think of corporations as gender neutral, men's power and masculine imagery are built into such organizations. For one, many people continue to adopt a **masculine worker norm,** that is, an assumption that the ideal worker is a man, especially in jobs that involve intelligence, leadership, or physical force. Due to racial exclusion, these workers are assumed not only to be men but also to be *white* men. As mentioned in Chapters 1, 2, and 7, the masculine worker norm is linked to presumptions about a man's role in the family. For instance, corporations often expect employees to work long hours, organize their time around their jobs, and prioritize work, assuming, implicitly, that someone else (their wives) takes care of domestic responsibilities. To the extent women workers still take more responsibility than men for care work, they may be framed as incapable of meeting the norm of work devotion (see Chapter 7).

The masculine worker norm was strengthened by the Fordist organization of work in the 20th century U.S. Under Fordism (named after the Ford Motor Company), men worked in assembly line manufacturing of standardized goods such as cars, and most earned enough wages to afford the products they made. Under the ideology of Fordism, one income supported an entire family. In return for a "family wage," the man was expected to devote his life to the company while his wife took care of reproduction and consumption in the home. Still, as this form of work and family came to be seen as a norm for white workers, immigrants and African American men rarely earned enough to make a family wage.

In conjunction with the masculine worker norm, managers also draw on gendered tropes to encourage employees to work harder. One such trope, the *hardworking man,* depicts workers as men dedicated to work, without obligations. This trope encourages workers to embrace an ethic of commitment to work and engage in intense competition in the workplace, not only meeting but also exceeding job requirements. Silicon Valley, which is arguably the heart of hegemonic masculinity in the workplace today, offers an example. Many Silicon Valley corporations portray their coders and entrepreneurs using the trope of warriors. Thus they demand aggressive displays of technical self-confidence, skill, and balance. In addition, they expect workers to be on the job 90 hours a week (Cooper 2000). Instead of traditional hierarchies, such corporations judge workers by the numbers of hours they put into a team, framing those hours as tests of stamina.

Women workers face pressure to meet the masculine worker norm as well, such as by putting in long hours or by acting aggressive and competitive.[1] As mentioned in Chapter 1, Sheryl Sandberg, the chief operating officer for Facebook, participated in creating this pressure through her 2013 bestseller, *Lean In.* Sandberg argued that women could achieve equity with men in the workplace if they embraced work as their primary vocation and assumed the kinds of leadership qualities typically celebrated in men but derided in women. Sandberg gave the example of the chief executive officer (CEO) of Yahoo, Marissa Mayer. One of Mayer's first acts as Yahoo CEO was to prohibit working from home, making work especially difficult for new mothers. Mayer herself also returned to work just two weeks after giving birth. Though she had a nursery built into her own office for her baby, Mayer refused to adapt to the needs of other women with fewer resources at work. Even as Sandberg and Mayer claimed to promote gender equality in the workplace, they still held women to a norm that starkly separated work from home and ignored people's obligations outside of work. They made it seem that women had lower salaries and rates of promotion than men because they had failed to meet a masculine standard, rather than due to ongoing discrimination or the unrealistic character of the masculine worker norm.[2]

Occupational Segregation by Sex

In many organizations, masculine worker norms intertwine with ongoing presumptions about which kinds of jobs are feminine or masculine. The effect is **occupational sex segregation,** namely, the concentration of men and women in occupations that predominantly employ workers of one gender or the other. In the U.S., as of 2010, the top jobs for women were in administrative positions, nursing, teaching, retail, customer service, bookkeeping, and housekeeping. Today, 81.7% of elementary and middle school teachers are women, along with 81.7% of social workers, and 76.2% of event planners. By contrast, men predominate in other industries. For instance, men make up 64% of postal workers, 65.9% of reporters, 66.2% of doctors, and 95.7% of airline pilots. In order to end sex segregation across industry, 40% of U.S. workers would have to change jobs (and more, if you desegregate by job role). Colloquial language reflects this gendering: Though jobs were once distinguished as *white collar* (professional) or *blue collar* (manual), a new category has been added—*pink collar*—to refer to jobs primarily staffed by women, particularly in the service industry.

There can also be sex segregation within a given industry or plant. As Chapter 1 suggested, each industry has a set of ideas about gender that structure who does what. In manufacturing, for instance, even though half of all assemblers are women, women assemblers tend to work on lower-paid electronic goods, while more men work on higher-paid motor vehicles. Similarly, in sales, women often sell small goods while men sell big-ticket items such as furniture or cars. Though half of professional workers are women, most professional women work in healthcare or education, not in higher-paying professions such as law or business. By placing women disproportionately in support positions and ensuring their subordinate status, institutions devalue women's work.

Sociologist Evelyn Nakano Glenn (1992) used the hospital setting to illustrate the ongoing, gendered hierarchy of care. She noted that doctors tend to be white men, senior nurses with the most qualifications are usually white women, and nurses' aides or junior nurses with one year of qualification—the people charged with day-to-day grunt work and the dirtiest, unskilled tasks—are often women of color. In the first half of the 20th century, restrictions prohibited women from becoming doctors and introduced grading for nurses so that women of color could enter only the lowest rank. While these formal constraints are gone, their effects linger, maintaining divisions today.

The Glass Ceiling and the Glass Escalator

The restrictions placed on women who attempt to transcend sex segregation to rise in the workplace hierarchy are referred to as **the glass ceiling.** Legally (according to Title VII of the Civil Rights Act of 1964), employers can discriminate based on gender only if there is some occupational requirement that requires a woman or a man (e.g., surrogacy). Therefore, restrictions on women's advancement remain invisible, like glass. Yet barriers to women's professional advancement still exist. Often, managers do not promote women because they are concerned that single women may leave when they get married, that married women may leave when they have children, and that mothers may have too many responsibilities to be effective managers. The effect of the glass ceiling is that while women change positions more often than men, their moves tend to be lateral rather than upward.

In addition to the glass ceiling, some women face a **sticky floor** at work, a phenomenon in which women tend to remain trapped in lower-level positions. For example, a female secretary may become an office supervisor but will not be able to move to a professional job classification such as administrative assistant or manager, even though the skill levels for these jobs may be the same. In the U.S. Supreme Court case *Hopkins vs. Price Waterhouse* in 1989, Ann Hopkins, an accountant, was passed over for promotion to partner. Even though she brought in more business that any of the men who were promoted, Hopkins did not fit partners' ideas of what a female employee should look like. Instead, she was perceived as abrasive and macho. Her colleagues reportedly said that she could benefit from a course at charm school, where she might learn to be more feminine in dress and speech. Hopkins won the case, and her employer, Price Waterhouse, was held liable for sex discrimination.

Such limits on women's advancement are not specific to the United States. For example, Yuko Ogasawara (1998) found that in large Japanese corporations, men and women also encountered two separate career tracks. Women were the "flowers of the workplace," restricted to clerical work and exempted from the traditional lifetime employment guarantees and opportunities for advancement afforded to men.

For white men, meanwhile, traditionally feminized workplaces operate in the reverse. Christine Williams (1992) described this effect as a **glass escalator**: a subtle, unseen force that helps boost men to higher-ranked positions in fields dominated by women. Williams showed that white men who entered professions such as nursing, social work, or education were often fast-tracked into managerial positions, with employers showing a marked preference for hiring and promoting men. In such jobs, men's token status—the fact that they were underrepresented—acted as an advantage, creating preferences for men rather than discrimination. Likewise, because men were often supervisors in such fields, male employees could build relationships of camaraderie with their bosses, providing another mechanism for advancement. However, as Adia Harvey Wingfield (2009) pointed out, the glass escalator was also racialized: In contrast to white men, Black men in traditionally feminized workplaces faced tense relations with colleagues and supervisors and barriers to promotion.

Job segregation by sex limits the occupational opportunities of both men and women. However, it is particularly disadvantageous for women; indeed, half of the pay gap between men and women (discussed below) can be attributed to their segregation into different kinds of jobs.

Explaining Sex Segregation at Work

What explains occupational sex segregation? The Supreme Court case of *EEOC v. Sears, Roebuck and Co.* (1988) offers some insights. In the mid-1980s, the Equal Employment Opportunity Commission (EEOC) filed the largest employment discrimination suit ever tried against Sears, Roebuck and Co. The EEOC argued that women were underrepresented in the best-paying commissioned sales jobs at Sears (Milkman 1986). Feminist historians Rosalind Rosenberg and Alice Kessler-Harris acted as expert witnesses on opposing sides. Rosenberg testified for Sears, arguing that women and men were segregated at Sears because they naturally had different preferences and values, and women simply preferred to work in the less-competitive, lower-paid sales positions. By contrast, Kessler-Harris argued that one could not know what women's choices actually were, since women's exclusion from opportunities had constrained their choices. When given the opportunity, Kessler-Harris added, women *had* taken better-paying jobs. Sears won the case, reflecting the normalization of a gender hierarchy that claims that women naturally enter into niches that "just happen" to be undervalued compared to men's.

These lawyers' arguments embody ongoing debates about the sources of sex segregation. Like Rosenberg, many people today believe that women prefer to be mothers, caregivers, and supporters. They claim that women are inherently better at certain lower-paid and lower-status jobs, such as teaching, childcare, and so on. By contrast, others suggest that employers benefit from keeping women in jobs where they are easier to exploit. They argue that the idea that certain jobs are natural for women help legitimate their subordination to employers or men. Feminists such as Heidi Hartmann (1976) add that occupational sex segregation reinforces men's control, ensuring that women will have lower wages and therefore continue to depend on men.

Finally, many social scientists suggest that there are two labor markets in the United States. The *primary labor market* includes professional, skilled, high-paid jobs with expectations of upward mobility. The *secondary labor market*, meanwhile, is made up of entry-level jobs that require little training and receive low pay, including sectors such as retail, services, and cleaning. In the secondary sector, additional experience often results in little increase in earnings. Gender theorists have argued that women are predominantly relegated to the secondary labor market. Yet both labor markets are also intersectional. The primary labor market benefits employers, men, and well-off women, as racial divisions drive low-income immigrants and people of color into the secondary labor market.

Together, the combination of employers' interests, men's interests, women's choices, and the dual labor market—all of which draw on different gender norms at different time periods—fuels ongoing occupational sex segregation. In turn, sex segregation has critical implications for economic inequality, giving men—on the whole—more money and power than women.

The Gender Wage Gap

One of the most important effects of women's relegation to the private sphere, devalued work, and lower-paying jobs is the **gender wage gap:** a persistent disparity between men's and women's pay. As sociologist Paula England (1992) and others have demonstrated, employers pay men and women unequal wages for the same work. The biggest difference between men's and women's incomes occurs among people who earn over $100,000 per year. Among CEOs, the pay ratio of women to men is 69%; among hospital administrators, it is 77%.

Even as women's wages are increasing relative to men's, the shifts obscure ongoing inequalities. In 1970, in the United States, women made 59 cents for every dollar earned by a man; by 2013, they made roughly 80 cents on the dollar. Still, even when women have similar education and work experience to their men peers, and even when they work in jobs that require equivalent skill, effort, and responsibility in equally demanding conditions, they earn less than men. Compared to male counterparts of the same race, as of 2013, white women earned 80 cents on the dollar, Black women earned 83 cents on the dollar, Asian women 74 cents, and Hispanic women 94 cents.

Are these pay differences due to gender discrimination? Some scholars argue that inequities are not a sign of discrimination but instead the logical outcome of different educational backgrounds and sets of skills. For instance, such scholars argue, women often take time off to care for children and families, so they gain less education and work experience than men. When a child with a working mother and father is sick, the woman often stays home. As a result, women accumulate fewer years of work experience and work fewer hours per year. They are less likely to work a full-time schedule, and they leave the labor force for longer periods of time than men. So, some conclude, women and men develop different *human capital*, or sets of skills.

Other scholars argue that wage differences may reflect women's preferences for certain lower-paying jobs. Such scholars concur with Rosalind Rosenberg, who argued on behalf of Sears in the mid-1980s that women seek out jobs with feminine traits, sorting themselves into different occupations and different industries. They suggest that the explanation is not discrimination at work itself, but that from a young age, women learn a predilection for certain kinds of work. Whether women opt into such jobs due to innate instincts or gender socialization, these scholars believe, their own choices land them in positions that pay less than men.

Nevertheless, evidence suggests that even when men and women have *the same* human capital—the same training, years on the job, and experience—and even when they opt into the same jobs, women still earn only 80% of what men do. That difference is commonly attributed to discrimination. The more educated people are, the wider the pay gap between men and women with similar levels of education and skill. Thus, as the table below shows, when people have less than a high school diploma, women earn 79 cents per dollar for men, whereas among people with master's, professional, and doctoral degrees, women earn only 73 cents per dollar for men (U.S. Bureau of Labor Statistics 2014a).

Table 8.1 Women's to Men's Earnings Ratios and Wage Gap by Educational Attainment, 2014

	Women's to Men's Earnings Ratio
Less Than a High School Diploma	79.1
High School Graduates, No College	77.0
Some College or Associates Degree	75.8
Bachelor's Degree Only	77.3
Advanced Degree*	72.7

*Advanced degree includes people with master's, professional, and doctoral degrees.

Source: U.S. Bureau of Labor Statistics 2014a.

Note: Based on median weekly earnings of full-time wage and salary workers, 25 years and older.

A 2011 book by sociologist Kristen Schilt called *Just One of the Guys? Transgender Men and the Persistence of Gender Inequality* used transgender men's and women's experiences to illustrate how discrimination persists within workplaces. The men and women in the study had gone to school and made their career choices prior to transitioning to a different gender identity. Some of them changed jobs after they transitioned, and some stayed in the same jobs. Some were "out" to their employers as transgender; others started new jobs without discussing past experiences of gender. Regardless, the overall pattern was very clear: Transgender women paid a wage penalty, and transgender men received additional pay after they shifted from identifying as women to identifying as men.

Schilt observed that once employers and colleagues saw workers as *men,* they were perceived as more competent and began to earn better pay. While transgender women were seen as less competent and lost respect and recognition after transitioning, transgender men received better performance reviews and more recognition for hard work. For example, when one scientist transitioned his gender identity from woman to man, a colleague who was unaware of the transition reported to their superior that the scientist's "brother" was a much better replacement. Likewise, Schilt interviewed a transgender attorney who had transitioned his identity from woman to man. As a younger attorney, the lawyer had been called Susan; now he was Thomas. He told Schilt that after his transition, another lawyer mistakenly believed that Susan had been fired and replaced by Thomas. The other lawyer commended the firm's boss for the replacement. He said Susan had been incompetent, but "the new guy," he added, was "just delightful." Ben Barres, a neurobiology professor at Stanford who transitioned his identity from woman to man, told the *Wall Street Journal* of a similar experience. An attendee at one of his lectures leaned over to a colleague and said, "Ben Barres's work is much better than his sister's."

Schilt underscored that the benefits of masculine self-presentation varied by race. For example, transgender men who were Black discovered that they had gone from being dismissed (as Black women) to feared (as Black men). Thus, the benefits of gender were intertwined with and conditional on hierarchies of race.

Other Forms of Discrimination

Gender discrimination occurs not only in the treatment of workers but also in the process of recruitment. For one, men employees have a tendency to seek to hire others like them, which some sociologists refer to as **homosocial reproduction**, and others colloquially call an "old boys network." Gendered organization theory helps make sense of these differences by showing how gender expectations and discrimination are embedded in organizations, the interactions between coworkers, and the relationships between employers and employees. A famous example of an organization overcoming gender bias is symphony orchestras. Until the 1970s, symphony orchestras had only 5% women. Then they began holding blind auditions in which the musicians played behind a screen. The number of women being hired immediately tripled, and today, many top orchestras have to 25% to 30% women performers.

In addition to favoring men, workplaces often penalize mothers in hiring and wage decisions. Correll, Benard, and Paik (2007) tested whether discrimination plays a factor in the lower wages of mothers. They created résumés and other materials for hypothetical job seekers and then asked 192 Cornell undergraduates to evaluate these résumés as candidates for a position as marketing director for a start-up communications company. Correll described the research process thus: "We created two applicant profiles that were functionally equivalent. Their résumés were very strong; they were very successful in their last jobs. In pretesting, no one preferred one applicant over the other; they were seen as equally qualified."

Next, Correll, Benard, and Paik added a memo to one of the profiles, mentioning that the applicant was a mother of two children, and her résumé was modified to show that she was an officer in a parent–teacher association. The memo and résumé in the second applicant's materials made no mention of children. When asked if they would hire these applicants, 84% of participants said they would hire the women without children, but only 47% said they would hire the mothers. In assigning a starting salary to the applicants, given a pay range appropriate for the job, participants offered non-mothers an average of $11,000 more than mothers. Women with children were also held to a harsher performance standard than women without: The participants allowed mothers significantly fewer days of missed work before they would not be seen as management material.

By contrast, fathers got a bonus. In the second round of the study, participants were given the same information in the résumés and memos and were asked the same questions, but men's names replaced women's on the applications. The researchers hoped to discover whether it was parents who suffered a penalty, or mothers alone. They found that fathers were in no way disadvantaged. On the contrary, fathers earned *benefits* on several measures, such as being seen as more committed to their jobs than men who were not fathers. Being a breadwinning man was correlated with more respect on the job.

Not only do women confront perceptions that they are less competent as well as barriers to advancement, particularly as mothers, but they also face **workplace sexual harassment.** The U.S. EEOC defines workplace sexual harassment as unwelcome sexual advances or conduct of a sexual nature that unreasonably interferes with the performance of a person's job or creates an intimidating, hostile, or offensive work environment.

Harassment can take two forms: (1) quid pro quo, in which women get treated as sexual objects in exchange for other favors (for instance, women might be given time off or office perks by a male supervisor who touches them against their wishes), or (2) a hostile environment, such as when sexist comments are made in public spaces at work. As of 2011, one in four women in the United States said they had experienced such harassment. Both forms of harassment are especially pervasive in jobs where women are in the minority; in addition to the statistics on sexual assault in the military discussed in Chapter 6, up to 80% of women in the military have been harassed. Such harassment undermines the goal of gender equity by making workplaces hostile environments for women.

Barriers to Union Organizing

Women can also be particularly vulnerable to exploitation because they face greater barriers than men to union organizing. Being in a union increases the likelihood that workers will have job protections. Even though women started to form unions in the 19th century, men historically dominated unions in the United States. In the 1930s and 1940s, as the Congress of Industrial Organizations (CIO) union emerged, many women sought to join, yet the union primarily sought to organize men. As more women entered the U.S. workforce in the 1960s and 1970s, the unions began to pay more attention to them. In 1973, the American Federation of Labor and Congress of Industrial Organizations (AFL-CIO) endorsed the Equal Rights Amendment, which would have guaranteed equal rights by gender and ended legal distinctions between men and women (it never passed). In 1974, the Coalition of Labor Union Women was formed to deal with issues of child care, affirmative action, equal pay, and other issues often associated with working women. They found that not only were these issues absent from union agendas but also that women were highly underrepresented among union workers.

As the women's movement grew, unions faced increasing pressure to take up feminist issues. Today, the gap in union membership is closing; as of 2015, 10.6% of women workers belong to a union compared to 11.5% of men workers. According to research by Kate Bronfenbrenner (2005) of Cornell University, women have outpaced men as new members of unions for the last 20 years, and workplaces with a majority of women workers are more likely to win organizing campaigns. Indeed, from 1997 to 2001, 425,000 women joined the U.S. labor movement. At the same time, men's participation in unions has declined.

Some women also face barriers to organizing due to the nature of the labor sectors in which they are overrepresented. In many countries, care workers work on a temporary basis in private homes. Not only are they fragmented from each other, but there is also no one employer or factory head whom they can collectively address to demand rights. In the U.S., domestic workers were also excluded from formal labor rights according to the 1935 Social Security Act, barring them from the kinds of benefits available to workers in other sectors. After years of fighting for labor rights, housekeepers, nannies, and other caretakers are only beginning to get recognition for their work.

Gendering Neoliberal Globalization

In the context of neoliberal globalization, production has been reorganized along new, gendered lines. As discussed in Chapter 1, neoliberal globalization has been defined by the withdrawal of state support and the liberalization of economic markets. In turn, production has been reorganized. Manufacturing and mass production have been offshored from the United States, so that industrial jobs that were once located in U.S. cities and considered masculine are now concentrated in global factories in countries such as Mexico and China and considered particularly suitable for women. In the United States, this transformation has coincided with the rise of the service sector and the tech sector. Neoliberalism has also encouraged the **flexibilization of labor,** that is, the pressure for workers to take less stable, shorter-term jobs with fewer benefits. In developing countries, meanwhile, international institutions such as the World Bank and International Monetary Fund (IMF) have promoted market policies, export economies, and reduced state support for disadvantaged segments of their populations.

Neoliberal ideology and policies have also shrunk public assistance for the poor, especially for mothers with children. In the U.S., the 1996 Personal Responsibility and Work Opportunity Reconciliation Act (PRWORA) ended Aid to Families with Dependent Children (AFDC), as described in Chapter 1. As a result, the U.S. and other countries have seen a feminization of poverty, with women representing a disproportionate percentage of the poor. Meanwhile, even though the male breadwinner model described in Chapter 1 was always confined to a select few white men, this model became even less viable as wages stagnated and union participation declined. Most families now need two incomes to survive. The number and proportion of working women has expanded dramatically across the world. To make it possible for women to work outside the home, some governments have even made what Andrews and Shahrokni (2014) called *patriarchal accommodations,* adapting historical gender inequalities to the new realities of women's work. Ideas about masculinity and femininity in the workplace have also shifted, emphasizing women's capacity as low-wage workers and their ability to take responsibility for civil services once provided by the government.

At the same time, globalization has created a "feminized" economy. In the United States, professions long labeled as *feminine*, particularly service work, have seen significant growth in recent years, while "masculine" professions such as manufacturing have eroded. Globally, women's low social and political status has helped forge new, feminized production networks, especially in the low-wage areas of domestic service, manufacturing, and informal work. As a result, women have also come to predominate in many unskilled, poorly paid, insecure, and informal jobs (Enloe 1989; Roy 2010; Sassen 1988). Such jobs give many women workers new wages and new leverage in their households; at the same time, the idea that work is liberating for women can help justify their exploitation. The following sections examine various sectors of the feminized economy.

Gendered Migration and the Global Care Chain

As well-off women in the Global North entered the working world, many turned to the international division of reproductive labor to make their own work possible. Today, as discussed in Chapter 7, working women in countries such as the United States often depend on migrant women from developing countries to care for their children. Thus, an important gendered component of contemporary globalization has been women's migration as domestic workers. While migration from countries such as Mexico and the Philippines was once seen as the domain of men, women now represent about 48% of all migrants and their migration is instrumental to keeping the global economy afloat (Donato and Gabaccia 2016). Women from the Philippines look after children in Italy, Dubai, Singapore, and the U.S.; women from Sri Lanka clean homes in Saudi Arabia; and rural women in India and Peru travel to the metropolises to cook, clean, and look after the children of middle-class and wealthy families. In the Philippines, where the migrant labor stream involves primarily women, women's remittances are critical to the economic health of the nation. In other countries such as Pakistan, where most international migrants are men, migrants depend on their wives and mothers to care for their families and belongings while they are away (Enloe 1989).

Migrant domestic work is deeply imbalanced by race and class. As of 2006, according to a study of domestic workers in New York conducted by Domestic Workers United and Datacenter, 77% of domestic employers are white and 76% are U.S. citizens. By contrast, 95% of domestic workers are people of color; 93% are women and 76% are not U.S. citizens. Fifty-one percent of live-in workers move away from their countries because they cannot support their families at home. Their work is backbreaking, with 35% working more than 60 hours per week and another 43% working more than 50 hours per week.

As affluent families in the U.S. and Europe turn to immigrant women to look after their children, mothering, love, and care have not only become purchasable commodities—as Chapter 7 described—but have also gone global. In her book *Doméstica,* Pierrette Hondagneu-Sotelo (2001) described how women from Mexico and Central America come to states such as California and Texas to work as maids and nannies. Many of these women are transnational mothers, leaving children back home in their native countries to provide a better future for those children by working in the United States and sending money home.

These migrant mothers often pass care work down what sociologists Rhacel Parreñas (2001) and Arlie Hochschild (2005) referred to as **the global care chain:** a series of connections among women, where well-off working women depend on poor working women, who in turn depend on paid or unpaid care workers back home. In *Servants of Globalization: Women, Migration, and Domestic Work,* for instance, Parreñas (2001) examined how this global interdependence of women affects the lives of Filipina migrants in Rome and Los Angeles. Parreñas pointed out that to avoid depriving their children in the Philippines of parental care, many migrant women hire their own domestic workers. Thus, a woman executive in Rome may hire a Filipina domestic worker who has left her children in her home city in the Philippines. That worker, in turn, may hire a nanny from a small village, who has, in turn, left her own children with a sister or other relative.

The same way that scholars speak of a "brain drain," with highly educated workers from places such as India migrating to the United States, Parreñas described a "care drain." While migrant women pour love onto other women's children—the ones they see every day—the children they leave behind end up with worse health and educational outcomes. Thus, families in the first world literally extract love (and opportunities) from the developing world.

These global care chains are reinforced by the realities of unequal globalization, which puts economic pressure on poor women in the Global South to migrate. When people in the Global North stereotype women from poor countries as naturally more loving or as choosing to migrate for opportunities, or when they claim that the women who work in their homes as nannies are just like family, they obscure the pressures and impossible choices such women face. As one nanny from Barbados, living in New York, put it,

> We have been forced here because U.S. foreign policy has created poverty in our home countries. Once we are here in the U.S., searching for a way to survive, we are pushed into exploited jobs where our work is not recognized, respected or protected. (Domestic Workers United and Datacenter 2006)

As the historical forces of imperialism have created drastic divisions of wealth, they have also made women into key employers and links in the global care chain.

The Global Factory and the New Feminine Worker

Neoliberal globalization has also altered norms of gender within global factories. In 2013, an eight-story factory in Rana Plaza in Dhaka, Bangladesh collapsed, killing more than 1,000 people. Many hundreds more were seriously injured. The building housed thousands of workers who sewed garments for European and American companies such as Mango, Primark, J.C. Penney, and Benetton. While this was not the first tragedy of this sort, its scale shocked the world as it brought the human cost of cheap labor sharply to the forefront. To keep labor cheap, employers often ignore safety regulations, allow brutal working conditions, and abuse workers' rights.

This kind of labor exploitation is sustained in part by **feminine worker tropes**—images of workers as docile, dependable, or otherwise feminine that replace the old masculine worker norm. One such image is **the third world woman worker trope,** that is, the idea that women from the Global South are ideal, low-cost workers who are responsible and subservient to managers' demands. In her 2003 book *Genders in Production: Making Workers in Mexico's Global Factories,* Leslie Salzinger examined the use of this trope in the *maquilas* (factories) in the city of Juarez, close to the U.S.–Mexico border. She showed that even when employers were unable to find female workers, they advertised explicitly for *señoritas* (young women) and persistently invoked the superiority of women workers. For instance, one manager told Salzinger (2001), "Eighty-five percent of the labor force is made up of women, since they're more disciplined, pay more attention to what they do, and get bored less than men do," while another said, "Men are not inclined to sit. Women are calmer about sitting" (14).

Despite these stereotypes, Salzinger explained, women were not born submissive. Rather, the gendered ideas and practices within factories made them vulnerable. For instance, managers controlled labor by placing workers inside a fishbowl-style factory, where they became hypervisible and self-conscious. In turn, managers would stroll the floor to talk and joke with the women, focusing on workers' appearance rather than the work itself. The effect was to encourage women to present themselves as feminine, not only working hard but coming to work with perfectly painted nails and so on. Even when men worked in such factories, managers used similar feminine worker tropes to keep them in line. By the time of Salzinger's research, women's strikes had led to labor shortages, and nearly half of *maquila* workers were men. Nevertheless, these men workers might be placed at the edges of the factory. If they misbehaved, they would be told, "That's not manly," or disciplined by being placed among the girls, where they joked about how bad things were.

In sum, under the third world woman worker trope, manufacturers actively sought to employ women for their presumed characteristics as workers, including the idea that women—unlike male breadwinners—were *not* responsible for earning a family wage. At the same time, men in factories were also emasculated as a means to keep them docile. In reality, though, this workforce is far from docile; as Chapter 9 describes, garment and shoe workers continue to wage strikes around the world from Bangladesh to China to Vietnam.

Microfinance, the "Responsible Woman," and the Triple Burden of Public Service

In low-income countries, a second trope has also helped legitimate the withdrawal of government support from families. This is the **responsible woman trope**. As Ananya Roy argued in her 2010 piece "Millennial Woman: The Gender Order of Development," international development today frames poor women as heroic entrepreneurs, selfless altruists, and devoted mothers. These norms presume that women are responsible to children and family, while implying that men—especially men of color in the Global South—are selfish and wasteful. In turn, investors and donors believe that women will use money wisely so that their families are fed, while men will spend it on a night of drinking.

New York Times journalist Nicolas Kristof (2010) illustrated the idea that fathers in countries such as India or the Congo make choices to the detriment of their children in an article entitled "Moonshine or the Kids?" Kristof reported on a 43-year-old father named Fulbert Mfouna in the Congolese village of Mont-Belo, where school fees cost $2.50 a month and rent costs $6.00. While Mfouna's children have had to drop out or repeat grades for lack of school fees—his eldest son, Jude, repeating first grade five times—Mfouna spent $2 a day on alcohol and cigarettes, reportedly telling Kristof, "If possible, I drink every day." Given the profligacy of such fathers, Kristof argued, the solution to poverty is to encourage women to become entrepreneurs in their communities.

Major international organizations such as the World Bank, IMF, nongovernmental organizations (NGOs), and socially responsible businesses have also placed the responsible woman trope at the center of their efforts to confront poverty. These institutions spent the past several decades encouraging governments to cut support to small farms and withdraw public services ranging from government-funded water supplies to development grants, in order—ostensibly—to promote economic growth. At the same time, they have held women up as responsible, often promoting programs that offer women loans so that they might take charge of their own well-being. In turn, poor women have had to take on a triple burden: not only their paid work and household work but also the burden of performing civic duties once taken care of by the state.

Microfinance offers a key example of the responsible woman trope. Microfinance entails offering small loans to poor people, primarily women, to enable them to start businesses. The most common model of microfinance ensures that women will pay back these loans with interest by rotating loans among groups of women. If one woman fails to pay, the other women in the group will not receive loans and will have to pay on her behalf, so the group members push the first woman to pay. Therefore, the lender earns interest while exerting little effort to ensure that the women pay back their loans. One key organization promoting microfinance globally is the Grameen Foundation. Started in 1976 by Mohammed Yunus and the Grameen Bank in Bangladesh, the Grameen Foundation aims to alleviate poverty and empower the poor through lending to women in turns within a community. Organizations such as the Grameen Foundation argue that such loans give women access to finances they might not otherwise have had and enable them to start small businesses that lift them up economically. Nevertheless, microfinance can also use the poor—and their debt—to grow the wealth of the lenders. In recent years, microfinance has burgeoned as a neat response to poverty, in which poor people do not have to depend on state assistance—and in which a portion of the resources generated through their labor flows back to wealthy lenders.

As Katherine Rankin (2001) explained, microfinance relies on the idea of a woman who is rational, free willed, and self-governing—that is, *entrepreneurial*—and who is also responsible enough to feel an obligation to her community and to pay back her loans. Smitha Radhakrishnan (2015) likewise showed in her study of the global microfinance industry that microfinance organizations assumed "a universalized construction of a feminine entrepreneur" rather than seeing who their clients actually were. The idea of third world women is central to this picture. Visiting the Grameen Foundation website (http://www.grameenfoundation.org), one is instantly greeted with images of poor women in traditional dress, smiling broadly or with intense, dignified expressions.

However, making business the solution, and putting women in charge, can have adverse implications. Microfinance organizations often expect women to convert very small loans into successful businesses with little education or support in impoverished places that have access to few would-be buyers. If the women fail, their fellow borrowers may turn against them, since microfinance institutions often hold the whole group responsible when one member does not repay her loan. In nations such as India, there have been a wave of suicides among microfinance borrowers who are unable to repay their loans and are left feeling ashamed and desperate. Critics argue that while the original intention of microfinance organizations may be noble, their current version abandons the principles of educating women about smart investment and ways to repay loans. Instead, major international banks have begun to act as loan sharks, treating the poor as an untapped market, or what C. K. Prahalad (2006) has referred to as the "fortune at the bottom of the pyramid." As Ananya Roy (2012) puts it, such women become "the figure of resilience charged with converting poverty into enterprise" (136).

Government social policy has also come to rely on the responsible woman trope, as increasing numbers of governments make state funding conditional on women's performance as good mothers. In Mexico, for instance, the star social policy for the poor is a program called *Oportunidades* ("Opportunities"), which grants conditional cash transfers to poor families. That is, the government gives small amounts of money to the poor on the condition that they meet certain requirements. In Mexico's case, women must attend workshops teaching them to be responsible for their families, and they must bring their children to doctor's appointments and school (Molyneux 2006). If women fail to meet these requirements, the government cuts off their monthly payments. Likewise, in the United States, welfare-to-work programs require that women seek and find paid work; these programs cut off their support if they fail to do so. While such programs extend government support to women, they also construct women as mothers, making the funds contingent on women's successful performance of responsible motherhood.

Gender Transformations in the Informal Economy

As gender relations have shifted in the areas of domestic service, factory work, and international development, gender has also been transformed by the decline of the Fordist economy and the dramatic increase in the **informal economy**, that is, the sphere of work outside of sectors such as factories. Today, many people around the world work in unstable, short-term jobs with few labor protections or benefits. Across the developing world, the informal economy represents more than half of nonagricultural employment. In sub-Saharan Africa, informal workers comprise 73% of the nonagricultural labor force, rising to over 90% in parts of West Africa (Meagher and Lindell 2013). The rise of the informal economy has altered work for women and men, albeit in gender-specific ways.

Women do much of this informal work. Indeed, as Cynthia Enloe (1989) explained, a country's ability to tolerate the withdrawal of government support has depended on women's skill and willingness to find new ways to make ends meet. As the World Bank and IMF promoted neoliberal policies, women often carried the burden of lost government safety nets by working in the informal sector. Enloe (1989) reflected,

> An indebted government can institute the IMF prescriptive package [of structural adjustment] and not suffer political destabilization if women can figure out ways to stretch the kerosene and cooking oil, if women can find more ways to earn a bit of money in the casual labor sector, if women can provide demoralized men in their families with emotional support, if women are willing to care for a sick child without resort to the public clinic. Thus the politics of international debt is not simply something that has an *impact* on women in indebted countries. The policies of international debt won't work in their current form *unless* mothers and wives are willing to behave in ways that enable nervous regimes to adopt cost-cutting measures without forfeiting their political legitimacy. (184–185)

Thus, the disappearance of well-paying, unionized factory jobs and the shift to the informal sector has hinged on the labor of women.

As manufacturing has moved to new places and government institutions have closed down, other workers—even those who were previously exploited or devalued in their paid work—are now excluded from the workforce altogether. While women have traditionally dominated the informal economy, today the paradigmatic member of the global *precariat* (a working class with permanently insecure jobs) is the young urban man. Traditionally masculine factory jobs have disappeared for men, and economic restructuring has been particularly acute for racial minorities and the poor. In turn, among low-income communities of the United States and in the Global South, neoliberalism has triggered a crisis of masculinity.

This crisis can take many forms. Some of the conservative backlash in the U.S. and Western Europe (such as the rise of President Trump in the U.S.; Brexit, the movement in the UK to leave the European Union; the increased popularity of white nationalist parties in countries such as France) can be attributed to white, working class men who experience the decline of breadwinning jobs as a decline of their masculinity and who misattribute the cause of the decline to immigrants and foreigners instead of to the workings of the capitalist economy.

Meanwhile, African American men in the U.S. have also experienced being made redundant. In the first half of the 20th century, African American men from the U.S. South migrated north to enter manufacturing jobs during the Great Migration. However, the factory jobs they gained began to disappear in the 1970s and work relocated from the urban centers where Black populations lived to the service-oriented economies of quickly expanding white suburbs (Wilson 1987). Loïc Wacquant (2009) argued that Black men's overrepresentation in prison (described in Chapter 6) is a reflection of closed labor opportunities: Shut out from the formal economy, Black men turned to the informal sector to make ends meet, participating in activities such as drug dealing that the criminal justice system aggressively pursued under the "War on Crime."

Another example is men in postcolonial countries. In parts of Africa, 75% of men now work in the informal sector, previously considered appropriate only for women or struggling migrants. For such men, work is no longer a point of pride but instead an act of desperation. In an article titled "Men Doing 'Women's Work': Masculinity and Gender Relations among Street Vendors in Maputo, Mozambique," Victor Agadjanian (2002) explored how the rise of the informal economy has affected masculine identity. In the colonial era, men in colonized countries typically worked in wage-earning trades, while women more often performed informal-sector tasks that did not earn a steady salary, were dismissed as feminine, and were not considered real work. Yet market-oriented policies gutted the government sector and the majority of opportunities for steady work in African cities. Insecure work such as street vending took the place of formal work as men's primary economic option.

The shift challenged men's dignity. Agadjanian (2002) explained,

> Although the contraction of the formal sector has affected both men and women once employed there, men's mass ejection from it has greater implications for gender relations than does women's. This is because in the context of an entrenched patriarchal gender hierarchy, women's employment in the formal sector still tends to be seen as unusual, whereas for men, formal sector jobs constitute not only the most appropriate and desirable type of work, but also part of their masculine status. (261)

Moreover, the low earnings in informal, precarious work have made it harder for men to perform traditional masculine tasks, such as paying bridewealth (money given to a bride's family by the bridegroom) and acting as family breadwinners. In the informal sector, Agadjanian (2002) concluded, men's inability to earn enough money to support their families has undermined their economic and social supremacy. Because masculine identity had been rooted in the formal economy and feminine identity outside, poor men struggled to live up to gendered norms.

Reconstructing Masculinities on the Margins

On the margins of the global economy, men unable to be family breadwinners have sought to redefine masculinity beyond the realm of paid work. In *Those Who Work, Those Who Don't: Poverty, Morality and Family in Rural America* (2009), for instance, Jennifer Sherman examined a community in the U.S. Pacific Northwest, where environmental protections in the early 1990s outlawed once-abundant logging, and sawmill jobs disappeared. As men lost their capacity to be breadwinners, Sherman found, many became deeply frustrated and clung rigidly to a traditional masculinity, turning, for instance, to domestic abuse. However, others tried to redefine masculinity through moral norms, including being a good family man who has the time, by virtue of not working, to impart skills and values to his children.

In the West African nation of Ivory Coast, men have also appropriated cultural symbols as a means to identify as men in the absence of dignifying work. While Ivory Coast was seen as an "economic miracle" in the 1980s due to its successful coffee and cocoa industries, the informal economy now predominates, leaving men to feel the same sting as the street vendors Agadjanian examined in Mozambique or the loggers studied by Sherman. Due to its history of rapid economic growth, Ivory Coast once made lavish spending a mark of "civilization." If a man was well off, he might spend money on his wife or mistress to illustrate his masculine identity. Men who could afford it used the provider ideal to assert power over women.

Today, instead of work, some men have turned to conspicuous consumption to make themselves visible in a global economy that appears to have forgotten them. In the city of Abidjan, Jordanna Matlon (2011, 2016) showed, men in the informal sector contest their denigrated working identities by constructing counter-narratives of a consumerist Black masculinity inspired by hip-hop culture. By purchasing and showing images of hip-hop style "bling" (big gold jewelry) and celebrating iconic Black American personalities such as Barack Obama, they locate themselves in the same position as socioeconomically marginal but culturally powerful Black men from the United States.

In South Africa, meanwhile, Mark Hunter (2010) linked the spread of AIDS to men's chronic unemployment amid persistent expectations of wage-earner masculinity. Because South African women were historically dependent on their partner's salaries, romantic and sexual relations were linked to economic exchange. But with men working less, it is now common for men to be without partners and for one man, a "sugar daddy" who is typically older and already married, to have many partners. Hunter wrote,

> As a consequence of the increasingly winner-takes-all sexual economy—in which wealth can secure many girlfriends and poverty none—men marginalized from the productive economy also face marginalization from the sexual economy. . . . This close connection between money and sex reveals that class consciousness, long searched for on the shop floor, is constructed today in the sexual and not simply the productive economy. (167–168)

These gender imbalances, Hunter argued, implicate sex with "material benefits for unmarried women but also feelings of love and a wide range of moral and reciprocal obligations" that drive the spread of AIDS (2010: 6).

The End of Men? Or More Glass Ceiling?

As global production has become feminized and masculinity de-linked from work, some observers suggest that a new era has begun, heralding, as journalist Hanna Rosin (2012) put it, the "end of men." In the United States, popular literature laments disappointing trends in men's economic and social roles. As jobs once held by men have been lost, women's rates of college graduation are rising, along with their employment and their presence in male-dominated fields such as business and politics. In school, boys' performance is poor compared to girls' from kindergarten through university. As of 2015, women earned 58% of bachelor's degrees in the United States. Likewise, even though women in the workforce still make lower wages than men, women's wages have risen while men's have stagnated. Today, men in their prime are unemployed at the striking rate of 1 in 5, compared to 1 in 20 in 1950 (Homans 2012).

Hanna Rosin's (2012) bestselling book, *The End of Men: And the Rise of Women*, takes the position that feminine qualities are better adapted to the new service economy. Men, she claims, are stiff as "cardboard" and women are flexible like "plastic." Unlike Sandberg's call for women to lean in and be more *like* men at work, Rosin suggests that as women overtake men, the workplace has become a woman's world. As a result, she argues, women have won the gender war, pulling decisively ahead (of men) by almost every measure. Women not only predominate in U.S. schools and workplaces, but, according to Rosin, they also find themselves competent and capable in these spaces. Rosin suggests, "Women are not just catching up anymore, they are becoming the standard by which success is measured" (11). Patriarchy, Rosin hints, is coming to an end.

Other scholars view the situation differently. For example, historian Stephanie Coontz (2012) supplies a host of figures disputing this portrait of women's ascendancy at men's expense. The real issue, she counters, is what she calls the *masculine mystique*. In her account, men's "overinvestment in their gender identity" has created a *masculine* gender mystique that is now equally restrictive as the *feminine mystique* Betty Friedan described in the 1960s (see Chapter 3), which pressured women to stay at home and act as nurturing partners. Coontz argues that the masculine mystique penalizes boys who study and men who pursue traditionally feminine careers or actively participate in childcare and housework. She concludes, "Men need to liberate themselves from the pressure to prove their masculinity."

Regardless of whether such a masculine mystique exists, white men still dominate corporate power positions. Even as production has become feminized, transnational circuits of capital are still controlled by men who embody a particular brand of hegemonic masculinity. Women's entry into paid work has not ended occupational sex segregation or the glass ceiling. Women still only make up 4.6% of Fortune 500 CEOs and sit on 16.9% percent of Fortune 500 corporate boards, the key decision-making positions in global industry (Warner 2014). Even fewer of these economic powerholders are women of color. Meanwhile, when women *do* serve as CEOs in Fortune 500 companies, they earn less than men CEOs, and when they talk about their positions of power, their likability falls. Although women as a group have made substantial gains in wages, educational attainment, and prestige over the past three decades, the economists Betsey Stevenson and Justin Wolfers (2009) show that women are less happy today than their predecessors were in 1972, both in absolute terms and relative to men. This picture does not look like the end for all men.

Beyond the Gendered Economy

Examining the gendered economy leaves sociologists of gender with a set of questions: Are things getting better thanks to women's entry into paid work and the end of the family wage? Where does neoliberal globalization help, and where do inequalities persist?

As this chapter has shown, gender shapes the power relationships between labor and capital. On one hand, these power relationships rely on a long history of public/private divides in which workers are still framed as breadwinners, with few care work responsibilities. These divides reverberate in ongoing inequities, such as occupational sex segregation, the wage gap, and the exclusion of women from positions of power. Gender-egalitarian policies and business practices could help transform such dynamics. Specifically, laws and businesses might aggressively enforce wage equality and help draw women into positions of power. They might also revalue child-rearing, offering more time off for both mothers and fathers, equitable pay and promotions for mothers, and more flexible hours and paid family leave.

On the other hand, the relationship between gender and the economy is complex and dynamic, incorporating new gendered terms and tropes such as the third world woman worker for labor control or the responsible woman for international development. To break down the relationship between gender and the economy, sociologists of gender must go beyond framing issues of gender and work in terms of the differences between women and men. Remembering that gender is about power, position, representation, and practice, sociologists must also question how gendered tropes reinforce the subordination of labor to capital as well as the relationships of power among women, such as in the global care chain.

When asking whether globalization and employment have made women better off, it is important to remember that the implications vary by social position. Gender is multifaceted, taking different forms for women across race and class. For instance, white and well-off women's ability to enter positions held by white and well-off men in the workplace—to the extent they have done so—has depended on women of color. The expansion of finance and the withdrawal of government support also have varying implications for women around the world. Even among women in the Global South, the changes are uneven: Some women can earn wages if an employer lives in their area; some face reinforced gender segregation at work; and others, such as migrant domestic workers, have to move to sell their labor. Throughout this global economy, poor women—stuck in export work, domestic service, and informal labor—continue to have little power to determine the fates of their own lives, let alone the balance between their families and jobs. For these women, there is little hope in Sheryl Sandberg's call to lean in.

In a critique of Sheryl Sandberg, feminist activist and scholar bell hooks (2013) argued that the goal of feminism is not to adapt women to patriarchal capitalism but to move beyond it. While media icons such as Oprah Winfrey and women's groups across the country have taken Sandberg's *Lean In* as a new feminist manifesto, Sandberg's feminism continues to insist that women act more like the ideal masculine worker, remaining silent on issues of race and class. As a result, Sandberg's idea of gender equality remains tied to the status quo rather than seeking to challenge the current gender order. As hooks (2013) writes,

> [Sandberg] makes it seem that that privileged white men will eagerly choose to extend the benefits of corporate capitalism to white women who have the courage to "lean in." It almost seems as if Sandberg sees women's lack of perseverance as more the problem than systemic inequality. Sandberg effectively uses her race and class power and privilege to promote a narrow definition of feminism that obscures and undermines visionary feminist concerns.

hooks suggests that the male-dominated media have embraced Sandberg's vision precisely because it reframes feminism in masculinist terms. By leaving the normative gendered order as is and making it women's responsibility to change themselves (with the idea that women at the top will encourage women's empowerment at all levels), Sandberg is advocating a neoliberal feminist solution.

Instead of celebrating women as the new entrepreneurs, hooks argues, feminists must undo the technologies of production that rely on gendered norms to ensure the continued functioning of global capital. They must go beyond fighting for equal opportunities within the system to working to dismantle patriarchal capitalism altogether. Instead of pursuing the same opportunities available to men, hooks believes, women must transform the gender norms used by capital—and the profound inequalities they create—to build a system that is more equitable for all men and women, across nation, race, and class.

KEYWORDS

Exploitation 148
Feminine worker tropes 161
Flexibilization of labor 158
Gender wage gap 154
Gendered tropes 149
Glass ceiling 152
Glass escalator 152
Global care chain 159
Homosocial reproduction 156
Masculine worker norm 150
Occupational sex segregation 151
Pink collar jobs 151
Responsible woman trope 161
Sex segregation of work 148
Sticky floor 152
Third world woman worker trope 161
Workplace sexual harassment 157

QUESTIONS

- There are various gender *tropes* in places of work. Think of a place where you or a family member has worked. What gendered expectations did your boss (or your family member's boss) have? For instance, did they ask you to be submissive or caring, in a feminized role, even if you or other workers were men? Or did they approach workers in more masculine terms, for instance, encouraging them to be tough or competitive? Perhaps there were elements of both. Reflect on how gendered terms and expectations have shaped your work experience.

- Give an example of an area where sex segregation of work still occurs in the contemporary United States. Why does such sex segregation still occur? How is it intersectional by race and class?
- Does the question "Can women (or men) have it all?" make sense? Why or why not? How is the way people think about this question changing?
- What might a world in which men are not considered the main breadwinners look like in terms of gender relationships and family life?

ASSOCIATED READINGS

- Acker, Joan. 1990. "Hierarchies, Jobs, Bodies: A Theory of Gendered Organizations." *Gender & Society* 4 (2): 139–158.
- England, Paula. 2005. "Gender Inequality in Labor Markets: The Role of Motherhood and Segregation." *Social Politics: International Studies in Gender, State & Society* 12 (2): 264–288.
- Hartmann, Heidi. 1976. "Capitalism, Patriarchy and Job Segregation by Sex." *Signs: Journal of Women in Culture and Society* 1 (3): 137–169.
- Hondagneu-Sotelo, Pierrette. 2001. *Doméstica: Immigrant Workers Cleaning and Caring in the Shadows of Affluence*. Berkeley: University of California Press.
- Hochschild, Arlie. 2005. *Global Women: Nannies, Maids, and Sex Workers in the New Economy.* London, UK: Macmillan.
- Milkman, Ruth. 1986. "Women's History and the Sears Case." *Feminist Studies* 12 (2): 375–400.
- Glenn, Evelyn Nakano. 1992. "From Servitude to Service Work: Historical Continuities in the Racial Division of Paid Reproductive Labor." *Signs: Journal of Women in Culture and Society* 18 (1): 1–43.
- Rosin, Hanna. 2012. *The End of Men: And the Rise of Women.* New York: Riverhead Hardcover.
- Salzinger, Leslie. 2003. *Genders in Production: Making Workers in Mexico's Global Factories*. Berkeley: University of California Press.
- Schilt, Kristen. 2010. *Just One of the Guys? Transgender Men and the Persistence of Gender Inequality*. Chicago: The University of Chicago Press.
- Williams, Christine L. 1992. "The Glass Escalator: Hidden Advantages for Men in the 'Female' Professions." *Social Problems* 39 (3): 253–267.

NOTES

1. In her 1949 classic, *Male and Female*, anthropologist Margaret Mead argued that men were unsexed (made to feel less masculine) by failure; while women were unsexed by success. implying that when women became economically successful, they lost their femininity and thereby appeared masculine.
2. After the death of her husband in 2015, Sheryl Sandberg acknowledged that for women like her to lean in required significant economic privilege as well as support in the household either from partners or from paid care workers.

CHAPTER

9

Politicizing Gender

Gowri Vijayakumar and Katherine Maich

The previous chapters have examined how gendered norms, practices, ideologies, and institutions shape social life. This chapter explores how movements create changes in gender relations by tracing the history of feminist activism since the late 19th century. Feminist activism is typically described as involving three "waves": the first wave of the late 1800s and early 1900s, when women organized for voting and other legal rights; the second wave of the 1960s and 1970s, when women organized for workplace equality and against sexual violence; and the third wave of the 1990s and beyond, when the category of "woman" increasingly became contested and feminists of color pushed for an understanding of gender and sexuality as linked to race, class, and colonialism. This chapter takes a different approach: Instead of describing feminist movements as consecutive waves, we will look at feminist movements as involving multiple "currents" that sometimes intersect, sometimes join, and sometimes emerge in tension with one another. The chapter shows that like other social movements, feminist activism has historically been influenced by and reproduced multiple social inequalities. Though the chapter primarily examines feminisms in the United States, it also looks at the global context for feminist activism and the powerful influence of feminists in Europe, Asia, Latin America, and Africa on U.S. feminisms. The chapter concludes by showing how activists around the world challenge and transform gender relations in many ways, including in ways not typically defined as feminist.

Introduction

On Valentine's Day in 2013, activists in 207 countries around the world gathered to protest violence against women. They called the march "One Billion Rising." The event was designed as an activist response to recent incidents of violence against women that captured media attention and sparked outrage around the world—a gang rape in Steubenville, Ohio, in the United States; the shooting of Malala Yousafzai, an activist for girls' education in northwestern Pakistan; and a gang rape and murder in New Delhi, India. It emphasized that by coming together and telling their stories, women could rise up against such violence. The famous organizer of One Billion Rising, Eve Ensler, who was also the author of the *Vagina Monologues*, explained in the newspaper *The Guardian* that the event aimed to "transform the mindset that has normalized this violence, to bring women survivors into their bodies, their strength, their determination, their energy and power and to dance up the will of the world to finally make violence against women unacceptable" (Ensler 2013).

While One Billion Rising sought to emphasize women's ability to overcome violence, feminist activist critics pointed out that the event silenced some women while elevating others, promoting a narrow vision of feminism. These critics suggested that by claiming that individual women could rise up against violence, One Billion Rising obscured the structural constraints they faced. For instance, a **feminist** from the Democratic Republic of Congo (DRC) argued that it was insulting to expect rape survivors to turn up in the face of atrocities and in order to tell their stories to the rest of the world. An Iranian feminist pointed out, "Who is someone else to come to my country and claim to 'help' me by telling me to 'rise' above the experiences I have had?!" (Gyte 2013).

These critiques articulated long-standing tensions in feminist activism. Previous chapters showed that even as feminists of the 1960s and 1970s—mostly white and middle class—challenged women's subordination to their husbands, their "liberation" through professional work often depended on the subordination of other women. By contrast, women of color and working-class activists articulated the need for feminisms that incorporated race, class, sexuality, and colonialism—some rejecting the term *feminist* altogether.

This chapter looks at how feminist activists have organized politically to both disrupt and reproduce the various power relations that are inextricably linked to gender. Focusing on a few specific movements and struggles that highlight key historical moments in feminist activism, the chapter explores the internal power dynamics of feminism as a social movement. It considers how the category of *woman* has served as a useful tool for organizing but also as a tool for exclusion. The chapter also uses the words of feminist activists to describe the multiple dimensions of **feminist praxis**—that is, the ways in which feminist critiques and theories are embodied and practiced through collective action. This praxis holds important lessons for the intellectual project of the sociology of gender that we reflect on at the end of the chapter.

Rethinking the History of Feminism: Waves and Currents

Scholars and activists typically describe the history of feminist movements in the United States as involving three consecutive phases: *first-*, *second-*, and *third-wave* feminism. According to this model, from the 1840s through the 1920s, **first-wave feminism** focused on basic citizenship rights for women equal to those of men—such as suffrage and property rights. Then, from the 1960s to the 1990s, **second-wave feminism** focused on issues such as workplace inequalities, sexual harassment, reproductive rights (such as the right to choose an abortion), domestic violence, and rape. Finally, starting in the 1990s, **third-wave feminism** challenged the idea that women shared a single experience and instead expanded conversations within feminism to consider relationships between gender and race, class, sexuality, and colonialism. (See Figure 9.1.)

Figure 9.1 Feminist Activism in Three "Waves"

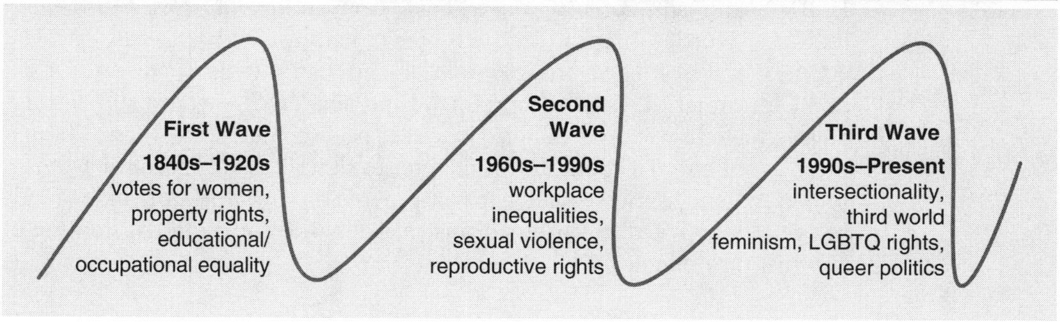

Figure 9.2 Feminist Activism as a Set of Intersecting Currents

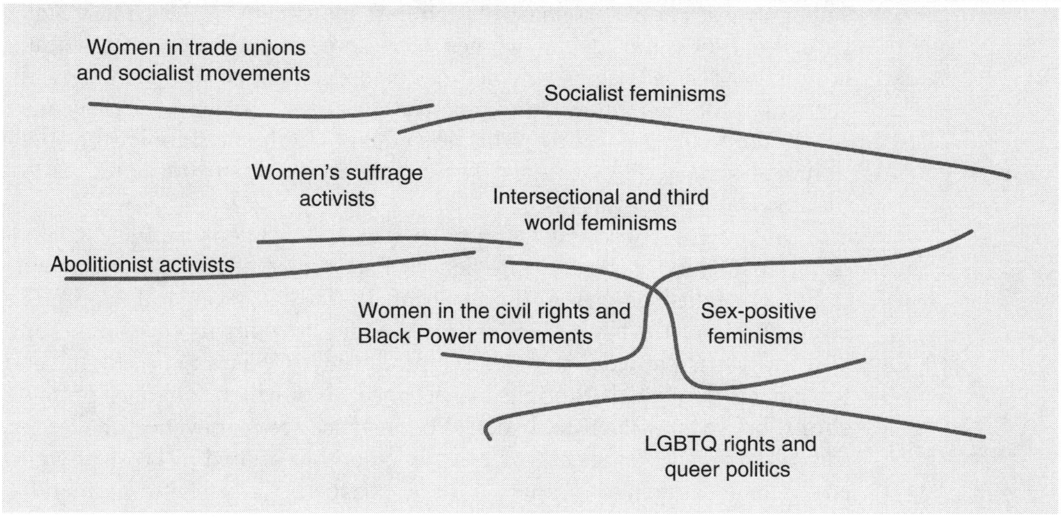

This chapter moves away from the metaphor of waves to conceptualize feminist politics as involving a series of intersecting and overlapping currents. **Feminist currents** describe particular movements and struggles around gendered power relations. For instance, currents include everything from socialist feminism to women's suffrage to lesbian, gay, bisexual, transgender, and queer (LGBTQ) rights to Black feminism. While all currents are related to gender, they tie gender to different goals, ranging from sexual freedom to labor rights. In turn, they also adopt different strategies. These currents build on and enhance one another, but they can also diverge and come into conflict. At times, one current has obscured or even subordinated another current. Within each time period, we trace different currents and their relationships to one another. (See Figure 9.2.)

Conventional histories often use a narrow definition of feminist movements that is focused on women's collective action for legal, economic, or social rights as *women* (rather than as immigrants, laborers, or nationalists).

Yet women's political struggles have taken many forms. Women around the world have played key roles in labor, communist, abolitionist, nationalist, LGBTQ, and anti-colonial movements. Conventional histories also often focus on North American and European feminist activism and pay less attention to histories of struggle around gender and sexuality in Africa, Asia, and Latin America. Finally, activism around gendered power relations is not always waged by women but also by queer people, men, and others. Though there is not enough room in this chapter to describe every form of activism linked to gender and sexuality, it will provide a framework for understanding gender activism in various forms that defy the conventional framing of feminist movements.

Nineteenth- and Early 20th-Century Gender Activism in the United States

Though most people associate the feminist movement in the United States with the 1960s and 1970s, women (and some men) had been advocates around gender issues for many decades before the rise of feminism *per se*. In particular, the currents of gender activism prior to the feminist movement centered on women's voting rights and equality in the household, the abolition of slavery, and labor rights. These currents are often considered part of the first wave of feminism.

One of the most critical moments in the women's suffrage current occurred in July of 1848 at the Seneca Falls Convention, led by women's rights advocates Susan B. Anthony, Elizabeth Cady Stanton, and others. The convention was the first in U.S. history to focus on women's equal rights and political participation. The delegates produced a Declaration of Rights and Sentiments that listed 18 points of grievance, all of which sought to promote equity between women and men. For instance, one grievance challenged the "tyranny" of men over women, while another argued in favor of women's right to vote. The primary author, Elizabeth Cady Stanton, amended Thomas Jefferson's writing by affirming that "All men *and women* are created equal," nearly 75 years after the signing of the Declaration of Independence.

The Seneca Falls Convention itself had been inspired by women's involvement in advocating the abolition of slavery. Indeed, Convention organizer Elizabeth Cady Stanton first met Lucretia Mott, a founder of the Philadelphia Female Anti-Slavery Society at the World Anti-Slavery Convention in London in 1840. Frustrated at the exclusion of women from the deliberations in London, Mott and Stanton began to discuss women's rights and then decided to hold the Seneca Falls meeting. In turn, a number of prominent abolitionists attended the Seneca Falls Convention, including Frederick Douglass, the black famous intellectual who had been enslaved as a young man, and Sarah and Angelina Grimké, white Southern sisters who renounced their family's slaveholding practices to become abolitionists and fixtures in the women's equality movement (McMillen 2008). Though women would not achieve political suffrage throughout the U.S. for another 75 years, the Seneca Falls Convention launched a series of conversations on social reforms to extend voting rights and end slavery.

In addition to the anti-slavery movement and the women's rights movement, perhaps the most prominent current of gender activism prior to the 1960s revolved around labor. Although unions are conventionally associated with men, women were also active in the U.S. labor movement, even in the 19th century, when women textile workers formed the Lowell Female Labor Reform Association to testify before the legislature about working conditions in 1843, and freed Black women formed a union of laundresses in Jackson, Mississippi, in 1866. In 1909, many women workers participated in the "Uprising of the Thirty Thousand," a mass strike by New York women garment workers. The strike compelled many factories to accept union demands, such as maintaining open doors and better fire escapes. Yet the Triangle Shirtwaist Factory held out. Then, in 1911, a fire at that factory killed 123 women and 23 men, who were trapped behind its locked doors. The fire drew attention to the hostile conditions garment workers faced and the importance of unionization.

Rose Schneiderman, a Jewish socialist feminist and shop-floor unionist, survived the Triangle Shirtwaist fire and went on to fight for unionization by forging cross-class alliances. A 4'9" capmaker with flaming red hair and legendary speaking power, Schneiderman deftly connected the exploitation of male factory workers and young, immigrant female workers in textile mills (Orleck 1995). Thus, her advocacy helped draw attention to the 1912 textile workers' strike in Lawrence, Massachusetts, in which over twenty thousand textile mill workers protested wage cuts and poor working conditions. Vying for an expansive working-class movement beyond the narrow vision that characterized men labor leaders at the time, Schneiderman famously stated, "The woman worker needs bread, but she needs roses, too." In other words, workers fought for *bread*—meaning safer working conditions, medical care, a shorter workday, affordable housing, and food; the basic human needs for survival—and *roses*—access to culture and education, meaningful work, and equality; the enjoyment of life (Orleck 1995). This demand for "**bread and roses**" soon took on a cultural life of its own in songs, slogans, poetry, and film. Schneiderman later became New York Secretary of Labor and a member of the National Labor Advisory Board. She advocated social security benefits for domestic workers, supported the unionization of restaurant workers, and championed labor regulation of women's work in the home, not only the factory.

While advocacy such as Schneiderman's drew attention to the plight of women workers, they remained stymied by ongoing sexual harassment, labor exploitation, and norms about women's positions in the home. As Ken Loach's 2000 film, *Bread and Roses,* attests, many similar issues persist today. The film depicts the Los Angeles Justice for Janitors campaign of the late 1990s, focusing on how women janitors navigate sexual harassment, threats of deportation, and the quest for dignity at work. Nevertheless, women's involvement in movements such as those for women's suffrage, abolition, and labor persisted throughout the first half of the 20th century and helped lay the groundwork for the U.S. feminist movement in the 1960s and 1970s.

Feminisms in the United States during the 1960s and 1970s

In the 1960s and 1970s, women continued to be active in antiracist, civil rights, Black Power, LGBTQ, and labor movements as well as in women's liberation organizations. While the more dominant feminist currents in this period continued to assume a white, middle-class subject, excluding women of color, working-class women, and others from feminist struggle, they also pioneered new ways of understanding women's labor, bodies, and politics.

In the 1960s and 1970s, feminists built on the long tradition of women's labor activism in the United States. Women in leftist social movements of this era fought for workers' rights and civil rights and protested the Vietnam War. Women were actively involved in student movements, civil rights organizations, and leftist reform groups such as Students for a Democratic Society (SDS) and the Student Nonviolent Coordinating Committee (SNCC) that actively fought for economic and racial justice in the United States. Yet women were often left out of these groups' leadership circles and relegated to "feminine" caretaking tasks. Tensions mounted between women and their male allies in these movements.

One example of the dismissive attitude of leftist men toward women's liberation was their reaction to women's feminist statements at the National Convention of SDS in 1967, where women led a "Women's Liberation Workshop." Women called for communal childcare centers, contraception and abortion care, and a more aggressive commitment to women's liberation within SDS. At the convention, many men reacted angrily. When the women's demands were published in the *New Left Notes* the next week, they were illustrated with a cartoon of a girl with earrings, a polka dot mini-dress, and matching visible undergarments, holding a sign saying, "We want our rights and we want them now," (Echols 1989: 45; Rosen 2000). For the women activists, the cartoon was belittling and dismissive of their struggles.

Another catalytic moment in the relationship between women and leftist organizations occurred at the National Conference for the New Politics in Chicago. At the conference, 2,000 activists met to discuss a range of issues, including the role of Black Power and Black activists within the New Left. Women's demands continued to be overlooked at the conference. Ti-Grace Atkinson and Shulamith Firestone drafted a resolution demanding 51% of convention votes for women; an official endorsement of progressive marriage, divorce, and property laws; and reproductive rights for women. Their resolution was initially excluded from the convention's agenda. When they began reading their manifesto at the conference, the chairman patted Firestone on the head and said, "Move on little girl; we have more important issues to talk about here than women's liberation," (Echols 1989: 49). These insults eventually led to the formation of autonomous radical women's organizations dedicated to both class and race politics and women's liberation.

Even as women were being marginalized within leftist organizations, new energy was building around feminist activism in the United States. As discussed in Chapter 3, in 1963, American feminist Betty Friedan published *The Feminine Mystique*, speaking to the loneliness and frustration of white

American housewives caught in post–World War II norms of domesticity. Friedan urged women to seek more personally fulfilling lives outside the home, and many reacted enthusiastically. In 1966, Friedan became the first president of the **National Organization for Women (NOW)**, a key organization in feminist politics.

Building on the insights of European feminists such as Simone de Beauvoir (see Chapter 7), the feminists of organizations such as NOW sought to understand why women were positioned as subordinate to men. Armed with the insight that "the personal is political," these feminists worked on *consciousness raising*, exploring their experiences of sexual objectification in small groups to reveal and undo patterns of power relations. Rather than imposing a top-down theory of power, consciousness-raising groups sought to build a theory of sexuality and women's subordination from women's own points of view (MacKinnon 1982: 535).

Feminists also sought to regain control over their bodies and reproduction. In 1966, women activists founded the Association to Repeal Abortion Laws (now NARAL Pro-Choice America), and in the following year, at least 25 state legislatures discussed abortion reform bills (Morgen 2002: 4). Feminist networks around the country worked to make abortion legal and safe. In 1973, in a major success for these activists, the Supreme Court's decision in *Roe v. Wade* ordered states to lift restrictions on abortions until the third trimester of pregnancy (with exceptions for maternal health).

This landmark decision provided new momentum for activists around the country who had been advocates for women's control over their health. In 1970, the Boston Women's Health Book Collective, a group of 12 feminist activists, published a pamphlet called *Women and Their Bodies*. The book aimed to subvert the scientific expertise of male physicians about women's bodies by providing accessible women's health information. Built on women's own accounts and experiences, the book was immensely popular and influential. After selling 350,000 copies, it was published as *Our Bodies, Ourselves* in 1973 (Morgen 2002; Norsigian 2005). *Our Bodies, Ourselves* articulated the core themes of a broader feminist health movement: In the 1970s, and especially after *Roe v. Wade*, some fifty feminist health clinics opened around the country to provide abortions and feminist reproductive health care (Newman 2007).[1]

In the 1970s, the Comparable Worth Movement also challenged institutionalized gender discrimination in the labor market. Feminists involved in the Comparable Worth Movement sought to revalue traditionally feminine occupations, such as nursing, teaching, and other "pink-collar" jobs (see Chapter 8). Launched by mainly white liberal feminists, the movement demanded an equal salary for men and women with comparable skills. They asked why tree trimmers should earn more money than childcare providers or why electricians (an occupation largely dominated by men) should earn more than librarians (an occupation largely dominated by women). Throughout the 1970s and 1980s, scholars, activists, and women workers continued to critique gender pay gaps, the glass ceiling, and occupational sex segregation. They noted that the subjective nature of job evaluations opened opportunities for discrimination, and they critiqued a general devaluation of skills considered to be women's work (such as caregiving, nurturing, and other soft skills embedded in forms of emotional labor).

Similarly, the Wages for Housework campaign directly took on issues of labor and work and had active chapters internationally and in New York. By demanding wages in exchange for housework, the campaign positioned housewives and women who worked outside the home in the same category: as women workers whose labor was devalued. By drawing this link, the campaign positioned all women as working women and demanded workers' rights for women in all forms of work. Wages for Housework also made a symbolic claim to radical gender equality in all areas of life. As Silvia Federici, an Italian Marxist feminist and one of the founders of the movement, wrote,

> Wages for housework is only the beginning, but its message is clear: from now on they have to pay us because as females we do not guarantee anything any longer. We want to call work what is work so that eventually we might rediscover what is love and create what will be our sexuality, which we have never known. (Federici [1975] 2012: 20)

Organizations such as NOW maintained a middle-class white orientation. Many of the organization's aims, such as winning the right for women to work outside the home, were irrelevant to working-class women and women of color who already worked for low wages and whose occupations—such as domestic labor—were excluded from campaigns for equal pay. Middle-class white feminism also tended to overlook ways in which class and race operated intersectionally with gender in producing oppressive social relations. However, white housewives and professional women were not the only people mobilizing around gender inequality during this period.

Black Women's Organizing: "A Woman's Place Is in the Struggle"

Black women were very active in the Civil Rights movement and in shaping movements such as the Black Panther Party (BPP), which organized and mobilized out of Oakland, California, to protest police oppression and brutality against Black communities. As Salamishah Tillet (2015) notes, though mainstream white American media tended to depict the Black Panthers as militant Black men clad in leather coats with berets on their heads and rifles tucked beneath their arms, in fact, by the early 1970s, two-thirds of BPP members were women.

The first woman Black Panther, Joan Tarika Lewis, utilized her artwork to depict women as strong warriors and heroes of the community, which opened up space for women in the struggle (Martin 2014). Likewise, Ericka Huggins, the first woman to establish a BPP chapter and the widow of slain BPP leader John Huggins, explained that the women who were drawn to the Panthers

> were all feminists; not in the way that feminism is looked at today, in which you have to go step by step in order to claim yourself as a feminist. But we generally believed in the political, social, economic and sexual equality of women and girls. (Tillet 2015)

However, Black women struggled with their male counterparts in the movement over gender issues. As in the (white) leftist organizing discussed above, gender in the BPP often took a backseat to broader concerns of racial justice and class, which were central to the Panthers' platform. Tensions also emerged around whether women should bear arms as part of the movement.

Furthermore, toward the end of the BBP's most active years in the late 1960s, the police and Federal Bureau of Investigation (FBI) began to target male Black Panthers through violent attacks. In turn, women Black Panthers kept alive a strong organizing base in Oakland. They struggled for equal housing, the Free Breakfast for All program, liberation schools, and political education classes designed to end gender bias in the Black community. As the state targeted men, women also moved from their original positions behind the scenes into central BPP leadership (Tillet 2015).

These Black Panther women organized for anti-racist movement building that included community health and safety issues affecting women and children. Black Panther women's articles, circulated among membership, include photographs of women members smiling with fists raised in front of the central office in Oakland, proudly standing underneath the words, "The Sky's the Limit." These images demonstrate a sisterhood united against their shared racialized, classed, and gendered oppression.

In the 1970s, other Black women and women of color also organized against white biases within the feminist movement. In 1970, the Black Women's Alliance, which had originated with women members of the anti-racist SNCC, grew frustrated with racism within the feminist movement. They joined a group of Puerto Rican feminists to form the Third World Women's Alliance. The group built connections to feminists around the world and promoted unity among Black and brown feminists. In 1973, the Comisión Femenil Mexicana Nacional (CFMN, National Commission of Mexican Women) was formed by a group of women who felt that gender had been marginalized within the Chicano movement.

As feminist efforts gained momentum in the middle and late 1970s, women of color continued to demand greater attention to their concerns. The United Nations proclaimed 1975 the International Women's Year and, as part of a series of events intended to promote gender equality, Congress provided funding for a National Women's Conference in 1977 in Houston, Texas. The conference included many prominent feminists and women politicians, such as three First Ladies, Coretta Scott King, Betty Friedan, and Maya Angelou, among others, but it paid relatively little attention to women of color. In response, a group of Black feminists formed the Black Women's Agenda, which developed the Black Women's Action Plan. At the conference, women who faced racial injustice joined together in supporting the Action Plan, creating a shared position as women of color (Ross 2011).

Another influential group of Black socialist feminist activists, the **Combahee River Collective**, argued for new formations of political struggle that acknowledged the interlocking nature of their oppression along lines of race, class, gender, and sexuality. The Combahee River Collective's statement, part of which appears below, demanded a feminist politics that acknowledged the interlocking nature of oppression.

The Combahee River Collective Statement (1978)

We are a collective of Black feminists who have been meeting together since 1974. During that time, we have been involved in the process of defining and clarifying our politics, while at the same time doing political work within our own group and in coalition with other progressive organizations and movements. The most general statement of our politics at the present time would be that we are actively committed to struggling against racial, sexual, heterosexual, and class oppression, and see as our particular task the development of integrated analysis and practice based upon the fact that the major systems of oppression are interlocking. The synthesis of these oppressions creates the conditions of our lives. As Black women, we see Black feminism as the logical political movement to combat the manifold and simultaneous oppressions that all women of color face. . . .

Our politics initially sprang from the shared belief that Black women are inherently valuable, that our liberation is a necessity not as an adjunct to somebody else's . . . [but] because of our need as human persons for autonomy. This may seem so obvious as to sound simplistic, but it is apparent that no other ostensibly progressive movement has ever considered our specific oppression as a priority or worked seriously for the ending of that oppression. . . .

In the practice of our politics, we do not believe that the end always justifies the means. Many reactionary and destructive acts have been done in the name of achieving "correct" political goals. As feminists, we do not want to mess over people in the name of politics. We believe in collective process and a nonhierarchical distribution of power within our own group and in our vision of a revolutionary society. We are committed to a continual examination of our politics as they develop through criticism and self-criticism as an essential aspect of our practice. . . . As Black feminists and lesbians, we know that we have a very definite revolutionary task to perform and we are ready for the lifetime of work and struggle before us.

In short, just as white feminist currents pushed against exclusion in labor and New Left advocacy, Black feminists and feminists of color pushed for greater influence in both racial justice and feminist movements.

Speaking, Singing, and Performing Gender: Creatively Challenging the "Relations of Ruling"

Feminists in the 1960s and 1970s also sought to find creative spaces through which to critique existing power relations. Feminist artists and scholars thus became as much a part of political movement building as those marching and demonstrating.

Following Virginia Woolf's call in 1929 for women to forge "a room of one's own" (claim their own literary voices), women songwriters of this era expressed their politics through their writing and performance. Notable examples include Roberta Flack's soul and gospel-turned-pop hits and Laura Nyro and Carole King's folk songs, which championed equal pay for equal work and dealt with themes of pregnancy, birth control, and women's freedom. Joan Baez delivered strong messages of social justice via acoustic guitar, including covers of Chile's ethnomusicologist and folklorist Violeta

Parra, while Aretha Franklin's 1967 hit, "Do Right Woman, Do Right Man," urged gender equality and recognition as Franklin crooned, "A woman's only human, this you should understand." Sounding out a call for respect, Franklin declared, "She's not just a plaything, she's flesh and blood—just like her man!" And in a track on Joni Mitchell's 1976 album *Hejira*, "Amelia," a tribute to the lost pilot Amelia Earhart, Mitchell soulfully identified with the pilot's longing for another world through musical parallels of guitar strings and "songs so wild and blue." She mused about Earhart, "A ghost of aviation, she was swallowed by the sky—or by the sea, like me, she had a dream to fly."

The historically white, masculine, and elite institution of academia also began to respond to feminist organizing. The first university-level women's studies courses were offered in the late 1960s at Cornell, and in the early 1970s, women's, gender, or feminist studies programs, departments, and concentrations spread rapidly. There are now over 400 such programs in the U.S. and over 900 globally. Interdisciplinary in nature, these programs draw from the humanities and social sciences. Many offer courses in sexualities, LGBTQ studies, critical race theory, queer and feminist theory, and feminist perspectives on biology, history, literature, technology, and research methods. The institutionalization of these departments and the creation of doctoral degree–granting women's studies programs in the 1960s and 1970s demonstrated the importance of gender as a serious topic of study and a critical lens on the social world.

Nevertheless, as feminists, Black Panthers, LGBTQ movements, and singers fought for liberation in the 1960s and 1970s, dominant feminist currents continued to assume a white, middle-class subject. Such activists often assumed that the concept of *woman* provided a common denominator across multiple experiences. Yet their idea of *woman* continued to exclude women of color, working-class women, and others. These dynamics would continue to be key points of tension in the 1980s and 1990s.

The 1980s and 1990s: Critiques of White Feminism, Queer Politics, and Transnational Solidarities

In the 1980s and 1990s, many of the currents of feminism that had addressed race, class, sexuality, and colonialism gathered force and came into direct conflict with the white middle-class currents that had previously been dominant. Women of color had organized to bring race and class to the forefront of feminist activism since the 1970s, but they often remained excluded from the dominant currents of feminist organizing. Indeed, women of color faced a triple exclusion: sexism from antiracist activists and racism and classism from middle-class white feminists. It was not until the early 1990s that mainstream feminist activism began to incorporate an intersectional perspective that included questions of race, class, sexuality, and colonialism. Intersectionality (recall Chapter 2) destabilized the one-dimensional understanding of gender that had run through dominant feminisms in the 1960s and 1970s. As white feminists responded to challenges from multiple quarters, many came to rethink the category of *woman*, highlighting that it was produced in relation to multiple intersecting dynamics.

Feminist scholars of color were active in the movement to bring race and class analysis to feminism. In 1981, for instance, two Chicana feminists, Cherríe Moraga and Gloria Anzaldúa, published an edited anthology of writings from women of color called *This Bridge Called My Back*. The book included reflections from diverse women of color in the United States. It challenged the dominance of white middle-class experience in feminist activist and intellectual realms and argued for a politics that took into account the divisions and inequalities among women rather than assuming that they shared a single experience. The editors called for a new way of thinking about feminist, anti-racist, class, and sexuality politics as dynamically interconnected. They also moved beyond typical academic writing by including poetry, essays, and fiction; emphasizing third world women's subjective experiences; and using accessible language.

Feminist scholars of color also placed their activism in an international context. In 1983, two graduate students at the University of Illinois, Chandra Talpade Mohanty and Ann Russo, organized a conference called "Common Differences: Third World Women and Feminist Perspectives." The conference and the resulting book, *Third World Women and the Politics of Feminism* (Mohanty, Russo, and Torres 1991) provided a transnational perspective on feminism, seeking to link the struggles of women of color in the U.S. and Europe to the struggles of those in Latin America, Asia, and sub-Saharan Africa. We will discuss their work further in Chapter 10.

Meanwhile, women of color activists also challenged dominant white feminism more directly. Some women of color even questioned the term *feminist* as an overly narrow conception of what women's concerns looked like. For example, Alice Walker, in her book, *In Search of Our Mother's Gardens,* famously wrote, "Womanist is to feminist as purple is to lavender" and celebrated the womanist, "a black feminist or feminist of color" who "Loves music. Loves dance. Loves the moon. *Loves* the Spirit. Loves love and food and roundness. Loves struggle. *Loves* the Folk. Loves herself" (1983: xi–xii).

A key catalytic moment in the consolidation of intersectional feminism came in 1991 with the Senate hearings preceding the confirmation of the Supreme Court justice Clarence Thomas, described in detail in Chapter 2. When Anita Hill, a Black woman, testified that Thomas, who was also Black, had sexually harassed her while he had been her supervisor, controversy erupted. Many Black leaders accused Hill of betraying the Black community by bringing an accusation against a Black man who had the opportunity to gain power within white political structures. Meanwhile, many white women feminists supported Hill, but without acknowledging the place of racism in Hill's vulnerability to harassment and in her treatment by senators during the hearings. The case pointed to the gaps within both dominant anti-racism (which assumed a Black masculine subject) and dominant feminism (which assumed a white middle-class feminine subject), neither of which could speak to Hill's experience (Crenshaw 1991).

Soon after Hill's testimony, Rebecca Walker, a 22-year-old student at Yale University, wrote an essay in *Ms.* Magazine titled "Becoming the Third Wave," in which she called for an invigoration of feminist activism:

> I write this as a plea to all women, especially the women of my generation: Let Thomas' confirmation serve to remind you, as it did me, that the fight is far from over. Let this dismissal of a woman's experience move you to anger. Turn that outrage into political power. . . . I am not a postfeminism feminist. I am the Third Wave. (1992: 41)

Rebecca Walker's call reflected the growing challenge to the assumption that white middle-class women's concerns were a default experience. This challenge had developed alongside white middle-class feminism in the 1970s, but by 1992, it had attained new visibility and become influential in both academic feminist scholarship and mainstream feminist organizations.

The Politics of Sexuality in the 1980s and 1990s

In the 1960s, there was considerable tension around the participation of LGBTQ people in the feminist movement. While the 1969 Stonewall riots (see Chapter 5) helped catalyze LGBTQ politics and spark a newly invigorated gay liberation movement, the relationship between gay liberation and women's liberation politics was not always smooth. In the late 1960s, Betty Friedan at NOW had been uncomfortable with lesbians participating in the feminist movement and termed them a "*lavender menace*," leading many lesbians to leave the organization. Eventually, in 1971, in response to pressure from the few remaining lesbian members, NOW passed a resolution acknowledging the oppression of lesbians as a feminist issue.

In the 1980s and 1990s, the dominant, currents within feminism also began to embrace new thinking about sexuality and sexual freedom, and the inclusion of sex workers' rights in feminist politics became less fraught than it was during the "Sex Wars," as discussed in Chapter 5. Sex workers' rights activism, which had roots in the 1970s and 1980s, gained broader acceptance. Anthologies of writings by sex workers published in the 1990s argued that sex work was like any other work and that sex workers had a key role to play in feminist politics (Chapkis 1997; Delacoste and Alexander 1998). These accounts offered a more nuanced view of sex work as a possible site of violence but also a site of self-expression, creativity, connection, and pleasure—or simply as another way to make a living.

LGBTQ politics also gained momentum in the 1980s and 1990s. In the period after the 1969 Stonewall Riots, marches for gay liberation took place around the country, making LGBTQ people's demands more visible at the local level. The first LGBTQ March on Washington in 1979 marked a new era of LGBTQ organizing aimed at transforming national policy; an estimated 75,000 to 125,000 LGBTQ people attended (Ghaziani and Baldessari 2011). The march marked a step on the way to forming a shared national LGBTQ identity that sought to unite multiple groups—gay, lesbian, transgender, bisexual, and queer people.

LGBTQ movements achieved some legal gains in the 1980s and 1990s. In 1982, Wisconsin was the first U.S. state to outlaw discrimination on the basis of sexual orientation. In 1993, the Department of Defense issued its "Don't Ask, Don't Tell" policy, which prohibited the military from excluding potential recruits on the basis of sexual orientation, so long as they did not engage in homosexual acts or talk publicly about homosexuality. This policy opened up some space for inclusion while still severely limiting the participation of LGBTQ people in the military. LGBTQ movements also suffered major setbacks. For example, in 1996, the Defense of Marriage Act signed by President Bill Clinton officially defined legal marriage as a union between a man and a woman. Since then, LGBTQ movements have gained important cultural visibility, especially through movements for marriage equality, as discussed in Chapter 5.

Nevertheless, exclusions persisted within the LGBTQ movement. For example, lesbians, working-class LGBTQ people, LGBTQ people of color, and transgender people in general were often marginalized from white male LGBTQ politics in San Francisco (Armstrong 2002). While such groups advocated same-sex marriage, transgender and gender queer people hoped instead to promote alternative family arrangements and move beyond marriage altogether. Similarly, LGBTQ people of color and working-class LGBTQ people felt that white gay male advocacy did not adequately address the exclusions they faced (Hunter 2013).

LGBTQ movements often worked in tandem with other currents of the feminist movement. However, there were continuing debates among lesbian and queer feminists and straight feminists about how the two currents should relate to one another. Some theorists saw sexuality politics and women's movements as intrinsically interconnected (e.g., Rich 1980), while others saw sexuality as requiring a distinct political space (e.g., Rubin 1997). Sometimes queer feminists simply felt overlooked within dominant feminist spaces. These tensions would continue as LGBTQ politics gained more momentum in the 2000s.

The Sounds of Feminist Politics in the 1980s and 1990s: Women as Cultural Producers

Toward the end of the 20th century, women musicians expressed their feminist claims through alternative kinds of performance, songwriting, and radical messaging. Women's involvement in underground punk, post-punk, and indie rock movements in Washington, DC, and the Pacific Northwest through the "riot grrrl movement" dealt with feminist themes of patriarchy, gender relations, power, authority, women's rights, and "subversive" sexualities. Indicative of the many variants of feminism in this period, these movements blended feminist, LGBTQ, gender queer, and trans protest and politics through zines (independently produced magazines), poetry, and music. Their activism challenged masculine domination in mainstream cultural production rather than directly targeting the state with rights-based claims as had earlier waves of feminist protest. This movement was built on, and also inspired, fellow underground punk feminist bands in the UK, Brazil, Australia, and other countries.

Avant-garde, minimalist, and androgynous fashion characterized sectors of the moment, and women pushed traditional narrative songwriting boundaries and challenged musical form and content by singing, chanting, shrieking, screaming, and otherwise producing discordant, powerful sounds. London-based Siouxsie Sioux of Siouxsie and the Banshees, for instance, urged a collective identity rather than singling out their lead singer in the late 1970s, and though Siouxsie later became known for dramatic makeup and elaborate costumes on stage, Steward and Garratt (1999) note that "[f]or a long time, the Banshees refused to be interviewed separately and resisted using pictures of themselves on record-sleeves or in press ads" (31–32).

In the 1990s, the band Bikini Kill infamously coined the term *girl power*, which soon took on a discursive life of its own. Bikini Kill and other feminist punk and rock bands took on this challenge in a more raucous way than traditional women folk, pop, and blues artists of previous generations, reflecting Mary Katzenstein's (1998) observation that feminist protests involve an "effort to reinterpret, reformulate, rethink, and rewrite the norms and practices of society and the state," (17). Several independent record labels, including K Records in Olympia, Washington, opened up new space for women in music to critique inequality, express political and social frustrations, and reshape the gender politics of the industry. Riot grrrls also demanded an end to masculine domination, pushed for equal participation in music and broader society, and offered other critiques of social and economic relations of exchange.

The riot grrrl movement exemplified the contested nature of the institution of music and pointed to Katzenstein's conception of a politics of identity in which feminists ask, "Who am I? Who are we as women? In what ways are women different from men, and from each other? In what ways do gendered identities and experiences shape political understandings and authorize different groups to speak?" (1998: 18). Regarding the significance of women's creative politics, Sue Steward and Sheryl Garratt (1999), authors of *Signed, Sealed, and Delivered: True Life Stories of Women in Pop,* conclude, "Women are not condemned to be passive, swooning onlookers while the boys have all the fun on stage." Indeed, the riot grrrl movement and beyond demonstrate that the creative nature of protest and politics is alive and well in collective feminist expression.

Thinking Globally: Transnational Feminisms and North–South Alliances

Another important shift in feminism in the 1980s and 1990s was a stronger relationship—as well as more critical debates—between Western feminists and postcolonial feminists. Throughout the 20th century, women's participation in anti-colonial movements in South Asia and Africa created space to articulate claims to gender justice as women activists grew frustrated with the failure of newly independent states to address gender concerns in meaningful ways (see Chapter 10). Postcolonial and anti-colonial women's movements were extremely diverse. Geraldine Heng (1997) argues that, because of its complex relationships to nationalism and modernity, third world feminism is "a chimerical, hydra-headed creature, surviving in a plethora of lives and guises" (30).

While a small number of women in the West provided support to women's anti-colonial and postcolonial activism in other nations throughout the 20th century, transnational feminist partnerships grew wider and more varied in the 1990s, with women from Africa, Asia, and Latin America becoming increasingly linked to transnational feminist advocacy networks (Keck and Sikkink 1998). In these alliances, which we refer to as

transnational feminisms, international partnerships sometimes enabled grassroots feminist groups to utilize international pressure to influence their national states or other targets. Margaret Keck and Kathryn Sikkink (1998) call this ability to reach around the home state *the boomerang effect*. For example, sweatshop workers in Mexico who were unable to directly influence their employers to improve working conditions garnered support by reaching out to students in the United States to put pressure on retailers that buy their products.

Transnational feminism also involved conflicts and tensions. Feminists from postcolonial contexts critiqued their Western counterparts for dominating the agenda and addressing them in ways they found condescending and patronizing. At the United Nations Conferences on Women in Mexico in 1975 and Copenhagen in 1980, activists struggled to find common ground. Keck and Sikkink (1998) argue that at the Nairobi United Nations Conference on Women in 1985, violence against women became a central organizing theme that allowed transnational feminist networks to bridge their differences and move past this impasse. The topic of violence bridged a wide range of concerns relevant to distinct settings, from dowry killings to political prisoners to domestic violence and marital rape. Even sex-selective abortion and infanticide could be defined as violence against women. Violence also suggested bodily harm to vulnerable people, a cause around which diverse constituencies could unite. Thus, diverse groups of feminists could mobilize around the issue of violence in distinct settings, supporting each other's struggles while addressing the particularities of their political, social, and cultural contexts. This adaptation demonstrated how Western feminists slowly began to shift in the face of critiques of feminists from the Global South—even if the alliance between the two continued to be fraught.

The 2000s and Beyond: Institutionalization, Backlash, and New Directions

In the 2000s, feminism took even more complex directions. On one hand, feminism faced backlash from those who considered it annoying or irrelevant. On the other hand, the idea of women's rights became a mainstay of institutions from the state to employers. Meanwhile, new currents extended feminist ideas to a wider variety of movements and began to bridge the myriad issues faced by feminists around the world.

The F Word: The Feminist Backlash

By the 2000s, public debate increasingly positioned feminism as irrelevant and outdated. After the legal advances of the 1970s and the social shifts of the 1980s and 1990s, which brought women into professions previously dominated by men, the word *feminist* was increasingly cast as old-fashioned or extreme. Feminist critics, however, argued that these shifts had occurred in the realm of cultural attitudes but not in the realm of practice: Women were still overrepresented in underpaid professions and subject to sexual harassment and violence.

In 2003, journalist Anna Quindlen (2003) responded to the growing dismissal of feminism in an article in the mainstream magazine *Newsweek* that asked a provocative question: Do we still need the "*F* word" (feminism)? She argued that feminism is indeed still necessary, as contemporary U.S. society is marked by sexual harassment, inequality in the workplace, gender-based violence, and eating disorders. Citing a study from Duke University that found women students spending an enormous amount of effort, money, and time on clothes, shoes, workout programs, and diets (recall Chapter 3) as well as "hiding their intelligence in order to succeed with their male peers," Quindlen concluded that the *F* word is not an "expletive, but an ideal—one that still has a way to go."

Critics from within feminist movements pointed out that the progress still left to be made by feminism included a recommitment to class-based justice, arguing that contemporary cultural shifts in feminism supported forms of neoliberal capitalism that earlier feminists would have rejected (Eisenstein 2005; Fraser 2007, 2009). In 2009, for instance, the feminist philosopher Nancy Fraser published an essay called "Feminism, Capitalism and the Cunning of History." She argued that whereas feminist movements of the 1960s and 1970s had woven together economic, cultural, and political dimensions of gender injustice, feminist cultural claims had grown separated from demands for economic equality. In particular, Fraser worried about the assumption that work could be liberating for women. She was also concerned about framing jobs such as those in the *maquilas*—discussed in Chapter 8—as a path to freedom. Today, she suggested, corporations could absorb women as low-waged labor and argue that giving women work empowered them and advanced gender equality. While certain elements of second-wave feminism had succeeded, these critics argued, a broader vision of feminist social justice had been left behind.

Bridging Locations, Interests, and Movements

Transnational feminist partnerships continued to grow in the 2000s. However, transnational feminisms faced tensions as they sought to bridge constituencies and avoid reproducing unequal power relations. Despite the successes of transnational networks in pushing some feminist concerns onto the agenda of the United Nations, international donors, and national states, inequalities persisted among feminist groups positioned differently in the world economy.

The relationships between feminisms and globalization can be complex, and globalization can both help and hurt feminist causes. Manisha Desai (2007), for instance, showed that globalization can further women's subordination by supporting war and neoliberal economic policies, but women can also draw on economic and cultural opportunities that emerge within globalization to improve their lives and further their agency. At the same time, within transnational feminist networks, especially those connected to the United Nations, people who speak English and who are formally educated might become privileged in providing gender expertise, excluding other feminists in the process.

The growing number of global, feminist non-governmental organizations (NGOs) embodies these unequal relations of power within transnational feminist partnerships. Many organizations in the Global South, which began as protest organizations without any funding, have now become NGOs, which rely on funding from donors in order to exist. This has, in many cases, meant that they cannot be as political or radical as they would like, since they are now reliant on external sources (usually from the U.S. and Europe) for support. In an ethnography of Brazilian feminist organizations, Millie Thayer (2009) provided an in-depth look at power relations within such transnational feminist networks. Focusing on two organizations, one middle-class urban NGO and one rural women's movement, both of which received funding from North America, Thayer argued that Brazilian feminists were able to use tools from the West to further their agenda even as Western concerns might eclipse their own. The middle-class urban NGO was "expert" and professionalized and was able to connect with donors from the Global North in a way that the rural women's movement members were not. Though the middle-class NGO staff were concerned about issues that might be thought of as conventionally *women's* issues—such as violence against women—the rural women's movement was concerned with issues around class and labor. Their definitions of "women's" issues were thus very different. Thayer showed, though, that these inequalities did not mean that solidarity was impossible. The rural social movement was able to define its own politics in collaboration with the urban NGO staff. It was also able to use the discourse of gender and women's issues from the West as a tool for challenging gendered power relations in their local setting, drawing on Joan Scott's feminist theories to build their own agenda for struggle. Yet, Thayer concluded, just as the rural social movement needed the North American funding agency, so too did the funding organization need them. It was by funding a movement so obviously poor and rural that the North American organization was able to retain its own legitimacy.

The role of NGOs has been a major point of debate among feminists, particularly in their relationships to grassroots activists. Sonia Alvarez (1999, 2009) provides another perspective on the complexities of feminist NGOs in Latin America. In her 1999 article on the "feminist NGO 'boom,'" Alvarez argues that "NGOization" was a key challenge to feminist movements, causing them to become professionalized and disconnected from their roots. Often, feminist NGOs positioned themselves as "gender experts," turning women's concerns into technical problems of expertise rather than issues for debate and participation from grassroots women. State governments and international organizations saw NGOs as replacements for soliciting input from a diversity of actors and activists. Finally, governments also used NGOs to carry out programs, making it difficult for NGOs to be critical of state policies. Instead, NGOs became dependent on the state and carried out technical projects rather than challenging the government and offering a more radical version of feminism.

However, Alvarez also showed that NGOs could play complex, hybrid roles in feminist movements. Their work varied across national contexts, depending on the state's particular relationship to NGOs. If NGOs could resist the tendency to become professionalized and sustain their connections to feminist movements, they could draw on the resources of international funding and state attention while also advancing the agenda of grassroots feminists. In her 2009 article "Beyond NGOization?" Alvarez is more hopeful, suggesting that in Latin America, the feminist movement is now moving beyond NGOization. She also shows that NGOs do important movement work, building links across feminist groups and helping articulate shared concerns. Alvarez's examples of transnational feminist linkages show that there are no simple models for bridging power divides in women's mobilization.

New Struggles over Sexuality around the World

The global LGBTQ movement is another example of these kinds of complexities. Just as the category of *woman* is contested in transnational feminisms, the category of *gay* has been challenged in various contexts. *Gay* is just one of a number of sexual identity categories people use around the

Negotiating Alliances in the Sexual Minority Movement
A Perspective from an Indian Activist

Akkai Padmashali is a human rights activist, transgender woman, and former sex worker based in Bangalore, India.

As a transgender person, you face it every second, every minute, you face that discrimination, that untouchability, that stigma. You are completely marginalized. You are oppressed. Why? . . . Because of your gender orientation. . . .

[Class] is a huge barrier between communities, because when you talk about sexual minorities, there are people from upper-class backgrounds as well, and then the majority are from working class backgrounds. . . . [T]en years ago I had been to an upper class sexual minority platform . . . and people were laughing, because I was wearing low-cost slippers. I was not dressed properly, you know? . . . And people were laughing! . . . If you did not speak English, you were discriminated against in that meeting. Then I felt that this was not my space. . . .

My long vision is, how are we going to fight back, and how are we going to battle the class discrimination happening within the community and outside the community? How are we going to bring this diversity of identities to a platform? . . . People from upper class backgrounds do exist [in] the sexual minority category. But who is vulnerable? There is this demand for gay marriages. But for working class sexual minorities, marriage is not important. Identity is important; your livelihood is important. Your social rejection is important. You are a person on the street, struggling daily, doing sex work and begging daily, to fulfill your bread and butter, for clothing and housing. How many upper-class sexual minorities could understand these issues? . . .

[I]t could be Dalit groups, women's groups, disabled groups, many, many community movements of people who are oppressed due to their class, caste, gender, sexuality, ethnicity, race, etc. We, as a movement-based organization, we were trying to build up networks with those movements. . . . It's kind of a by and take [give and take]. Where you are coming to a platform to understand each other. . . . So I think that's the moment where we are now. We will definitely bring about social change. Now any human rights violations happening against sexual minorities, we are here to show solidarity. . . . We are trying to build up a new world of all these oppressed communities. . . . When a person or a community has been rejected because of ethnicity, class, caste, sexuality, or gender, that is against social justice.

world. Some groups prefer to use alternative conceptualizations, from *two-spirit* to *kothi*, and reject the term *gay*. At the same time, gay identity has been increasingly internationalized, and activists in various locations must use categories such as *gay* and *lesbian* to access dominant networks and monetary resources. Sometimes, they can leverage those resources to influence their national governments (Altman 1996). Global feminist and LGBTQ movements have also highlighted the relationships between sexuality and other dynamics of inequality. For example, Akkai Padmashali, a human rights activist based in India, has fought to link class, caste, gender, sexuality, religion, and ability politics. At the same time, she has faced challenges in bridging divides within social movements and has often felt excluded from activist spaces on the basis of class. Padmashali describes her story in the boxed text on the previous page.

In the 2010s, transgender rights also became a major topic of mainstream discussion in the U.S., as described in Chapter 4 in regard to the "bathroom debates." When North Carolina Governor Pat McCrory eliminated antidiscrimination protections for LGBTQ people in 2016, activists across the country responded vehemently in opposition.

These injustices against transgender people, along with everyday forms of discrimination, have exposed new conflicts between different currents of U.S. feminist movements. Some middle-class, cisgender white feminists who identify as second-wave feminists have expressed discomfort with transgender rights. In 2015, Caitlyn Jenner, formerly Bruce Jenner, a reality television star and Olympic athlete, came out as transgender. In a controversial article in the *New York Times*, Elinor Burkett, a journalist and former women's studies professor, referred to Caitlyn Jenner as *him* and argued against Jenner's "notion . . . that some sort of gendered destiny is encoded in us," saying, "that's the kind of nonsense that was used to repress women for centuries" (2015: SR1).

Transgender activists fired back against this characterization of Jenner, calling Burkett and her allies transphobic, or TERFs (Trans-Exclusionary Radical Feminists). Transgender activists argued that TERFs were intolerant and abusive by making transgender people out to be suspect; questioning the true, essential nature of transgender people; and rejecting trans women as women, thus subjecting others' bodies and identities to judgment and scrutiny. They argued that second-wave feminist terms were now being used to delegitimize, exploit, endanger, and mis-gender trans and gender-nonconforming people. That is, for many contemporary feminists, queer activists, and transactivists, this exclusionary, violent rush to mis-categorize people has reproduced and reified the same dominant binary oppressions that movements for gender identity and freedom of expression have struggled against for decades.

In Samantha Allen's 2013 article in *Jacobin*, she—as a trans woman—likens herself to an endangered species and criticizes TERFs' practice of "openly discriminating against the transgendered while clinging to a reactionary definition of sex." Allen's contribution points to the continued tensions and divergences in feminist activism, as different currents must navigate and question the power of language, naming, and discourse as linked to material consequences, including emotional trauma, sexual violence, and other mistreatment. This process is more difficult for some currents than others, as these claims to legitimacy are historically rooted and culturally produced.

Conclusion

This chapter has traced a number of debates that shaped the histories of feminist activism and women's politics in the U.S. while also highlighting the sociopolitical context for particular struggles. By working through key examples, the chapter illustrated how power relations are intertwined with feminist activism. Women's organizing in the United States has been influenced by conversations with global women's movements, which have led to new articulations of the relationships among gender, class, race, nationality, and sexuality.

Activists, organizers, scholars, and workers of different backgrounds approach the term *feminist* in very different ways. As the arguments between TERFs and transgender activists suggest, the term *feminist* can take on new meaning and create new forms of hierarchy and difference. Contemporary feminists sometimes echo Betty Friedan's treatment of lesbians as a "lavender menace" by isolating and marginalizing those who fall into categories they view as challenging. Yet the history of activism around gender also provides lessons for a more just politics. Activism around gender relations is most powerful when it incorporates the variations in women's experiences—and the variations in their marginalization.

This chapter shifted away from the traditional metaphor of *waves* to instead conceptualize distinct moments in women's organizing as *currents*. Whereas waves suggest a linear, chronological path, this chapter pointed to recurring trends and moments of resurgence and continuity over time. The notion of currents suggests overlap and interaction as opposed to the stricter demarcation between waves. Finally, the notion of *currents* breaks away from the idea that women's activism is uniform in character in different time periods. Feminist activism is anything but monolithic or homogenous. Women's political achievements are built through a long and complex history of struggle—but their story is not simply one of growth but also of divergence and tension. The currents of gender activism continue to move women's variegated struggles both closer together and further apart.

KEYWORDS

Bread and roses 175
Combahee River Collective 179
Feminist 172
Feminist currents 173
Feminist praxis 172
First-wave feminism 172
National Organization for Women (NOW) 177
Second-wave feminism 172
Third-wave feminism 172
Transnational feminisms 186

QUESTIONS

- When did you first hear the term *feminist*? In what context? Was it in a positive or negative light?
- Did anything surprise you about the history of feminist movements? How does it shed light on contemporary struggles around gender?
- This chapter demonstrated long-standing tensions but also solidarities among LGBTQ movements, labor movements,

racial justice movements, and feminist movements. What links have you observed among these areas of struggle?

- Think about a version of feminism you've encountered (e.g., in popular culture, on your campus, or in your own activism). Which currents were present? Which were not? Did you see any conflicts emerging among different groups or individuals?
- Consider the city/metropolitan area closest to you. What place did it have in shaping feminist movements? Was it home to any of the protests or struggles around labor, sexuality, or political rights discussed in this chapter? Conduct some historical research into your city's connections to the history of feminist movements.

ASSOCIATED READINGS

- Alarcón, Norma. 1991. "The Theoretical Subject(s) of This Bridge Called My Back and Anglo-American Feminism." In *Criticism in the Borderlands: Studies in Chicano Literature, Culture and Ideology*, edited by Hector Calderon and Jose David Saldivar. Durham: Duke University Press.
- Collins, Patricia Hill. 1990. *Black Feminist Thought: Knowledge, Consciousness, and the Politics of Empowerment*. New York: Routledge.
- Delacoste, Frederique, and Priscilla Alexander. 1998. *Sex Work: Writings by Women in the Sex Industry*. San Francisco: Cleis Press.
- Desai, M. 2007. "The Messy Relationship between Feminisms and Globalizations." *Gender & Society* 21 (6): 797.
- Federici, Silvia. (1975) 2012. *Revolution at Point Zero: Housework, Reproduction, and Feminist Struggle*. Oakland: PM Press.
- Friedan, Betty. 1963. *The Feminine Mystique*. New York: W.W. Norton.
- Ghaziani, Amin. 2008. *The Dividends of Dissent: How Conflict and Culture Work in Lesbian and Gay Marches on Washington*. Chicago: University of Chicago Press.
- Heng, Geraldine. 1997. "'A Great Way to Fly': Nationalism, the State, and the Varieties of Third-World Feminism." In *Feminist Genealogies, Colonial Legacies, Democratic Futures*, edited by M. Jacqui Alexander and Chandra Talpade Mohanty, 30–45. London, UK: Routledge.
- Orleck, Annelise. 1995. *Common Sense and a Little Fire: Women and Working-Class Politics in the United States, 1900–1965*. Chapel Hill: University of North Carolina Press.
- Ray, Raka, and Anna Korteweg. 1999. "Movements in the Third World: Identity, Mobilization, and Autonomy." *Annual Review of Sociology* 25: 47–71S.
- Thayer, Millie. 2001. "Transnational Feminism: Reading Joan Scott in the Brazilian Sertao." *Ethnography* 2 (2): 243–271.
- Walker, Rebecca. 1992. "Becoming the Third Wave." *Ms. Magazine* (January/February): 39–41.

NOTE

1. With feminist health care perpetually under threat, only about 15 of these clinics still exist today.

CHAPTER 10

Decolonizing Gender

Raka Ray

Gender is shaped, represented, and positioned through world politics both in the past and in the present. The preceding chapters showed that problems of gender must be understood in relation to other social forces. This chapter looks at the global nature of those social forces through a focus on two central ideas: geopolitical domination *and* the politics of knowledge. *First, the chapter traces how the history of* colonialism *shaped the contemporary construction of gender and global women's movements. Second, the chapter examines world politics to show how the gender hegemony in any one society is connected to other gender hegemonies around the globe. Finally, the chapter engages with feminists around the world to show that Western conceptions of gender and gender norms are not universal. The ideals of* freedom *and* agency *that are foundational to Western feminism are culturally constructed, and, at least as formulated by Western feminists, they are not held by all women in all contexts. The chapter ends by reflecting on what the global diversity of women's ideals means for our understanding of gender, feminism, and feminist activism.*

Introduction

In 2012, *New York Times* reporter Nicholas Kristof and his wife Sheryl WuDunn published a PBS documentary film titled *Half the Sky: Turning Oppression into Opportunity for Women Worldwide*, based on their 2008 book by the same title. The book and film explored violence against women in postcolonial countries: sex trafficking in Cambodia, female genital mutilation in Senegal, and maternal mortality in Somalia. To connect these foreign contexts with Western empathy, Kristof and WuDunn took U.S. celebrities—including Meg Ryan, America Ferrera, Olivia Wilde, and Eva Mendes—to the filming sites. In several scenes, these actors are shown reacting in shock or with tears to the difficult conditions faced by women and children in other countries. Sometimes, as in a now-iconic photograph of Olivia Wilde, they are shown hugging children. For many Americans, the book and the documentary were a wake-up call, an important commentary on the work that needs to be done to save women around the world from gender-based violence.

By contrast, many people living in the parts of the world covered by the film reacted with dismay and anger. Sayantani Dasgupta, an Indian-born physician who lives in the United States, wrote a blog in which she accused Kristof and WuDunn of exhibiting the "your women are oppressed but ours are awesome" syndrome. The "syndrome" Dasgupta identified treats violence against women as something that exists only in other parts of the world—not in the U.S. Dasgupta also pointed out that women in the book and the film were subjected to a sort of voyeurism that would not be tolerated in the US. She asked,

> For example, would Kristof, a middle-aged male reporter, so blithely ask a 14-year-old U.S. rape survivor to describe her experiences in front of cameras, her family, and other onlookers? Would he sit smilingly in a European woman's house asking her to describe the state of her genitals to him? Yet, somehow, the fact that the rape survivor is from Sierra Leone and that the woman being asked about her genital cutting is from Somaliland, seems to make this behavior acceptable in Kristof's book. (Dasgupta [2012] 2013)

Critics such as Dasgupta pointed out that while Kristof and WuDunn may have intended to bring attention to the suffering of women and children, they in fact reproduced a colonial relationship. Ignoring the work of women's organizations in Senegal and Cambodia, the couple (and Kristof in particular) presented themselves as the saviors of these women and children.

This chapter unpacks the meaning of actions taken by Westerners to represent and to rescue women in postcolonial contexts. It also considers postcolonial critics' reactions to these actions. What does it mean to reproduce a colonial relationship, and what do those relationships have to do with gender? How should scholars and activists in the U.S. think about gender inequities and injustices in postcolonial contexts such as India, the Middle East, and Africa, and what is the responsibility of Western feminists to help women across the globe?

This chapter begins from the premise that gender is shaped, represented, and positioned through world politics, both in the past and in the present. Previous chapters showed that gender in the U.S. is co-constituted with the legal system, national politics, and the economy. Gender relations also shape and are shaped by international political and economic imperatives. In this chapter, we show how understanding the historical and contemporary relationship between gender and world politics complicates taken-for-granted assumptions about the relationship between U.S. women and women in other countries. First, the chapter looks at how the history of colonialism shaped the contemporary construction of gender and global women's movements. Next, it examines world politics to show how the gender order in any one society is connected to other gender orders around the globe. Then, the chapter engages with feminists around the world to show that Western conceptions of women's freedom and agency are not universal. It ends by reflecting on what the global diversity of women's ideals and aspirations means for our understanding of gender, feminism, and feminist activism.

Constructing the Global World Order

Capitalism is a global economic system that relies on and reinforces an imbalance of power among nations in the world system (Sassen 1984; see also Chapters 1 and 8). Some nations have more power than others to determine their own futures and the futures of other nations. In the present moment, the rules that govern the world economy favor the U.S. and some nations in Europe and East Asia over other countries. These dominant nations established their power over the previous two centuries through the process of colonialism.

The Oxford Dictionary defines **colonialism** as "the policy or practice of acquiring full or partial political control over another country, occupying it with settlers, and exploiting it economically." Following this definition, the terms *colonial powers* or *colonists* refer to the countries and the people from those countries that participated in the process of colonizing other countries. The *colonized* refers to people in the countries that were occupied and exploited by the colonizers. This chapter uses primarily the term *postcolonial* to refer to the formerly colonized countries, although reflecting the diversity of terms among scholars, it sometimes uses the phrases *third world*, *developing*, or *Global South* to refer to these same countries. The term *postcolonial* implies not only that these countries are no longer colonized but also that the experience of having been colonized continues to shape their economy, culture, and politics.

Colonialism was a political and economic enterprise with long-lasting cultural effects. By the early 20th century, England, France, the Netherlands, Belgium, and Germany had colonized much of the rest of the world, dividing up the continents of Africa, the Americas, and Asia among a handful of European nations. In the 18th and 19th centuries, European armies, bureaucracies, merchants, and travelers occupied the nations now known as India, the Congo, Vietnam, Mexico, and Mauritius with the intent of capturing natural resources—such as copper and iron—to fuel Europe's industrial economy. Colonialism quickly became a source of employment and other opportunities for Europeans. As the colonies consolidated their power over the occupied territory, they imposed new laws on the colonized countries based on their own laws, fundamentally altering the lives of the people whose countries they colonized.

How Colonialism Reconstituted Gender Hegemonies

The populations of the colonial powers understood themselves as fundamentally superior to those who were colonized. In most cases, colonizing countries approached the colonized populations under a civilizing mission to Christianize, educate, and otherwise transform supposedly inferior people to be more like Europeans. As described in Chapter 1, this civilizing mission was based on the notion that Western ways of being represented the pinnacle of human development; other ways of being and behaving represented backwardness. This dichotomous construction of the civilized colonizer and the savage colonial subject became more entrenched with time and as the colonizers entered new societies. Many of the colonized societies constructed gender differently than their European colonizers. Following the reasoning of the civilizing mission, Europeans saw those gender practices as backward and sought to change them.

When Europeans entered the colonies, they also entered into a complex set of sexual relationships with colonized women (as Chapters 5 and 7 have shown). So doing, they altered the social arrangements of power that existed between men and women of the colonies before the arrival of

Europeans. They also created families and established unequal guardianship rights over the children. When colonized women and European men had children together, they did not share equal status as legal parents. European men who held low-level civil service positions frequently took on women in 19th-century colonies as concubines—not legal wives—but the law gave those men greater claim on any children that might result from these relationships. Women in these arrangements had limited rights and could be exchanged among men or dismissed without notice. According to the Indies Civil Code of 1848, for instance, "native women 'had no rights over children recognized by a white man'" (Stoler 2002: 49).

In postcolonial countries today, gender relations reflect colonial interventions in a myriad of ways. In India, for example, the amount a woman can inherit, the terms of her marriage and divorce, and the right to be guardian of her child all depend on the religion into which she was born. The laws governing these family-related topics are called *personal laws*, and the personal laws differ based on religion (Hindu, Christian, Muslim, or Zoroastrian) as a direct result of decisions made by British colonists. When the British came to India, they were confronted by many kingdoms and rulers of different religions. To ease the transition to British colonialism, the British decided to allow native elite men to keep the practices of their community. While they created criminal and other civil laws to apply uniformly to all people, they did not do so in the arena of the family. By turning customary practice into family law on the basis of religion, the British legally subsumed Indian women to their religions.

Several examples in this book have already shown that while the transition to colonial laws did benefit some women (for example, the abolition of *sati*, mentioned in Chapter 1), the laws were actually focused on bringing colonized societies in line with the colonialists' gendered expectations. These expectations were necessarily limited by the colonists' perspective as elite, European men. The height of British colonialism in the late 19th century, for example, was the era in which conservative and masculine-dominant Victorian moral gender politics prevailed. The British tried to bring their colonies in line with this rigid sexuality. In India, the British imposed a law prohibiting a married woman from refusing to have sex with her husband. In addition, because the British believed that men needed to have sex with women to remain manly, they also created a system of prostitution in India to provide colonists with access to women's bodies, as did the Dutch in the Dutch Indies, discussed in Chapter 5.

To legitimate their aggression, as introduced in Chapter 1, the colonists represented themselves as ideal men, virile and strong, protectors of the weak, and as fathers to the "natives." English poet Rudyard Kipling (1899) captured this attitude during the Philippine–American War (1899–1909) in a poem called "The White Man's Burden," urging Americans to look after people of the Philippines the way that Britain looked after its colonial subjects (recall also the colonial advertisements discussed in Chapter 3):

Take up the White Man's burden—

Send forth the best ye breed—

Go send your sons to exile

To serve your captives' need

To wait in heavy harness

On fluttered folk and wild—

Your new-caught, sullen peoples,

Half devil and half child.

The poem described colonized people—both men and women—as infantile and savage: bad children who needed a "White Man's" supervision and discipline. In everyday practice, colonists similarly infantilized colonized people, referring to grown men as *boys*. This form of representation positioned the colonists as benevolent patriarchs. Here, gender acts as a racialized *signifier*, asserting that the relationship between colonist and colonized was one of natural dependence.

Inasmuch as masculinity implies some degree of power and control, this representation of power symbolically emasculated men who were colonial subjects by subjecting them to the rule of others and positioning them as lower than both men *and* women of the colonial power. This emasculation produced feelings of frustration and resentment. In *Black Skin, White Masks*, Franz Fanon ([1952] 2008), an Afro-descendant psychiatrist and revolutionary thinker from the former French colony of Martinique, captured the effect of this emasculation on Black men's psyche. Fanon asked, "What does a man want? What does the black man want? At the risk of arousing the resentment of my colored brothers, I will say that the black is not a man" (8). Fanon's statement asserts that colonialism denies both the masculinity and the humanity of colonized men. The frustration he articulated stemmed from the many ways in which he was made to feel inferior, scorned for his color, infantilized, and considered lacking as an adult man in a colonial situation.

Colonialism benefited men and women in the colonizing countries. European men who had not achieved economic success in their own countries, or younger sons who would not inherit from their parents, were able to travel to the colonies to make a better living as colonists. Imperial travel also benefited women. In Europe, women were treated as the weaker sex. They could not vote, and their sexuality was policed. In colonized countries, women were able to imagine themselves as part of the "superior race" and enjoy adventure and power in their capacity as colonial administrators' wives, travelers, or missionaries. Many willingly undertook the responsibility of instilling the values of their own culture in foreign lands.

The colonial encounter thus reconstituted gender and class hegemonies both in the colonies and in the colonizing countries. By turning customary practices into law and by considering their laws to indicate the only appropriate ways to be, colonialism reconstituted the gender hegemonies of the countries they colonized. At the same time, men and women of the colonial powers who went to the colonies experienced powers and freedoms that they lacked at home, and they returned home with new wealth and influence.

Breaking the Power of Indigenous Women: Colonialism in North America

Though colonialism is typically associated with Asia, Africa, and Latin America, it also transformed gender relations in North America. Before the arrival of British, French, and Spanish colonists, women formed the backbone of many indigenous communities in North America. Native American feminist Paula Allen Gunn (1986) shows that contrary to stereotypes and Western movies, traditional native societies were not masculine-dominated warrior cultures before contact with the Europeans. Instead, many Native American women acted as leaders, fought in battles, and made key decisions about war and peace and about daily life. Among the Haudenosaunee, for example, the 50 extended family clans were each headed by a clan mother, and these women formed the main council within the confederacy (Jaimes and Halsey 1997: 303). Among the Lakota, women were the primary property owners; all a Lakota woman needed to do if she wanted to divorce her husband was to put his possessions outside the door of their home (Powers 1986: 89). Unlike Judeo-Christian religions, most cosmologies of North American indigenous groups had many powerful female elements.

To conquer and weaken the indigenous nations, European colonists in North America focused on reducing the status of women. When the French entered the St. Lawrence Valley, they noted,

> Women have great power. . . . A man may promise you something, and if he does not keep his promise, he thinks he is sufficiently excused when he tells you that his wife did not wish him to do it. (Thwaites, quoted in Jaimes and Halsey 1997: 306)

Starting in 1633, however, the French sent Jesuit missionaries, who represented a strong tradition of patriarchy, to the region. They supported the missionaries with military power, forcing the creation of a new economy more reliant on fur-trapping and trading, activities at the time relegated to men. The Jesuits imposed monogamy on indigenous nations, forbade divorce, refused to accept women as representatives of the community, and insisted that families live in the homes of men and not women (thus shifting the society from matrilocality to patrilocality).

British colonialists in North America also imposed their gender hierarchies on native groups. In *Cherokee Women: Gender and Culture Change, 1700–1835*, historian Theda Perdue (1999) details the ways in which the colonial government repeatedly tried to "civilize" the Cherokee, who followed a matrilineal kinship system and whose women owned and farmed the land. Colonists forced the Cherokee to adopt Euro-American gender roles, patrilineal kinship, and individual rather than communal ownership of land. While the Cherokee did resist, a small group of Cherokee men adapted to British ways and soon became the elite, adopting European values that included diminishing the status of women and African American people. In the meantime, these leaders and the colonists also encouraged Cherokee women and girls to pursue chastity, Protestant values, and domesticity (rather than farming), thus altering the Cherokee gender order.

Through a combination of economic pressure, warfare, and active cultural work, colonialism systematically undermined women's positions in native communities across North America. While native women remained powerful within households, as the colonial authorities strengthened their hands against native communities, women's power as political players vastly diminished.

This history has produced considerable tensions between Native American feminists and white feminists to this day. On one hand, white feminists have criticized masculine domination among Native Americans. On the other hand, native feminists assert that native cultures are unfairly represented as brutal and misogynist. They argue that white women historically benefited from the exploitation of native peoples and the disfranchisement of native women. They also argue that white culture helped *create* misogyny among the indigenous. Finally, they resent white feminists for asking indigenous women to leave their culture to participate in mainstream feminism. For instance, Pam Colorado, a member of the Oneida nation, asserts, "Nothing I've encountered in feminist theory addresses the fact of our colonization or the wrongness of white women's stake in it" (Colorado, quoted in Jaimes and Halsey 1997: 318).

The Effects of Struggles around Decolonization

Colonialism eventually came to an end in most parts of the world. The demise of colonialism was triggered by the struggles of colonized peoples. Ideas about gender played a major role in these struggles, which were both violent and nonviolent. Subsequently, the struggles shaped how women in formerly colonized nations thought about the global women's movement.

For example, consider how the film *Battle of Algiers* graphically depicted the anticolonial war against French colonists in Algeria. When the film first aired in 1966, it set off shock waves for revealing the brutality of French colonial rule as well as the violence of anticolonial struggles. In particular, the film showed Algerian women participating in the long and bitter struggle for freedom from French colonialism. The film demonstrates how Algerian women hid guns and bombs in their clothes and deliberately wore veils so the French army would not suspect them. As sociologist Marnia Lazreg (1994) argues, in the war against the French, Algerian women, no less than men, chose to engage in a struggle that transcended their everyday lives for the idea of a free nation.

Women's participation in resistance to colonialism was not a figment of filmic imagination; all over the colonized world, from West Africa to India, thousands of women participated in anticolonial struggles using both non-violent and violent means. For example, in 1932, a young woman called Pritilata Wadedar led a raid against the British in India. On realizing that she was about to be caught, Wadedar killed herself. Before she did so, she left a note that read,

> I earnestly hope that our sisters would no longer nurse the view that they are weak. Armed women of India will demolish thousand hurdles, disregard thousand dangers and join the rebellion and the

armed struggle for freedom and will prepare themselves for it. With this hope in my heart I am proceeding today for self-immolation. (Bandopadhyay 1991: 32).

Just as U.S. women's participation in the abolition and Civil Rights movements led them to become advocates for their political rights as women (as described in Chapter 9), struggles against colonial rule led many women in colonized countries to demand freedom against male domination. Millions of women around the world were first politicized as they demanded the right to self-governance. Through anticolonial struggle, many women came to see that they, too, deserved the right to govern their lives as women, out from under the rule of husbands or fathers. Yet as the colonial powers withdrew, women—who had been crucial participants in anticolonial movements—often found themselves with fewer rights than formerly colonized men. Many newly independent states only partially implemented policies beneficial to women. This failure prompted women, who were now politicized, to create independent women's movements in India, Algeria, and other postcolonial countries (Jayawardena 1986; Kumar 1993; Lazreg 1994). As the initial exhilaration of winning the struggle for national independence waned, a new struggle for women's independence was born. In later liberation struggles such as the fight against apartheid in South Africa, women were not only at the forefront of the movement but were also vocal about women's rights.

Women active in anticolonial struggles saw women from the colonizing countries as the beneficiaries and even perpetrators of colonial oppression. Just a few decades after the decolonization, Western feminists called for a feminist sisterhood among women around the world. Given their relationships to colonialist women, however, many women in postcolonial countries found the idea difficult to accept. The idea of a global sisterhood, they insisted, hid relations of power. In anticolonial struggles, women colonizers and colonized women faced off on opposite sides, locked in a battle over land, ways of life, and freedom. Thus, instead of simply embracing Western-led feminism, women who had been involved in the struggles for national independence developed their interests as women in their societies and fought for their own rights to a nation free from colonialism.

Today, few countries in the world are colonizers or colonized. An intense period of decolonization took place between the 1940s and the 1960s, though some countries (such as American Samoa, Guam, and the Cayman Islands) are still ruled by imperial powers such as the United States. Nevertheless, in place of colonialism, there now exists a radically unequal world that still reflects differences stemming from colonial histories. Colonial history helps explain why women from places such as Mexico and the Philippines go to countries like the U.S. and Italy, often countries with which they had colonial connections, to work as domestic workers (as described in Chapter 8). It also helps understand why sex tourism flourishes in the U.S. military bases in Southeast Asia. These colonial remnants mean that the term *women's rights* takes on different meanings in different contexts.

The ongoing inequalities among nations in a postcolonial context introduce a form of intersectionality (see Chapter 2). Under colonialism, the interests of colonial women and colonized women were directly opposed.

But even today, despite efforts to create a common cause such as the International Conferences on Women's Rights and campaigns such as One Billion Rising (see Chapter 9), global divides among women remain.

Colonial Positions and the Politics of Knowledge

Not only did colonization reshape gender, it also influenced the ways people understood the world. If social position shapes a person's understandings of the world, as discussed in Chapter 2, then how did the colonial encounter influence knowledge? This section discusses the **politics of knowledge**, the power involved in who gets to create knowledge about whom. In the 19th and early 20th centuries, women in North America and Europe derived their understanding of gender in other places through World's Fairs (carnivals that offered simulations of colonial countries) and by attending talks and reading accounts from missionaries, travelers, explorers, and military members who served abroad during the colonial period. Today, women in North America and Europe learn about gender in other places from these past accounts, from film, the Internet, and television, and—for some—by travel. Colonialist representations shape contemporary understandings in Europe and North America about gender relations in postcolonial countries. That is, the ideological constructions of men and women in the colonies that justified colonialism continue to exert weight today. The persistence of these ideologies is a source of tension between women's movements around the world, as women in Europe and North America often misunderstand and misrepresent women and men in postcolonial countries. In an influential article called "Under Western Eyes," Chandra Talpade Mohanty (1988, 2003) argued that women in colonial countries erased the diversity of women in postcolonial areas. Despite the good intentions of feminists in places such as the U.S. and Europe, Mohanty suggested, they often stereotyped women in other countries under the third world women trope, with *third world* being a common term for poor, postcolonial countries (recall that this trope was discussed in Chapter 8 in the context of work). In other words, white feminists from Europe and North America imagined women in other countries to be poor, uneducated, and oppressed, while envisioning themselves as liberated, educated, and middle class. Mohanty argued that these accounts silenced postcolonial women. They also echoed colonial relations by positioning white European and North American women as saviors and third world women as victims in need of rescue, as did the colonial civilizing mission.

The third world woman trope also implied that postcolonial women were timeless and placeless. In other words, while European and North American women progressed with and participated in changes in the economy and culture, women in postcolonial contexts held the same values and lived the same lifestyle as existed even before the colonial encounter. They were pre-constituted outside of social relations. This meant that economic differences, cultural specificities, and racial and ethnic variation were imagined to matter little to third world women. The third world woman was timeless; she had no history.

Many writers, journalists, feminists, and do-gooders in Europe and North America perpetuate this trope today. For instance, the book and film *Half the Sky*, discussed in the opening of the chapter, portray women in Cambodia, India, and Somalia as sharing the same characteristics of dependency. *Half the Sky* represents all such women as victims of patriarchy. This trope of the third world woman denies that postcolonial women may have complex thoughts or belong to a nation where, prior to colonialism, women might have been more powerful than men. The trope also reduces the multiplicity of real women across different postcolonial contexts to a unified representation.

For example, Annie Griffiths, one of the first women photographers for *National Geographic*, a magazine generally known for its cultural sensitivity, portrays herself very differently from the women she photographs in postcolonial countries. In Griffiths' photographs of herself, she looks like she has agency. For instance, in Photo 10.1, Griffiths is holding the camera and smiling, as she appears to contemplate taking her next picture. By contrast, the women she takes pictures of appear to *be seen* rather than *seeing* (see Chapter 3). Photo 10.2, also taken by Griffiths, shows a nameless girl peeking from behind a cloth. *National Geographic* takes particular care to present non-caricatured and respectful representations of people around the world; yet photographs like these reinforce the idea that women from postcolonial countries are to be looked at, while men and women from Europe and North America perform the act of looking.

In sum, colonial histories and power differences between countries structure the ways people perceive and understand the world. In particular, colonial histories can perpetuate the stereotype of the third world woman, which renders women in postcolonial countries as victims of their men, while allowing European and U.S. women to maintain the ability to act. These politics of knowledge enable ongoing inequities and global relations of domination.

Photo 10.1

Source: Linda Makarov/ National Geographic Creative.

Photo 10.2

Source: Annie Griffiths/ National Geographic Creative.

The Geopolitical Construction of Gender

Tropes of colonized and postcolonial women as victims have been used as justification for colonial intervention. In 1927, a book called *Mother India* (Mayo [1927] 2000) denounced the treatment of Indian women by Indian men, thus justifying the continuation of colonial rule by Britain. The author, Katherine Mayo, wrote,

> We stop at the bedside of a young girl who looks at us with the eyes of a hungry animal. . . . [M]arried as a baby, sent to her husband at ten, the shock of her incessant use was too much for her brain. . . . All she could do was crouch in a corner, a little twisted heap, panting. . . . [H]er husband, in despair and rage . . . cast her among the scrub thicket at the edge of the jungle to die. (55)

The book continued, however, to say that an English woman rescued the girl from the edge of the jungle. Under the care of the English woman, the Indian girl eventually began "to blossom into normal intelligence" (55).

In 1927, when *Mother India* was written, India was still occupied by British colonists, though the struggle against colonialism was well underway. The over-200-page book provided a scathing critique of Indian culture, especially the condition of Indian women, and galvanized American and English public opinion in support of victimized Indian women. The colonialists capitalized on this support to argue that the condition of Indian women proved that India was not yet ready for self-rule. At the same time, Mahatma Gandhi and other leaders of the freedom struggle—including women—condemned the book as one-sided and deliberately sensationalist.

The book's author, Katherine Mayo, was a conservative American woman who was hostile to immigrants, Blacks, and Catholics and supported the Asian Exclusion Acts passed in the U.S. in the late 19th century. Historian Mrinalini Sinha (2000) writes that Mayo conducted the investigation for her book with the direct support of the British colonial administration, which had "encouraged her to write a book critical of Indian habits and traditional Indian practices, partly as a rejoinder to Gandhi, who was making major strides in building a mass-movement to end British rule" (627). Thus, while American and British women read *Mother India* as a direct and moving documentary account of the social situation in India, the book was in fact a direct act of pro-colonial propaganda.

Because North America and Europe remain politically and economically dominant, even today, the representations of gender in these nations influence policies throughout the globe. Consider, for example, U.S. concern with Afghan women under the Taliban. Even prior to the 9/11 terrorist attacks and the subsequent U.S. war on Afghanistan, feminists in the U.S. were worried about the Taliban's power in Afghanistan because of the Taliban's terrible reputation for gender oppression. In early 2001, an urgent e-mail circulated throughout progressive circles in the U.S. It read,

> Subject: HELP: war upon women
>
> The government of Afghanistan is waging a war upon women. Since the Taliban took power in 1996, women have had to wear burqua [sic] and have been beaten and stoned in public for not having the proper attire, even if this means simply not having the mesh covering in front of their eyes. One woman was beaten to death by an angry mob of fundamentalists for accidentally exposing her arm(!) while she was driving. . . . At one of the rare hospitals for women, a reporter found still, nearly lifeless bodies lying motionless on top of beds, wrapped in their burqua, [sic] unwilling to speak, eat, or do anything, but slowly wasting away. Others have gone mad and were seen crouched in corners, perpetually rocking or crying, most of them in fear. . . . Husbands have the power of life and death over their women relatives, especially their wives, but an angry mob has just as much right to stone or beat a woman, often to death, for exposing an inch of flesh or offending them in the slightest way. . . . Everyone has a right to a tolerable human existence, even if they are women in a Muslim country. If we can threaten military force in Kosovo in the name of human rights for the sake of ethnic Albanians, citizens of the world can certainly express peaceful outrage at the oppression, murder and injustice committed against women by the Taliban.

The email goes on to describe a situation in which even highly educated Afghan women were not allowed to practice their professions, and to state that depression and suicide rates for women were extraordinarily high. It describes, in short, a barbaric situation: Afghan women are hungry, powerless, and being driven insane. Instead of calling for humanitarian aid, the e-mail asks for a response of "peaceful outrage." Such framings use the issue of women's rights to legitimate going to war.

Like *Mother India*, the e-mail about women in Afghanistan is an example of the effects of the politics of knowledge. Given the historical depictions of women in India and Afghanistan, Western readers are primed to believe stories such as these, and women's rights and gender oppression can be used to justify global geopolitical endeavors. In the contemporary era, less than a month after Al-Qaeda operatives attacked the World Trade Center in New York City, President George W. Bush announced Operation Enduring Freedom, a military intervention aimed at removing the ruling Taliban regime in Afghanistan. The Bush administration referred to the Taliban's brutal treatment of women to explain the moral motivation for military intervention. In a radio address on Voice of America in November 2001, First Lady Laura Bush noted, "Because of our recent military gains in much of Afghanistan, women are no longer imprisoned in their homes. They can listen to music and teach their daughters without fear of punishment." Laura Bush was celebrated for her work on behalf of Afghan women after the U.S. invaded Afghanistan.

Feminists around the world were bitterly divided in their response to this reference to women's rights to justify military intervention. Some organizations, such as the U.S.-based Feminist Majority Foundation, which had been working since the mid-1990s to end gender oppression in Afghanistan, welcomed the Bush administration's military action. The Feminist Majority Foundation argued that the U.S. intervention had liberated Afghan women, though they also affirmed that the Bush administration should maintain a commitment to supporting Afghan women during reconstruction. However, the Revolutionary Association of the Women of Afghanistan (RAWA), a feminist organization based in Afghanistan, openly criticized the Feminist Majority Foundation, its former ally, for overlooking the contributions of Afghan feminists to gender change in that country. RAWA argued that U.S. military forces were as dangerous to Afghan women as the Taliban. In 2002, in an open letter to *Ms. Magazine*, which was owned by the Feminist Majority Foundation, one RAWA supporter, Elizabeth Miller, accused the Feminist Majority Foundation of being a "mere mouthpiece of hegemonic, U.S.-centric, ego driven, corporate feminism." In subsequent years, other prominent U.S.-based feminists, such as Sonali Kolhatkar of the Afghan Women's Mission, continued to criticize the Feminist Majority Foundation, arguing that "feminists around the world must refuse to allow the good name of feminism to be manipulated to provide political cover for yet another war of aggression" (Kolhatkar and Rawi 2009).

The historically constructed third world women trope leaves no room to consider the consequences of actions taken to "save" these women. The idea of Afghan women as victims of the Taliban justified military intervention as a rescue tactic, despite the death and destruction that war brought to these same women. The American "analysis of the situation" (to use another term from Chandra Mohanty) was rooted in the logic of colonialism. Many in the U.S. blamed Afghan women's subordination on the Taliban Muslim patriarchy's extreme restrictions, drawing on the notion that other cultures are backward. By focusing on the Taliban, however, they overlooked the role of geopolitics in determining women's positions in Afghanistan.

Indeed, the colonial enterprise helped *create* the idea that Afghans were backward and traditional. A better understanding of women's lives in that country would pay attention to history. In particular, understanding gender requires analyzing the **geopolitical construction of gender**: the ways political history and conflicts between nations shape gender relationships in a given time and place.

Take the case of Afghan women. Attention to history shows that in the 1960s and 1970s, Afghanistan was one of the most progressive countries in the region for women. Women in Afghanistan were educators, doctors, and lawyers. Then in 1979, the Soviet Union (or USSR) invaded Afghanistan. Alarmed by the expansion of Soviet influence during the Cold War, the U.S. responded by seeking to block the Soviet Union from establishing a base in Afghanistan, founding, training, and arming a militant Islamic group called the *Mujahideen* (Freedom Fighters). By 1989, the Mujahideen drove the Soviet Union to withdraw its military from Afghanistan. Later, however, fighters involved in the Mujahideen helped form the Taliban. The Taliban shared the Mujahideen's ideology, and, importantly, they were armed with American as well as Russian weaponry. In 1996, the Mujahideen cum Taliban turned against the U.S. and took over their own country. Therefore, the image of Afghan women's lives presented in the e-mail quoted above was not simply the product of local backwards beliefs about gender but rather was the effect of a geopolitical conflict between the Soviet Union and the U.S. that helped give the Taliban its power.

The example of the Taliban and Afghanistan offers an important lesson for the sociology of gender. It reminds sociologists that gendered events and practices need to be situated in global history to be understood. Otherwise, one may wrongly assume that observed cultural differences are long-standing and unchanging. It reveals that those of us situated in the U.S. or Europe must be careful about calling on militaries to "help" women in other countries. Even with good intentions, military action may result in women and apparent feminism becoming pawns in a larger geopolitical game. Well-intentioned people without an understanding of global history can support a war against an entire people, resulting in years of destruction.

Contextualizing Our Concepts: Ideas Mediated by Culture

Geopolitical power relations can weigh heavily on feminist movements as well. Despite the critiques of white, middle-class feminism and the growing attention to intersectionality, many feminist projects still frame women's issues as universal. Often, feminists in Europe and North America believe that women constitute a group with distinct concerns, regardless of whether all women are aware of their membership in this group or not (Orloff, Ray, and Savci 2016). These feminists imagine a core of similarity among women that transcends differences in race, class, nation, and so on, so that all women have similar interests. In particular, these feminists presume that all women share a desire for **freedom**, even if the specific contexts of this desire (the workplace, the family, and so forth) vary. These feminists look for proof of freedom in women's **agency**, the independent exercise of their will. These two concepts—freedom and agency—form the backbone of white, middle-class feminism and remain central to many contemporary feminist projects.

In what follows, we first discuss the concepts of freedom and agency while keeping in mind the importance of cultural context. In this context, we consider two cases: **female genital surgeries** (FGS) and **veiling** (referring to the various ways many Muslim women cover their heads). Both FGS and veiling have become sites of cross-cultural feminist interventions. The complex consequences of these interventions teach certain lessons:

1. Any social practice must be seen as part of a larger social fabric and not in isolation. Before being condemned, a practice must be understood from within the logic of a social system.
2. The history of colonialism by European countries and the United States has long-lasting effects that may make feminist interventions coming from these countries unintentionally counterproductive.
3. Women in postcolonial countries must be seen as actors in their own right, both in the ways they defend existing, gendered practices and in the ways they advocate changing or ending such practices. Women in postcolonial countries are not victims waiting to be saved by people of the former colonial powers.

Freedom

The Introduction to this book discussed the banning of the *burkini*—or burqa/bikini—in France. The French believed that by banning covering garments worn by Muslim women, such as the burkini, they would liberate women to wear what they wanted. The French read these garments as standing in for an absence of freedom. The irony of this belief is that, in fact, the ban meant that women were *not* free to wear the burkini.

The concept of *freedom* is central to feminist theory. Women's freedom has long been one of the core goals of feminist activism in Europe and North America. For instance, in the 19th century, women's rights activist Susan B. Anthony explained to a journalist why she never married by appealing to freedom: "I never felt I could give up my life of freedom to become a man's housekeeper" (Harper [1898] 1908). Freedom, in the sense Susan B. Anthony used the term and in the understanding of women's rights activism of the time, meant individual autonomy: the right to go to school, to wear what one wants, and to work or participate in politics rather than cook or clean for one's husband.

This is a very specific definition of freedom. Freedom came to be defined as individual autonomy in 18th- and 19th-century Europe with the emergence of the philosophy of liberalism and the market economy. Since that time, North American and European political philosophy has been largely premised upon the belief that human beings have an innate desire for freedom and seek out autonomy when allowed to do so (Mahmood 2005). In this understanding, freedom is individual, not communal. Individual autonomy is considered to stand in opposition to societal considerations.

Though this definition remains dominant in many European and North American societies, other understandings of freedom also exist. For example, for Karl Marx, freedom did not mean individual autonomy but rather the freedom of a group or class of people (workers) from exploitation by another class (capitalists). Marx valued freedom *from exploitation* rather than freedom *to be autonomous*.

However, both liberal and Marxist understandings treat freedom as a natural human instinct; both assume that all humans have a core desire to be free. For the liberal philosopher John Locke, a decision is free when the person arrives at that decision of his or her own will and not by coercion, regardless of the content of the decision. The philosopher Isaiah Berlin (1958) explained the presumed fundamental human desire to make such decisions in the following way:

> I wish to be the instrument of my own, not of other men's, acts of will. I wish to be a subject, not an object; to be moved by reasons, by conscious purposes, which are my own, not by causes which affect me . . . from the outside. I wish to be . . . deciding, not being decided for, self-directed and not acted upon by external nature or by other men. (23)

Zygmunt Bauman (1989) adds that in capitalist society, freedom appears as the natural condition, and it is *unfreedom*, or the lack of freedom, that must be explained. Does this mean that self-realization is possible only in liberal, modern societies? Bauman makes clear that the desire for freedom is not specific to such places, but he underscores that only Western nations (such as those in Europe and North America) think of freedom in terms of self-realization. What marks the modern idea of freedom as distinct from other ideas is its association with the *individual* and with *market economy*. This philosophy suggests that North American and European feminists opposed veiling and burkinis because they represented a lack of freedom. In the U.S., unlike in France, head coverings are not banned because of the First Amendment; nevertheless, there is still considerable dismay in the U.S. about women who wear veils. Those who argue against covering garments say that they represent the imposition of tradition (or society's will) against an individual woman's will. North American and European feminists who argue *for* veils also base their arguments in the liberal idea of freedom. They argue that all women should have the right to choose what to wear: They should have the freedom to wear veils or not as they wish.

However, the antagonism between the individual and society is only one way of conceiving of freedom. Freedom can be collective as well as individual. An example of a collective sense of freedom is the Hindu idea of renunciative freedom, which was common in India before contact with the British. Renunciative freedom is freedom from the material world, believed to lead to spiritual strength. Only through discipline and practice *within* the

Hindu tradition could one achieve this freedom from material things and thus become enlightened and self-realized. Here, freedom was generated through discipline and practice within a tradition, not through individual autonomy. Similarly, in Buddhist Zen philosophy, freedom requires the transcendence of the *ego*, or the self.

For many Muslim women, veiling likewise reflects a desire to live a pious life. Anthropologist Saba Mahmood (2005) shows that in contemporary Egypt, women exercise agency not to find individual freedom but to participate in collective efforts to become pious, including through the practice of deferring to their husbands. From this vantage point, the individual desire to achieve freedom as an expression of agency is a Western assumption rather than a universal phenomenon.

Agency

One of the other most widely used concepts in Western liberal thought and feminist theory is that of agency. *Agency* is defined as the ability to act and to make choices. In both sociology and feminist theory, this definition has been extended to imply acting independently of, or even in opposition to, social structure. Thus, for a woman to have agency, she must act against custom, tradition, and other obstacles (Mahmood 2005: 8). If a woman acts according to tradition, many feminists see her as without agency. When Saba Mahmood studied women in the Mosque movement in Cairo, she found that women not only believed devoutly in Islam, but they also studied it, thought about what the Quran—the holy book of Islam—implied about their daily lives, and argued the finer points of Quranic law. These women actively worked to make themselves more pious. Most feminist analyses would not treat these women as agentic. Instead, many feminists would see these women as submissive to the control of Islam and their husbands.

Through her careful ethnography, Mahmood challenges this typical feminist explanation as well as its underpinnings in the belief that agency and freedom (in her study, defined as individual opposition to societal constraint) are uniformly defined and universally desired. Instead, Mahmood argues that ideas about humans' innate desire for freedom should be seen as mediated by culture. There are many acts that can be interpreted one way if they are seen through Western feminist eyes but another way if they are seen through a different lens.

One example Mahmood offers is that of Hajja Faiza, a woman who leads other women in collective prayers in her mosque. One of the four schools of thought in Islam frowns upon the practice of allowing women to lead prayers, and Faiza's local imam subscribes to this school of thought. Yet when Faiza is told about the imam's disapproval of this practice, she responds by saying that she is comfortable leading prayers because it is allowed by three other schools of Islamic thought. Mahmood notes that Faiza does not argue that it is her individual *right* to lead prayers. Rather, she offers an argument that falls within the accepted practices of Islam.

Similarly, in Mahmood's book, the women wore *hijab* (headscarves, which are considered a form of veiling), but not because their husbands told them to do so. They wore headscarves because they believed that doing so enabled them to achieve the Islamic ideal of modesty. They saw modesty as a difficult attribute to reach, but one that God desired and that therefore had to be striven for. Wearing the *hijab* was a practice that helped the women attain a level of modesty. Here, Mahmood suggests that agency is not simply resistance but the ability to make choices and to act; therefore, these women do, indeed, have agency. They have a project that they aspire toward (that is, piety), and they act with discipline and effort to attain it. Though they are not acting in opposition to social structure, they are acting nonetheless. Because people in Europe and North America view veils as symptoms of Muslim women's oppression, they do not see the veils as religiously symbolic clothing, such as a yarmulke on a Jewish man or a turban on a Sikh man (Mahmood 2005: 75), that devout women would want to wear.

Rather than attributing practices associated with *hijab* to a universal desire for autonomy, Mahmood shows that these acts take their meaning from within specific cultural settings. In turn, she compels readers to consider whether they can ever really understand people's agency in profoundly different cultural settings. In particular, she challenges thinkers in North American and European traditions to think of agency as including not only resistance but also conscious and willful adherence to norms, and the adoption of deliberate action and thought toward a norm.

The Problem of Female Genital Surgeries

To recognize that action occurs within a specific cultural setting is not to say that the norms guiding such action are unchanging. All cultures change. Starting from the understanding that all ideas occur within specific social and cultural settings, it is still possible to ask how and when participants in those settings may challenge and change the existing set of ideas.

Consider the example of the practice of female genital surgeries (FGS). Female genital surgeries have received enormous attention in North America and Europe not only in the present moment but for over 100 years. These surgeries are performed in several parts of Africa, the Middle East, and Southeast Asia, though they are primarily seen as an African phenomenon. Today, FGS are understood in the West primarily as destructive surgeries performed upon women's genitals with the primary purpose of inhibiting women's sexual pleasure and therefore ensuring their chastity.

The surgeries are often called *female genital mutilation* and have been popularly described in the following way:

> This is what it usually includes: the partial or total excision of the clitoris and all or parts of the labia minora and labia majora, plus the sewing or pinning together of both sides of the vulva, by catgut or thorns, and the obliteration of the vaginal entrance except for a tiny passage. The male equivalent would be the removal of the penis. . . . The purpose is to insure virginity and destroy sexual pleasure. It is a form of male control, perhaps the ultimate except for murder. (Rosenthal 1995)

The particular procedure Rosenthal describes is used in about 10% of cases, but it has come to stand in for a far more complex set of processes. Most genital surgeries remove part of the labia and part or all of the clitoral hood and tissue. The idea of such surgeries is repugnant to many in the West, and there are numerous organizations and websites dedicated to abolishing this practice (see, for example, http://desertflowerfoundation.org and http://www.endfgm.eu). According to these websites, FGS is fundamentally cruel, demeaning, and patriarchal—and therefore worthy of universal condemnation.

To understand this reaction to FGS, one must consider colonial history. In her study of colonial Sudan, anthropologist Janice Boddy (2007) writes that the British who governed Sudan condemned the practice of FGS as a sign of Sudanese backwardness. The British tried (but failed) to abolish FGS, arguing that FGS led to childbirth complications and population decline (310). At that time, because the British needed a higher birthrate to increase Sudan's labor force, they denounced the practice. Today, this same practice is condemned for a different reason: inhibiting women's sexual pleasure (311). Though North Americans and Europeans still treat FGS as a sign of Africa's backwardness, the reason for their discomfort has changed with the changing values of the West.

The women's movement and sexual revolution that occurred in the 1970s in the U.S., Canada, and Western Europe changed those societies' perceptions of women's sexual pleasure such that sexual pleasure is now understood as an individual right and as centered on the clitoris. In these contexts, a surgery that involves the clitoris came to be seen as pleasure destroying. But the sources of feelings of sexual pleasure may not be universal. In other words, it is possible that the belief that FGS destroys sexual pleasure stems from a particular, culturally rooted sense of where sexual pleasure comes from.

In an attempt to increase understanding of FGS, the Public Policy Advisory Network published a report on FGS that clarifies several misconceptions. The report notes that a high percentage of women who have had genital surgery have rich sexual lives, with no evidence of reduced frequency of sexual activity or pleasure. Indeed, the report argues that in African cultures that practice FGS, along with male genital surgeries, it is viewed by many insiders as an aesthetic enhancement of the body and not as mutilation. Indeed, FGS can be compared to male circumcision in the U.S. Though male circumcision may have minor health benefits, it is considered a primarily aesthetic procedure by the American Association of Pediatrics. Still, more than 80% of U.S.-born men are circumcised. FGS can also be compared to female surgery for cosmetic purposes, such as labiaplasty (plastic surgery altering the labia), which is gaining popularity in North America.

The Public Policy Advisory Network argues that because FGS in the areas of Africa that practice it is typically managed and controlled by women, health care providers interested in the health and safety of FGS recipients should work with the women conducting the surgeries. In an essay outlining culturally sensitive feminist responses to FGS, Isabelle Gunning (1992), a professor of law, suggests an approach that involves (1) understanding one's own historical context; (2) appreciating how the "other" might perceive

Western feminists, especially with regard to their colonial/imperial heritage; and (3) recognizing the complexities of the life and circumstances of the "other" woman in her particular context. In other words, Western feminists need to understand their own social contexts, the contexts of others, and the relationships between the two. In discussing FGS, Gunning uses the term *surgeries* rather than the more commonly used *mutilation* to lower the level of value judgment involved. Though Gunning is herself not particularly comfortable with the practice, she recognizes that her discomfort comes from her own historical context and is aware that she does not fully understand the contexts within which such surgeries occur. Rather than considering FGS as nothing more than an outlandish practice, Gunning concludes that FGS must be seen in the context of the health, economy, and culture of each society in which it is practiced.

Furthermore, in their haste to condemn FGS from an outside perspective, many Western accounts also miss African feminists' work to change the practice. Some are against all versions of FGS, while others oppose versions of the surgery that cause health risks or painful scarring. Given that these feminists have been working on the issue for many years, some argue that recent outrage from the West has been counterproductive. According to Seble Dawit and Salem Mekuria (1993: 27), North American and European activists have advocated the use of force to stop FGS, creating a natural backlash in countries with histories of colonial and imperial oppression. In addition, Western opposition to FGS has reiterated notions of Western superiority and African backwardness and tyranny. Thus, vocal opposition to FGS from the West makes the work of African activists seeking to change or end the practice more difficult.

Conclusion

As Chapter 9 showed, gender-based inequalities have provoked millions of people to participate in social movements against gender injustice. Extending Chapter 9, this chapter further underscores that gender does not function on its own but in relation to other forces, particularly political power relations. Gender relations take their meaning from both local context and geopolitical history. How, then, is it possible to fight against gender injustice globally?

Every year, hundreds of women from American universities go to once-colonized countries to volunteer in NGOs that help women. On one hand, the urge to help those who are less fortunate or to fight against injustice is a good one. On the other hand, given the complex history of global gender relations and the difficulty in knowing what women in other countries really need or desire, sometimes the rush to help women outside North America and Europe is not well-advised. There are many reasons for this. Given global history, such help may be interpreted as patronizing or unwelcome; it may be mistrusted; and it may backfire. At the same time, it may also help individual women.

This chapter suggested that the sorts of interventions that should be avoided—exemplified by Nicholas Kristof and Sheryl Wudun's film, *Half the Sky*, discussed at the opening of this chapter—are those that fail to acknowledge history and/or the actual feminist struggles taking place within the countries they visit. Refusing to participate in activism that ignores history and context does not mean ending all transnational activism; instead, it means connecting local injustice to global inequalities.

Feminist activism that is informed by the sociology of gender seeks to better understand the global connections between the lives of women (and men) in North America and Europe and the lives of women (and men) in other parts of the world. Feminists need to take the time to understand that former colonial powers remain tied to postcolonial nations through contemporary global capitalism as well as through histories of colonial rule and war. These realities pose challenges to solidarity among women. Yet solidarity is not impossible. Attention to women's interconnected histories and to the cultural specificities of freedom and agency can give rise to different kinds of solidarity and different types of knowledge: harder won, but more enduring.

KEYWORDS

Agency 207
Colonialism 195
Female genital surgeries (FGS) 207
Freedom 207
Geopolitical construction of gender 206
Politics of knowledge 201
Third world woman trope 201
Veiling 207

QUESTIONS

- Take a look at the website for *Half the Sky* (http://www.halftheskymovement.org/) and analyze the photographs and text. What do they convey about women in postcolonial countries? What emotions do they seem designed to evoke in viewers who live in the U.S.?
- Now that you have read this chapter, explore online appeals to aid women in postcolonial countries. What do they convey about freedom and agency? Do they address global histories of colonialism?
- Contextualizing our own ideas can be a very difficult thing to do. Name your culture's ideas about a better life and world. Where do you think these ideas come from? Can you think of other possibilities for ideas about a better life and world?
- Imagine an activist campaign to make the world a better place for women, transgender people, and other gender minorities that also takes into account historical and contemporary inequalities between countries. What would such a campaign need to consider to create a truly transnational practice?

ASSOCIATED READINGS

- Enloe, Cynthia. (1989) 2002. *Bananas, Beaches and Bases: Making Feminist Sense of International Politics*. Berkeley: University of California Press.
- Gunn, Paula Allen. 1986. *Sacred Hoops: Recovering the Feminine in American Indian Traditions*. Boston: Beacon Press.
- Gunning, Isabelle R. 1992. "Arrogant Perception, World-Travelling and Multicultural Feminism: The Case of Female Genital Surgeries." *Columbia Human Rights Law Review* 23: 189.
- Jayawardena, Kumari. 1986. *Feminism and Nationalism in the Third World*. London, UK: Zed Books
- Kristof, Nicholas, and WuDunn, Sheryl. 2008. *Half the Sky: Turning Oppression into Opportunity for Women Worldwide*. New York: Knopf Doubleday
- Mahmood, Saba. 2005. *Politics of Piety: The Islamic Revival and the Feminist Subject*. Princeton: Princeton University Press.
- McClintock, Anne. 1995. *Imperial Leather: Race, Gender and Sexuality in the Colonial Context*. New York: Routledge.
- Mohanty, Chandra Talpade. 1988. "Under Western Eyes: Feminist Scholarship and Colonial Discourses." *Feminist Review* 30 (Autumn): 61–88.
- Sinha, Mrinalini. 2006. *Specters of Mother India: The Global Restructuring of an Empire*. Durham: Duke University Press.

References

Acker, Joan. 1990. "Hierarchies, Jobs, Bodies: A Theory of Gendered Organizations." *Gender & Society* 4 (2): 139–158.

African American Policy Forum (AAPF). 2017. "Say Her Name." *African American Policy Forum*. July 5, 2017. http://www.aapf.org/sayhername/

Agadjanian, Victor. 2002. "Men Doing 'Women's Work': Masculinity and Gender Relations among Street Vendors in Maputo, Mozambique." *The Journal of Men's Studies* 10 (3): 329–342.

Agathangelou, Anna, and L.H.M Ling. 2003. "Desire Industries: Sex Trafficking, UN Peacekeeping, and the Neo-Liberal World Order." *Brown Journal of World Affairs* X (1): 133–148.

Agustin, Laura. 2007. *Sex at the Margins: Migration, Labour Markets and the Rescue Industry*. New York: Zed Books.

Alarcón, Norma. 1991. "The Theoretical Subject(s) of This Bridge Called My Back and Anglo-American Feminism." In *Criticism in the Borderlands: Studies in Chicano Literature, Culture, and Ideology*, edited by H. Calderon and J. D. Saldivar, 140. Durham: Duke University Press.

Allen, Samantha. 2013. "Counterpunch and the War on the Transgendered." *Jacobin*. July 10, 2013. https://www.jacobinmag.com/2013/07/counterpunch-and-the-war-on-the-transgendered/

Almeling, Rene, and Miranda Waggoner. 2013. "More and Less Equal: How Men Factor in the Reproductive Equation." *Gender & Society* 27 (6): 821–842.

Altman, Dennis. 1996. "Rupture or Continuity? The Internationalization of Gay Identities." *Social Text* 48: 77–94.

Altman, Dennis. 2001. *Global Sex*. Chicago: University of Chicago Press.

Alvarez, Sonia. 1999. "Advocating Feminism: The Latin American Feminist NGO 'Boom.'" *International Feminist Journal of Politics* 1 (2): 181–209.

Alvarez, Sonia. 2009. "Beyond NGO-Ization? Reflections from Latin America." *Development* 52 (2): 175–184.

American Psychiatric Association. 2013. *Gender Dysphoria*. https://www.psychiatry.org/File%20Library/Psychiatrists/Practice/DSM/APA_DSM-5-Gender-Dysphoria.pdf

American Society for Aesthetic Plastic Surgery. 2016. "American Society for Aesthetic Plastic Surgery Reports More Than $13.5 Billion Spent for the First Time Ever." *The American Society for Aesthetic Plastic Surgery*. March 8, 2016. http://www.surgery.org/media/news-releases/american-society-for-aesthetic-plastic-surgery-reports-more-than-135-billion-spent-for-the-first-time-ever

Anderson, Elijah. 1999. *Code of the Street: Decency, Violence and the Moral Life of the Inner City*. New York: W.W. Norton & Company.

Andrejevic, Mark. 2008. "Watching Television Without Pity: The Productivity of Online Fans." *Television New Media* 9 (1): 24–46.

Andrews, Abigail, and Nazanin Shahrokni. 2014. "Patriarchal Accommodations: Women's Mobility and Policies of Gender Difference from Urban Iran to Migrant Mexico." *Journal of Contemporary Ethnography* 43 (2): 1–28.

Andrijasevic, Rutvica. 2010. *Migration, Agency, and Citizenship in Sex Trafficking*. New York: Palgrave Macmillan.

Anzaldúa, Gloria. 1990. "La Conciencia de la Mestiza: Towards a New Consciousness." In *Making Face, Making Soul/Haciendo Caras: Creative and Critical Perspectives by Feminists of Color*, edited by Gloria Anzaldúa, 270–274. San Francisco: Aunt Lute Foundation Books.

Apple, Rima D. 1987. *Mothers and Medicine: A Social History of Infant Feeding, 1890–1950*. Madison: University of Wisconsin Press.

Armstrong, Elizabeth A. 2002. *Forging Gay Identities: Organizing Sexuality in San Francisco, 1950–1994*. Chicago: University of Chicago Press.

Baer, Drake. 2015. "The Most Popular Plastic Surgery Operation in South Korea Has a Controversial Past." *Business Insider*. October 6, 2015. http://www.businessinsider.com/the-most-popular-plastic-surgery-in-korea-2015-10

Bales, Kevin. 2000. *Disposable People*. Berkeley: University of California Press.

Balogun, Oluwakemi. 2012. "Cultural and Cosmopolitan: Idealized Femininity and Embodied Nationalism in Nigerian Beauty Pageants." *Gender & Society* 26 (3): 357–381.

Bandopadhyay, Sandip. 1991. "Women in the Bengal Revolutionary Movement (1902–1935)." *Manushi* 65 (July–August): 30–35.

Banet-Weiser, Sarah. 1999. *The Most Beautiful Girl in the World: Beauty Pageants and National Identity*. Berkeley: University of California Press.

Banks, Tyra. 2007. Tyra Confronts Her Fat Tabloid Photos. *The Tyra Banks Show*, Season 2, Episode 87. Burbank, CA: Warner Bros.

Barber, Kristen. 2008. "The Well-Coiffed Man." *Gender & Society* 22 (4): 455–476.

Barry, Kathleen. 1995. *The Prostitution of Sexuality.* New York: New York University Press.

Battle of Algiers. 1966. *Directed by Gillo Pontecorvo*. Los Angeles: Rialto Pictures.

Bauman, Zygmunt. 1989. *Freedom*. Minneapolis: University of Minnesota Press.

Beauboeuf-Lafontant, Tamara. 2003. "Strong and Large Black Women? Exploring Relationships between Deviant Womanhood and Weight." *Gender & Society,* 17 (1): 111–121.

Beauvoir, Simone de. (1949) 1989. *The Second Sex*. New York: Vintage Books.

Belkin, Lisa. 2003. "The Opt-Out Revolution." *New York Times Magazine*. October 26, 2003. http://www.nytimes.com/2003/10/26/magazine/the-opt-out-revolution.html

Belknap, Joanne, and Kristi Holsinger. 2006. "The Gendered Nature of Risk Factors for Delinquency." *Feminist Criminology* 1 (1): 48–71.

Bentham, Jeremy. 1791. *Panopticon or the Inspection House*. Lausanne, Switzerland: University of Lausanne.

Berger, John. 1992. *Ways of Seeing*. New York: Penguin Modern Classics.

Berlin, Isaiah. "Two Concepts of Liberty." Lecture at University of Oxford, October 31, 1958. http://faculty.www.umb.edu/steven.levine/courses/Fall%202015/What%20is%20Freedom%20Writings/Berlin.pdf

Bernard, April. 2013. "The Intersectional Alternative: Explaining Female Criminality." *Feminist Criminology* 8 (1): 3–19.

Bernstein, Elizabeth, and Elena Shih. 2014. "The Erotics of Authenticity: Sex Trafficking and 'Reality Tourism' in Thailand Social Politics." *Social Politics: International Studies in Gender, State & Society* 21 (3): 430–460.

Bernstein, Elizabeth. 2007. *Temporarily Yours: Intimacy, Authenticity, and the Commerce of Sex*. Chicago: University of Chicago Press.

Bernstein, Mary. 2002. "Identities and Politics: Toward a Historical Understanding of the Lesbian and Gay Movement." *Social Science History* 26 (3): 531–581.

Bianchi, Suzanne, Liana Sayer, Melissa Milkie, and John Robinson. 2012. "Housework: Who Did, Does or Will Do It, and How Much Does It Matter?" *Social Forces* 91 (1): 55–63.

Bianchi, Suzanne, Melissa Milkie, Liana Sayer, and John Robinson. 2000. "Is Anyone Doing the Housework? Trends in the Gender Division of Labor." *Social Forces* 79 (1): 191–228.

Blair-Loy, Mary. 2003. *Competing Devotions: Career and Family among Women Executives*. Cambridge: Harvard University Press.

Bledsoe, Caroline. 1993. "The Politics of Polygyny in Mende Education and Child Fosterage Transactions." In *Sex and Gender Hierarchies*, edited by B. D. Miller, 170–192. New York: Cambridge University Press.

Boddy, Janice. 2007. *Civilizing Women: British Crusades in Colonial Sudan*. Princeton: Princeton University Press.

Boero, Natalie. 2012. *Killer Fat: Media, Medicine, and Morals in the American "Obesity Epidemic."* New York: Rutgers University Press.

Boggis, Terry. 2001. "Affording Our Families: Class Issues in Family Formation." In *Queer Families, Queer Politics: Challenging Culture and the State*, edited by M. Bernstein and R. Reimann, 175–181. New York: Columbia University Press.

Boon, Kevin Alexander. 2003. "Men and Nostalgia for Violence: Culture and Culpability in Chuck Palahniuk's *Fight Club*." *The Journal of Men's Studies* 11 (3): 267–276.

Bordo, Susan. 1993. *Unbearable Weight: Feminism, Western Culture, and the Body*. Berkeley: University of California Press.

Boskin, Joseph. 1988. *Sambo: The Rise and Demise of an American Jester.* Oxford: Oxford University Press.

Botelho, Greg. 2012. "Seventeen Magazine Vows Not to Alter Images, to 'Celebrate Every Kind of Beauty.'" *CNN*. July 5, 2012. http://www.cnn.com/2012/07/05/us/seventeen-photoshopping/

Bowers v. Hardwick. 478 U.S. 186. 1986.

Branch, John. 2015. "Dutee Chand, Female Sprinter with High Testosterone Level, Wins Right to Compete." *New York Times*. July 28, 2015. http://www.nytimes.com/2015/07/28/sports/international/dutee-chand-female-sprinter-with-high-male-hormone-level-wins-right-to-compete.html?_r=0

Bread and Roses. 2000. *Directed by Ken Loach*. Santa Monica: Lionsgate.

Brennan, Denise. 2001. "Selling Sex for Visas: Sex Tourism as Tourism as a Stepping Stone to International Migration." In *Global Woman: Nannies, Maids, and Sex Workers in the New Economy*, edited by Barbara Ehrenreich and Arlie Hochschild, 154–168. New York: Henry Holt and Company.

Brennan, Denise. 2004. *What's Love Got to Do with It? Transnational Desires and Sex Tourism in the Dominican Republic*. Durham: Duke University Press.

Brennan, Denise. 2005. "Methodological Challenges in Research with Trafficked Persons: Tales from the Field." *International Migration* 43 (1/2): 35–54.

Brennan, Denise. 2014. *Life Interrupted: Trafficking into Forced Labor in the United States*. Durham: Duke University Press.

Bridges, Tristan. 2014. "A Very 'Gay' Straight?" *Gender & Society* 28 (1): 58–82.

Bridges, Tristan, and C. J. Pascoe. 2014. "Hybrid Masculinities: New Direction in the Sociology of Men and Masculinities." *Sociology Compass* 8 (3): 246–258.

Bronfenbrenner, Kate. 2005. "Organizing Women: The Nature and Process of Union-Organizing Efforts Among U.S. Women Workers Since the Mid-1990s." *Work and Occupations* 32 (4): 441–463.

Brown, Anna. 2017. "5 Key Findings about LGBT Americans." *Pew Research Center.* July 4, 2017. http://www.pewresearch.org/fact-tank/2017/06/13/5-key-findings-about-lgbt-americans/

Brown, Wendy. 1995. *States of Injury: Power and Freedom in Late Modernity.* Princeton: Princeton University Press.

Brownmiller, Susan. (1975) 2013. *Against Our Will: Men, Women and Rape*. New York: Open Road Media.

Bumiller, Kristin. 2008. *In an Abusive State: How Neoliberalism Appropriated the Feminist Movement against Sexual Violence*. Durham: Duke University Press.

Burkett, Elinor. "What Makes a Woman?" *The New York Times*, June 7, 2015.

Butler, Judith. (1990) 2011. *Gender Trouble: Feminism and the Subversion of Identity*. New York: Routledge.

Butler, Judith. (1993) 2011. *Bodies That Matter: On the Discursive Limits of Sex*. Abingdon, UK: Taylor & Francis.

Cabezas, Amalia. 2009. *Economies of Desire: Sex and Tourism in Cuba and the Dominican Republic*. Philadelphia: Temple University Press.

Cadet, Danielle. 2013. "Rachel Jeantel, Trayvon Martin Friend: Teen Was Trying to Escape George Zimmerman." *The Huffington Post*. June 27, 2013. http://www.huffingtonpost.com/2013/06/26/rachel-jeantel-trayvon-martin_n_3505587.html

California Penal Code. 1991. Section 646.9.

Carlen, Pat. 2010. *A Criminological Imagination: Essays on Justice, Punishment and Discourse*. London, UK: Ashgate.

Carlson, Jennifer, and Jessica Cobb. 2017. "From Play to Peril: A Historical Examination of Media Coverage of Accidental Shootings Involving Children." *Social Science Quarterly* 98 (2): 397–412.

Carlson, Jennifer. 2015. *Citizen-Protectors: The Everyday Politics of Guns in an Age of Decline*. New York: Oxford University Press.

Carmon, Irin. 2014. "For Eugenic Sterilization Victims, Belated Justice." *MSNBC*. June 27, 2014. http://www.msnbc.com/all/eugenic-sterilization-victims-belated-justice

Carrington, Christopher. 1999. *No Place Like Home: Relationships and Family Life among Lesbians and Gay Men*. Chicago: University of Chicago Press.

Catalano, Shannan, Erica Smith, Howard Snyder, and Michael Rand. 2009. *Bureau of Justice Statistics: Selected Findings. Female Victims of Violence.* September 2009 U.S. Department of Justice: Office of Justice Programs. https://www.bjs.gov/content/pub/pdf/fvv.pdf

Centers for Disease Control and Prevention (CDC). 2014. *The National Intimate Partner and Sexual Violence Survey (NISVS)*. https://www.cdc.gov/violenceprevention/pdf/NISVS-Fact-Sheet-2014.pdf

Centers for Disease Control and Prevention (CDC). 2015. "National Marriage and Divorce Rate Trends." *National Vital Statistics System*. http://www.cdc.gov/nchs/nvss/marriage_divorce_tables.htm

The Central Park Five. 2012. *Directed by Ken Burns*. Arlington County: PBS.

Cermele, Jill, and Martha McCaughey. 2016. "What's Wrong with the CDC's Public Health Model for Rape Prevention." *Gender & Society*, February 16, 2016. https://gendersociety.wordpress.com/2016/02/16/whats-wrong-with-the-cdcs-public-health-model-for-rape-prevention/

Chaib, Fadéla, Jenny Orton, Keletso Ratsela, and Katie Steels. 2013. "Violence against Women: A 'Global Health Problem of Epidemic Proportions.'" *World Health Organization*, June 20, 2013. http://www.who.int/mediacentre/news/releases/2013/violence_against_women_20130620/en/

Chancer, Lynn. 1993. "Prostitution, Feminist Theory, and Ambivalence: Notes from the Sociological Underground." *Social Text* 37 (1): 143–171.

Chapkis, Wendy. 1997. *Live Sex Acts: Women Performing Erotic Labor*. New York: Taylor & Francis.

Chatters, Linda M., Rober Joseph Taylor, and Rukmalie Jayakody. 1994. "Fictive Kinship Relations in Black Extended Families." *Journal of Comparative Family Studies* 25 (3): 297–312.

Chen, Feinian, Guangya Liu, and Christine A. Mair. 2011. "Intergenerational Ties in Context: Grandparents Caring for Grandchildren in China." *Social Forces* 90 (2): 571–594.

Cheng, Sealing. 2010. *On the Move for Love: Migrant Entertainers and the U.S. Military in South Korea*. Philadelphia: University of Pennsylvania Press.

Chesney-Lind, Meda. 1987. "Girls and Violence: An Exploration of the Gender Gap in Serious Delinquent Behavior." In *Childhood Aggression and Violence*, edited by David Crowell, Ian Evans, and Clifford O'Donnell, 207–229. New York: Springer US.

Chesney-Lind, Meda. 2006. Patriarchy, Crime, and Justice: Feminist Criminology in an Era of Backlash. *Feminist Criminology* 1 (1): 6–26.

Childress, Sarah. 2013. "Why the Military Has a Sexual Assault Problem." *PBS*. May 10, 2013. http://www.pbs.org/wgbh/frontline/article/why-the-military-has-a-rape-problem/

Chin, Christine. 2013. *Cosmopolitan Sex Workers: Women and Migration in a Global City*. New York: Oxford University Press.

Chin, Ko-Lin, and James Finckenauer. 2012. *Selling Sex Overseas: Chinese Women and the Realities of Prostitution and Global Sex Trafficking*. New York: New York University Press.

Chiricos, Ted, and Sarah Eschholz. 2002. "The Racial and Ethnic Typification of Crime and the Criminal Typification of Race and Ethnicity in Local Television News." *Journal of Research in Crime and Delinquency* 39 (4): 400–420.

Chou, Rosalind. 2012. *Asian American Sexual Politics: The Construction of Race, Gender, and Sexuality*. Lanham: Rowman & Littlefield.

Chuang, Janie. 2013. "Exploitation Creep and the Unmaking of Human Trafficking Law." Labor Law Research Network Inaugural Conference, Pompeu Fabra University, Barcelona, Spain, June 13–15, 2013.

Clarey, Christopher. 2009. "Gender Test after a Gold-Medal Finish." *The New York Times*. August 20, 2009. http://www.nytimes.com/2009/08/20/sports/20runner.html

Cohn, D'Vera, Gretchen Livingston, and Wendy Wang. 2014. "Chapter 4: Public Views on Staying at Home vs. Working." *Pew Social Trends*. http://www.pewsocialtrends.org/2014/04/08/chapter-4-public-views-on-staying-at-home-vs-working/

Collins, Patricia Hill. 1986. "Learning from the Outsider Within: The Sociological Significance of Black Feminist Thought." *Social Problems* 33 (6): 14–32.

Collins, Patricia Hill. 1989. "The Social Construction of Black Feminist Thought." *Signs: Journal of Women in Culture and Society* 14 (4): 745–773.

Collins, Patricia Hill. 2000. *Black Feminist Thought: Knowledge, Consciousness, and the Politics of Empowerment*, 2nd edition. New York: Routledge.

Collins, Patricia Hill. 2004. *Black Sexual Politics: African Americans, Gender, and the New Racism*. New York: Routledge.

The Combahee River Collective. 1978. "Black Feminist Statement." In *Capitalist Patriarchy and the Case for Socialist Feminism*, edited by Zilla Eisenstein. New York: Monthly Review Press.

Comella, Lynn. 2017. *Vibrator Nation: How Feminist Sex-Toy Stores Changed the Business of Pleasure*. Durham: Duke University Press.

Connell, Raewyn W. 1987. *Gender and Power: Society, the Person and Sexual Politics*. Berkeley: University of California Press.

Connell, Raewyn W. 1992. "A Very Straight Gay." *American Sociological Review* 57 (6): 735–751.

Connell, Raewyn W. 1995. *Masculinities*. Stanford: Stanford University Press.

Connell, Raewyn W. 1997. "Why Is Classical Theory Classical?" *American Journal of Sociology* 102 (6): 1511–1557.

Connell, Raewyn W. 2001. "Understanding Men: Gender Sociology and the New International Research on Masculinities." *Social Thought & Research* 24 (1/2): 13–31.

Connell, Raewyn W. 2005. "Hegemonic Masculinity: Rethinking the Concept." *Gender & Society* 19 (6): 829–859.

Connell, Raewyn. 2009. *Gender (Short Introductions)*. Cambridge: Polity Press.

Contreras, Randol. 2012. *The Stickup Kids: Race, Drugs, Violence, and the American Dream*. Berkeley: University of California Press.

Coontz, Stephanie. 1993. *The Way We Never Were: American Families and the Nostalgia Trap*. New York: Basic Books.

Coontz, Stephanie. 2012. "The Myth of the Male Decline" *The New York Times*, September 29, 2012. http://www.nytimes.com/2012/09/30/opinion/sunday/the-myth-of-male-decline.html

Cooper, Frank Rudy. 2009. "Who's the Man?" Masculinities Studies, Terry Stops, and Police Training. *Columbia Journal of Gender and Law* 18 (3): 671.

Cooper, Marianne. 2000. "Being the "Go-To Guy": Fatherhood, Masculinity, and the Organization of Work in Silicon Valley." *Qualitative Sociology* 23 (4): 379–405.

Correll, Shelley J., Stephen Benard, and In Paik. 2007. "Getting a Job: Is There a Motherhood Penalty?" *American Journal of Sociology* 112 (5): 1297–1338.

Costigliola, Frank. 1997. "Unceasing Pressure for Penetration: Gender, Pathology and Emotion in George Kennan's Formation of the Cold War." *Journal of American History* 83 (4): 1309–1339.

Courtney, Alice E., and Sarah Wernick Lockeretz. 1971. "A Woman's Place: An Analysis of the Roles Portrayed by Women in Magazine Advertisements." *Journal of Marketing Research* 8 (1): 92–95.

Cox, Laverne. 2015. "The May 29, 2014, Issue of Time Magazine." *Official Laverne Cox Tumblr.* June 2, 2015. http://lavernecox.tumblr.com/post/120503412651/on-may-29-2014-the-issue-of-timemagazine

Crenshaw, Kimberlé. 1991. "Mapping the Margins: Intersectionality, Identity Politics and Violence Against Women of Color." *Stanford Law Review* 43 (6): 1241–1299.

Crenshaw, Kimberlé. 1992. "Whose Story Is It Anyway? Feminist and Antiracist Appropriations of Anita Hill." In *Race-in Justice, Engendering Power*, edited by T. Morrison, 402–440. New York: Pantheon.

Crime after Crime. 2011. *Directed by Yoav Potash*. New York: Virgil Films and Entertainment.

Currie, Dawn. 1997. "DECODING FEMININITY: Advertisements and Their Teenage Readers." *Gender & Society* 11 (4): 453–477.

Currier, Danielle M. 2013. "Strategic Ambiguity: Protecting Emphasized Femininity and Hegemonic Masculinity in the Hookup Culture." *Gender & Society* 27 (5): 704–727.

Danet, Brenda. 1998. "Text as Mask: Gender, Play, and Performance on the Internet." In *Cybersociety 2.0: Revisiting Computer-Mediated Communication and Community*, edited by Steven G. Jones, 129–158. Thousand Oaks: SAGE.

Dasgupta, Sayantani. (2012) 2013. "'Your Women Are Oppressed but Ours Are Awesome': How Nicolas Kristoff and *Half the Sky* Use Women against Each Other." *Racalious*. http://www.conspireforchange.org/?p=964

Davidson, Julia O'Connell. 1998. *Prostitutions, Power, and Freedom*. Ann Arbor: University of Michigan Press.

Davis, Angela. 1983. *Women, Race, and Class*. New York: Vintage.

Davis, Bre. 2014. Pinterest Envy. *The Motherhood Collective,* February 9, 2014. http://www.themotherhood collective.org/blog/pinterest-envy

Dawit, Seble, and Salem Mekuria. 1993. "The West Just Doesn't Get It." *New York Times*, December 7, 1993.

Delacoste, Frederique, and Priscilla Alexander. 1998. *Sex Work: Writings by Women in the Sex Industry*. San Francisco: Cleis Press.

Desai, M. 2007. "The Messy Relationship between Feminisms and Globalizations." *Gender & Society* 21 (6): 797.

Dill, Karen E., and Kathryn P. Thill. 2007. "Video Game Characters and the Socialization of Gender Roles: Young People's Perceptions Mirror Sexist Media Depictions." *Sex Roles* 57 (11): 851–864.

Dixon, Travis L., and Daniel Linz. 2000. "Overrepresentation and Underrepresentation of African Americans and Latinos as Lawbreakers on Television News." *Journal of Communication* 50 (2): 131–154.

Doe v. Commonwealth's Attorney for City of Richmond. 403 F. Supp. 1199. E.D. Va. 1975.

Domestic Workers United and Datacenter. 2006. *Home Is Where the Work Is: Inside New York's Domestic Work Industry.* http://www.datacenter.org/reports/homeiswheretheworkis.pdf

Donato, Katharine M., and Donna Gabaccia. 2016. *The Global Feminization of Migration: Past, Present, and Future*. Migration Policy Institute. http://www.migrationpolicy.org/article/global-feminization-migration-past-present-and-future

Dow, Dawn Marie. 2015. "Negotiating 'The Welfare Queen' and 'The Strong Black Woman': African American Middle-Class Mothers' Work and Family Perspectives." *Sociological Perspectives* 58: 36–55.

Dow, Dawn Marie. 2016a. "Caring for Them Like Family: Examining How Structure and Culture Simultaneously

Influence Kin and Community Childcare Choices of Contemporary African American Middle- and Upper-Middle-Class Mothers." *Sociology of Race and Ethnicity* 2: 72–86.

Dow, Dawn Marie. 2016b. Enacting Black Feminist Thought on African American Mommy Blogs. Paper presented at the meeting of the American Sociological Association, Seattle, WA.

Dow, Dawn Marie. 2016c. "Integrated Motherhood: Beyond Traditional Ideologies of Motherhood." *Journal of Marriage and Family* 78 (1): 180–196.

Dow, Dawn Marie. 2016d. "The Deadly Challenges of Raising African American Boys: Navigating the Controlling Image of the 'Thug.'" *Gender & Society* 30: 161–218.

Dreby, Joanna. 2010. *Divided by Borders: Mexican Migrants and Their Children.* Berkeley: University of California Press.

Durfee, Alesha. 2011. "'I'm Not a Victim, She's an Abuser' Masculinity, Victimization, and Protection Orders." *Gender & Society* 25 (3): 316–334.

Durham, Aisha. 2012. "'Check on It': Beyoncé, Southern Booty, and Black Femininities in Music Video." *Feminist Media Studies* 12 (1): 35–49.

Durkheim, Émile. 1997. *The Division of Labor in Society.* New York: Free Press.

Dworkin, Andrea. 1981. *Pornography: Men Possessing Women.* New York: Plume.

Dworkin, Shari L. 2001. "'Holding Back': Negotiating a Glass Ceiling on Women's Muscular Strength." *Sociological Perspectives* 44 (3): 333–350.

Echols, Alice. 1989. *Daring to be Bad: Radical Feminism in America 1967–1975.* Minneapolis: University of Minnesota Press.

Edin, Kathryn, and Laura Lein. 1997. "Work, Welfare, and Single Mothers' Economic Survival Strategies." *American Sociological Review* 62 (2): 253–266.

Edlund, Jonas, and Ida Öun. 2016. "Who Should Work and Who Should Care? Attitudes towards the Desirable Division of Labour between Mothers and Fathers in Five European Countries." *Acta Sociologica* 59 (2): 151–169.

EEOC v. Sears, Roebuck & Co., 839 F. 2d 302 1988.

Ehrenreich, Barbara, and Deirdre English. (1978) 2005. *For Her Own Good: Two Centuries of Experts' Advice to Women.* New York: Anchor Books.

Eisenstein, Hester. 2005. "A Dangerous Liaison? Feminism and Corporate Globalization." *Science & Society* 69 (3): 487–518.

Elders, M. Jocelyn, David Satcher, and Richar Carmona. 2017. *Re-Thinking Genital Surgeries on Intersex Infants.* San Francisco: Palm Center: Blueprints for Public Policy. http://www.palmcenter.org/wp-content/uploads/2017/06/Re-Thinking-Genital-Surgeries-1.pdf

Engber, Daniel. 2016. "Should Caster Semenya Be Allowed to Compete Against Women?" *Slate,* August 5, 2016. http://www.slate.com/articles/sports/fivering_circus/2016/08/should_caster_semenya_be_allowed_to_compete_against_women.html

England, Paula. 1992. *Comparable Worth: Theories and Evidence.* New York: Aldine de Gruyter.

England, Paula. 2005. "Gender Inequality in Labor Markets: The Role of Motherhood and Segregation." *Social Politics: International Studies in Gender, State & Society* 12 (2): 264–288.

Enloe, Cynthia. (1989) 2002. *Bananas, Beaches and Bases.* Berkeley: University of California Press.

Enloe, Cynthia. 2000. *Maneuvers: The International Politics of Militarizing Women's Lives.* Berkeley: University of California Press.

Ensler, Eve. 2013. "What Is One Billion Rising? Founder Eve Ensler Explains." *The Guardian,* February 14, 2013. https://www.theguardian.com/society/blog/2013/feb/14/what-is-one-billion-rising-founder-eve-ensler-explains

Epp, Charles R., Maynard-Moody, Steven, and Haider-Markel, Donald P. 2014. *Pulled Over: How Police Stops Define Race and Citizenship.* Chicago: University of Chicago Press.

Epstein, Steven G. 1999. "Gay and Lesbian Movements in the United States: Dilemmas of Identity, Diversity, and Political Strategy." In *The Global Emergence of Gay and Lesbian Politics: National Imprints of a Worldwide Movement,* edited by Barry Adam, Jan W. Duyvendak, and Andre Krouwel, 30–90. Philadelphia: Temple University Press.

Faludi, Susan. (1991) 2006. *Backlash: The Undeclared War against American Women,* 15th Anniversary Edition. New York: Three Rivers Press.

Fanon, Frantz. (1952) 2008. *Black Skin, White Masks.* New York: Grove/Atlantic.

Farr, Kathryn. 2005. *Sex Trafficking: The Global Market in Women and Children.* New York: Worth Publishers.

Farrag, Hebah, Richard Flory, and Brie Loskota. 2014. "Evangelicals and Human Trafficking: Rescuing, Rehabilitating, and Releasing One Individual at a Time." In *Human Trafficking Reconsidered: Rethinking the Problem, Envisioning New Solutions,* edited by Kimberly Kay

Hoang and Rhacel Parreñas, 116–122. New York: The International Debate Education Association.

Fausto-Sterling, Anne. 2000. *Sexing the Body: Gender Politics and the Construction of Sexuality*. New York: Basic Books.

Federal Bureau of Investigation (FBI). 2016. *2015: Crime in the United States*. Washington, DC: U. S. Department of Justice. https://ucr.fbi.gov/crime-in-the-u.s/2015/crime-in-the-u.s.-2015/resource-pages/crime-clock

Federici, Silvia. (1975) 2012. *Revolution at Point Zero: Housework, Reproduction, and Feminist Struggle*. Oakland: PM Press.

Ferraro, Kenneth F. 1996. "Women's Fear of Victimization: Shadow of Sexual Assault?" *Social Forces* 75 (2): 667–690.

Field, Connie. 1980. *The Life and Times of Rosie the Riveter*. Minneapolis: Clarity Films.

Foucault, Michel. 1975. *Discipline and Punish: The Birth of the Prison*. New York: Pantheon Books.

Foucault, Michel. 1976. *The History of Sexuality: Volume I*. New York: Vintage Books.

Franke-Ruta, Garance. 2013. "The Amazing 1969 Account of the Stonewall Uprising." *The Atlantic*, January 24, 2013.

Franklin, Aretha. 1967. "Do Right Woman, Do Right Man." *I Never Loved a Man the Way I Love You*. New York: Atlantic Recording Studios.

Fraser, Nancy, and Linda Gordon. 1994. "A Genealogy of Dependency: Tracing a Keyword of the U.S. Welfare State." *Signs: Journal of Women in Culture and Society* 19 (2): 309–336.

Fraser, Nancy. 2007. "Feminist Politics in the Age of Recognition: A Two-Dimensional Approach to Gender Justice." *Studies in Social Justice* 1 (1): 23–35.

Fraser, Nancy. 2009. "Feminism, Capitalism, and the Cunning of History." *New Left Review* 56: 87–104.

Freud, Sigmund. 1995. "Three Contributions of the Theory of Sex." In *The Basic Writings of Sigmund Freud*, edited by A.A. Brill. New York: Modern Library

Friedan, Betty. 1963. *The Feminine Mystique*. New York: W.W. Norton & Company.

Fukushima, Annie. 2014. "Beyond Supply & Demand: The Limitations of End-Demand Strategies." In *Human Trafficking Reconsidered: Rethinking the Problem, Envisioning New Solutions*, edited by Kimberly Kay Hoang and Rhacel Parreñas, 91–101. New York: The International Debate Education Association.

Fuller-Thomson, Esme, Meredith Minkler, and Diane Driver. 1997. "A Profile of Grandparents Raising Grandchildren in the United States." *The Gerontologist* 37 (3): 406–411.

Gagnon, John, and William Simon. (1973) 2017. *Sexual Conduct: The Sources of Human Sexuality*. New York: Routledge.

Garcia, Lorena. 2012. *Respect Yourself, Protect Yourself: Latina Girls and Sexual Identity*. New York: New York University Press.

Garfinkel, Harold. (1967) 2006. "Passing and the Managed Achievement of Sex Status in an 'Intersexed' Person." In *The Transgender Studies Reader*, edited by S. Stryker and S. Whittle, 58–93. New York: Routledge.

Gates, Gary. 2013. *LGBT Parenting in the United States*. http://williamsinstitute.law.ucla.edu/wp-content/uploads/LGBT-Parenting.pdf

Gathings, M. J., and Kylie Parrotta. 2013. "The Use of Gendered Narratives in the Courtroom: Constructing an Identity Worthy of Leniency." *Journal of Contemporary Ethnography* 42 (6): 668–689.

Gay Lib v. University of Missouri. 558 F. 2d 848. 8th Cir. 1977.

General Social Survey (GSS). 2012. *1972–2014 Cumulative Datafile*. http://www.icpsr.umich.edu/icpsrweb/ICPSR/studies/36319

Ghaziani, Amin, and Delia Baldessari. 2011. "Cultural Anchors and the Organization of Differences: A Multi-Method Analysis of LGBT Marches on Washington." *American Sociological Review* 76 (2): 179–206.

Gibson, Priscilla A. 2005. "Intergenerational Parenting from the Perspective of African American Grandmothers." *Family Relations* 54 (2): 280–297.

Glenn, Evelyn Nakano. 1992. "From Servitude to Service Work: Historical Continuities in the Racial Division of Paid Reproductive Labor." *Signs: Journal of Women in Culture and Society* 18 (1): 1–43.

Goffman, Erving. (1959) 2008. "The Presentation of Self in Everyday Life: Selections." In *Sociology: Exploring the Architecture of Everyday Life Readings*, edited by D. M. Newman and J. O'Brien, 56. Thousand Oaks: SAGE.

Golash-Boza, Tanya, and Pierrette Hondagneu-Sotelo. 2013. "Latino Immigrant Men and the Deportation Crisis: A Gendered Racial Removal Program." *Latino Studies* 11 (3): 271–292.

Goldsby, Jacqueline. 1996. "The High and Low Tech of It: The Meaning of Lynching and the Death of Emmett Till." *The Yale Journal of Criticism* 9 (2): 245–282.

Gramsci, Antonio. 1971. *Selections from the Prison Notebooks*. Translated and edited by Quintin Hoare and Geoffrey Nowell Smith. New York: International Publishers.

Griswold v. Connecticut. 381 U.S. 479. 1965.

Groesz, Lisa M., Michael P. Levine, and Sarah K. Murnen. 2002. "The Effect of Experimental Presentation of Thin Media Images on Body Satisfaction: A Meta-Analytic Review." *International Journal of Eating Disorders* 31 (1): 1–16.

Gunn, Paula Allen. 1986. *Sacred Hoops: Recovering the Feminine in American Indian Traditions*. Boston: Beacon Press.

Gunning, Isabelle R. 1992. "Arrogant Perception, World-Travelling and Multicultural Feminism: The Case of Female Genital Surgeries." *Columbia Human Rights Law Review* 23: 189.

Guzman, Isabel Molina, and Angharad N. Valdivia. 2004. "Brain, Brow, and Booty: Latina Iconicity in U.S. Popular Culture." *The Communication Review* 7 (2): 205–211.

Gyte, Natalie. 2013. "Why I Won't Support One Billion Rising." *The Huffington Post UK*, February 16, 2013. http://www.huffingtonpost.co.uk/natalie-gyte/one-billion-rising-why-i-wont-support_b_2684595.html

Haag, Pamela. 2016. *The Gunning of America: Business and the Making of American Gun Culture*. New York: Basic Books.

Haas, Ann, Philip Rodgers, and Jody Herman. 2014. *Suicide Attempts among Transgender and Gender Non-Conforming Adults*. The American Foundation for Suicide Prevention and the Williams Institute at UCLA Law. http://williamsinstitute.law.ucla.edu/wp-content/uploads/AFSP-Williams-Suicide-Report-Final.pdf

Halberstam, Judith Jack. 2011. *The Queer Art of Failure*. Durham: Duke University Press.

Halberstam, Judith Jack. 2012. *Gaga Feminism: Sex, Gender, and the End of Normal*. New York: Beacon Press.

Haley, Sarah. 2013. "'Like I Was a Man': Chain Gangs, Gender, and the Domestic Carceral Sphere in Jim Crow Georgia." *Signs: Journal of Women in Culture and Society* 39 (1): 53–77.

Halliwell, James Orchard. 1844. *The Nursery Rhymes of England*. London, UK: John Russell Smith.

Hamblin, James. 2016. "Trump is a Climax of American Masculinity," *The Atlantic*, August 8, 2016. http://www.theatlantic.com/health/archive/2016/08/trump-masculinity-problem/494582/

Hamilton, Laura, and Elizabeth A. Armstrong. 2009. "Gendered Sexuality in Young Adulthood Double Binds and Flawed Option." *Gender & Society* 23 (5): 589–616.

Haney, Lynne. 2010. *Offending Women: Power, Punishment, and the Regulation of Desire*. Berkeley: University of California Press.

Hannah-Moffat, Kelly. 2001. *Punishment in Disguise: Penal Governance and Federal Imprisonment of Women in Canada*. Toronto, Canada: University of Toronto Press.

Haraway, Donna. 1988. "Situated Knowledges: The Science Question in Feminism and the Privilege of Partial Perspective." *Feminist Studies* 14 (3): 575–599.

Harding, Sandra. 1986. *The Science Question in Feminism*. Ithaca: Cornell University Press.

Harper, Ida Husted. (1898) 1908. *The Life and Work of Susan B. Anthony: Including Public Addresses, Her Own Letters and Many from Her Contemporaries during Fifty Years*. Indianapolis: The Hollenbeck Press.

Harrison, Kristen, and Joanne Cantor. 1997. "The Relationship Between Media Consumption and Eating Disorders." *Journal of Communication* 47 (1): 40–67.

Hartmann, Heidi. 1976. "Capitalism, Patriarchy, and Job Segregation by Sex." *Signs: Journal of Women in Culture and Society* 1 (3): 137–169.

Hartmann, Heidi. 1981. "The Family as the Locus of Gender, Class, and Political Struggle: The Case of Housework." *Signs: Journal of Women in Culture and Society* 6 (3): 366–394.

Hartsock, Nancy. 1983. "The Feminist Standpoint: Developing the Ground for a Specifically Feminist Historical Materialism." In *Discovering Reality: Feminist Perspectives on Epistemology, Metaphysics, and Philosophy of Science*, edited by S. Harding and M. B. Hintikka, 283–310. New York: Springer.

Haynes, Dina. 2014. "The Celebritization of Human Trafficking." *Annals of the American Academy of Political and Social Science* 653 (1): 25–45.

Hays, Sharon. 1996. *The Cultural Contradictions of Motherhood*. New Haven: Yale University Press.

Hazell, Vanessa, and Juanne Clarke. 2008. "Race and Gender in the Media: A Content Analysis of Advertisements in Two Mainstream Black Magazines." *Journal of Black Studies* 39 (1): 5–21.

Hegel, Geord Wilhelm Friedrich. 1977. "Lordship and Bondage." In *The Phenomenology of Spirit*, translated by A.V. Miller. Oxford: Clarendon Press.

Heldman, Caroline, and Lisa Wade. 2010. "Hook-Up Culture: Setting a New Research Agenda." *Sexuality Research and Social Policy* 7 (4): 323–333.

Heneghan, Helen M., Leslie Heinberg, Amy Windover, Tomasz Rogula, and Philip R. Schauer. 2012. "Weighing the Evidence for an Association between Obesity and Suicide Risk." *Surgery for Obesity and Related Diseases* 8 (1): 98–107.

Heng, Geraldine. 1997. "'A Great Way to Fly': Nationalism, the State, and the Varieties of Third-World Feminism." In *Feminist Genealogies, Colonial Legacies, Democratic Futures*, edited by M. J. Alexander and C. T. Mohanty, 30–45. New York: Psychology Press

Herbert, Steve. 1997. *Policing Space: Territoriality and the Los Angeles Police Department*. Minneapolis: University of Minnesota Press.

Higginbotham, Elizabeth, and Lynn Weber. 1992. "Moving Up with Kin and Community: Upward Social Mobility for Black and White Women." *Gender & Society* 6 (3): 416–440.

Hoang, Kimberly Kay. 2010. "Economies of Emotion, Familiarity, Fantasy and Desire: Emotional Labor in Ho Chi Minh City's Sex Industry." *Sexualities* 13 (2): 255–272.

Hoang, Kimberly Kay. 2014. "Competing Technologies of Embodiment: Pan-Asian Modernity and Third World Dependency in Vietnam's Contemporary Sex Industry." *Gender & Society* 28 (4): 513–536.

Hoang, Kimberly Kay. 2015. *Dealing in Desire: The Hidden Currencies in Global Sex Work*. Oakland: University of California Press.

Hoang, Kimberly Kay, and Rhacel Parreñas, eds. 2014. *Human Trafficking Reconsidered: Rethinking the Problem, Envisioning New Solutions*. New York: International Debate Education Association.

Hochschild, Arlie. 1997. *The Time Bind: When Work Becomes Home and Home Becomes Work*. New York: Holt.

Hochschild, Arlie. 2005. *Global Women: Nannies, Maids, and Sex Workers in the New Economy*. London, UK: Macmillan.

Hochschild, Arlie, and Anne Machung. (1989) 2003. *The Second Shift*. New York: Penguin Books.

Hoigard, Cecile, and Liv Finstad. 1992. *Backstreets: Prostitution, Money, and Love*. University Park: The Pennsylvania State University Press.

Hollander, Jocelyn A. 2001. "Vulnerability and Dangerousness: The Construction of Gender through Conversation about Violence." *Gender & Society* 15 (1): 83–109.

Homans, Jennifer. 2012. "A Woman's Place" *The New York Times*, September 13, 2016. http://www.nytimes.com/2012/09/16/books/review/the-end-of-men-by-hanna-rosin.html

Hondagneu-Sotelo, Pierrette. 2001. *Doméstica: Immigrant Workers Cleaning and Caring in the Shadows of Affluence*. Berkeley: University of California Press.

hooks, bell. 1984. *Feminist Theory: From Margin to Center*. Boston: South End Press.

hooks, bell. 1990. "Postmodern Blackness." *Postmodern Culture* 1(1).

hooks, bell. 2013. "Dig Deep: Beyond Lean In." *The Feminist Wire*. October 28, 2013. http://www.thefeministwire.com/2013/10/17973/

Hudson, Laura. 2013. "Die Like a Man: The Toxic Masculinity of Breaking Bad." *Wired*. October 5, 2013. https://www.wired.com/2013/10/breaking-bad-toxic-masculinity/

Hunter, Marcus Anthony. 2013. "Race and the Same-Sex Marriage Divide." *Contexts* 12 (3): 74–76.

Hunter, Mark. 2010. *Love in the Time of AIDS: Inequality, Gender, and Rights in South Africa*. Bloomington: Indiana University Press.

The Hunting Ground. 2015. *Directed by Kirby Dick*. New York: The Weinstein Company.

Inequality for All. 2013. *Directed by Jacob Kornbluth*. Los Angeles: 72 Productions.

Jacoby, Hanan G. 1995. "The Economics of Polygyny in Sub-Saharan Africa: Female Productivity and the Demand for Wives in Côte d'Ivoire." *Journal of Political Economy* 103 (5): 938–971.

Jaimes, M. Annette, and Theresa Halsey. 1997. "American Indian Women: At the Center of Indigenous Resistance in Contemporary North America." In *Dangerous Liaisons: Gender, Nation, and Postcolonial Perspectives*, edited by A. McClintock, A. Mufti, and E. Shohat, 301–344. Minneapolis: University of Minnesota Press.

Jayawardena, Kumari. 1986. *Feminism and Nationalism in the Third World*. London, UK: Zed Books

Jeffery, P. 1979. *Frogs in a Well: Indian Women in Purdah*. London, UK: Zed Press.

Jones, Nikki. 2008. "Working 'the Code': On Girls, Gender, and Inner-City Violence." *Australian & New Zealand Journal of Criminology* 41 (1): 63–83.

Jordan, Ann. 2009. Sex Trafficking: The Abolitionist Fallacy. *Human Rights Issue*. March 18, 2009. http://fpif.org/sex_trafficking_the_abolitionist_fallacy/

Kamo, Yoshinori. 2000. "Racial and Ethnic Differences in Extended Family Households." *Sociological Perspectives* 43 (2): 211–229.

Kandiyoti, Deniz. 1988. "Bargaining with Patriarchy." *Gender & Society* 2 (3): 274–290.

Kapidzic, Sanja, and Susan Herring. 2011. "Gender, Communication, and Self-Presentation in Teen Chatrooms Revisited: Have Patterns Changed?" *Journal of Computer-Mediated Communication* 17 (1): 39–59.

Katz, Jackson. 2003. "Advertising and the Construction of Violent White Masculinity." In *Gender, Race, and Class in Media: A Text Reader*, edited by Gail Dines and Jean M. Humez, 349–358. Thousand Oaks: SAGE.

Katzenstein, Mary Fainsod. 1998. *Faithful and Fearless: Moving Feminist Protest inside the Church and Military*. Princeton: Princeton University Press.

Keck, Margaret E., and Kathryn Sikkink. 1998. *Activists beyond Borders: Advocacy Networks in International Politics*. Ithaca: Cornell University Press.

Keenan, Kevin L. 1996. "Skin Tones and Physical Features of Blacks in Magazine Advertisements." *Journalism & Mass Communication Quarterly* 73 (4): 905–912.

Kelly, Joan B. 1994. "The Determination of Child Custody." *Children and Divorce* 4 (1): 121–142.

"Kelly Ripa's Electrolux Commercial." YouTube video, 0:30. Posted by ourdailyripa, April 16, 2008. YouTube. https://youtu.be/PDBMHz1Dthw

Kempadoo, Kamala. 2005. *Trafficking and Prostitution Reconsidered: New Perspectives on Migration, Sex Work and Human Rights*. Boulder: Paradigm Publishers.

Kimmel, Michael S., and Matthew Mahler. 2003. "Adolescent Masculinity, Homophobia, and Violence Random School Shootings, 1982–2001." *American Behavioral Scientist* 46 (10): 1439–1458.

Kimmel, Michael. 1994. "Masculinity as Homophobia." In *Theorizing Masculinities*, edited by Harry Brod and Michael Kaufman. Thousand Oaks: SAGE.

Kimmel, Michael. 2008. *Guyland: The Perilous World Where Boys Become Men*. New York: Harper.

Kimmel, Michael. 2012. "Masculinity, Mental Illness and Guns: A Lethal Equation?" *CNN*. December 19, 2012. http://www.cnn.com/2012/12/19/living/men-guns-violence/

Kinsey, Alfred. 1948. *Sexual Behavior in the Human Male*. Philadelphia: W.B Saunders.

Kinsey, Alfred. 1953. *Sexual Behavior in the Human Female*. Philadelphia: W.B. Saunders.

Kipling, Rudyard. 1899. "The White Man's Burden: The United States and the Philippine Islands." *McClure's Magazine*.

Kolb, Kenneth H. 2014. *Moral Wages: The Emotional Dilemmas of Victim Advocacy and Counseling*. Berkeley: University of California Press.

Kolhatkar, Sonali, and Mariam Rawi. 2009. "Why Is a Leading Feminist Organization Lending Its Name to Support Escalation in Afghanistan?" *AlterNet*, July 7, 2009. http://www.alternet.org/story/141165/why_is_a_leading_feminist_organization_lending_its_name_to_support_escalation_in_afghanistan

Korean Air. 2014. *All About You*. https://www.ispot.tv/ad/7TOB/korean-air-all-about-you

Kraska, Peter B. 1996. "Enjoying Militarism: Political/Personal Dilemmas in Studying U.S. Police Paramilitary Units." *Justice Quarterly* 13 (3): 405–429.

Kristof, Nicholas, and Sheryl WuDunn. 2008. *Half the Sky: Turning Oppression into Opportunity for Women Worldwide*. New York: Knopf Doubleday

Kristof, Nicholas. 2010. "Moonshine or the Kids?" *The New York Times*, May 22, 2010. http://www.nytimes.com/2010/05/23/opinion/23kristof.html?_r=0

Kruttschnitt, Candace, and Carbone-Lopez, Kristin. 2006. Moving beyond the Stereotypes: Women's Subjective Accounts of Their Violent Crime. *Criminology* 44 (2): 321–352.

Kumar, Radha. 1993. *The History of Doing: An Illustrated Account of Movements for Women's Rights and Feminism in India 1800–1990*. New Delhi, India: Zubaan.

Lachance-Grzela, Mylène, and Geneviève Bouchard. 2010. "Why Do Women Do the Lion's Share of Housework? A Decade of Research." *Sex Roles* 63 (11/12): 767–780.

Landry, Bart. 2000. *Black Working Wives: Pioneers of the American Family Revolution*. Berkeley: University of California Press.

Laslett, Barbara, and Johanna Brenner. 1989. "Gender and Social Reproduction: Historical Perspectives." *Annual Review of Sociology* 15: 381–404.

Laws of Indiana. 1907. *1907 Indiana Eugenics Law.* B050823. http://www.in.gov/history/markers/524.htm

Lazreg, Marnia. 1994. *The Eloquence of Silence: Algerian Women in Question*. New York: Routledge.

Lederer, Laura. 2012. "End Human Trafficking: A Contemporary Slavery." *2012 Election*. Princeton: The Witherspoon Institute.

Lee, Yean-Ju, and Isik A. Aytac. 1998. "Intergenerational Financial Support among Whites, African Americans, and Latinos." *Journal of Marriage and Family* 60 (2): 426–441.

Leslie, Michael. 1995. "Slow Fade to? Advertising in Ebony Magazine, 1957–1989." *Journalism & Mass Communication Quarterly* 72 (2): 426–435.

Lewis, Oscar. 1959. *Five Families: Mexican Case Studies in the Culture of Poverty*. New York: Basic Books.

Lilly Ledbetter Fair Pay Act of 2009. 2009. Public Law 111-2, 123 U.S. Statutes at Large 5.

Livingston, Gretchen, and D'Vera Cohn. 2015. "Share of Births to Unmarried Women Dips, Reversing a Long Trend." *Pew Research Center Fact Tank*. June 17, 2015. http://www.pewresearch.org/fact-tank/2015/06/17/share-of-births-to-unmarried-women-dips-reversing-a-long-trend/

Lois, Jennifer. 2006. "Role Strain, Emotion Management, and Burnout: Homeschooling Mothers' Adjustment to the Teacher Role." *Symbolic Interaction* 29 (4): 507–530.

Lorde, Audre. (1992) 2012. *Sister Outsider*. Freedom: Cross Press.

Lorde, Audre. 1984. *The Master's Tools Will Never Dismantle the Master's House*. Freedom: Cross Press.

Lori, Kendall. 2000. "'Oh No! I'm a Nerd!': Hegemonic Masculinity on an Online Forum." *Gender & Society* 14 (2): 256–274.

Lowery, Wesley. 2016. "Aren't More White People Than Black People Killed by Police? Yes, But No." *Washington Post*. Accessed July 11, 2016. https://www.washingtonpost.com/news/post-nation/wp/2016/07/11/arent-more-white-people-than-black-people-killed-by-police-yes-but-no/? utm_term=.a18491cd173e

Luker, Kristin. 1985. *Abortion and the Politics of Motherhood*. Berkeley: University of California Press.

Lyons, Christopher J., and Becky Pettit. 2011. "Compounded Disadvantage: Race, Incarceration, and Wage Growth." *Social Problems* 58 (2): 257–280.

MacKendrick, Norah. 2014. "More Work for Mother: Chemical Body Burdens as a Maternal Responsibility." *Gender & Society* 28 (5): 705–728.

MacKinnon, Catharine A. 1982. "Feminism, Marxism, Method and the State: An Agenda for Theory." *Signs: Journal of Women in Culture and Society* 7 (3): 515–544.

MacKinnon, Catharine. 1989. "Sexuality, Pornography, and Method: 'Pleasure under Patriarchy.'" *Ethics* 99 (2): 314–346.

Madriz, Esther I. 1997. "Images of Criminals and Victims: A Study on Women's Fear and Social Control." *Gender & Society* 11 (3): 342–356.

Mahmood, Saba. 2005. *Politics of Piety: The Islamic Revival and the Feminist Subject*. Princeton: Princeton University Press.

Malcolm, Hadley. 2016. "Dos Equis Retiring its 'Most Interesting Man in the World.'" *USA Today*. March 9, 2016. http://www.usatoday.com/story/money/2016/03/09/dos-equis-most-interesting-man-in-the-world-retiring/81432356/

Marling, Karal Ann. 1992. "Betty Crocker's Picture Cook Book: The Aesthetics of American Food in the 1950s." *Prospects* 17: 79–103.

Martin, Emily. 1991. "The Egg and the Sperm: How Science Has Constructed a Romance Based on Stereotypical Male–Female Roles." *Signs: Journal of Women in Culture and Society* 16 (3): 485–501.

Martin, Nicole. 2014. "Women Key in Shaping Black Panther Party: Historian Reveals How African American Women Transformed Gender Roles in the Black Power Movement." *The Clayman Institute for Gender Research*. http://gender.stanford.edu/news/2014/women-key-shapingblack-panther-party#sthash.UBfAobIu.dpuf.

Martin, Susan Ehrlich. 1999. "Police Force or Police Service? Gender and Emotional Labor." *The ANNALS of the American Academy of Political and Social Science* 561 (1): 111–126.

Marx, Karl, and Friedrich Engels. 2002. *The Communist Manifesto*. London: Penguin Classics.

Mason, Katherine. 2012. "The Unequal Weight of Discrimination: Gender, Body Size, and Income Inequality." *Social Problems* 59 (3): 411–435.

Mason, Katherine. 2016. "Responsible Bodies: Self-Care and State Power in the Women, Infants, and Children Program." *Social Politics* 23 (1): 70–93.

Massoni, Kelley. 2004. "Modeling Work: Occupation Messages in Seventeen Magazine." *Gender & Society 18* (1): 47–65.

Matlon, Jordanna. 2011. "Informality and Visibility on the Periphery." Photo essay. *Contexts* 10 (2): 58–63.

Matlon, Jordanna. 2016. "Racial Capitalism and the Crisis of Black Masculinity." *American Sociological Review* 81 (5): 1014–1038.

Mayo, Katherine. (1927) 2000. *Mother India*. Ann Arbor: The University of Michigan Press.

Mazama, Ama, and Garvey Lundy. 2012. "African American Homeschooling as Racial Protectionism." *Journal of Black Studies* 43 (7): 723–748.

McCaughey, Martha. 1998. "The Fighting Spirit: Women's Self-Defense Training and the Discourse of Sexes Embodiment." *Gender & Society* 12 (3): 277–300.

McClintock, Anne. 1995. *Imperial Leather: Race, Gender, and Sexuality in the Colonial Contest*. London, UK: Routledge.

McCorkel, Jill. 2003. "Embodied Surveillance and the Gendering of Punishment." *Journal of Contemporary Ethnography* 32 (1): 41–76.

McLaughlin, Tara L., and Nicole Goulet, Nicole, and Tara L. McLaughlin. 1999. "Gender Advertisements in Magazines Aimed at African Americans: A Comparison to Their Occurrence in Magazines Aimed at Caucasians." *Sex Roles* 40 (1): 61–71.

McMillen, Sally. 2008. *Seneca Falls and the Origins of the Women's Rights Movement*. New York: Oxford University Press.

McRobbie, Angela. 2004. "Post-Feminism and Popular Culture." *Feminist Media Studies* 4 (3): 255–264.

McRobbie, Angela, and Sarah L. Thornton. 1995. "Rethinking 'Moral Panic' for Multi-Mediated Social Worlds." *The British Journal of Sociology* 46 (4): 559–574.

Mead, Margaret. (1949) 2001. *Male and Female*. New York: Harper Collins.

Meadow, Tey. 2010. "'A Rose is a Rose': On Producing Legal Gender Classifications." *Gender & Society* 24 (6): 814–837.

Meagher, Kate, and Ilda Lindell. 2013. "Introduction." *African Studies Review* 56 (3): 57–76.

Mehaffy, Marilyn Maness. 1997. "Advertising Race/Racing Advertising: The Feminine Consumer (-Nation), 1876–1900." *Signs: Journal of Women in Culture and Society* 23 (1): 131–174.

Messner, Michael A., Max A. Greenberg, and Tal Peretz. 2015. *Some Men: Feminist Allies and the Movement to End Violence against Women*. Oxford: Oxford University Press.

Meyer, Madonna H. 2014. *Grandmothers at Work: Juggling Families and Jobs*. New York: New York University Press.

Milkman, Ruth. 1986. "Women's History and the Sears Case." *Feminist Studies* 12 (2): 375–400.

Miller, Elizabeth. 2002. "An Open Letter to the Editors of *Ms. Magazine*." http://www.rawa.org/tours/elizabeth_miller_letter.htm

Miller, Jody. 2001. *One of the Guys: Girls, Gangs, and Gender*. New York: Oxford University Press.

Miller, Michael. 2016. "'A Steep Price to Pay for 20 Minutes of Action': Dad Defends Stanford Sex Offender." *Washington Post*. https://www.washingtonpost.com/news/morning-mix/wp/2016/06/06/a-steep-price-to-pay-for-20-minutes-of-action-dad-defends-stanford-sex-offender/?utm_term=.59c43ded7761

Mirchandani, Rekha. 2006. "'Hitting Is Not Manly': Domestic Violence Court and the Re-Imagination of the Patriarchal State." *Gender & Society* 20 (6): 781–804.

Mitchell, Joni. 1976. Amelia. *Hejira*. Hollywood: A&M Studios.

Mohanty, Chandra Talpade. 1988. "Under Western Eyes: Feminist Scholarship and Colonial Discourses." *Feminist Review* 30 (Autumn): 61–88.

Mohanty, Chandra Talpade. 2003. "'Under Western Eyes' Revisited: Feminist Solidarity Through Anticapitalist Struggles." *Signs: Journal of Women in Culture and Society* 28 (2): 499–535.

Mohanty, Chandra Talpade, Ann Russo, and Lourdes Torres, eds. 1991. *Third World Women and the Politics of Feminism*. Bloomington: Indiana University Press.

Molyneux, Maxine. 2006. "Mothers at the Service of the New Poverty Agenda: *Progresa/Oportunidades*, Mexico's Conditional Transfer Programme." *Social Policy and Administration* 40 (4): 425–449.

Moon, Dawne. 2004. *God, Sex and Politics: Homosexuality and Everyday Theologies*. Chicago: University of Chicago Press.

Moore, Lori D., and Padavic, Irene. 2010. Racial and Ethnic Disparities in Girls' Sentencing in the Juvenile Justice System. *Feminist Criminology* 5 (3): 263–285.

Moore, Mignon. 2008. "Gendered Power Relations among Women: A Study of Household Decision Making in Black, Lesbian Stepfamilies." *American Sociological Review* 73: 335–356.

Moraga, Cherríe, and Gloria Anzaldúa. 1981. *This Bridge Called My Back: Writings by Radical Women of Color*. Watertown: Persephone Press.

Morgen, Sandra. 2002. *Into Our Own Hands: The Women's Health Movement in the United States, 1969–1990*. New Brunswick: Rutgers University Press.

Moynihan, Daniel Patrick. 1965. *The Negro Family: The Case for National Action*. Washington, DC: Office of Policy Planning and Research, U.S. Department of Labor.

Munir, Huma. 2011. "Media's Stereotyping of Black Athletes Creates High Standards, Professor Says." *The Daily*

Texan, February 24, 2011. http://www.dailytexanonline.com/2011/02/24/media%C2%92s-stereotyping-of-black-athletes-creates-high-standards-professor-says

Musto, Jennifer. 2014. "The Posthuman Anti-Trafficking Turn: Technology, Domestic Minor Sex Trafficking and Augmented Human-Machine Alliances." In *Human Trafficking Reconsidered: Rethinking the Problem, Envisioning New Solutions*, edited by Kimberly Hoang and Rhacel Parreñas. New York: IDEA.

Nagel, Joane. 2000. "States of Arousal/Fantasy Islands: Race, Sex, and Romance in the Global Economy of Desire." *American Studies* 41 (2/3): 159–181.

Najmabadi, Afsaneh. 2005. *Women with Moustaches and Men without Beards: Gender and Sexual Anxieties of Iranian Modernity*. Berkeley: University of California Press.

National Coalition of Anti-Violence Program. 2017. *Hate Violence against Transgender Communities*. https://avp.org/wp-content/uploads/2017/04/ncavp_transhv-factsheet.pdf

Newman, Amie. 2007. "Life Support for Feminist Health Care?" *Rewire*. https://rewire.news/article/2007/01/02/life-support-for-feminist-health-care/

Norsigian, Judy. 2005. *Our Bodies, Ourselves: A New Edition for a New Era*. New York: Touchstone.

Oakley, Ann. 1990. *Housewife*. London, UK: Penguin Books Ltd.

Obergefell v. Hodges. 576 U.S. ___ 2015.

Ocampo, Anthony. 2012. "Making Masculinity: Negotiations of Gender Presentation among Latino Gay Men." *Latino Studies* 10 (4): 448–472.

Ogasawara, Yuko. 1998. *Office Ladies and Salaried Men: Power, Gender, and Work in Japanese Companies*. Berkeley: University of California Press.

Ogden, Cynthia L., Cheryl D. Fryar, Mararet D. Carroll, and Katherine M. Flegal. 2004. *Mean Body Weight, Height, and Body Mass Index: United States 1960–2002*. Washington, DC: Department of Health and Human Services, Centers for Disease Control and Prevention, National Center for Health Statistics.

The Opportunity Agenda. 2011. *Media Representations and Impact on the Lives of Black Men and Boys*. New York: Author. http://www.racialequitytools.org/resourcefiles/Media-Impact-onLives-of-Black-Men-and-Boys-OppAgenda.pdf

Organization for Economic Cooperation and Development (OECD) Family Database. 2016. *Trends in Parental Leave Policies Since 1970*. https://www.oecd.org/els/family/PF2_5_Trends_in_leave_entitlements_around_childbirth.pdf

Orleck, Annelise. 1995. *Common Sense and a Little Fire: Women and Working-Class Politics in the United States, 1900–1965*. Chapel Hill: University of North Carolina Press.

Orloff, Ann Shola. 1996. "Gender in the Welfare State." *Annual Review of Sociology* 22: 51–78.

Orloff, Ann Shola, Raka Ray, and Evren Savci, eds. 2016. *Perverse Politics? Feminism, Anti-Imperialism, Multiplicity*. Bingley, UK: Emerald Group Publishing Limited.

Ortner, Sherry. 1972. "Is Female to Male as Nature Is to Culture?" *Feminist Studies* 1 (2): 5–31.

Parham-Payne. 2014. "Media Portrayals of Gun Violence Depend on Race, Leading to Often Very Disparate Policy Responses." *USApp—American Politics and Policy Blog*, November 19, 2014. http://eprints.lse.ac.uk/60413/

Paris is Burning. 1991. *Directed by Jennie Livingston*. Santa Monica: Miramax Films.

Parreñas, Rhacel. 2001. *Servants of Globalization: Women, Migration, and Domestic Work*. Stanford: Stanford University Press.

Parreñas, Rhacel. 2011. *Illicit Flirtations*. Stanford: Stanford University Press.

Parsons, Talcott, and Robert F. Bales. 1955. *Family Socialization and Interaction Process*. New York: Free Press.

Pascoe, C. J. 2011. *Dude, You're a Fag: Masculinity and Sexuality in High School, with a New Preface*. Berkeley: University of California Press.

Pascoe, C. J., and Hollander, Jocelyn A. 2016. "Good Guys Don't Rape: Gender, Domination, and Mobilizing Rape." *Gender & Society*, *30* (1): 67–79.

Pateman, Carole. 1988. *The Sexual Contract*. Stanford: Stanford University Press.

Payne, B. Keith. 2006. "Weapon Bias Split-Second Decisions and Unintended Stereotyping." *Current Directions in Psychological Science* 15 (6): 287–291.

Payne, Will. 2013. "My Son Is the Victim Here." *The Daily Mail*, October 17, 2013. http://www.dailymail.co.uk/news/article-2465458/Maryville-footballer-Matthew-Barnetts-mother-says-hes-victim.html

Perdue, Theda. 1999. *Cherokee Women: Gender and Cultural Change, 1700–1835*. Lincoln: Bison Books.

Pew. 2017. Fact Sheet: Changing Attitudes on Gay Marriage. *Pew Research Center*. July 4, 2017. http://

www.pewforum.org/fact-sheet/changing-attitudes-on-gay-marriage/

Pfeffer, Carla. 2010. "'Women's Work?': Women Partners of Transgender Men Doing Housework and Emotion Work." *Journal of Marriage and Family* 72 (1): 165–183.

Picton, Oliver. 2013. "The Complexities of Complexion: A Cultural Geography of Skin Colour and Beauty Products." *Geography* 98 (2): 85–92.

Power, Shannon. 2017. "'Stunning Victory' as US Surgeons General Call for an End to Intersex Surgery." *Gay Star News*. July 3, 2017. https://www.gaystarnews.com/article/us-surgeon-generals-call-end-intersex-surgery/

Powers, William K. 1986. "Counting Your Blessings: Sacred Numbers and the Structure of Reality." *Zygon* 21 (1): 75–94.

Prahalad, Coimbatore K. 2006. *Fortune at the Bottom of the Pyramid: Eradicating Poverty through Profits*. New Delhi, India: Dorling Kindersley Pvt Ltd.

Price Waterhouse v. Hopkins, 490 U.S. 228. 1989.

Prokos, Anastasia, and Irene Padavic. 2002. "'There Oughtta Be a Law Against Bitches': Masculinity Lessons in Police Academy Training." *Gender, Work & Organization* 9 (4): 439–459.

Protect Our Defenders. 2017. *Facts on United States Military Sexual Violence*. Retrieved July 5, 2017. http://www.protectourdefenders.com/wp-content/uploads/2013/05/1.-MSA-Fact-Sheet-170629.pdf

Public Broadcasting Service. 2002. *American Experience: Miss America*. http://www.pbs.org/wgbh/amex/missamerica/sfeature/sf_list.html

Puri, Jyoti. 1999. *Woman, Body, Desire in Post-Colonial India: Narratives of Gender and Sexuality*. New York: Routledge.

Pyle, Jean L., and Kathryne B. Ward. 2003. "Recasting our Understanding of Gender and Work During Global Restructuring." *International Sociology* 18 (3): 461–489.

Quindlen, Anna. 2003. "Still Needing the F Word." *Newsweek*, October 19, 2003. http://www.newsweek.com/still-needing-f-word-138627

Rabin, Roni Caryn. 2016. "More Teenage Girls Seeking Genital Cosmetic Surgery," *New York Times*. April 25, 2016. http://well.blogs.nytimes.com/2016/04/25/increase-in-teenage-genital-surgery-prompts-guidelines-for-doctors/?_r=0

Radhakrishnan, Smitha. 2015. "'Low Profile' or Entrepreneurial? Gender, Class, and Cultural Adaptation in the Global Microfinance Industry. *World Development* 74: 264–274.

Rankin, Katharine N. 2001. "Governing Development: Neoliberalism, Microcredit, and Rational Economic Woman." *Economy and Society* 30 (1): 18–37.

Rape, Abuse and Incest National Network (RAINN). 2009. "Marital Rape." *Rape, Abuse and Incest National Network*. http://www.rainn.org/public-policy/sexual-assault-issues/marital-rape

Rape, Abuse and Incest National Network (RAINN). 2017a. "About Sexual Assault." *Rape, Abuse and Incest National Network*. https://www.rainn.org/about-sexual-assault

Rape, Abuse and Incest National Network (RAINN). 2017b. "Campus Sexual Violence: Statistics." *Rape, Abuse and Incest National Network*. https://www.rainn.org/statistics/campus-sexual-violence

Rape, Abuse and Incest National Network (RAINN). 2017c. "The Criminal Justice System: Statistics." *Rape, Abuse and Incest National Network*. https://www.rainn.org/statistics/criminal-justice-system

Ray, Raka, and Seemin Qayum. 2009. *Cultures of Servitude: Modernity, Domesticity and Class in India*. Palo Alto: Stanford University Press.

Reich, Jennifer. 2014. "Neoliberal Mothering and Vaccine Refusal: Imagined Gated Communities and the Privilege of Choice." *Gender & Society* 28 (5): 679–704.

Rich, Adrienne. 1980. "Compulsory Heterosexuality and Lesbian Existence." *Signs: Journal of Women in Culture and Society* 5 (4): 631–660.

Roberts, Dorothy. 1997. *Killing the Black Body: Race, Reproduction, and the Meaning of Liberty*. New York: Random House.

Roberts, Dorothy. 2002. *Shattered Bonds: The Color of Child Welfare*. New York: Basic Civitas Books.

Robertson, Campbell. 2015. "History of Lynchings in the South Documents Nearly 4,000 Names." *New York Times*. February 10, 2015. https://www.nytimes.com/2015/02/10/us/history-of-lynchings-in-the-south-documents-nearly-4000-names.html?_r=0

Roby, Pamela. 1992. "Women and the ASA: Degendering Organizational Structures and Processes, 1964–1974." *The American Sociologist* 23 (1): 18–48.

Rollins, Judith. 1987. *Between Women: Domestics and Their Employers*. Philadelphia: Temple University Press.

Rosen, Ruth. 2000. *The World Split Open: How the Modern Women's Movement Changed America*. New York: Penguin.

Rosenthal, A. M. 1995. "The Possible Dream: Ending Female Genital Mutilation." *New York Times*, p. A25. January 13, 1995.

Rosin, Hanna. 2012. *The End of Men: And the Rise of Women*. New York: Riverhead Hardcover.

Ross, Loretta. "The Origin of the Phrase 'Women of Color.'" YouTube video, 3:00. Posted by Western States Center, February 15, 2011. https://www.youtube.com/watch?v=82vl34mi4Iw

Roy, Ananya. 2010. "Millennial Woman: The Gender Order of Development." In *International Handbook of Gender and Poverty: Concepts, Research, Policy*, edited by Sylvia Chant, 548–556. Northampton: Edward Elgar Publishing.

Roy, Ananya. 2012. "Subjects of Risk: Technologies of Gender in the Making of Millennial Modernity." *Public Culture* 24 (1): 131–155.

Roychowdhury, Poulami. 2013. "Stop Demonizing Indian Culture!" *Salon*, January 9, 2013. http://www.salon.com/2013/01/09/stop_demonizing_indian_culture/

Rubin, Gayle. 1997. "Thinking Sex: Notes for a Radical Theory of the Politics of Sexuality." In *Culture, Society and Sexuality: A Reader*, 143–79. New York: Taylor & Francis.

Rubin, Gayle. 2000. "Sites, Settlements, and Urban Sex: Archaeology and the Study of Gay Leathermen in San Francisco 1955–1995." In *Archaeologies of Sexuality*, edited by Robert Schmidt and Barbara Voss. London, UK: Routledge.

Rupp, Leila, Verta Taylor, Shiri Regev-Messalem, Alison C.K. Fogarty, and Paula England. 2014. "Queer Women in the Hookup Scene: Beyond the Closet?" *Gender & Society* 28 (2): 212–235.

SafeNetwork. 1999. *History of Battered Women's Movement*. California Department of Health Services, Maternal and Child Health Branch, Domestic Violence Section, and Intervace Children Family Services. http://www.icadvinc.org/what-is-domestic-violence/history-of-battered-womens-movement/

Saguy, Abigail C., and Kjerstin Gruys. 2010. "Morality and Health: News Media Constructions of Overweight and Eating Disorders." *Social Problems* 57 (2): 231–250.

Salzinger, Leslie. 2001. "Making Fantasies Real: Producing Women and Men on the Maquila Shop Floor." *NACLA Report on the Americas* 34 (5): 13–19.

Salzinger, Leslie. 2003. *Genders in Production: Making Workers in Mexico's Global Factories*. Berkeley: University of California Press.

Samara, Rachel. 2013. "What White People Don't Understand About Rachel Jeantel." *Global Grind*. https://globalgrind.cassiuslife.com/1984623/what-white-people-dont-understand-about-rachel-jeantel-trayvon-martin-blog/

Sandberg, Sheryl. 2013. *Lean In: Women, Work and the Will to Lead*. New York: Random House.

Sarkisian, Natalia, Mariana Gerena, and Naomi Gerstel. 2007. "Extended Family Integration among Euro and Mexican Americans: Ethnicity, Gender, and Class." *Journal of Marriage and Family* 69 (1): 40–54.

Sassen, Saskia. 1988. "New York City's Informal Economy." *Institute for Social Science Research*. UCLA: Institute for Social Science Research.

Sassen-Koob, Saskia. 1984. "Notes on the Incorporation of Third World Women into Wage–Labor through Immigration and Off-Shore Production." *The International Migration Review* 18 (4): 1144–1167.

Schaeffer, Felicity. 2012. *Love and Empire: Cybermarriage and Citizenship across the Americas*. New York: New York University Press.

Scheper-Hughes, Nancy. 1987. "The Cultural Politics of Child Survival." In *Child Survival*, edited by N. Scheper-Hughes, 1–29. Dordrecht, Holland: D. Reidel Publishing Company.

Scheper-Hughes, Nancy. 1989. "Death Without Weeping." *Natural History* 10: 8–16.

Schilt, Kristen. 2010. *Just One of the Guys? Transgender Men and the Persistence of Gender Inequality*. Chicago: The University of Chicago Press.

Schippers, Mimi. 2000. "The Social Organization of Sexuality and Gender in Alternative Hard Rock." *Gender & Society* 14 (6): 747–764.

Schradie, Jen. "The Gender Production Gap: Whose Voices Are in the Digital Public Sphere." Paper presented at the International Communication Association Annual Conference, May 30, 2011. Boston, Massachusetts.

Schvey, Natasha A., Rebecca M. Puhl, Katherine A. Levandoski, and Kelly D. Brownell. 2013. The Influence of a Defendant's Body Weight on Perceptions of Guilt. *International Journal of Obesity* 37 (9): 1275.

Scott, Joan Wallach. 1988. *Gender and the Politics of History*. New York: Columbia University Press.

Scott, Joan Wallach, and Louise Tilly. 1978. *Women, Work and Family*. New York: Holt, Rinehart and Winston.

Seelye, Katharine. 1995. "Gingrich 'Piggies' Poked." *New York Times*. January 19, 1995. http://www.nytimes.com/1995/01/19/us/gingrich-s-piggies-poked.html

Sennett, Richard. 1970. *The Uses of Disorder: Personal Identity & City Life*. New York: Alfred A. Knopf, Inc.

The Sentencing Project. 2013. Report of the Sentencing Project to the United Nations Human Rights Committee: Regarding Racial Disparities in the United States Criminal Justice System. *The Sentencing Project.* August 2013. http://sentencingproject.org/wp-content/uploads/2015/12/Race-and-Justice-Shadow-Report-ICCPR.pdf

Sherman, Jennifer. 2009. *Those Who Work, Those Who Don't: Poverty, Morality, and Family in Rural America.* Minneapolis: University of Minnesota Press.

Sherman, Lawrence W., and Heather M. Harris. 2015. "Increased Death Rates of Domestic Violence Victims from Arresting vs. Warning Suspects in the Milwaukee Domestic Violence Experiment (MilDVE)." *Journal of Experimental Criminology* 11 (1): 1–20.

Sherman, Lawrence W., and Richard A. Berk. 1984. *The Minneapolis Domestic Violence Experiment.* Washington, DC: Police Foundation.

Siddharth, Kara. 2009. *Sex Trafficking: Inside the Business of Modern Slavery.* New York: Columbia University Press.

Siebert, Valeria. 2014. "Michael Phelps: The Man Who Was Built to Be a Swimmer." *The Telegraph,* April 25, 2014. http://www.telegraph.co.uk/sport/olympics/swimming/10768083/Michael-Phelps-The-man-who-was-built-to-be-a-swimmer.html

Sinha, Mrinalini. 2000. "Refashioning Mother India: Feminism and Nationalism in Late-Colonial India" *Feminist Studies* 26 (3): 623–644.

Sinha, Mrinalini. 2006. *Specters of Mother India: The Global Restructuring of an Empire.* Durham: Duke University Press.

Slaughter, Anne-Marie. 2012. "Why Women Still Can't Have It All" *The Atlantic,* July/August. http://www.theatlantic.com/magazine/archive/2012/07/why-women-still-cant-have-it-all/309020/

Slotkin, Richard. 1992. *Gunfighter Nation: The Myth of the Frontier in Twentieth-Century America.* Norman: University of Oklahoma Press.

Smith, Andrea. 2013. "Beyond Eve Ensler: What Should Organizing Against Gender Violence Look Like?" *Personal Blog.* http://andrea366.wordpress.com/2013/12/13/beyond-eve-ensler-what-should-organizing-against-gender-violence-look-like/.

Smith, Dorothy. 1974. "Women's Perspective as a Radical Critique of Sociology." *Sociological Inquiry* 44 (1): 7–13.

Smith, Dorothy. 1987. *The Everyday World as Problematic: A Feminist Sociology.* Toronto, Canada: University of Toronto Press.

Smith, Dorothy. 1993. "The Standard North American Family: SNAF as an Ideological Code." *Journal of Family Issues* 14 (1): 50–65.

Smith, Kristin, Barbara Downs, and Martin O'Connell. 2001. "Maternity Leave and Employment Patterns: 1961–1995. *U.S. Census Bureau Household Economic Studies,* 70–79. https://www.census.gov/prod/2001pubs/p70-79.pdf

Solinger, Rickie. 1994. "Race and 'Value': Black and White Illegitimate Babies, 1945–1965." In *Mothering: Ideology, Experience, and Agency,* edited by E. N. Glenn, G. Chang, and L. R. Forcie, 287–310. New York: Routledge.

Somashekhar, Sandhya, Wesley Lowery, Keith L. Alexander, Kimberly Kindy, and Julie Tate. 2015. Black and Unarmed. *Washington Post.* August 9, 2015. http://www.washingtonpost.com/sf/national/2015/08/08/black-and-unarmed/? tid=a_inl&utm_term=.39592aca34a8

Spanjer, Noor. 2015. "These Five People Are Going to Have a Baby Together." *Vice.* August 4, 2015. http://www.vice.com/read/a-child-in-the-netherlands-is-going-to-have-five-parents-876

Sparke, Penny. 1995. *As Long as It's Pink: The Sexual Politics of Taste.* Ontario, Canada: Pandora.

Spohn, Cassia, and David Holleran. 2000. "The Imprisonment Penalty Paid by Young, Unemployed Black and Hispanic Male Offenders." *Criminology* 38 (1): 281–306.

Stacey, Judith, and Barrie Thorne. 1985. "The Missing Feminist Revolution in Sociology." *Social Problems* 32 (4): 301–316.

State of Florida v. George Zimmerman. No. 5D13–1233. 2013.

Steedman, Carolyn Kay. 1986. *Landscape for a Good Woman: A Story of Two Lives.* New Brunswick: Rutgers University Press.

Steffensmeier, Darrell, and Emilie Allan. 1996. "Gender and Crime: Toward a Gendered Theory of Female Offending." *Annual Review of Sociology* 22: 459–487.

Stein, Arlene, and Ken Plummer. 1994. "I Can't Even Think Straight. 'Queer' Theory and the Missing Sexual Revolution in Sociology." *Sociological Theory* 12 (2): 178–187.

Stein, Arlene. 1989. "Three Models of Sexuality: Drives, Identities and Practices." *Sociological Theory* 7 (1): 1–13.

Stein, Joel. 2015. "Nip. Tuck. Or Else." *Time.* June 18, 2015. http://time.com/3926042/nip-tuck-or-else/

Steinem, G. (1978) 1995. *Outrageous Acts and Everyday Rebellions*. New York: Macmillan.

Steiner, Leslie Morgan. 2006. *Mommy Wars: Stay-at-Home and Career Moms Face Off on Their Choices, Their Lives, Their Families*. New York: Random House.

Stepler, Renee. 2017. "Female Police Officers' On-The-Job Experiences Diverge from Those of Male Officers." *Pew Research Center.* January 17, 2017. http://www.pewresearch.org/fact-tank/2017/01/17/female-police-officers-on-the-job-experiences-diverge-from-those-of-male-officers/

Stevenson, Betsey, and Justin Wolfers. 2009. "The Paradox of Declining Female Happiness." *American Economic Journal: Economic Policy* 1 (2): 190–225.

Steward, Sue, and Sheryl Garratt. 1999. *Signed, Sealed, and Delivered: True Life Stories of Women in Pop*. Boston: South End Press.

Stoler, Ann Laura. 1995. *Race and the Education of Desire: Foucault's History of Sexuality and the Colonial Order of Things*. Durham: Duke University Press.

Stoler, Ann Laura. 2002. *Carnal Knowledge and Imperial Power: Race and the Intimate in Colonial Rule*. Berkeley: University of California Press.

Stone, Amy L. 2016. "Bathroom Panics and Guns." *Gender & Society,* July 1, 2016. https://gendersociety.wordpress.com/2016/07/01/bathroom-panics-and-guns/

Stone, Pamela. 2007. *Opting Out? Why Women Really Quit Careers and Head Home*. Berkeley: University of California Press.

Story, Mary, Simone A. French, Michael D. Resnick, and Robert W. Blum. 1995. "Ethnic/Racial and Socioeconomic Differences in Dieting Behaviors and Body Image Perceptions in Adolescents." *International Journal of Eating Disorders* 18 (2): 173–179.

Taylor, Paul, Gretchen Livingston, Kim Parker, Wendy Wang, and Daniel Dockterman. 2010. "Since the Start of the Great Recession, More Children Raised by Grandparents." *Pew Research Center Social & Demographic Trends Report*. September 9, 2010. http://www.pewsocialtrends.org/files/2010/10/764-children-raised-by-grandparents.pdf

Teo, Youyenn. 2009. "Gender Disarmed: How Gendered Policies Produce Gender-Neutral Politics in Singapore." *Signs: Journal of Women in Culture and Society* 34 (3): 533–557.

Thayer, Millie. 2009. *Making Transnational Feminism: Rural Women, NGO Activists, and Northern Donors in Brazil*. New York: Taylor & Francis.

Thomas, June. 2012. "Did Caster Semenya Lose the Women's 800 Meters on Purpose." *Slate*. August 11, 2012. http://www.slate.com/blogs/five_ring_circus/2012/08/11/caster_semenya_2012_olympics_did_the_south_african_runner_lose_the_women_s_800_meters_on_purpose_.html

Tillet, Salamishah. 2015. "The Panthers' Revolutionary Feminism." *New York Times*. October 2, 2015. http://nyti.ms/1jEkMmW

Trebay, Guy. 2008. "He's Pregnant, You're Speechless." *New York Times*. June 22, 2008. http://www.nytimes.com/2008/06/22/fashion/22pregnant.html

Trudell, Scott. 2013. "Breaking Bad: Masculinity as Tragedy." *OUPBlob*. August 9, 2013. http://blog.oup.com/2013/08/breaking-bad-masculinity-tragedy/

U.S. Bureau of Labor Statistics (BLS). 2014a. *Current Population Survey*. Accessed on September 7, 2017 at https://www.dol.gov/wb/stats/earnings.htm.

U.S. Bureau of Labor Statistics (BLS). 2014b. "Women in the Labor Force: A Databook." *BLS Reports,* Report 1049. http://www.bls.gov/cps/wlf-databook-2013.pdf

U.S. Census Bureau. 2016. *Current Population Survey, Annual Social and Economic (ASEC) Supplement: Table PINC-05: Work Experience in 2015—People 15 Years Old and Over by Total Money Earnings in 2015, Age, Race, Hispanic Origin, Sex, and Disability Status*. https://www.census.gov/data/tables/timeseries/demo/income-poverty/cps-pinc/pinc-05.html (Unpublished calculation based on the median annual pay for all women and men who worked full time, year-round in 2015.)

U.S. Department of Education. 2014. "U.S. Department of Education Releases List of Higher Education Institutions with Open Title IX Sexual Violence Investigations." *US Department of Education*. https://www.ed.gov/news/press-releases/us-department-education-releases-list-higher-education-institutions-open-title-i

U.S. Department of Veteran Affairs. 2012. "Strategies for Serving our Women Veterans." *US Department of Veteran Affairs*. https://www.va.gov/opa/publications/draft_2012_women-veterans_strategicplan.pdf

Utah v. Strieff. 579 U.S. ___. 2016.

Uttal, Lynet. 1996. "Custodial Care, Surrogate Care, and Coordinated Care: Employed Mothers and the Meaning of Child Care." *Gender & Society* 10 (3): 291–311.

Wacquant, Loïc. 2009. *Punishing the Poor: The Neoliberal Government of Social Insecurity*. Durham: Duke University Press.

Walby, Sylvia. 1997. *Gender Transformations*. London, UK: Routledge.

Walker, Alice. 1983. *In Search of Our Mothers' Gardens: Womanist Prose*. San Diego: Harcourt Books.

Walker, Rebecca. 1992. "Becoming the Third Wave." *Ms. Magazine*.

Ware, Helen. 1979. "Polygyny: Women's Views in a Transitional Society." *Journal of Marriage and Family* 41 (1): 185–195.

Warner, Judith. 2014. *The Women's Leadership Gap: Women's Leadership by the Numbers*. Report for the Center for American Progress. https://www.americanprogress.org/issues/women/reports/2014/03/07/85457/fact-sheet-the-womens-leadership-gap/

Warren, Elizabeth, and Amelia Warren Tyagi. 2003. *The Two-Income Trap: Why Middle-Class Parents Are Going Broke*. New York: Basic Books.

Weeks, Jeffrey. 1985. *Sexuality and Its Discontents: Meanings, Myths, and Modern Sexualities*. New York: Routledge.

Weiss, Karen G. 2010. "Too Ashamed to Report: Deconstructing the Shame of Sexual Victimization." *Feminist Criminology* 5 (3): 286–310.

Welter, Barbara. 1966. "The Cult of True Womanhood: 1820–1860." *American Quarterly* 18 (2): 151–174.

Wesely, Jennifer K. 2006. "Considering the Context of Women's Violence Gender, Lived Experiences, and Cumulative Victimization." *Feminist Criminology* 1 (4): 303–328.

West, Candace, and Don H. Zimmerman. 1987. "Doing Gender." *Gender & Society* 1 (2): 125–151.

Westbrook, Laurel, and Kristen Schilt. 2014. "Doing Gender, Determining Gender: Transgender People, Gender Panics, and the Maintenance of the Sex/Gender/Sexuality System." *Gender & Society* 28 (1): 32–57.

Wilder, Laura Ingalls. 1935. *Little House on the Prairie*. New York: Harper & Brothers.

Wilkins, Amy. 2009. "Masculinity Dilemmas: Sexuality and Intimacy Talk among Christians and Goths." *Signs: Journal of Women in Culture and Society* 34 (2): 343–368.

Williams, Christine L. 1992. "The Glass Escalator: Hidden Advantages for Men in the 'Female' Professions." *Social Problems* 39 (3): 253–267.

Williams, Hank Jr. 1982. A Country Boy Can Survive. *The Pressure Is On*. Nashville: Elektra/Curb.

Williams, Joan. 2001. *Unbending Gender: Why Family and Work Conflict and What to Do About It*. New York: Oxford University Press.

Williams, Raymond. 1977. "Hegemony." In *Marxism and Literature*, edited by Raymond Williams, 108–115. Oxford: Oxford University Press.

Wilson, William J. 1987. *The Truly Disadvantaged: The Inner City, the Underclass and Public Policy*. Chicago: University of Chicago Press.

Wingfield, Adia Harvey. 2009. "Racializing the Glass Escalator Reconsidering Men's Experiences with Women's Work." *Gender & Society* 23 (1): 5–26.

Wolf, Naomi. (1991) 2002. *The Beauty Myth: How Images of Beauty Are Used against Women*. New York: William Morrow & Co.

Wolfgang, Marvin, and Marc Riedel. 1973. "Race, Judicial Discretion, and the Death Penalty." *The Annals of the American Academy of Political and Social Science* 407 (1): 119–133.

Wyse, Jessica B. 2013. "Rehabilitating Criminal Selves: Gendered Strategies in Community Corrections." *Gender & Society* 27 (2): 231–255.

Young, Iris Marion. 1980. "Throwing Like a Girl: A Phenomenology of Feminine Body Comportment Motility and Spatiality." *Human Studies* 3 (1): 137–156.

Young, Iris Marion. 2003. "The Logic of Masculinist Protection: Reflections on the Current Security State." *Signs: Journal of Women in Culture and Society* 29 (1): 1–25.

Zimring, Frank. 2017. *When Police Kill*. Cambridge: Harvard University Press.